A GUIDEBOOK ON MAPPING POVERTY THROUGH DATA INTEGRATION AND ARTIFICIAL INTELLIGENCE

APRIL 2021

ADB

ASIAN DEVELOPMENT BANK

© 2021 Asian Development Bank
6 ADB Avenue, Mandaluyong City, 1550 Metro Manila, Philippines
Tel +63 2 8632 4444; Fax +63 2 8636 2444
www.adb.org

Some rights reserved. Published in 2021.

ISBN 978-92-9262-785-0 (print); 978-92-9262-786-7 (electronic); 978-92-9262-787-4 (ebook)
Publication Stock No. SPR210131-2
DOI: http://dx.doi.org/10.22617/SPR210131-2

The views expressed in this publication are those of the authors and do not necessarily reflect the views and policies of the Asian Development Bank (ADB) or its Board of Governors or the governments they represent.

ADB does not guarantee the accuracy of the data included in this publication and accepts no responsibility for any consequence of their use. The mention of specific companies or products of manufacturers does not imply that they are endorsed or recommended by ADB in preference to others of a similar nature that are not mentioned.

By making any designation of or reference to a particular territory or geographic area, or by using the term "country" in this document, ADB does not intend to make any judgments as to the legal or other status of any territory or area.

Please contact pubsmarketing@adb.org if you have questions or comments with respect to content, or if you wish to obtain copyright permission for your intended use that does not fall within these terms, or for permission to use the ADB logo.

Corrigenda to ADB publications may be found at http://www.adb.org/publications/corrigenda.

Note:
In this publication, "$" refers to United States dollars.

Cover design by Francis Manio.

Printed on recycled paper

CONTENTS

Table, Figures, and Box   iv
Foreword   v
Abbreviations   vii

1   INTRODUCTION   1

2   HARDWARE AND SOFTWARE REQUIREMENTS AND SETUP   5
     Software Requirement Setup   5
     R and RStudio   5
     Chrome Browser   9
     Google Account   9
     Google Earth Engine   9

3   DATA PREPARATION   11
     Daytime Satellite Imagery Processing   11
     Downloading the Shapefiles   11
     Generating Centroids for Satellite Imagery   14
     Downloading Satellite Imagery   26
     Converting Format of Satellite Imagery   79
     Nighttime Satellite Imagery Processing   88
     Binning Luminosity Values and Splitting Dataset   124

4   TRAINING OF CONVOLUTIONAL NEURAL NETWORK   147

5   CONVOLUTIONAL NEURAL NETWORK MODEL FEATURE EXTRACTION   193

6   RIDGE REGRESSION   215

7   RESCALING OF POVERTY ESTIMATES AND VISUALIZATION   237

BIBLIOGRAPHY   263

TABLE, FIGURES, AND BOX

TABLE

Description of Required R Packages   7

FIGURES

1   Road Map of Methodology for Predicting Poverty Using Satellite Imagery   2
2   Machine Learning and Published Poverty Rate Maps of the Philippines, 2015   261
3   Machine Learning and Published Poverty Rate Maps of Thailand, 2015   261

BOX

Steps in Adjusting Weights of Cross Entropy Loss Function   179

FOREWORD

Since the Sustainable Development Goals (SDGs) were launched in 2015, both traditional and innovative types of data have become imperative in understanding the progress that has been made in achieving those goals. By providing more timely, granular, and comprehensive information, innovative sources complement traditional ones that are often constrained by high data collection costs. Conventional household or enterprise surveys, for instance, constitute a major data source for SDGs, but these often have sample sizes too small to provide enough granularity for highly targeted analyses. High costs also mean that these surveys are conducted too infrequently for timely measurement of indicators. On the other hand, conventional surveys and censuses serve as quality benchmarks for representativeness of data and adherence to statistical principles and standards that enable reliable inferences.

Indeed, to obtain timely, granular, and credible data entails integrating traditional with innovative data sources. Poverty statistics is an area where there have been several initiatives to blend multiple types of data. One noteworthy initiative involves using satellite imagery to provide more geographically disaggregated data than those published by government agencies. This approach leverages state-of-the-art computer imaging techniques to predict specific development indicators based on features on the ground.

The Asian Development Bank (ADB) designed a knowledge and support technical assistance called Data for Development in 2017 that aims to strengthen the capacity of national statistics offices to meet the increasing data demands for policymaking and monitoring of development goals and targets. One of its components focuses on subnational disaggregation of SDG indicators, particularly poverty statistics, that draws from recent studies combining geospatial data, satellite imagery, and powerful machine learning algorithms with traditional data sources and conventional methods to estimate the magnitude of poverty in specific locations. Such data are critical in aiding government and development agencies to distribute social assistance more efficiently. In the study, statisticians from ADB's Statistics and Data Innovation Unit within the Economic Research and Regional Cooperation Department worked with the Philippine Statistics Authority, National Statistical Office of Thailand, and World Data Lab to examine the feasibility of poverty mapping using satellite imagery and geospatial data.

This guidebook documents the study's key approaches step-by-step. It serves as a valuable reference for national statistics offices on how to use easily accessible resources such as satellite imagery to enhance the compilation of poverty statistics. The Key Indicators for Asia and the Pacific Special Supplement 2020 is recommended reading for users of this guidebook. The publication team was led by Arturo Martinez Jr. and Ron Lester Durante, under the overall direction of Elaine Tan. It was written by Ron Lester Durante, Arturo Martinez Jr., Mildred Addawe, Marymell Martillan, Joseph Bulan, Tomas Sako, and Martin Hofer, with valuable research and technical support from Katharina Fenz and Thomas Mitterling. Iva Lohovska from World Data Lab also provided insightful feedback on improving the guidebook, while Ma. Roselia Babalo, Rose Anne Dumayas, Raymond Adofina, and Ephraim Cuya provided operational support through its preparation. The cover of this publication was designed by Francis Manio. Manuscript editing was performed by Raynal Squires, while the publication's layout, page design, and typesetting were carried out by Judy Yñiguez.

We hope this guidebook will serve as a useful reference for national statistics offices across Asia and the Pacific in mapping the spatial distribution of poverty using a combination of traditional and innovative data sources.

Yasuyuki Sawada
Chief Economist and Director General
Economic Research and Regional Cooperation Department
Asian Development Bank

ABBREVIATIONS

CNN	convolutional neural network
Colab	Google Colaboratory
CRS	Coordinate Reference System
CSV	comma-separated values
DMSP-OLS	Defense Meteorological Program Operational Line-Scan System
GADM	Database of Global Administrative Areas
GB	gigabyte
GCS	Geographic Coordinate System
GDAL	Geospatial Data Abstraction Library
GEE	Google Earth Engine
GMM	Gaussian Mixture Model
GPU	graphics processing unit
GUI	graphical user interface
HDX	Humanitarian Data Exchange
JSON	java script object notation
NOAA	National Oceanic and Atmospheric Administration
NTL	nighttime lights
PCS	Projected Coordinate System
VIIRS	Visible Infrared Imaging Radiometer Suite

1 INTRODUCTION

Properly compiled data in poverty statistics provides visibility for socioeconomically disadvantaged people in society. It sheds light on their demographic profiles, their magnitude, location, and their needs, all of which are critical inputs for the design of interventions in a development agenda.

In developing countries, poverty statistics are typically derived from household surveys designed to provide reliable estimates at national, regional, provincial, or other highly aggregated levels. However, as better disaggregated data can facilitate more effective targeting of socioeconomic programs, it is important to explore alternative data sources that can complement these surveys.

Satellite imagery is a potentially useful source of alternative data which may be used to enhance the granularity of poverty statistics compiled from household surveys. The emergence of satellite data has invigorated efforts to measure poverty on a gridded level from space. A novel approach entails using artificial intelligence to predict the prevalence of poverty (or other indicators) based on satellite image features.[1] Since data from images are naturally unstructured, noisy, and difficult to process statistically, one can design computer vision techniques to extract patterns that may be used to associate them with poverty.

Mapping Poverty through Data Integration and Artificial Intelligence: A Special Supplement of the Key Indicators for Asia and the Pacific, a report published by the Asian Development Bank (ADB), documents the results of using computer vision techniques to map the spatial distribution of poverty in the Philippines and Thailand.[2] The country-specific reports, Mapping the Spatial Distribution of Poverty Using Satellite Imagery in the Philippines and in Thailand, provide more detailed discussion on the methodology.[3] The first step of the methodology entails training a convolutional neural network (CNN)—an advanced type of machine learning algorithm commonly used for image classification-related tasks—to predict nighttime light data using daytime images as input. Intensity of lights at night is a good proxy for wealth and human interaction on the ground and this kind of abundant, granular information meets the high-volume data requirement for training machine learning algorithms. In the process of learning to "predict" nighttime light intensity, the CNN learns to detect general features in images, or latent variables, related to light intensity that can be used for other tasks, like estimating poverty measures. To maintain consistency with published official statistics, the condensed, image-based information can be averaged on a coarser level to align with the level of information available in government-published poverty estimates. To speed up learning and reduce the amount of data needed for the process, a CNN that has already been trained on some image databases is used to assign labels to larger databases of images.

---

[1]   N. Jean et al. 2016. Combining Satellite Imagery and Machine Learning to Predict Poverty. *Science*. 353 (6301). pp 790–794.

[2]   Asian Development Bank (ADB). 2020. *Mapping Poverty through Data Integration and Artificial Intelligence: A Special Supplement of the Key Indicators for Asia and the Pacific*. Manila.

[3]   ADB. 2021. *Mapping the Spatial Distribution of Poverty Using Satellite Imagery in the Philippines*. Manila; and ADB. Forthcoming. *Mapping the Spatial Distribution of Poverty Using Satellite Imagery in Thailand*. Manila.

In the second step, prediction of nighttime light intensity is discarded and the trained CNN alone is used to summarize the complex multidimensional input of image data into a single vector. This vector has hundreds of features, each assigned a single value in every image. These features are a representation of what the network detects in an image. They have several advantages over raw pixel values, most notably that convolutional layers scan over the image using kernels so that it does not matter where features are placed on the image.

To combine grid-based image features with survey-based poverty data, the value of each feature within the given survey areas is averaged. The final training step uses a ridge regression to find the relationship between the image features and survey-based poverty statistics. The trained CNN and ridge parameters can then be used to predict poverty using only a daytime image as input. The process is illustrated in Figure 1.

Figure 1: Road Map of Methodology for Predicting Poverty Using Satellite Imagery

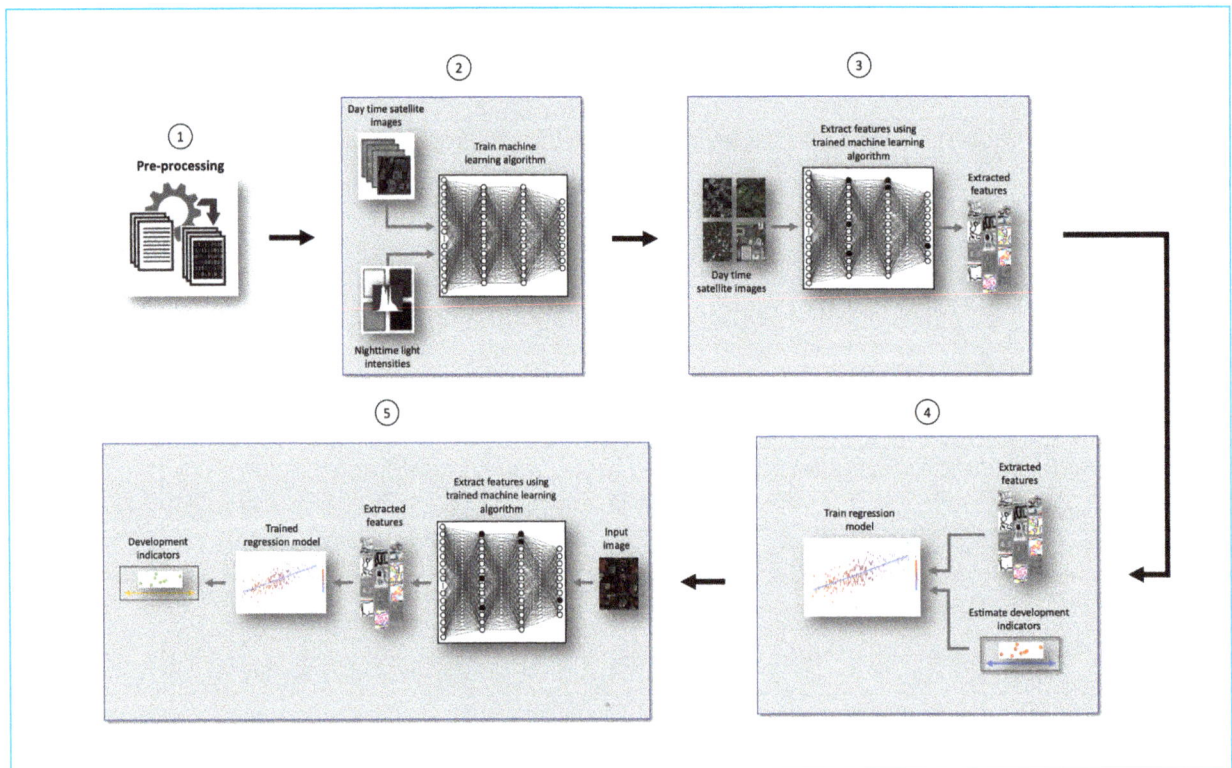

Notes: The procedure requires three types of data: geographically disaggregated poverty statistics, daytime satellite imagery, and images of earth at night. After pre-processing and cleaning these data (Step 1), Step 2 trains an algorithm to classify (daytime) satellite images into different classes of night light intensity. Step 3 extracts the image features from the last layer of the trained algorithm. In Step 4, the image features are averaged so the space enclosed in grids corresponds to the level at which poverty-labeled images are available. These are regressed using the target variable of the survey to find the relationship between features and the target variable. Step 5 summarizes the full pipeline from input image to target variable.

Source: Graphics generated by the study team.

This guidebook outlines the step-by-step procedure summarized in Figure 1. The guidebook is intended as a one-stop reference for researchers and other development practitioners (particularly from national statistics offices) who wish to apply these methods for exploratory studies using tools that are readily accessible and without significant cost. Because we strongly believe in the straightforward methods and tools described here, other (sometimes proprietary) tools that may be more effective in conducting larger-scale poverty mapping initiatives are not discussed.

Users of this guidebook are encouraged to first read the ADB report (footnote 2), particularly the section describing the methodology, before going through the step-by-step procedure outlined here. Users are also advised to check for updates to the software and services referred to and pictured in screenshots in this guidebook. The discussions in this guidebook are meant for educational purposes. It should be noted that trademarks of tools and resources used are owned solely by the respective developers, and this guidebook is not endorsed by or affiliated with these companies in any way.

2 HARDWARE AND SOFTWARE REQUIREMENTS AND SETUP

Hardware

- *Minimum system requirements*: 1.6 gigahertz 4-core processor or better, 8 gigabytes (GB) RAM, 10 GB of free hard disk space with reliable internet connection

Software

- R version 4 or higher
- RStudio version 1.4 or higher
- R Packages: caret, fasterize, gdalUtilities, mclust, raster, rasterVis, sf, tidyverse
- Google Chrome browser version 79.0.3945 or higher
- Fastai Python library version 1.0.61
- Gmail account, Google Drive with at least 5 GB free space, and Google Earth Engine account

Software Requirement Setup

R and RStudio

For step-by-step procedure in downloading and installing R and Rstudio, refer to this page: https://rstudio-education.github.io/hopr/starting.html.

Installing Rtools

Rtools is used to build R and R packages because some of the packages are downloaded as source code and need to be compiled.

For information on how to install and test Rtools, refer to this page: https://cran.r-project.org/bin/windows/Rtools/.

Installing R packages

The required packages are caret, fasterize, gdalUtilities, mclust, raster, rasterVis, sf, and tidyverse. Table 1 provides a description of these packages.

To install these packages, type the following commands in the Source Panel:

install.packages(c("caret",
                                 "fasterize",
                                 "gdalUtilities",
                                 "mclust",
                                 "raster",
                                 "rasterVis",
                                 "sf",
                                 "tidyverse"),
                         dependencies = T)

Then click the ⬄ Source ▾ icon to execute the entire script.

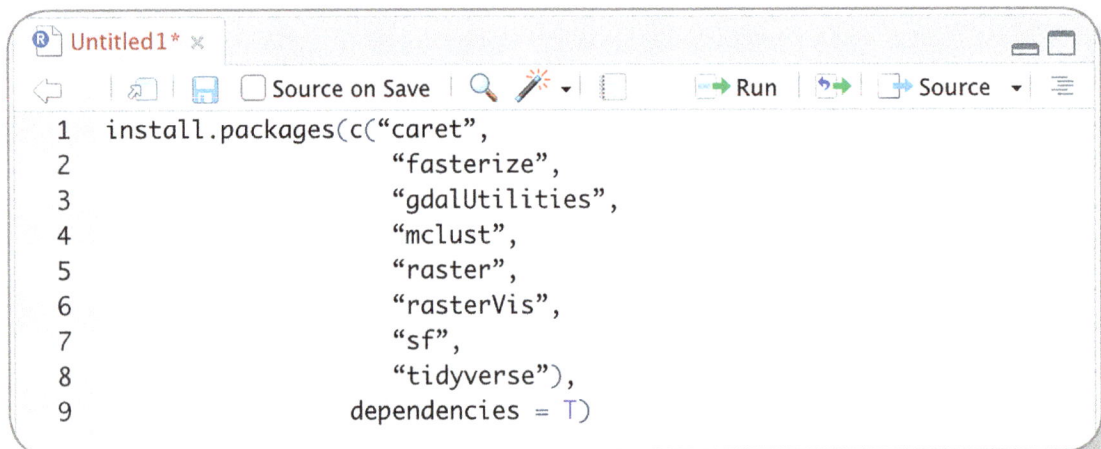

```
1  install.packages(c("caret",
2                      "fasterize",
3                      "gdalUtilities",
4                      "mclust",
5                      "raster",
6                      "rasterVis",
7                      "sf",
8                      "tidyverse"),
9                dependencies = T)
```

Table 1: Description of Required R Packages

Package Name	Description
caret	Short for **C**lassification **A**nd **RE**gression **T**raining. It contains functions for creating predictive modeling. It also includes tools for data splitting, pre-processing, feature selection, model tuning using resampling, and variable importance estimation.
fasterize	A faster alternative to **rasterize()** function of the package **raster**. However, it is currently limited to rasterizing polygons of sf-type objects.
gdalUtilities	It utilizes the self-contained Geospatial Data Abstraction Library (GDAL) utilities of the package *sf.* It provides a wrapper that mirrors the GDAL command line interface. (Wrapper is a function that calls another function/library that performs the actual operation but provides a different interface.)
mclust	A model-based clustering, classification and density estimation that uses finite normal mixture modeling.
raster	A package for reading, writing, manipulating, analyzing, and modeling spatial data.
rasterVis	A package complement to the raster package for visualization and interaction. It provides visualization methods for quantitative and qualitative data, for both univariate and multivariate rasters.
sf	A package support for simple features, which is a standardized way of spatial vector data encoding. It also has GDAL bindings for reading and writing data, GEOS bindings for geometrical operations, and PROJ bindings for projection conversions and datum transformations.
tidyverse	A collection of the following R packages used for data analyses: ***ggplot2*** – used for data visualization; ***dplyr*** – used for data manipulation; ***tidyr*** – used to create a tidy data where a column is variable, a row is an observation and a cell is a single value; ***readr*** – provides a way to read delimited text data; ***purr*** – provides tools for working with functions and vectors; ***tibble*** – a tweaked **data.frame()** function used for large datasets; ***stringr*** – provides functions for working with strings like searching, matching, concatenating, replacing, etc.; and ***forcats*** – provides tools to handle factors or categorical variables.

Some of the packages and/or their dependencies need to be installed from source through the help of Rtools. A dialog box will ask permission to install packages from source.

Click **Yes** to start package download and installation.

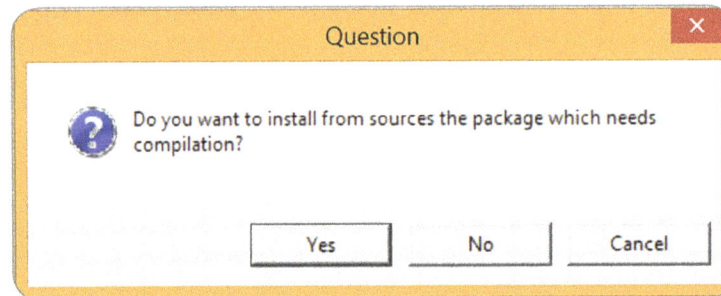

```
Question                                              ×

    [?]   Do you want to install from sources the package which needs
          compilation?


                    Yes          No          Cancel
```

```
Console   Terminal ×   Jobs ×                              _ □
~/ ⇨
8.zip'
Content type 'application/zip' length 188026 bytes (183 KB)
downloaded 183 KB

trying URL 'https://cran.rstudio.com/bin/windows/contrib/4.0/rgdal_1.5-12.z
ip'
Content type 'application/zip' length 36678484 bytes (35.0 MB)
downloaded 35.0 MB

trying URL 'https://cran.rstudio.com/bin/windows/contrib/4.0/sf_0.9-4.zip'
Content type 'application/zip' length 42821115 bytes (40.8 MB)
```

The Console Panel will revert to prompt once all packages are installed. Review the **Console Panel** outputs to check for errors in package installations.

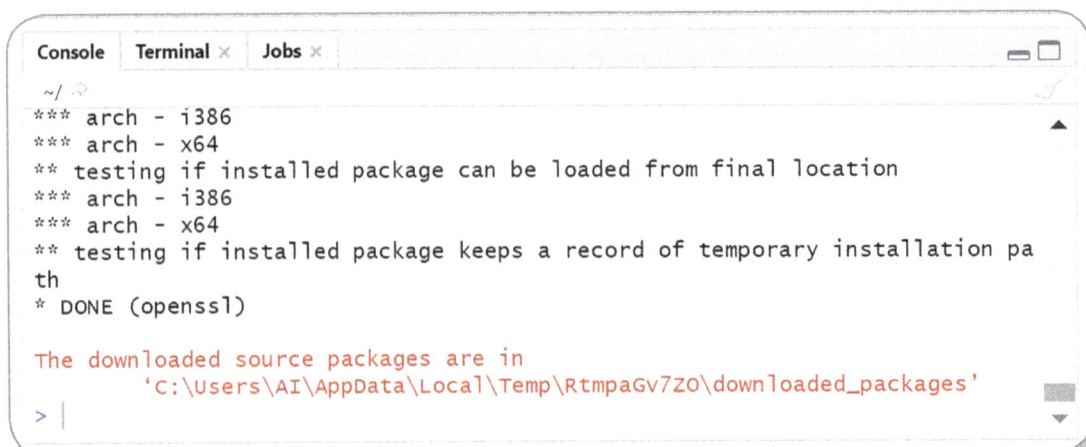

```
Console   Terminal ×   Jobs ×                              _ □
~/ ⇨
*** arch - i386
*** arch - x64
** testing if installed package can be loaded from final location
*** arch - i386
*** arch - x64
** testing if installed package keeps a record of temporary installation pa
th
* DONE (openssl)

The downloaded source packages are in
        'C:\Users\AI\AppData\Local\Temp\RtmpaGv7ZO\downloaded_packages'
> |
```

Chrome Browser

Install Google Chrome Web Browser version 79.0.3945 or higher.

For step-by-step procedure in downloading and installing Google Chrome, refer to this page: https://support.google.com/chrome/answer/95346.

Google Account

Setting up a new Google account.

For step-by-step procedure in creating a Google account refer to this page: https://support.google.com/accounts/answer/27441?hl=en#.

If you prefer to use an already existing Google account, verify that its associated Google Drive has at least 5 GB of free storage space.

Google Earth Engine

Google Earth Engine (GEE) is a cloud-based geospatial processing tool with built-in spatial datasets that goes back more than 4 decades. A sign-up is required using an active Google account to use the GEE service.

Refer to this page to sign up and get access for Google Earth Engine: https://signup.earthengine.google.com/.

Below is the Google Earth Engine Code Editor.

Search bar for datasets or places

Script manager

API documentation

Asset manager

Get a link (URL) to the script

Save script

Run script

Inspect locations, pixel values and objects on the map

Console output

Task manager

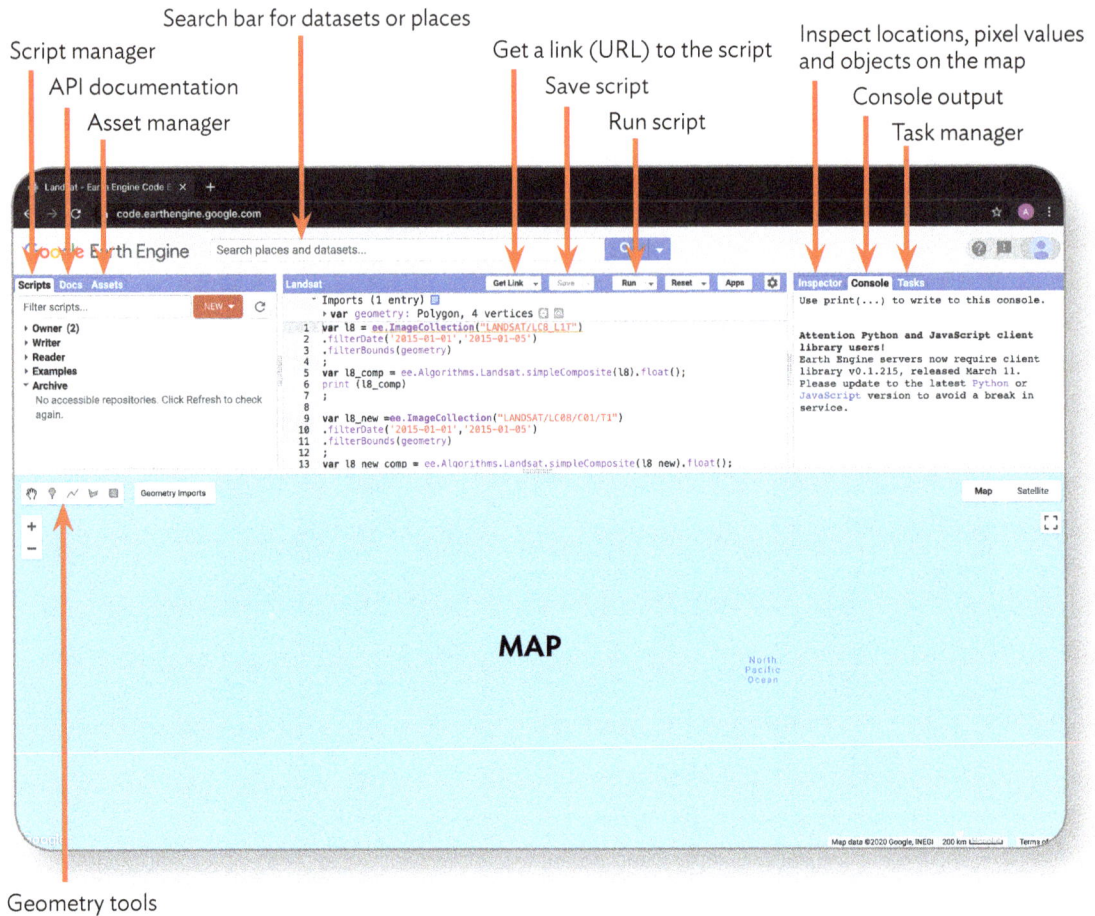

Geometry tools

3 DATA PREPARATION

Daytime Satellite Imagery Processing

Data Requirements
- Country shapefiles

Tools
- Google Colaboratory
- R and RStudio

Downloading the Shapefiles

A shapefile is a simple vector data storage format for storing the location, shape, and attributes of geographic features. The geographic features in a shapefile can be represented by points, lines, or polygons.[4] Shapefiles determine the extent of satellite imagery to download. The administrative boundaries of the shapefiles should be consistent with official statistical data.

Shapefiles can be downloaded from various sources, but the most common are the Humanitarian Data Exchange (HDX) (*www.humdata.org*) and Database of Global Administrative Areas (GADM) (*www.gadm.org*).

HDX is an open platform for sharing data across crises and organizations. Launched in July 2014 by the United Nations Office for the Coordination of Humanitarian Affairs, HDX aims to make humanitarian data easy to find and use for analysis. HDX shapefiles are derived from original datasets sourced from relevant government agencies (e.g., national statistics offices, mapping agencies) and attached with standard geographic codes. These shapefiles have been vetted, configured, and provided with live services by the Information Technology Outreach Services of the Carl Vinson Institute of Government - University of Georgia. These shapefiles are also updated every year.

GADM is a high-resolution database of country administrative areas that provides maps and spatial data for all countries and their subdivisions. The current version is 3.6, which delimits 386,735 administrative

---

[4] Environmental Systems Research Institute (ESRI). 1998. ESRI Shapefile Technical Description: An ESRI White Paper – July 1998. https://www.esri.com/Library/Whitepapers/Pdfs/Shapefile.pdf.

areas with high spatial resolution and an extensive set of attributes. One limitation of using GADM is that the administrative subdivisions could possibly differ on a country basis.

For the following steps, Thailand files are used for illustration.

STEP 1

In the browser address bar, type the HDX web address, www.humdata.org, and press **Enter**.

From the top bar, click **Search Datasets**. Type **<country_name> administrative boundary**.

For this illustration, type **Thailand administrative boundary** and press **Enter**.

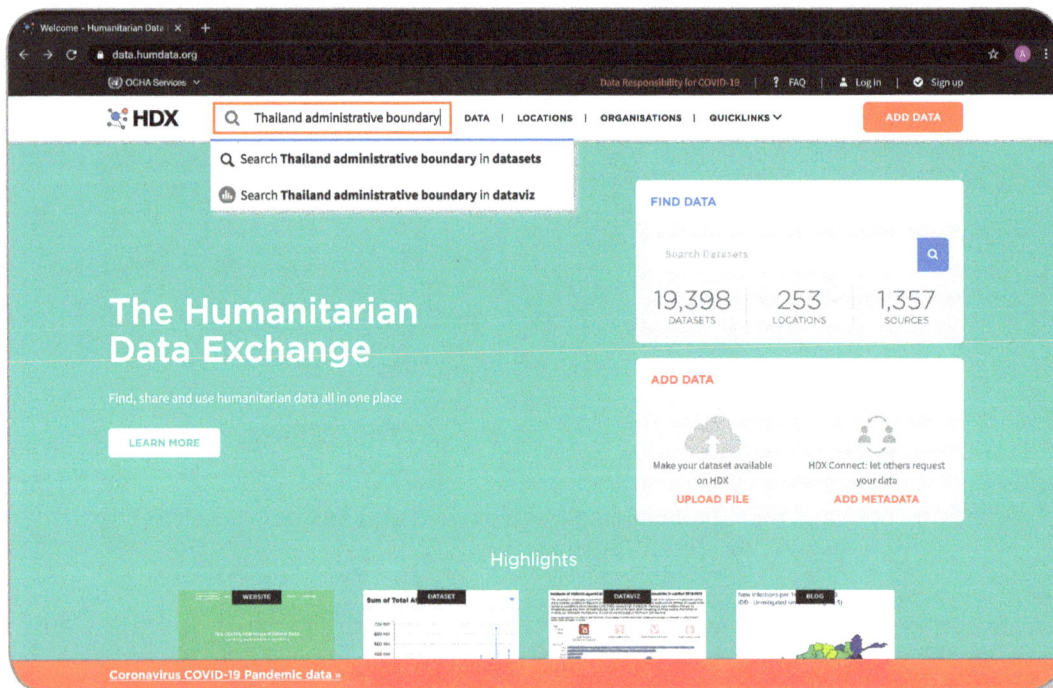

STEP 2

Click the link to the country's administrative boundary shapefile. Click **Thailand administrative levels 0-3 boundaries**.

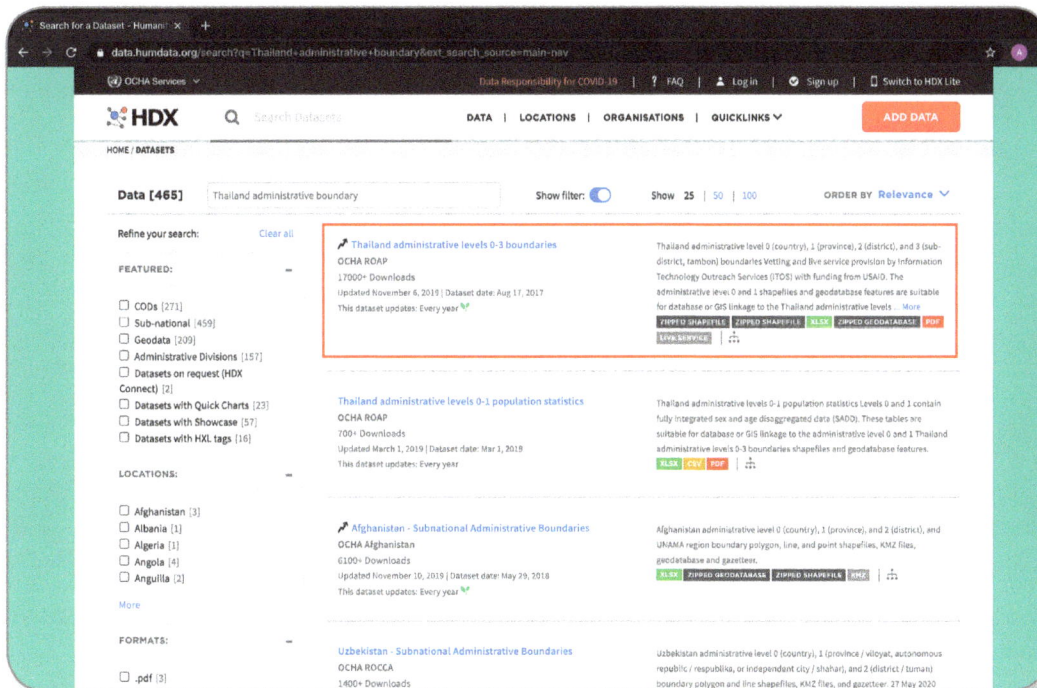

STEP 3

Browse and select the country-level shapefile and the administrative boundary shapefile coinciding with the published poverty estimates.

For this illustration, select **tha_adm_rtsd_itos_20190221_SHP_PART_2.zip**. Then click **Download.**

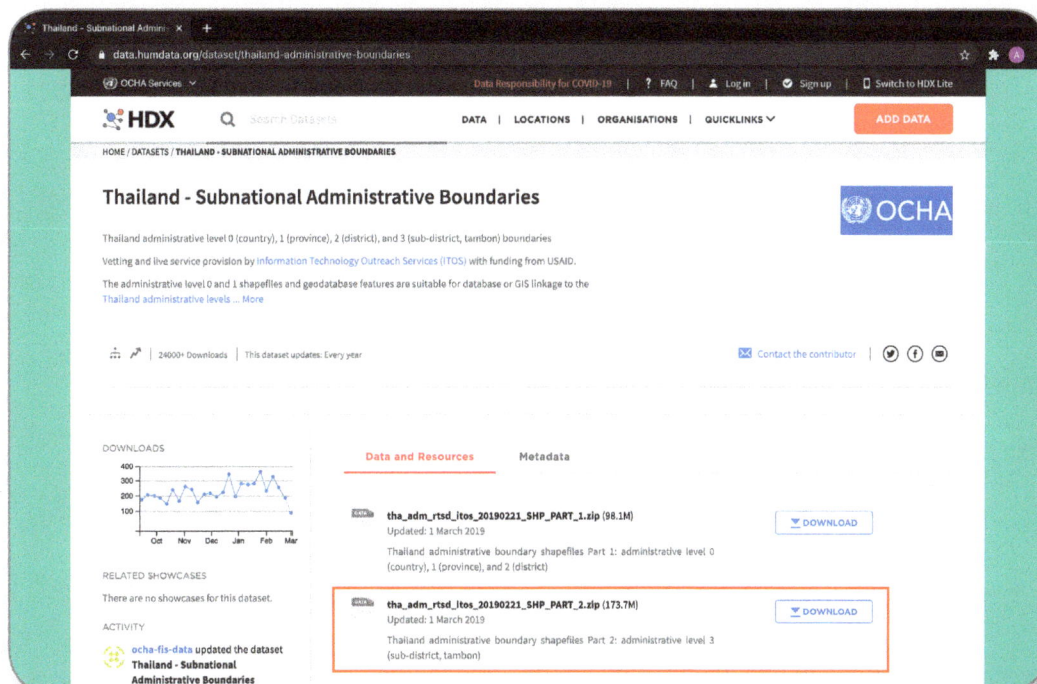

The shapefile is compressed in a ZIP file and automatically saved in the default download folder.

STEP 4

Open the Downloads folder. Extract the shapefile from the ZIP file. Check the information note attached to the ZIP file as different countries may have different notations.

In the case of Thailand, the following notations are used:

- adm0 – Country level
- adm1 – Provincial level
- adm2 – District level
- adm3 – Sub-district level (tambon)

Generating Centroids for Satellite Imagery

For this illustration, municipal boundary shapefiles are used to generate grids from raster pixels. Then centroids are obtained for each grid. Outputs are saved as comma-separated values (CSV) file.

Grid centroids will be used to determine the center of the daytime satellite imagery tile to be downloaded. Each tile will serve as input image for training the CNN model.

STEP 1

Open RStudio.

STEP 2

Click the **Open File** icon in the toolbar.

Search the R code: *grid_cell_selection.R* and click **Open**.

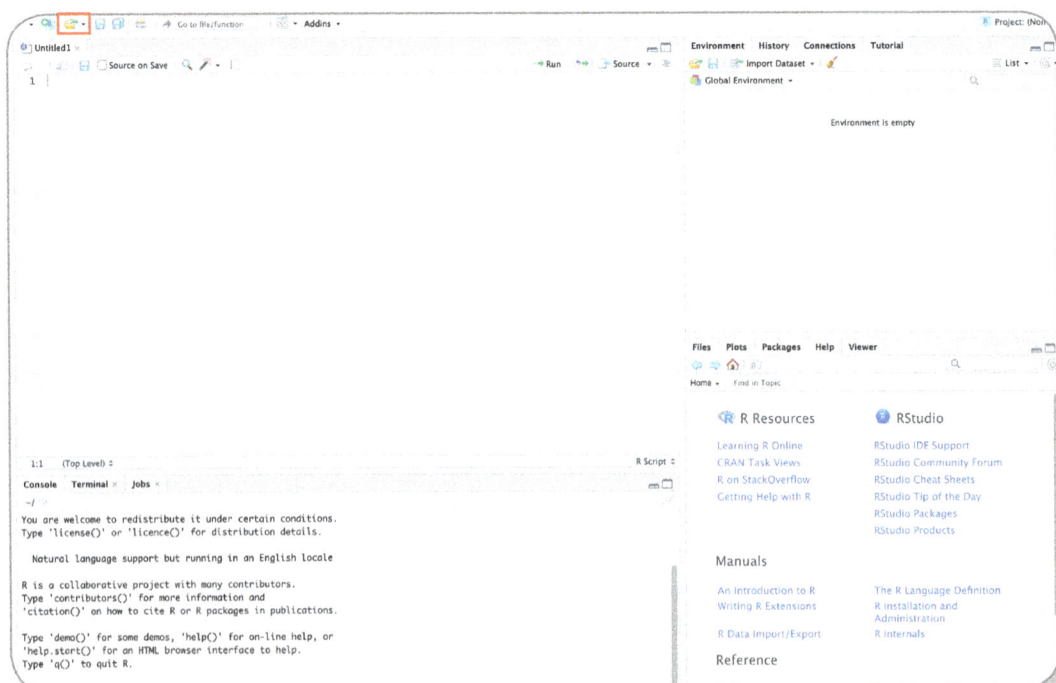

The administrative boundary shapefiles that correspond to the geographical level of the published poverty data will be used to generate grids from raster pixels. Obtain the centroids of each grid. Then generate the output as CSV file.

```r
# Grid cell selection

# load packages----
library(sf)
library(raster)
library(fasterize)
library(tidyverse)

# set working directory----
wd <- tcltk::tk_choose.dir(caption = "Select Working Directory")

setwd(wd)

# define country code-----
# THA = Thailand
# PHI = Philippines

country = ""


# Calculate grid size----

# The size per image is determined by ResNet34, the pretrained CNN model we used.
# ResNet34 has an image input of 256x256 pixel
# We use Landsat as our reference for grid computation since it has lower resolution (larger pixel size).
# This way we can have more coverage and image detail for the lower resolution imagery.
# For the higher resolution Sentinel 2 satellite, we will get more pixels per grid for the higher resolution imagery.
# For this we will just have to crop the grid to have exactly 256x256 pixel per image.

set.grid.resolution.px <- 256    # in pixel, image size required by CNN model
satellite.granularity   <- 15     # in meter/pixel,
                                  #   Landsat resolution after pansharpening

gridsize <- set.grid.resolution.px * satellite.granularity

# Select location of administrative boundary shapefile----
shp_path <-  tcltk::tk_choose.files(filters = matrix(c("SHP",".shp","All files","*"),2,2,byrow = T),
                                    caption = "Select Admin Boundary Shapefile")

# read shapefile to see which points are within the country border----
ADM_sf <- read_sf(shp_path)

# Generate a numeric "geocode" from the shapefile's ADM3_PCODE column----

# we use stringr package's str_extact() function to get the numeric portion of ADM3_PCODE entries
```

STEP 3

Load the R packages by typing *library(package)*. On the R console window, type the following commands and press **Enter**.

```r
# load packages----
library(sf)
library(raster)
library(fasterize)
library(tidyverse)
```

- **sf** is for interpreting and operations on vector shapefiles
- **raster** is for raster object operations
- **fasterize** is for rasterizing vectors
- **tidyverse** is for data manipulation

STEP 4

Select the working directory (i.e., the active computer folder) using the function **tk_choose.dir()** from the package **tcltk** (tcltk is a built-in package that provides the GUI for R; this command opens a window for selecting the target folder).

```
 9 ▾ # set working directory----
10   wd <- tcltk::tk_choose.dir(caption = "Select Working Directory")
11   setwd(wd)
```

Set the working directory by typing *setwd()*.

STEP 5

Set the code pertaining to the country of study by typing *country = "code"*.

```
14 ▾ # define country code-----
15   # THA = Thailand
16   # PHI = Philippines
17
18   country = "THA"
```

STEP 6

Calculate the grid size.

Grid size is the product of the satellite resolution (i.e., satellite granularity in meters/pixel) and the CNN input image size (i.e., set.grid.resolution.px in pixels).

Most of the CNN architecture is trained on ImageNet (http://www.image-net.org/), which is a database of human labeled images, like ResNet, which uses 256x256 pixel resolution. Though most have image input size of 224x224 pixels, these architectures can also benefit from higher resolution images such as 512x512 pixels, 1024x1024 pixels or higher. However, this increase in resolution also increases the file size of each image, constraining the graphics processing unit's (GPU) memory where it will be stored and processed during the CNN training process. The higher the resolution, the longer the training period since you may need to train the model in smaller batches of images.

Satellite granularity was based on Landsat's[5] resolution of **15 meters/pixel** after pansharpening.

---

[5] Landsat is the longest running program for acquisition of satellite imagery of Earth.

```
30   set.grid.resolution.px <- 256      # in pixel, image size required by CNN model
31   satelite.granularity    <- 15      # in meter/pixel,
32                                       #   Landsat resolution after pansharpening
33
34   gridsize <- set.grid.resolution.px * satelite.granularity
```

The grid size is equal to 3840 meters.

Landsat is used as reference for grid computation because it has lower resolution (i.e., larger pixel size), hence, more coverage and image detail. For the higher resolution Sentinel 2 satellite, more pixels can be derived for the same grid size.

STEP 7

Select the file path of the administrative boundary shapefile that is consistent with the granularity of the government-published estimates. Use the function **tk_choose.files()** to refer to GUI-based file selection.

```
36 ▾ # Select location of administrative boundary shapefile----
37   shp_path <-  tcltk::tk_choose.files(filters = matrix(c("SHP",".shp","All files","*"),2,2,byrow = T),
38                                 caption = "Select Admin Boundary Shapefile")
39
40 ▾ # read shapefile to see which points are within the country border----
41   ADM_sf <- read_sf(shp_path)
```

Next, load the shapefile using **sf** function's **read_sf()**.

STEP 8

Create a new column containing the numeric portion of the administrative boundaries' geographic code. The shapefile's PCODE usually contains a country code prefix. Thus, use a *stringr* package's **str_extact()** function to get only the numeric portion of ADM3_PCODE entries.

```
45   # we use stringr package's str_extract() function to get the numeric portion of ADM3_PCODE entries
46   ADM_sf$geocode <- as.numeric(str_extract(ADM_sf$ADM3_PCODE,"[0-9]+\\.*[0-9]*"))
```

```
> ADM_sf$ADM3_PCODE
  [1] "TH100101"   "TH100102"   "TH100103"   "TH100104"   "TH100105"   "TH100106"   "TH100107"   "TH100108"
  [9] "TH100109"   "TH100110"   "TH100111"   "TH100112"   "TH100201"   "TH100202"   "TH100203"   "TH100204"
 [17] "TH100206"   "TH100301"   "TH100302"   "TH100303"   "TH100304"   "TH100305"   "TH100306"   "TH100307"
 [25] "TH100308"   "TH100401"   "TH100402"   "TH100403"   "TH100404"   "TH100405"   "TH100502"   "TH100508"
 [33] "TH100601"   "TH100608"   "TH100701"   "TH100702"   "TH100703"   "TH100704"   "TH100801"   "TH100802"
 [41] "TH100803"   "TH100804"   "TH100805"   "TH100905"   "TH101001"   "TH101002"   "TH101101"   "TH101102"
 [49] "TH101103"   "TH101104"   "TH101105"   "TH101106"   "TH101203"   "TH101204"   "TH101301"   "TH101302"
 [57] "TH101303"   "TH101401"   "TH101501"   "TH101502"   "TH101503"   "TH101504"   "TH101505"   "TH101506"
 [65] "TH101507"   "TH101601"   "TH101602"   "TH101701"   "TH101702"   "TH101704"   "TH101801"   "TH101802"
 [73] "TH101803"   "TH101804"   "TH101901"   "TH101902.1" "TH101903.1" "TH101904"   "TH101905"   "TH101907"
 [81] "TH102004"   "TH102005"   "TH102006"   "TH102007"   "TH102009"   "TH102105"   "TH102107"   "TH102201"
 [89] "TH102202"   "TH102206"   "TH102207"   "TH102208"   "TH102209"   "TH102210"   "TH102302"   "TH102303"
 [97] "TH102401.1" "TH102402"   "TH102501"   "TH102502"   "TH102503"   "TH102504"   "TH102601"   "TH102701"
[105] "TH102704"   "TH102705"   "TH102801"   "TH102802"   "TH102803"   "TH102901"   "TH102902"   "TH103001"
```

```
> ADM_sf$geocode
  [1] 100101.0 100102.0 100103.0 100104.0 100105.0 100106.0 100107.0 100108.0 100109.0 100110.0 100111.0 100112.0
 [13] 100201.0 100202.0 100203.0 100204.0 100206.0 100301.0 100302.0 100303.0 100304.0 100305.0 100306.0 100307.0
 [25] 100308.0 100401.0 100402.0 100403.0 100404.0 100405.0 100502.0 100508.0 100601.0 100608.0 100701.0 100702.0
 [37] 100703.0 100704.0 100801.0 100802.0 100803.0 100804.0 100805.0 100905.0 101001.0 101002.0 101101.0 101102.0
 [49] 101103.0 101104.0 101105.0 101106.0 101203.0 101204.0 101301.0 101302.0 101303.0 101401.0 101501.0 101502.0
 [61] 101503.0 101504.0 101505.0 101506.0 101507.0 101601.0 101602.0 101701.0 101702.0 101704.0 101801.0 101802.0
 [73] 101803.0 101804.0 101901.0 101902.1 101903.1 101904.0 101905.0 101907.0 102004.0 102005.0 102006.0 102007.0
 [85] 102009.0 102105.0 102107.0 102201.0 102202.0 102206.0 102207.0 102208.0 102209.0 102210.0 102302.0 102303.0
 [97] 102401.1 102402.0 102501.0 102502.0 102503.0 102504.0 102601.0 102701.0 102704.0 102705.0 102801.0 102802.0
[109] 102803.0 102901.0 102902.0 103001.0 103002.0 103003.0 103004.0 103005.0 103101.0 103102.0 103103.0 103201.0
[121] 103202.0 103203.0 103301.0 103302.0 103303.0 103401.0 103501.0 103502.0 103503.0 103504.0 103602.0 103604.0
[133] 103605.1 103701.0 103702.0 103703.0 103704.0 103801.0 103802.0 103901.0 103902.0 103903.0 104001.0 104002.0
[145] 104003.0 104004.0 104101.0 104102.0 104201.1 104202.0 104203.0 104301.0 104302.0 104401.0 104501.0 104502.0
[157] 104503.0 104504.0 104601.0 104602.1 104603.0 104604.0 104605.0 104701.0 104801.0 104802.0 104901.1 104902.0
```

STEP 9

The Coordinate Reference System (CRS) is a system used to define the position on the earth's surface. It allows merging of spatial datasets accurately and facilitates calculation of distance and surface area properly. There are two types of CRS: the Geographic Coordinate System (GCS) and the Projected Coordinate System (PCS). GCS covers the entire globe, while PCS is localized to lessen visual distortion in a specific region. GCS is based on sphere coordinates and utilizes angular units (e.g., degrees, minutes, seconds), while PCS is plane-based and uses linear units (e.g., meter, feet). World Geodetic System 1984 (WGS84) is an example of GCS. Universal Transverse Mercator (UTM) is an example of PCS.

Define the CRS variables in Proj.4 format. There are several websites that host Proj.4 CRS of different projections, two of which are https://spatialreference.org/ and https://epsg.io/. Use the CRS to transform the shapefiles from GCS into PCS. Make sure to check the appropriate PCS for the country of study.

Type the following commands and press **Enter**.

```
49 ▾ # Define crs variables ----
50   # There are several websites that hosts Proj.4 CRS of different projections,
51   #  two of which are https://spatialreference.org/ and https://epsg.io/
52   WGS84 <- "+proj=longlat +datum=WGS84 +no_defs +ellps=WGS84 +towgs84=0,0,0"
53   UTM_CRS <- "+proj=utm +zone=47 +datum=WGS84 +units=m +no_defs" #Thailand is located at zone 47N
```

STEP 10

Check the projection information of the shapefile to verify its CRS.

```
56   # check the projection information of the shapefile
57   print(crs(ADM_sf))
```

```
> print(crs(ADM_sf))
CRS arguments: +proj=longlat +datum=WGS84 +no_defs
```

STEP 11

Transform the shapefile from GCS to PCS. Use **sf** package's **st_transform()** to change the shapefile's CRS.

```
59    # transform shapefile from WGS84 to UTM
60    ADM_UTM_sf <- st_transform(ADM_sf,UTM_CRS)
61
62    # check the projection information of the shapefile to verify CRS
63    print(crs(ADM_UTM_sf))
```

Then verify if transformation is successful using this command.

```
> print(crs(ADM_UTM_sf))
CRS arguments:
 +proj=utm +zone=47 +datum=WGS84 +units=m +no_defs +ellps=WGS84 +towgs84=0,0,0
```

Get the extents of the PCS and GCS shapefiles. This is needed to calculate the conversion factor (*meter_reciprocal_PCS2GCS*) from meters to degrees. Compute the conversion factor by getting the lagged differences of xmin and xmax and ymin and ymax for both PCS and GCS. Then compute the ratio of x's and y's of PCS and GCS, add the ratios, and get the average.

```
65    # get boundary box of the shapefile
66    PCS_ext <- extent(ADM_UTM_sf)
67    GCS_ext <- extent(ADM_sf)
68
69    # calculate conversion factor from degress to meters using bounding box
70    meter_reciprocal_PCS2GCS <- (diff(PCS_ext[1:2]) / diff(GCS_ext[1:2]) +
71                                 diff(PCS_ext[3:4]) / diff(GCS_ext[3:4]))/2
```

STEP 12

Create the grid in three steps:

First, generate an empty raster using **raster()** function through information from GCS extent, degrees-converted-gridsize as the resolution (pixel size) and define the CRS of the blank raster;

```
73    # create an empty raster of grid size granularity
74    ADM_raster <- raster (GCS_ext,
75                          res = gridsize/meter_reciprocal_PCS2GCS,
76                          crs = WGS84)
77
78    # rasterize the shapefile's geocode
79    geocode_raster <- fasterize(ADM_sf, ADM_raster, field = "geocode")
```

Second, rasterize the shapefile's geocode column. This creates a raster of all the shapefiles' features with the geocodes as raster values.

STEP 13

To get the coordinates of each centroid, convert the raster into dataframe using the function **as.data.frame()** with the option **xy=T** to generate the raster values (geocodes) and its corresponding centroid coordinates.

```
81   # get the centroids
82   geocode_df <- as.data.frame(geocode_raster, xy = T)
```

STEP 14

Use the **head()** command to check the dataframe generated and to learn its structure. The x and y columns are the centroid coordinates. The layer column is the rasterized shapefile attribute (geocode).

```
85   # check the created dataframe
86   head(geocode_df)
```

```
> head(geocode_df)
          x         y layer
1 97.36100 20.44744    NA
2 97.39627 20.44744    NA
3 97.43155 20.44744    NA
4 97.46683 20.44744    NA
5 97.50210 20.44744    NA
6 97.53738 20.44744    NA
>
```

STEP 15

Create a new dataframe. Use dplyr's functions and pipe operator (%>%) to perform a series of data manipulations.

First, use **filter()** function to remove all "NA" values in the layer column to get only the centroids inside the country borders.

```
87   selected.centroids <- geocode_df %>%      # create a new dataframe from geocode_df
88     filter(!is.na(layer)) %>%               # remove NA from the layer columns
89     mutate(id = 1:n()) %>%                  # generate grid ID
90     select(id,                              # rearrange the columns starting with ID
91            lon = x,                         # rename x centroid coordinate to lon
92            lat = y,                         # rename y centroid coordinate to lat
93            geocode = layer)                 # lastly, layer column renamed as geocode
```

Second, create a new column containing the grid ID.

```
87   selected.centroids <- geocode_df %>%      # create a new dataframe from geocode_df
88     filter(!is.na(layer)) %>%               # remove NA from the layer columns
89     mutate(id = 1:n()) %>%                   # generate grid ID
90     select(id,                               # rearrange the columns starting with ID
91           lon = x,                           # rename x centroid coordinate to lon
92           lat = y,                           # rename y centroid coordinate to lat
93           geocode = layer)                   # lastly, layer column renamed as geocode
```

Third, rearrange the column starting with ID, x, y, and layer. Rename "x", "y" and "layer" as "lon", "lat", and "geocode", respectively.

```
87   selected.centroids <- geocode_df %>%      # create a new dataframe from geocode_df
88     filter(!is.na(layer)) %>%               # remove NA from the layer columns
89     mutate(id = 1:n()) %>%                   # generate grid ID
90     select(id,                               # rearrange the columns starting with ID
91           lon = x,                           # rename x centroid coordinate to lon
92           lat = y,                           # rename y centroid coordinate to lat
93           geocode = layer)                   # lastly, layer column renamed as geocode
```

STEP 16

Generate the filename for the CSV file output. Indicate the following identifiers:

- country – refers to country code;
- "centroid" – refers to data content; and
- gridsize and "grid"– refer to the grid size.

```
96 ▾ # generate filename ----
97   file_name <- paste(country,
98                      "centroid",
99                      gridsize,
100                     "grid", sep = "_")
```

```
> file_name
[1] "THA_centroid_3840_grid"
>
```

STEP 17

Save the centroids dataframe as CSV file. Note that the output path will serve as the working directory.

```
102 ▾  # Output CSV----
103    write.csv(selected.centroids,
104              file = paste0(file_name,".csv"),
105              row.names = F)
```

The resulting CSV file should contain the grid ID, centroid coordinates (lon, lat), and the geocode.

	A	B	C	D
1	id	lon	lat	geocode
2	1	99.90088	20.4474357	570901
3	2	99.9361562	20.4474357	570901
4	3	99.9714323	20.4474357	570903
5	4	99.8656038	20.4121596	570906
6	5	99.90088	20.4121596	570906
7	6	99.9361562	20.4121596	570905
8	7	99.9714323	20.4121596	570903
9	8	100.006708	20.4121596	570903
10	9	99.4775661	20.3768834	571502
11	10	99.8656038	20.3768834	570904
12	11	99.90088	20.3768834	570904
13	12	99.9361562	20.3768834	570905
14	13	99.9714323	20.3768834	570905
15	14	100.006708	20.3768834	570905
16	15	100.041985	20.3768834	570804
17	16	100.077261	20.3768834	570801
18	17	100.253642	20.3768834	570310
19	18	100.288918	20.3768834	570310
20	19	100.324194	20.3768834	570310
21	20	99.5128422	20.3416073	571502

STEP 18

In the browser address bar, go to Google Drive[6] www.drive.google.com. Click ⟨ **+ New** ⟩ and then click **File upload**.

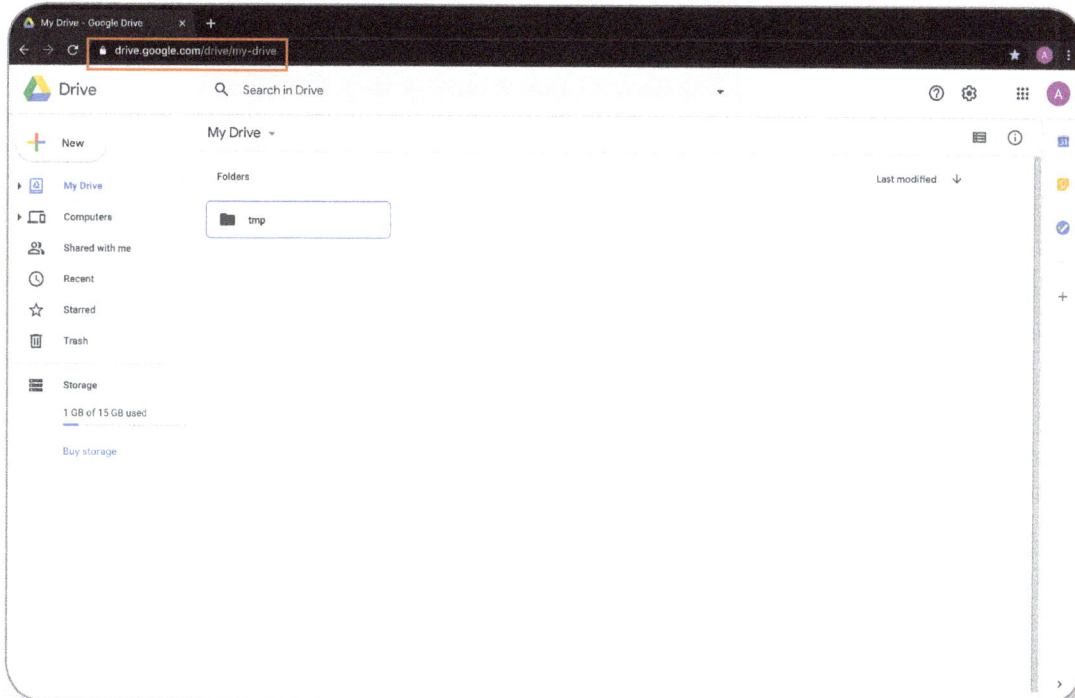

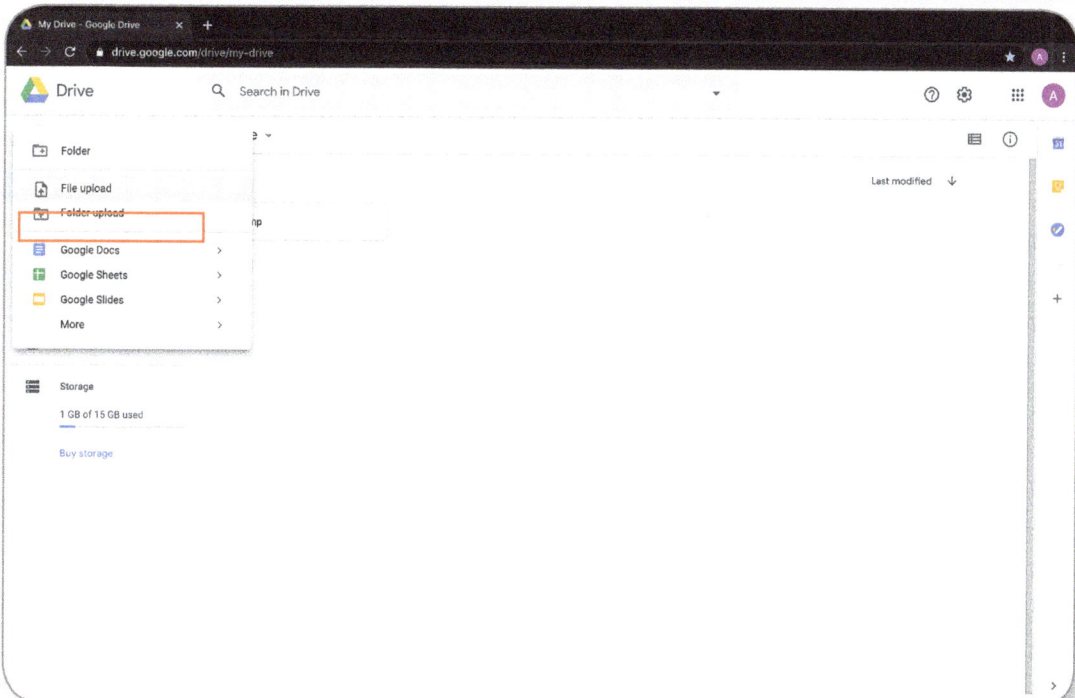

After the file is uploaded, locate the CSV file containing the centroid coordinates.

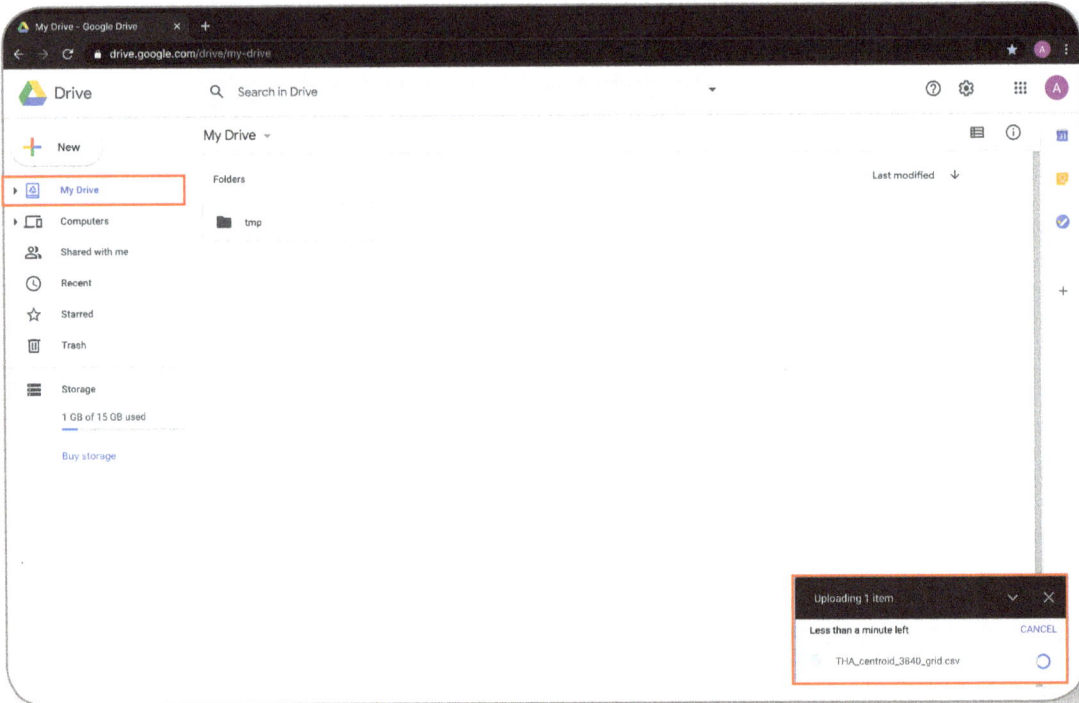

This file is needed for downloading the satellite imagery of each grid.

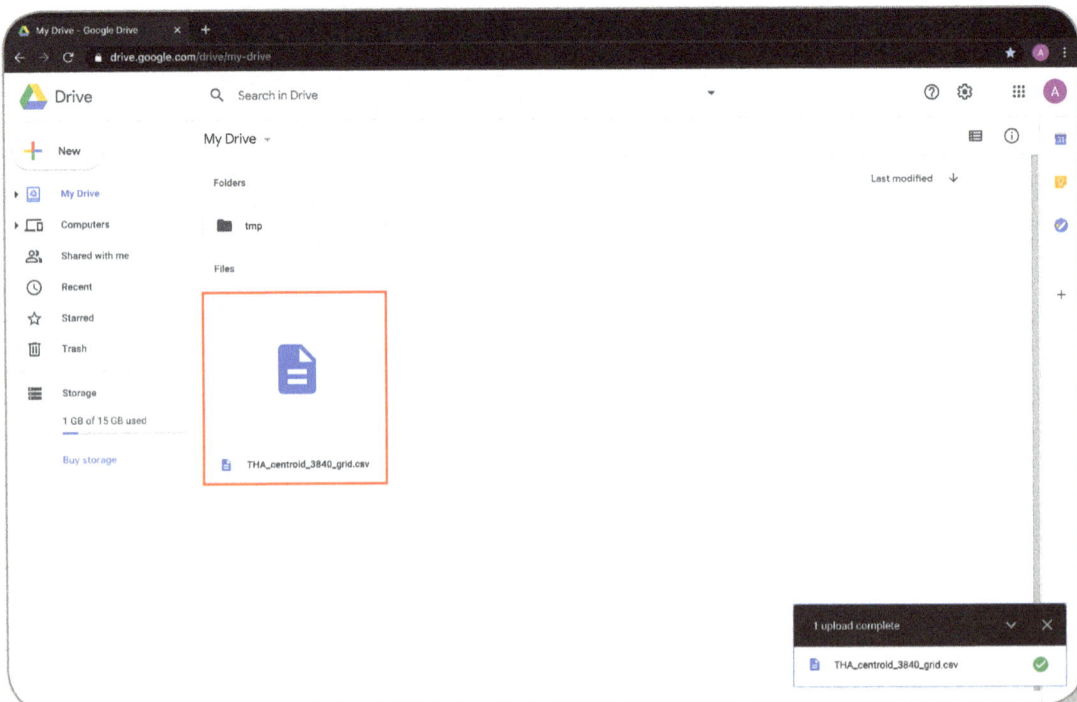

Repeat the steps using the country level shapefile. This time, upload the folder containing the country shapefile.

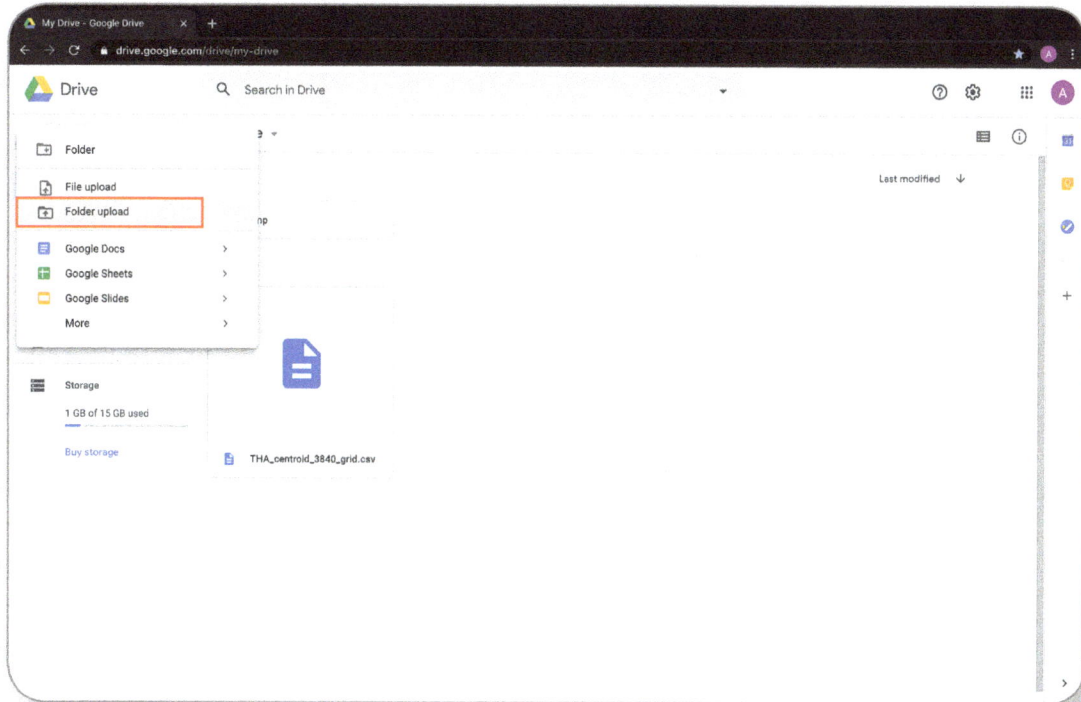

This folder is needed for determining the country boundary.

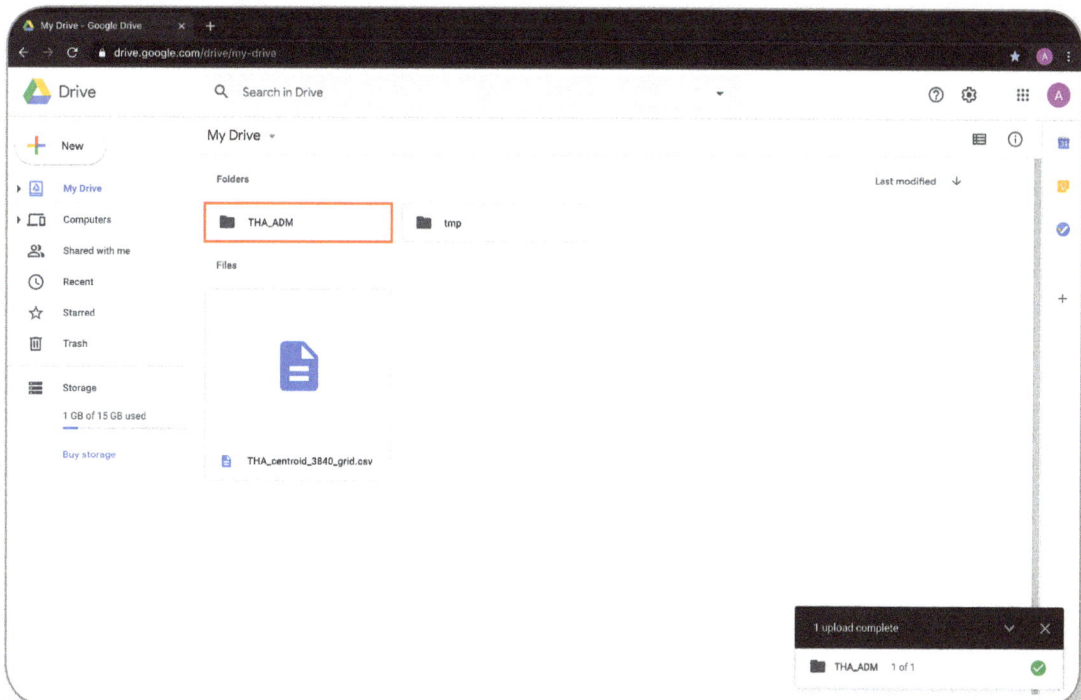

Downloading Satellite Imagery

STEP 1

In the browser address bar, input the Google Colaboratory (or Colab)[7] web address https://colab.research.google.com/ and press **Enter**.

Make sure to log in to your Google account. Then click **Upload**.

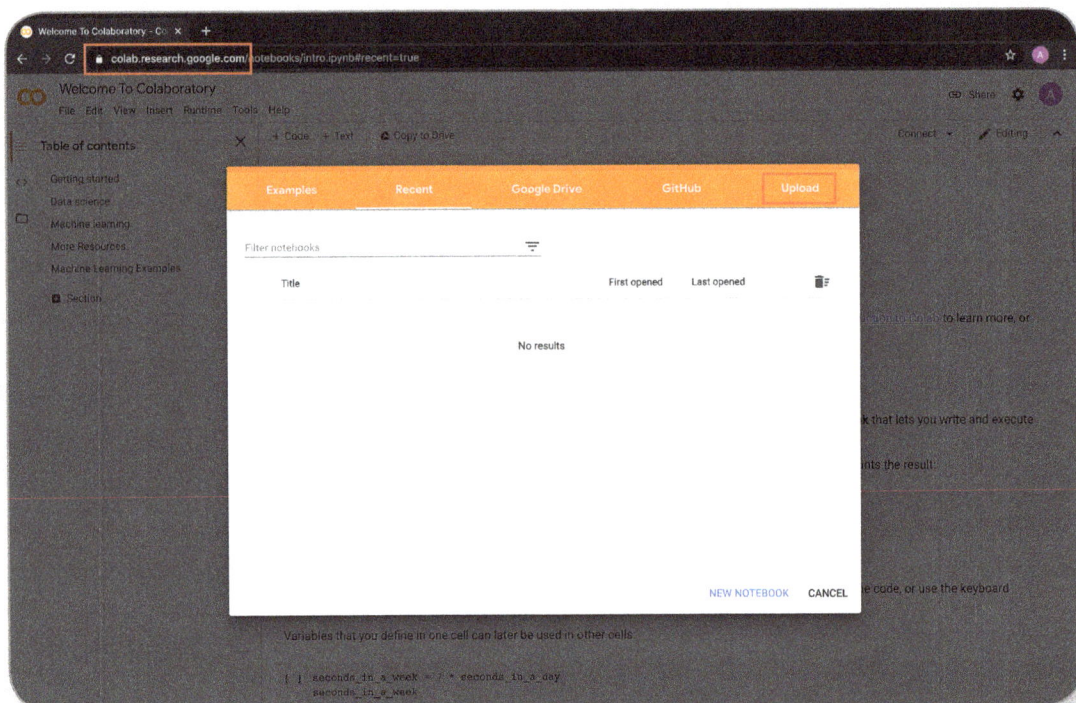

---

[7] Google Colab is a trademark of Google LLC.

STEP 2

Click **Choose File**.

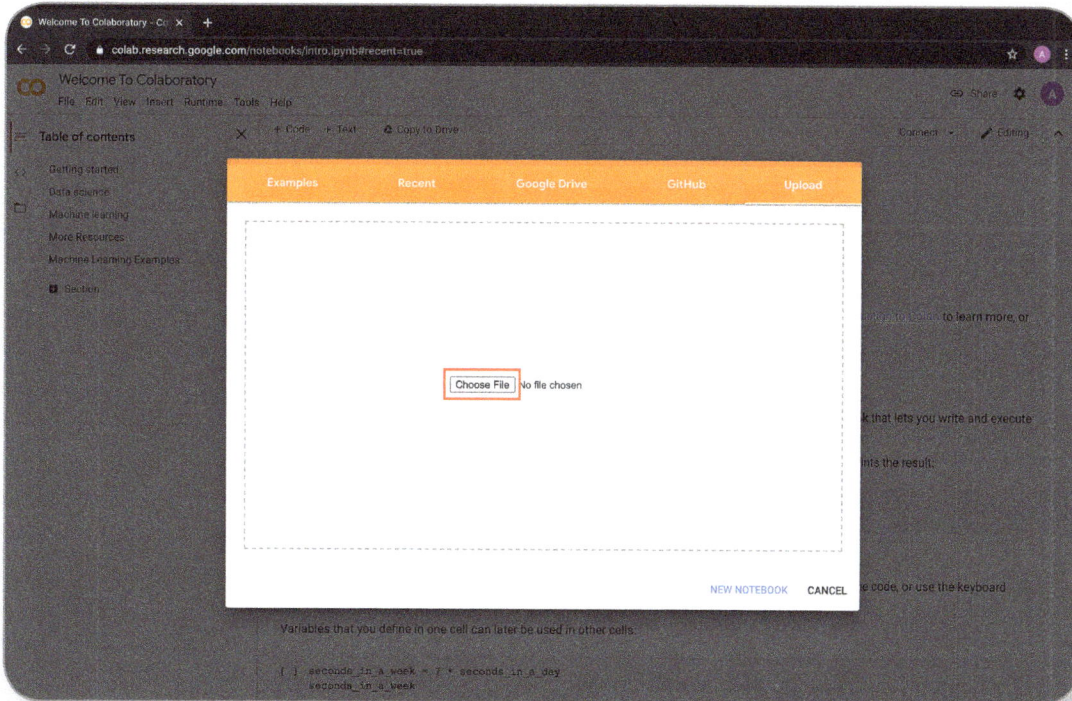

Locate the Jupyter Notebook file from the computer.

Use **Daytime_imagery_batch_download.ipynb**. Click **Open**.

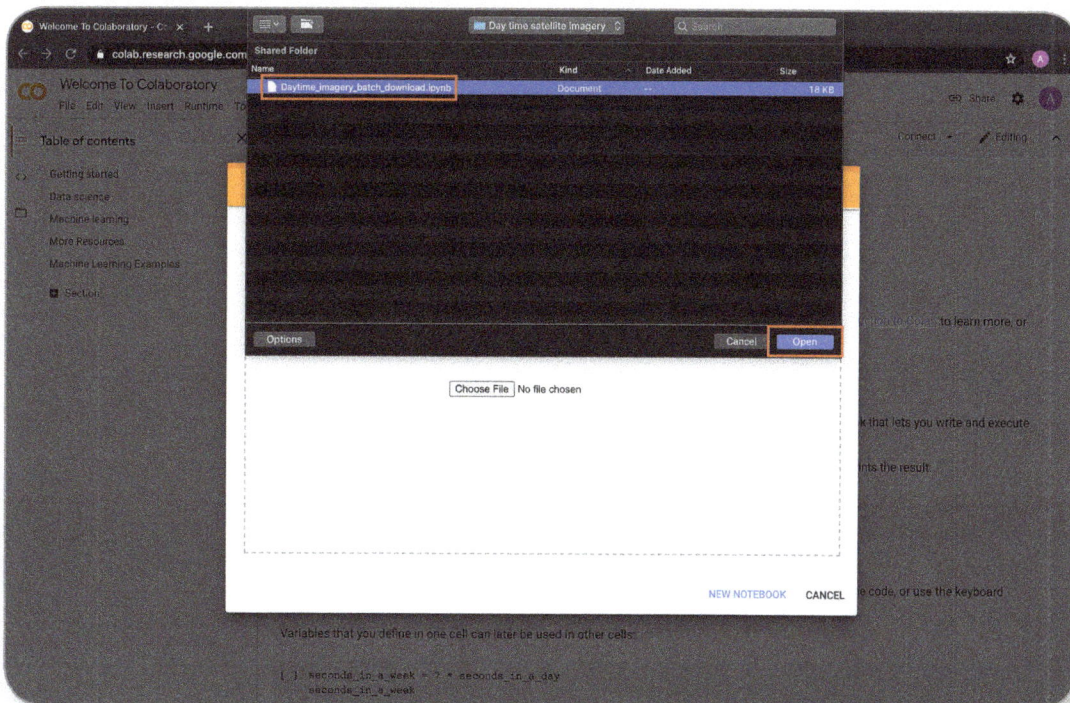

STEP 3

Click **Connect**.

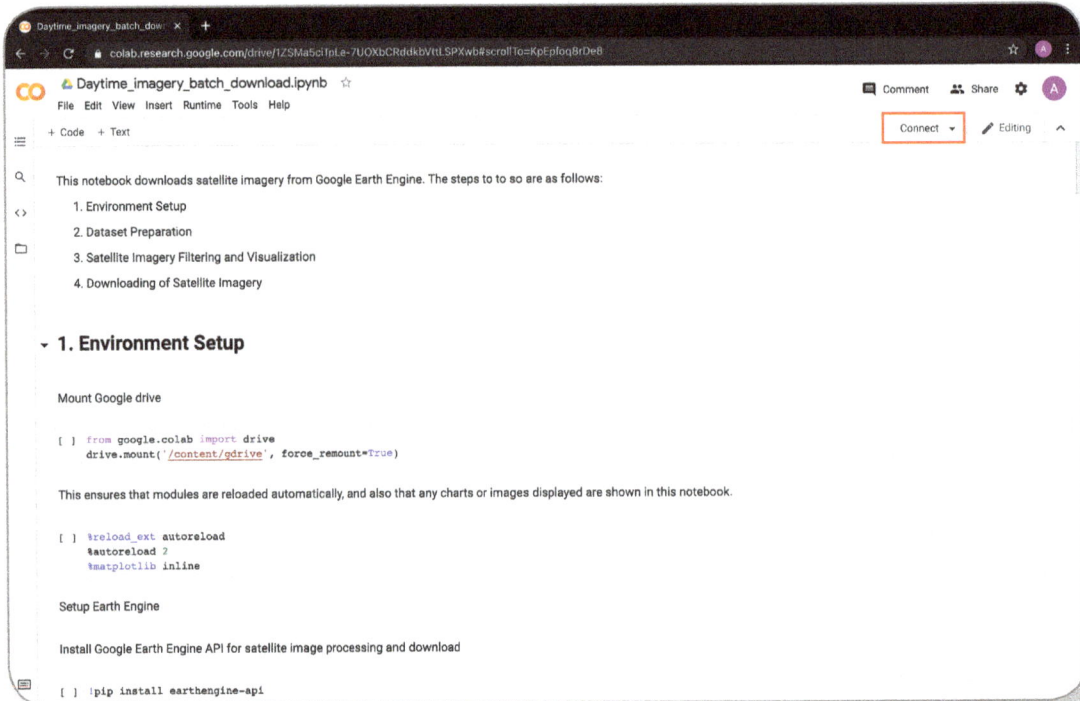

This will initialize the Colab's environment.

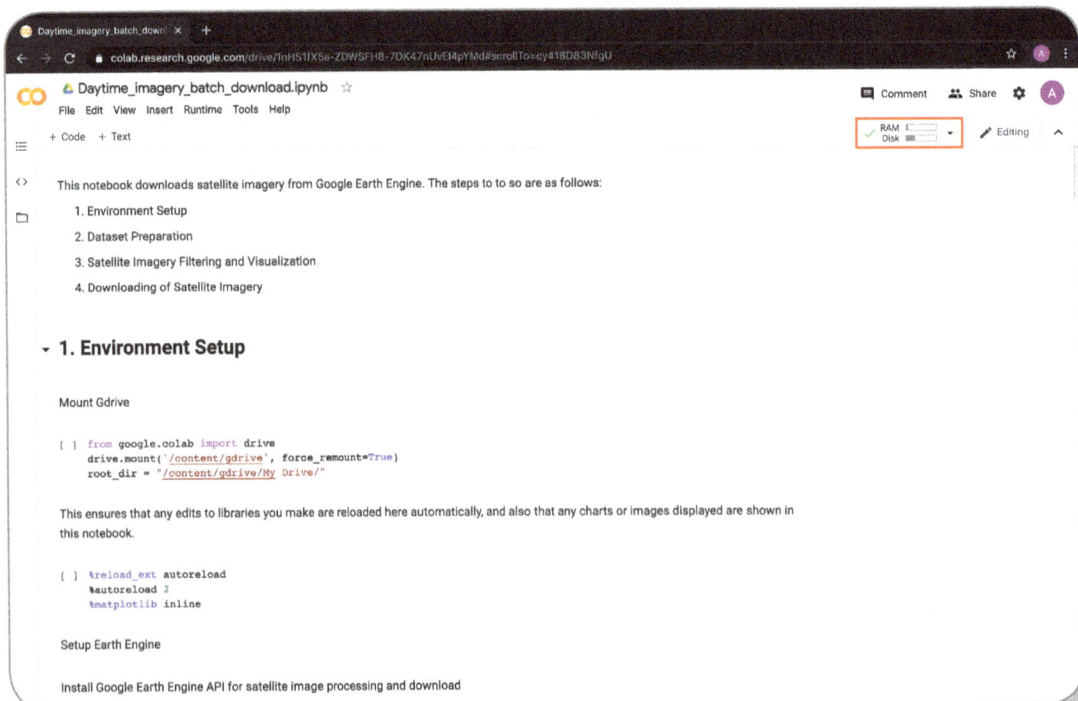

The Jupyter Notebook has two parts:

- Text cell is the non-executable part containing code descriptions or headers.

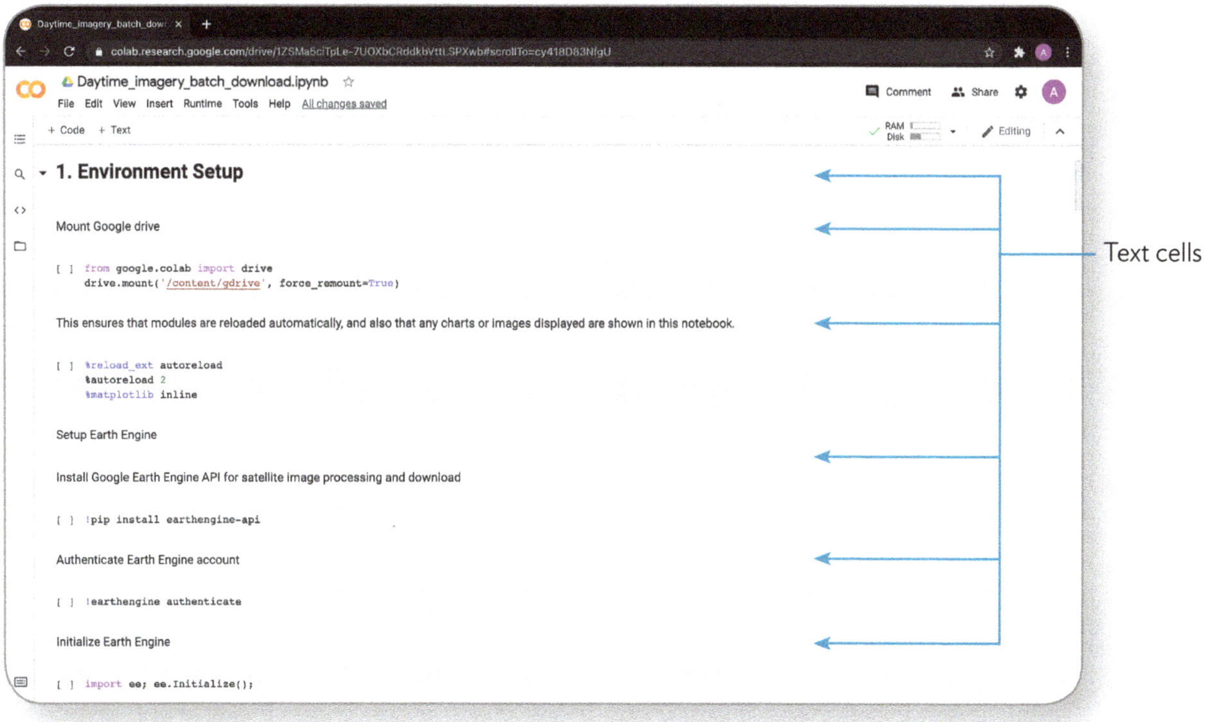

Text cells

- Code cell contains the Python commands and it is denoted by square brackets "[ ]".

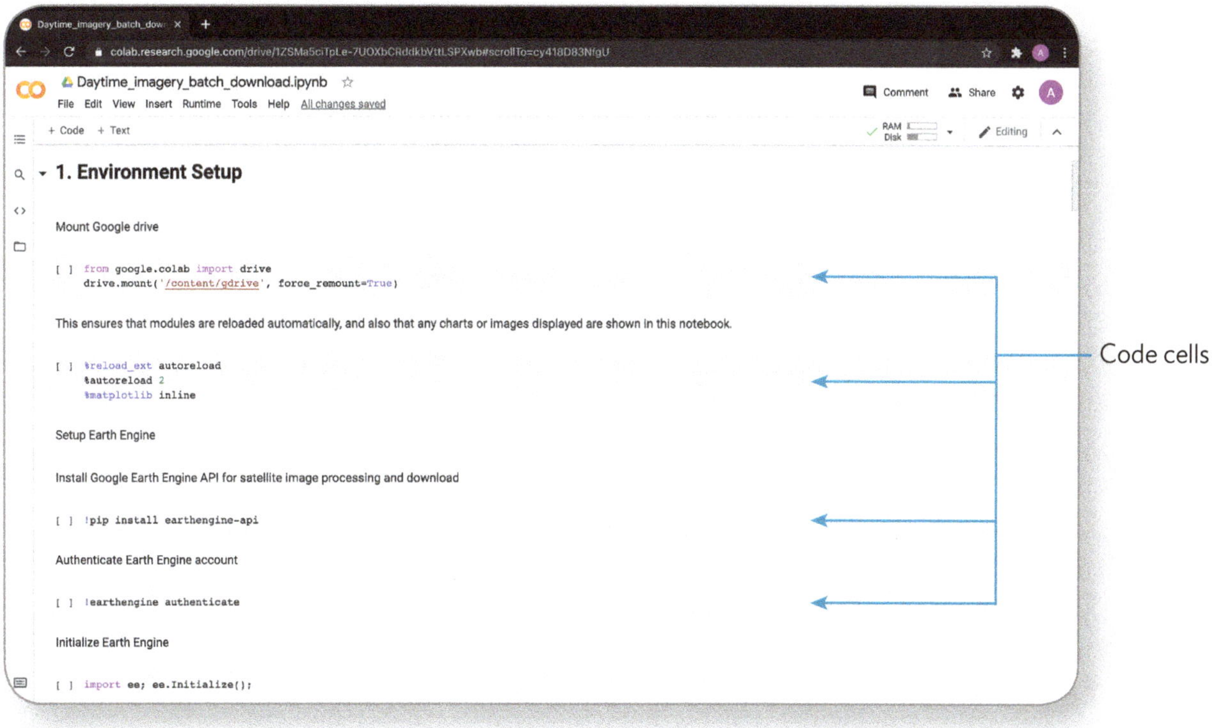

Code cells

To execute, click on each code cell and click ▶ button at the beginning of each code cell.

```
from google.colab import drive
drive.mount('/content/gdrive', force_remount=True)
```

The first code cell sets up and mounts the Google Drive. Click on the link.

```
from google.colab import drive
drive.mount('/content/gdrive', force_remount=True)

Go to this URL in a browser: https://accounts.google.com/o/oauth2/auth?client_id=947318989803-6bn6qk8qdgf4n4g3pfee6491hc0brc4i.apps.googleusercontent.com&red

Enter your authorization code:
```

STEP 4

In the browser, sign in to your Google account.

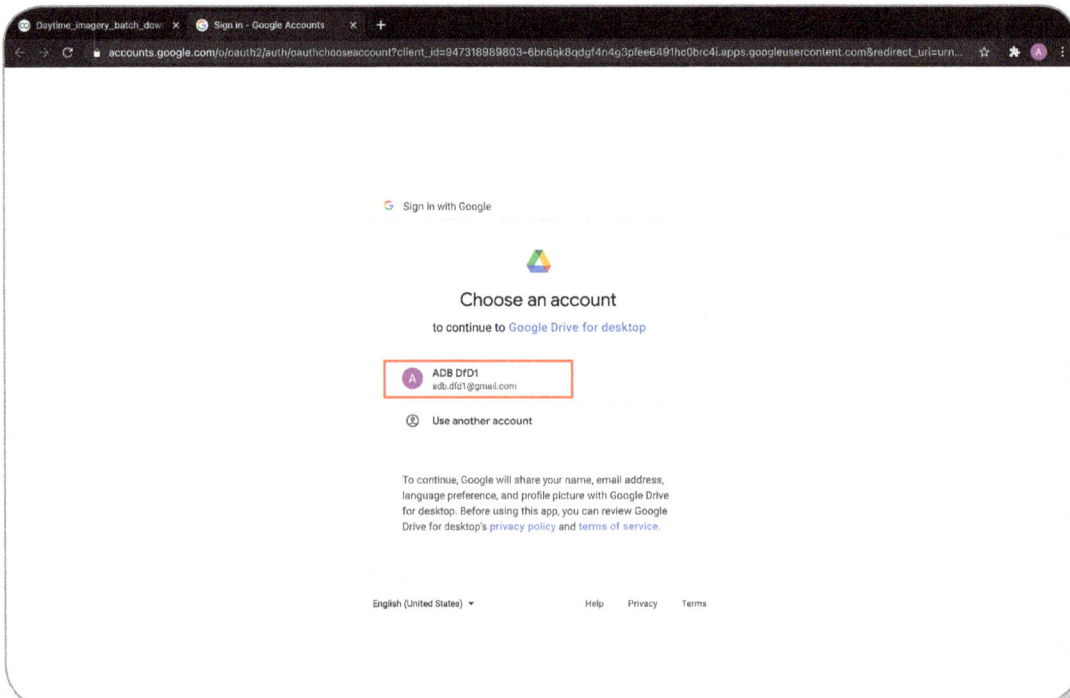

Click **Allow**.

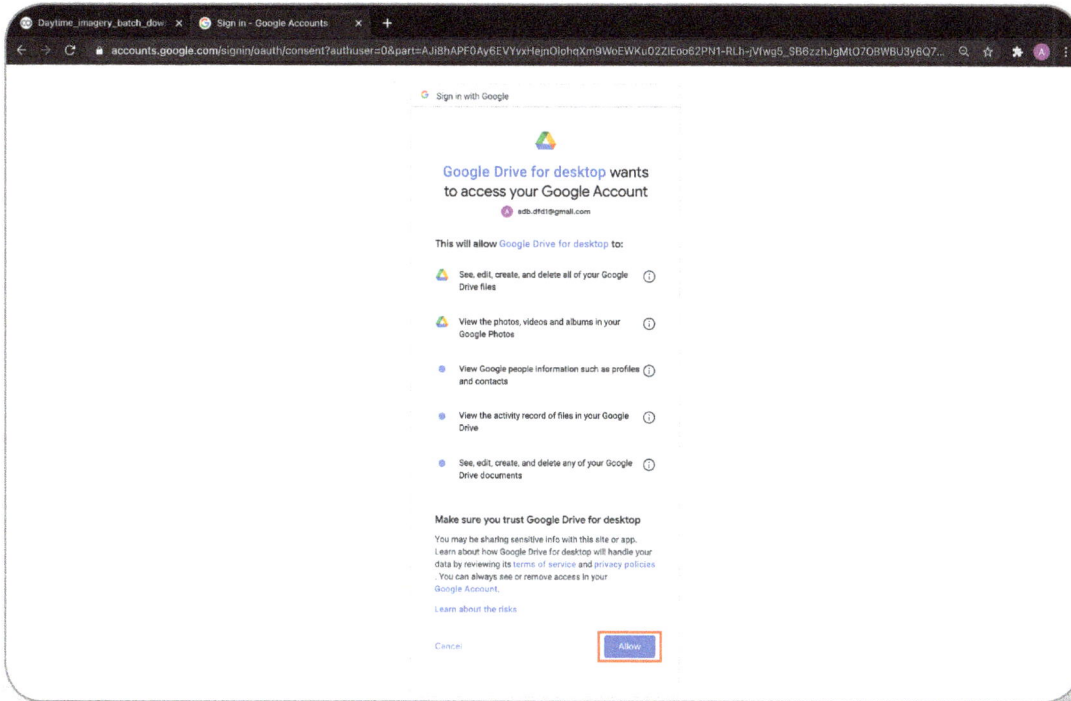

Click the **Copy** icon 🗐 to copy the code.

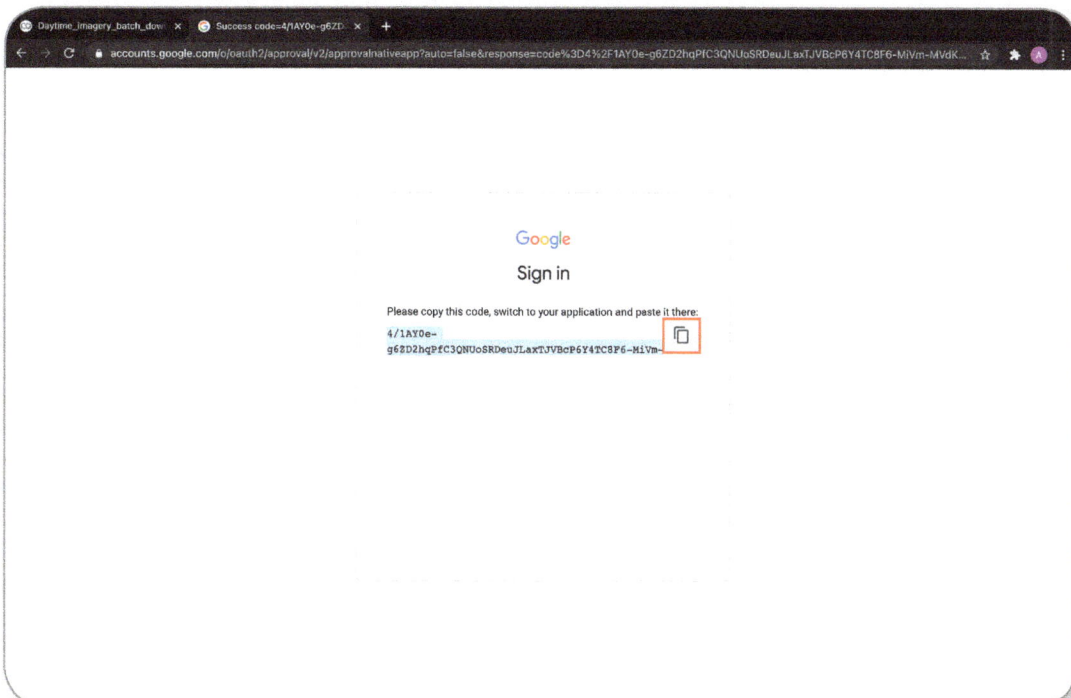

Return to the Colab browser tab. **Paste** the code in the text box. Then press **Enter**.

```
from google.colab import drive
drive.mount('/content/gdrive', force_remount=True)

... Go to this URL in a browser: https://accounts.google.com/o/oauth2/auth?client_id=947318989803-6bn6qk8qdgf4n4g3pfee6491hc0brc4i.apps.googleusercontent.com&red

Enter your authorization code:
aUgl_NlNg_zhsC_IZCJ8
```

A status will show the path where Google Drive is mounted.

```
from google.colab import drive
drive.mount('/content/gdrive', force_remount=True)

Mounted at /content/gdrive
```

STEP 5

Ensure that any edits made in the libraries are automatically reloaded and any charts or images displayed are shown in the notebook.

```
%reload_ext autoreload
%autoreload 2
%matplotlib inline
```

STEP 6

Setup the Google Earth Engine (GEE).[8]

```
Setup Earth Engine

Install Google Earth Engine API for satellite image processing and download

[ ]  !pip install earthengine-api

Authenticate Earth Engine account

[ ]  !earthengine authenticate

Initialize Earth Engine

[ ]  import ee; ee.Initialize();
```

---

8   Google Earth Engine is a trademark of Google LLC.

Install GEE Python library to the Colab virtual machine.

```
!pip install earthengine-api
```

Initialize the authentication of the GEE account by clicking on the link.

Authenticate Earth Engine account

```
!earthengine authenticate
```

WARNING:tensorflow:From /usr/local/lib/python3.6/dist-packages/tensorflow/python/compat/v2_compat.py:96: disable_resource_variables (from tensorflow.python.o
Instructions for updating:
non-resource variables are not supported in the long term
Running command using Cloud API. Set --no-use_cloud_api to go back to using the API

To authorize access needed by Earth Engine, open the following URL in a web browser and follow the instructions. If the web browser does not start automatica

https://accounts.google.com/o/oauth2/auth?client_id=517222506229-vsmmajv00ul0bs7p89v5m89qs8eb9359.apps.googleusercontent.com&scope=https%3A%2F%2Fwww.goog

The authorization workflow will generate a code, which you should paste in the box below.

Enter verification code:

STEP 7

In the browser, sign in to your Google account.

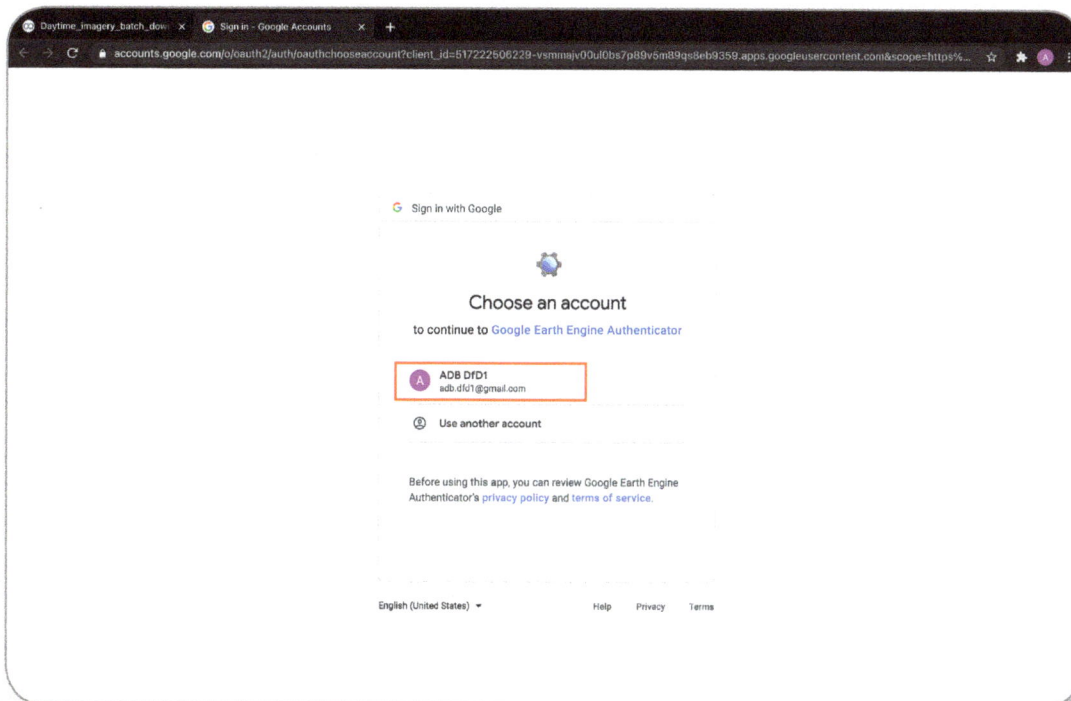

Click **Allow**.

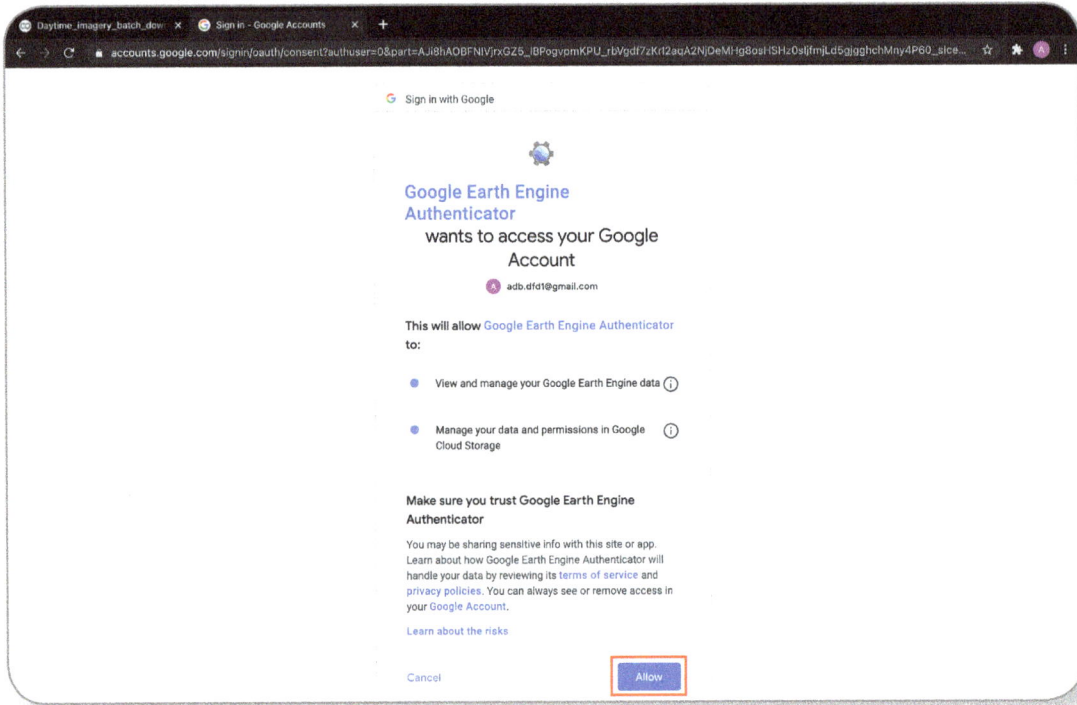

Click the **Copy** icon 🗐 to copy the code.

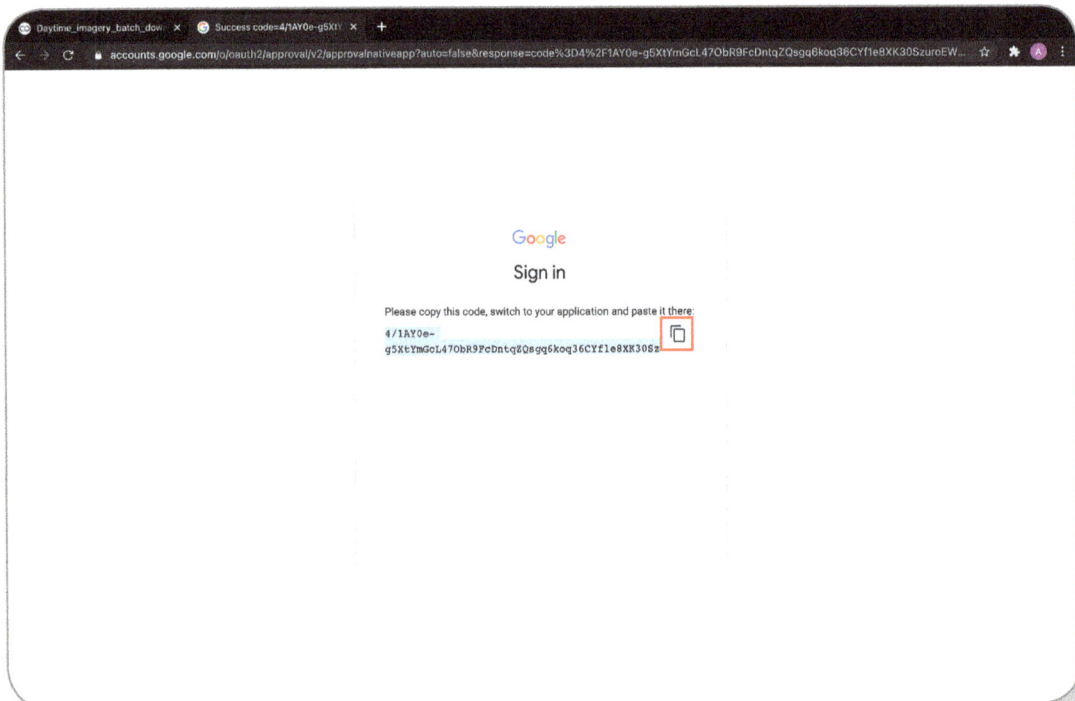

Return to the Colab browser tab. **Paste** the code in the text box. Then press **Enter**.

A status will show that the authorization token has been successfully saved.

STEP 8

Load the GEE library into the Python environment and initialize it.

```python
import ee; ee.Initialize();
```

STEP 9

Read the CSV file that contains the grid centroids.

```
▾ 2. Dataset Preparation

Import CSV from Google Drive

[ ]   import pandas as pd
      centroid_csv_path = '' #paste the link of csv file from your google drive
      df = pd.read_csv(centroid_csv_path)
      # Dataset is now stored in a Pandas dataframe

Check sample of CSV

[ ]   # Set the id = rownumber as index of the dataFrame
      df = df.set_index('id')
      df.head()

Get number of rows which is equal to the number of imagery centroid to be downloaded

[ ]   imagery_count = df.count()[1] + 1
      df.count()
```

Load the Python Data Analysis Library (Pandas) package that is used for reading external table files and manipulating data. Fetch the link of the CSV file that was previously uploaded to the Google drive and store it in the **centroid_csv_path** variable.

```
import pandas as pd
centroid_csv_path = '' #paste the link of csv file from your google drive
df = pd.read_csv(centroid_csv_path)
# Dataset is now stored in a Pandas dataframe
```

STEP 10

Click the **Files** icon 🗀 to show the **Files section**.

STEP 11

Click **gdrive** from the list of folders and expand the file directory tree to find the CSV file location.

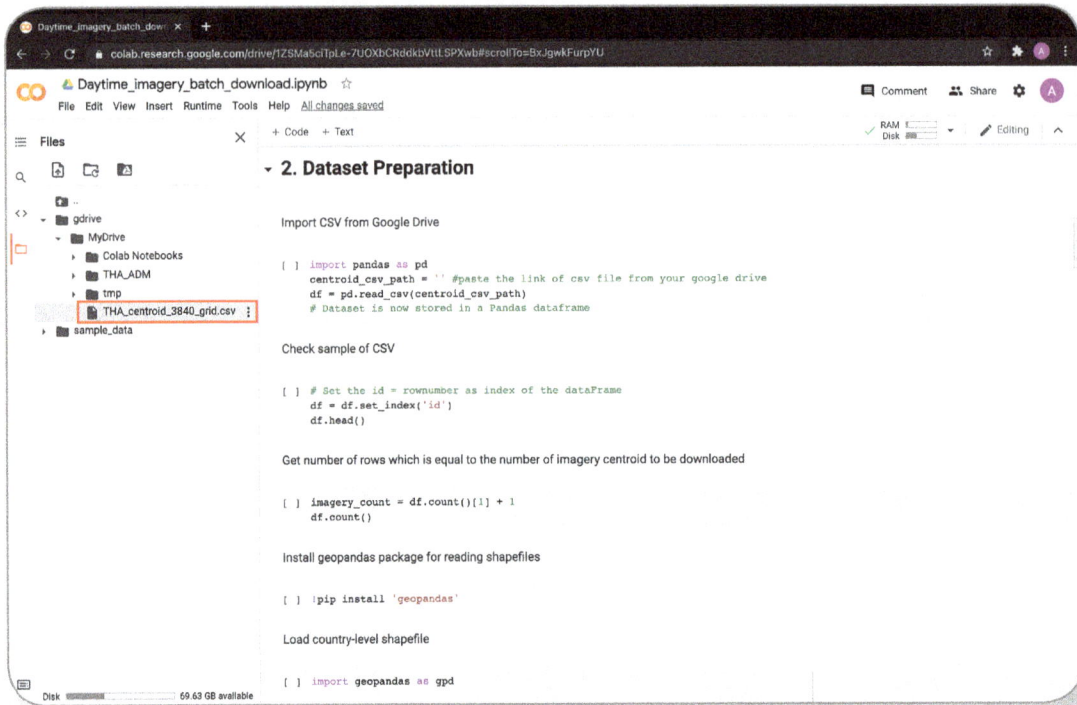

STEP 12

Click the vertical ellipsis to show more file options.

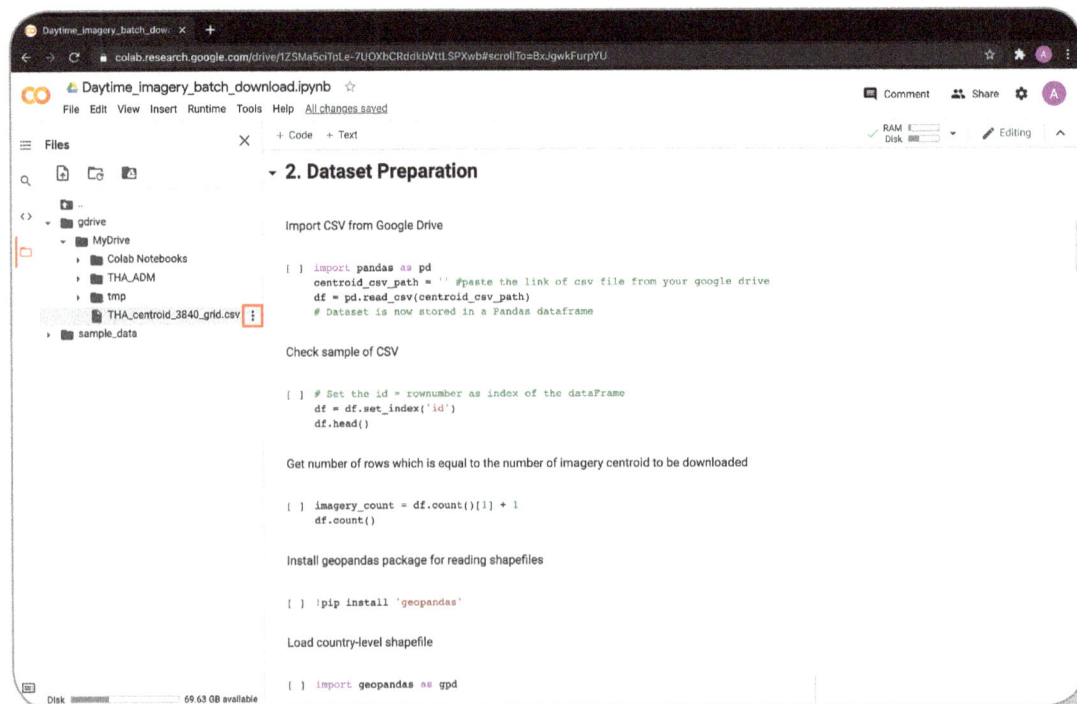

STEP 13

Click **Copy path**.

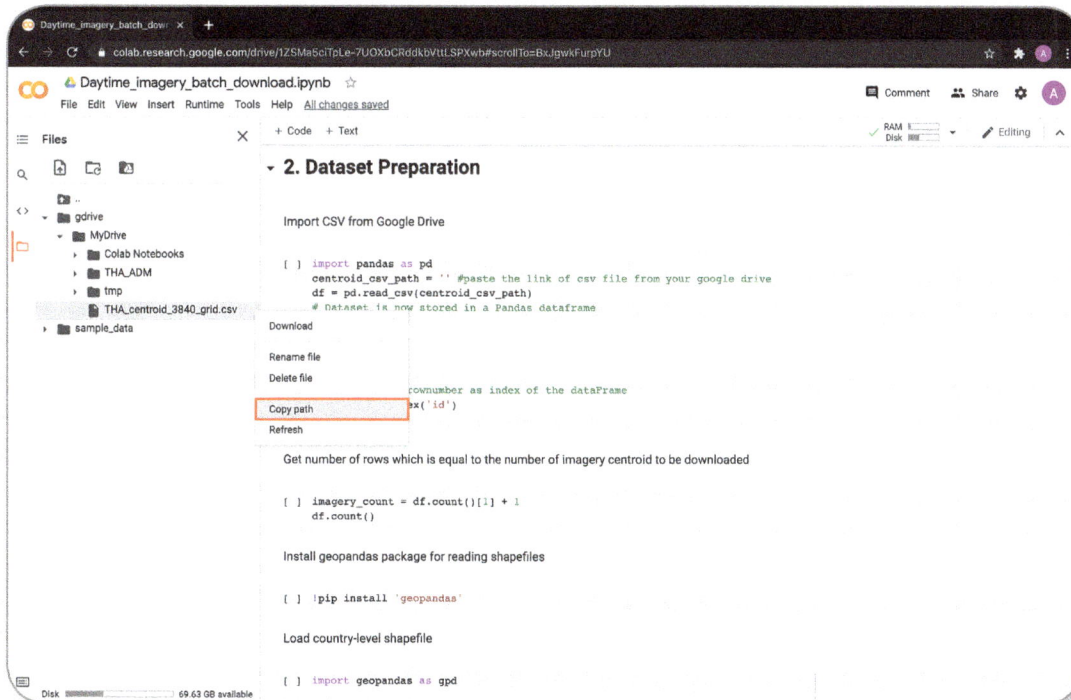

STEP 14

Paste the link on the blank space after the variable *centroid_csv_path* and enclose it in apostrophes.

```
import pandas as pd
centroid_csv_path = '/content/gdrive/MyDrive/THA_centroid_3840_grid.csv'
df = pd.read_csv(centroid_csv_path)
# Dataset is now stored in a Pandas dataframe
```

Then press ▶ to execute the code cell.

STEP 15

Execute the code cell to set the **id** column as the dataframe's row index and check the contents of the first five rows of the CSV file.

```
# Set the id = rownumber as index of the dataFrame
df = df.set_index('id')
df.head()
```

	lon	lat	geocode
id			
1	121.856175	20.825723	20902000
2	121.856175	20.790880	20902000
3	121.821332	20.756037	20902000
4	121.856175	20.756037	20902000
5	121.786490	20.721195	20902000

STEP 16

Determine the dataframe's row count using the **count()** function, which should be equal to the number of satellite imagery to be downloaded. The output is saved in the variable **imagery_count**.

```
imagery_count = df.count()[1] + 1
df.count()
```

```
lon         20090
lat         20090
geocode     20090
dtype: int64
```

STEP 17

Install the GeoPandas Python library in the Colab virtual machine. GeoPandas is an open source project that enables working with geospatial data in Python easier.

```
!pip install 'geopandas'
```

Load the GeoPandas library into the Python environment and then load the shapefile as **adm0_shp** variable. Display the first five rows of the shapefile's attribute table. To load the shapefile, fetch the link of the country level shapefile that was previously uploaded to Google Drive.

```
import geopandas as gpd

adm0_shp = gpd.read_file('') #paste the link of shapefile from your google drive
adm0_shp.head()
```

STEP 18

Click **Files** icon 🗀 to show the **Files section**.

STEP 19

Click **gdrive** from the list of folders and expand the file directory tree to find the folder containing the country level shapefile.

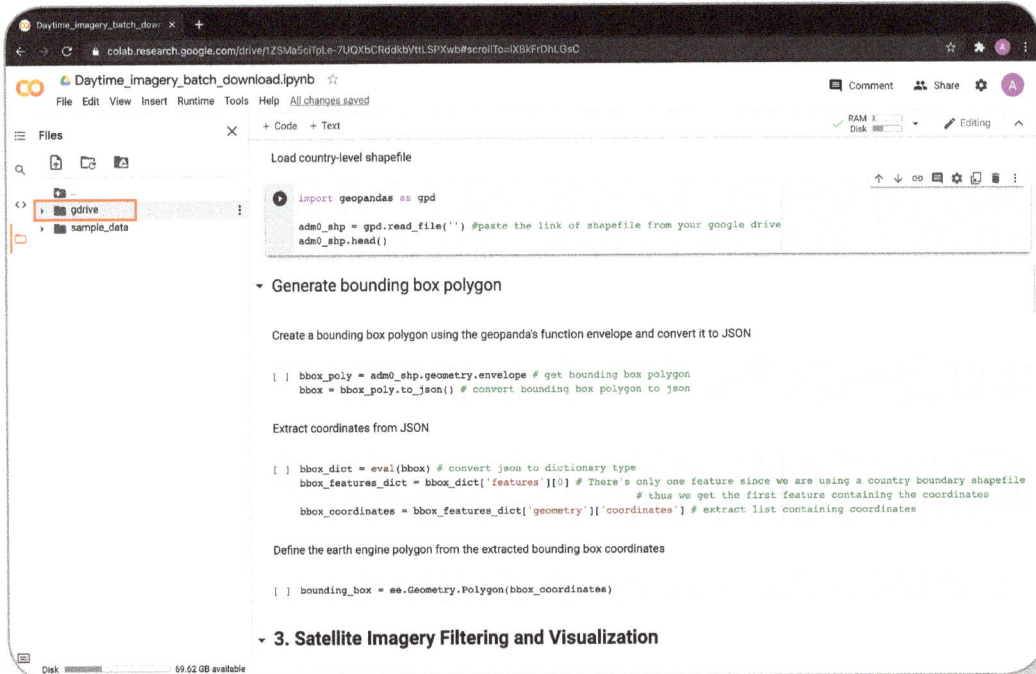

STEP 20

From the folder, select the country level shapefile (ADM0).

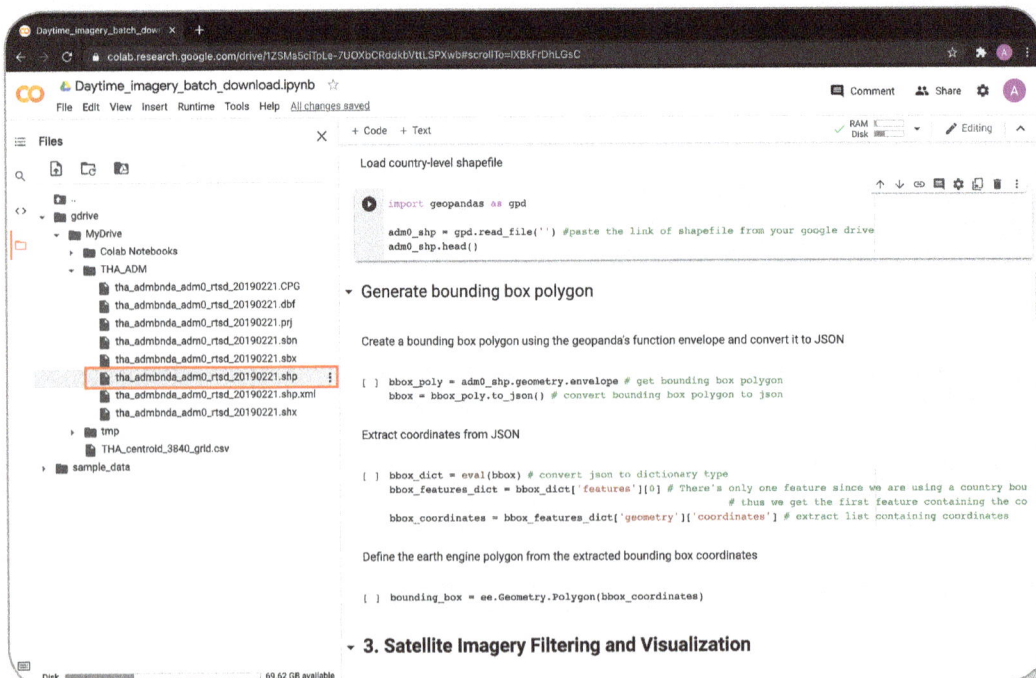

STEP 21

Click the vertical ellipsis to show more file options.

STEP 22

Click **Copy path**.

STEP 23

Paste the link on the blank space after the variable **adm0_shp** and enclose it in apostrophes.

```
import geopandas as gpd

adm0_shp = gpd.read_file('')  #paste the link of shapefile from your google drive
adm0_shp.head()
```

```
import geopandas as gpd

adm0_shp = gpd.read_file('/content/gdrive/MyDrive/THA_ADM/tha_admbnda_adm0_rtsd_20190221.shp')
adm0_shp.head()
```

STEP 24

Execute the code cell. The output shows the contents of the shapefile's attribute table. Only one row of features is displayed because it is a country level shapefile.

```
import geopandas as gpd

adm0_shp = gpd.read_file('/content/gdrive/MyDrive/THA_ADM/tha_admbnda_adm0_rtsd_20190221.shp') #paste the link of shapefile from your google drive
adm0_shp.head()
```

	Shape_Leng	Shape_Area	ADM0_EN	ADM0_TH	ADM0_PCODE	ADM0_REF	ADM0ALT1EN	ADM0ALT2EN	ADM0ALT1TH	ADM0ALT2TH	date	validOn	validTo	geometry
0	106.635862	43.403508	Thailand	ประเทศไทย	TH	None	None	None	None	None	2019-02-18	2019-02-21	None	MULTIPOLYGON (((100.09034 6.42574, 100.08995 6...

STEP 25

Generate the bounding box polygon. This code will limit the imagery download from GEE to the country boundaries.

▾ Generate bounding box polygon

Create a bounding box polygon using the geopanda's function envelope and convert it to JSON

```
[ ]  bbox_poly = adm0_shp.geometry.envelope # get bounding box polygon
     bbox = bbox_poly.to_json() # convert bounding box polygon to json
```

Extract coordinates from JSON

```
[ ]  bbox_dict = eval(bbox) # convert json to dictionary type
     bbox_features_dict = bbox_dict['features'][0] # There's only one feature since we are using a country boundary shapefile,
                                                   # thus we get the first feature. containing the coordinates
     bbox_coordinates = bbox_features_dict['geometry']['coordinates'] # extract list containing coordinates
```

Define the earth engine polygon from the extracted bounding box coordinates

```
[ ]  bounding_box = ee.Geometry.Polygon(bbox_coordinates)
```

First, create a bounding box polygon using the GeoPandas function envelope.

```
bbox_poly = adm0_shp.geometry.envelope # get bounding box polygon
bbox = bbox_poly.to_json() # convert bounding box polygon to json
```

Second, convert **bbox_poly** to java script object notation (JSON).

STEP 26

Extract bounding box coordinates from the JSON object.

First, convert the JSON object to a dictionary object.

```
bbox_dict = eval(bbox)
bbox_features_dict = bbox_dict['features'][0]

bbox_coordinates = bbox_features_dict['geometry']['coordinates']
```

Second, create a subset of the first feature containing the coordinates. *There is only one feature because it is a country level shapefile.*

Third, create a subset of the dictionary to get only the coordinate values of the bounding box.

STEP 27

Convert the bounding box coordinate into a GEE polygon object.

```
bounding_box = ee.Geometry.Polygon(bbox_coordinates)
```

STEP 28

View the composite imagery to check if the temporal filter used will generate a complete imagery, specifically for Sentinel-2 satellite imagery, covering the entire country.

Input the code pertaining to the country of study by typing country = "code". Then set the year of interest.

```
country = "THA" # country of study
year = "2015"
```

Use an if-else statement to select which satellite imagery to use based on the year of interest and to define the image resolution and image size of the corresponding satellite. Based on the satellite information, generate the folder name where the imagery will be stored in the Google Drive. Then generate the filename using the same information.

```
if int(year) >= 2015:
    day_sat="ST" # sentinel 2 satellite
    img_res = "384"
    img_size = str(int(img_res)*10)
else:
    day_sat = "LS" # Landsat
    img_res = "256"
    img_size = str(int(img_res)*15)

# Generate output directory---
drive_folder = "_".join(["CNN","IMGB",country,year,day_sat,img_res,"TIF",img_size])

# assemble DIMG filename
DIMG = "_".join(["CNN_DIMG",country,year,day_sat,img_res,img_size])
```

Print out the values of the variables to check if the outputs are correct.

```
print(day_sat)
print(img_res)
print(img_size)
print(drive_folder)
print(DIMG)

ST
384
3840
CNN_IMGB_THA_2015_ST_384_TIF_3840
CNN_DIMG_THA_2015_ST_384_3840
```

STEP 29

Specify the starting date of the coverage of satellite imagery.

```
# Specify coverage date
# Satellite imagery coverage starting date:
start_MM = "01"
start_DD = "01"
start_date = "-".join([year,start_MM,start_DD])
print("Coverage start date: "+start_date)

Coverage start date: 2015-01-01
```

Then specify the end date. The end date of the temporal imagery filter needs to be adjusted to have a longer temporal coverage in case it fails to generate a complete imagery for the entire country.

```python
# Change satellite imagery coverage end date if the composite image for the
# entire country is incomplete
# Satellite imagery coverage end date:
end_YYYY = "2016"
end_MM = "04"
end_DD = "30"

if int(end_YYYY)<int(year):
  end_YYYY=str(int(year)+1)
  print("Please specify end_YYYY")

end_date = "-".join([end_YYYY,end_MM,end_DD])
print("Coverage end date: "+end_date)
```

```
Coverage end date: 2016-04-30
```

STEP 30

Through the GEE Application Programming Interface (API), filter the satellite imagery collection based on the temporal range (i.e., **start_date** and **end_date**) and country boundary (i.e., **bounding_box**). Visualize the imagery to check if the temporal filter yields complete imagery for the entire country.

```python
# import folium library
import folium


if day_sat == "ST":

  def maskS2clouds(image):
    qa = image.select('QA60')
# Bits 10 and 11 are clouds and cirrus, respectively.
    cloudBitMask = 1 << 10
    cirrusBitMask = 1 << 11
# Both flags should be set to zero, indicating clear conditions.
    mask = qa.bitwiseAnd(cloudBitMask).eq(0).And(qa.bitwiseAnd(cirrusBitMask).eq(0))
    return image.updateMask(mask).divide(10000)

  rgbVis = {'min': 0.0,'max': 0.3,'bands': ['B4', 'B3', 'B2']}

  # Filter an image collection.
  cloud_masked = ee.ImageCollection('COPERNICUS/S2')\
  .filterDate(start_date, end_date)\
  .filterBounds(bounding_box).filter(ee.Filter.lt('CLOUDY_PIXEL_PERCENTAGE', 60))\
  .map(maskS2clouds)

  # Take median value
  satellite_imagery = cloud_masked.median().visualize(**rgbVis)

else:
  if int(year) < 2013:
      landsat_mission = 'LANDSAT/LE07/C01/T1' # Select Landsat 7
      LS_day_sat = "LS7"
  else:
      landsat_mission = 'LANDSAT/LC08/C01/T1' # Select Landsat 8
      LS_day_sat = "LS8"
```

STEP 31

First, import the Folium library in the Python environment. Folium is a Python visualization library for geospatial data.

```python
# import folium library
import folium
```

STEP 32

Using an if-else statement, select the appropriate filter for the satellite to be used. The satellite is selected based on the availability of coverage of the imagery. Landsat 7 covers the period January 1999 to present and Landsat 8 covers April 2013 to present, while Sentinel-2 imagery covers the period June 2015 to present.

```python
# import folium library
import folium


if day_sat == "ST":

    def maskS2clouds(image):
      qa = image.select('QA60')
    # Bits 10 and 11 are clouds and cirrus, respectively.
      cloudBitMask = 1 << 10
      cirrusBitMask = 1 << 11
    # Both flags should be set to zero, indicating clear conditions.
      mask = qa.bitwiseAnd(cloudBitMask).eq(0).And(qa.bitwiseAnd(cirrusBitMask).eq(0))
      return image.updateMask(mask).divide(10000)

    rgbVis = {'min': 0.0,'max': 0.3,'bands': ['B4', 'B3', 'B2']}

    # Filter an image collection.
    cloud_masked = ee.ImageCollection('COPERNICUS/S2')\
    .filterDate(start_date, end_date)\
    .filterBounds(bounding_box).filter(ee.Filter.lt('CLOUDY_PIXEL_PERCENTAGE', 60))\
    .map(maskS2clouds)

    # Take median value
    satellite_imagery = cloud_masked.median().visualize(**rgbVis)

else:
    if int(year) < 2013:
        landsat_mission = 'LANDSAT/LE07/C01/T1' # Select Landsat 7
        LS_day_sat = "LS7"
    else:
        landsat_mission = 'LANDSAT/LC08/C01/T1' # Select Landsat 8
        LS_day_sat = "LS8"

    # Landsat 7 and 8 imageries are available starting January 1999 and April 2013 to present

    filtered_shp = ee.ImageCollection(landsat_mission)\
    .filterDate(start_date, end_date)\
    .filterBounds(bounding_box)

    # Use inbuilt Earth Engine function to create big composite image from the Landsat tiles
    composite = ee.Algorithms.Landsat.simpleComposite(filtered_shp).float();

    # Pansharpening
    ###########################
    if LS_day_sat == "LS7":
      rgb = composite.select('B3', 'B2', 'B1').unitScale(0, 255)
      # For information on Landsat 7 bands,
      # please visit https://developers.google.com/earth-engine/datasets/catalog/LANDSAT_LE07_C01_T1_SR#bands
    if LS_day_sat == "LS8":
      rgb = composite.select('B4', 'B3', 'B2').unitScale(0, 255)
      # For information on Landsat 7 bands,
      # please visit https://developers.google.com/earth-engine/datasets/catalog/LANDSAT_LC08_C01_T1_SR#bands
    gray = composite.select('B8').unitScale(0, 155)

    # Convert to HSV, swap in the pan band, and convert back to RGB.
    huesat = rgb.rgbToHsv().select('hue', 'saturation')
    satellite_imagery = ee.Image.cat(huesat, gray).hsvToRgb()
```

Filter the imagery collection in GEE. If the basis is the reference year of the study, then employ Sentinel-2. Define the function **maskS2clouds()**. Using the Sentinel-2 QA60 band, create a cloud mask to filter over the imagery within the temporal range.

```python
if day_sat == "ST":

    def maskS2clouds(image):
        qa = image.select('QA60')
    # Bits 10 and 11 are clouds and cirrus, respectively.
        cloudBitMask = 1 << 10
        cirrusBitMask = 1 << 11
    # Both flags should be set to zero, indicating clear conditions.
        mask = qa.bitwiseAnd(cloudBitMask).eq(0).And(qa.bitwiseAnd(cirrusBitMask).eq(0))
        return image.updateMask(mask).divide(10000)

    rgbVis = {'min': 0.0,'max': 0.3,'bands': ['B4', 'B3', 'B2']}

    # Filter an image collection.
    cloud_masked = ee.ImageCollection('COPERNICUS/S2')\
    .filterDate(start_date, end_date)\
    .filterBounds(bounding_box).filter(ee.Filter.lt('CLOUDY_PIXEL_PERCENTAGE', 60))\
    .map(maskS2clouds)

    # Take median value
    satellite_imagery = cloud_masked.median().visualize(**rgbVis)
```

STEP 33

rgbVis defines the visualization parameters to be used in the filter.

- Min and max indicate the values to map red, green, and blue (RGB) 8-bit value to 0 and 255, respectively.
- Bands indicate the satellite bands to visualize.
  - B4 – refers to red band.
  - B3 – refers to green band.
  - B2 – refers to blue band.

```
if day_sat == "ST":

  def maskS2clouds(image):
    qa = image.select('QA60')
  # Bits 10 and 11 are clouds and cirrus, respectively.
    cloudBitMask = 1 << 10
    cirrusBitMask = 1 << 11
  # Both flags should be set to zero, indicating clear conditions.
    mask = qa.bitwiseAnd(cloudBitMask).eq(0).And(qa.bitwiseAnd(cirrusBitMask).eq(0))
    return image.updateMask(mask).divide(10000)

  rgbVis = {'min': 0.0,'max': 0.3,'bands': ['B4', 'B3', 'B2']}

  # Filter an image collection.
  cloud_masked = ee.ImageCollection('COPERNICUS/S2')\
  .filterDate(start_date, end_date)\
  .filterBounds(bounding_box).filter(ee.Filter.lt('CLOUDY_PIXEL_PERCENTAGE', 60))\
  .map(maskS2clouds)

  # Take median value
  satellite_imagery = cloud_masked.median().visualize(**rgbVis)
```

STEP 34

Apply filter to the **ImageCollection** (i.e., Sentinel 2, or COPERNICUS/S2 as used in this illustration).

- **filterDate()** defines the temporal coverage.
- **filterBounds()** uses the bounding box to limit the filter to the country boundaries.
- **filter(ee.Filter.lt('CLOUDY_PIXEL_PERCENTAGE', 60))** provides the filter to exclude images with more than 60% cloud cover.
- **map(maskS2clouds)** uses the function for creating cloud mask.

```
if day_sat == "ST":

  def maskS2clouds(image):
    qa = image.select('QA60')
  # Bits 10 and 11 are clouds and cirrus, respectively.
    cloudBitMask = 1 << 10
    cirrusBitMask = 1 << 11
  # Both flags should be set to zero, indicating clear conditions.
    mask = qa.bitwiseAnd(cloudBitMask).eq(0).And(qa.bitwiseAnd(cirrusBitMask).eq(0))
    return image.updateMask(mask).divide(10000)

  rgbVis = {'min': 0.0,'max': 0.3,'bands': ['B4', 'B3', 'B2']}

  # Filter an image collection.
  cloud_masked = ee.ImageCollection('COPERNICUS/S2')\
  .filterDate(start_date, end_date)\
  .filterBounds(bounding_box).filter(ee.Filter.lt('CLOUDY_PIXEL_PERCENTAGE', 60))\
  .map(maskS2clouds)

  # Take median value
  satellite_imagery = cloud_masked.median().visualize(**rgbVis)
```

STEP 35

Generate another object containing the median value of the filtered image collection and apply the visualization parameter.

```python
if day_sat == "ST":

  def maskS2clouds(image):
    qa = image.select('QA60')
  # Bits 10 and 11 are clouds and cirrus, respectively.
    cloudBitMask = 1 << 10
    cirrusBitMask = 1 << 11
  # Both flags should be set to zero, indicating clear conditions.
    mask = qa.bitwiseAnd(cloudBitMask).eq(0).And(qa.bitwiseAnd(cirrusBitMask).eq(0))
    return image.updateMask(mask).divide(10000)

  rgbVis = {'min': 0.0,'max': 0.3,'bands': ['B4', 'B3', 'B2']}

  # Filter an image collection.
  cloud_masked = ee.ImageCollection('COPERNICUS/S2')\
  .filterDate(start_date, end_date)\
  .filterBounds(bounding_box).filter(ee.Filter.lt('CLOUDY_PIXEL_PERCENTAGE', 60))\
  .map(maskS2clouds)

  # Take median value
  satellite_imagery = cloud_masked.median().visualize(**rgbVis)
```

STEP 36

For Landsat satellite imagery, use Landsat 7 for available imagery prior to 2013 and Landsat 8 for available imagery in 2013 and beyond. Assign the Landsat imagery collection to the variable **landsat_mission**.

LANDSAT/LE07/C01/T1 pertains to Landsat 7 imagery collection in GEE and LANDSAT/LC08/C01/T1 pertains to that of Landsat 8.

```python
else:
    if int(year) < 2013:
        landsat_mission = 'LANDSAT/LE07/C01/T1' # Select Landsat 7
        LS_day_sat = "LS7"
    else:
        landsat_mission = 'LANDSAT/LC08/C01/T1' # Select Landsat 8
        LS_day_sat = "LS8"

    # Landsat 7 and 8 imageries are available starting January 1999 and April 2013 to present

    filtered_shp = ee.ImageCollection(landsat_mission)\
    .filterDate(start_date, end_date)\
    .filterBounds(bounding_box)

    # Use inbuilt Earth Engine function to create big composite image from the Landsat tiles
    composite = ee.Algorithms.Landsat.simpleComposite(filtered_shp).float();

    # Pansharpening
    ###########################
    if LS_day_sat == "LS7":
        rgb = composite.select('B3', 'B2', 'B1').unitScale(0, 255)
        # For information on Landsat 7 bands,
        # please visit https://developers.google.com/earth-engine/datasets/catalog/LANDSAT_LE07_C01_T1_SR#bands
    if LS_day_sat == "LS8":
        rgb = composite.select('B4', 'B3', 'B2').unitScale(0, 255)
        # For information on Landsat 7 bands,
        # please visit https://developers.google.com/earth-engine/datasets/catalog/LANDSAT_LC08_C01_T1_SR#bands
    gray = composite.select('B8').unitScale(0, 155)

    # Convert to HSV, swap in the pan band, and convert back to RGB.
    huesat = rgb.rgbToHsv().select('hue', 'saturation')
    satellite_imagery = ee.Image.cat(huesat, gray).hsvToRgb()
```

STEP 37

Apply filter to the selected Landsat **ImageCollection**.

- **filterDate()** defines the temporal coverage.
- **filterBounds()** uses the bounding box to limit the filter to the country boundaries.

```python
else:
    if int(year) < 2013:
        landsat_mission = 'LANDSAT/LE07/C01/T1' # Select Landsat 7
        LS_day_sat = "LS7"
    else:
        landsat_mission = 'LANDSAT/LC08/C01/T1' # Select Landsat 8
        LS_day_sat = "LS8"

    # Landsat 7 and 8 imageries are available starting January 1999 and April 2013 to present

    filtered_shp = ee.ImageCollection(landsat_mission)\
    .filterDate(start_date, end_date)\
    .filterBounds(bounding_box)

    # Use inbuilt Earth Engine function to create big composite image from the Landsat tiles
    composite = ee.Algorithms.Landsat.simpleComposite(filtered_shp).float();

    # Pansharpening
    ###########################
    if LS_day_sat == "LS7":
      rgb = composite.select('B3', 'B2', 'B1').unitScale(0, 255)
      # For information on Landsat 7 bands,
      # please visit https://developers.google.com/earth-engine/datasets/catalog/LANDSAT_LE07_C01_T1_SR#bands
    if LS_day_sat == "LS8":
      rgb = composite.select('B4', 'B3', 'B2').unitScale(0, 255)
      # For information on Landsat 7 bands,
      # please visit https://developers.google.com/earth-engine/datasets/catalog/LANDSAT_LC08_C01_T1_SR#bands
    gray = composite.select('B8').unitScale(0, 155)

    # Convert to HSV, swap in the pan band, and convert back to RGB.
    huesat = rgb.rgbToHsv().select('hue', 'saturation')
    satellite_imagery = ee.Image.cat(huesat, gray).hsvToRgb()
```

STEP 38

Generate a composite image for the entire country using the filtered ImageCollection. *This command builds the composite from imagery with less cloud cover.*

```python
else:
   if int(year) < 2013:
      landsat_mission = 'LANDSAT/LE07/C01/T1' # Select Landsat 7
      LS_day_sat = "LS7"
   else:
      landsat_mission = 'LANDSAT/LC08/C01/T1' # Select Landsat 8
      LS_day_sat = "LS8"

   # Landsat 7 and 8 imageries are available starting January 1999 and April 2013 to present

   filtered_shp = ee.ImageCollection(landsat_mission)\
   .filterDate(start_date, end_date)\
   .filterBounds(bounding_box)

   # Use inbuilt Earth Engine function to create big composite image from the Landsat tiles
   composite = ee.Algorithms.Landsat.simpleComposite(filtered_shp).float();

   # Pansharpening
   ###########################
   if LS_day_sat == "LS7":
     rgb = composite.select('B3', 'B2', 'B1').unitScale(0, 255)
     # For information on Landsat 7 bands,
     # please visit https://developers.google.com/earth-engine/datasets/catalog/LANDSAT_LE07_C01_T1_SR#bands
   if LS_day_sat == "LS8":
     rgb = composite.select('B4', 'B3', 'B2').unitScale(0, 255)
     # For information on Landsat 7 bands,
     # please visit https://developers.google.com/earth-engine/datasets/catalog/LANDSAT_LC08_C01_T1_SR#bands
   gray = composite.select('B8').unitScale(0, 155)

   # Convert to HSV, swap in the pan band, and convert back to RGB.
   huesat = rgb.rgbToHsv().select('hue', 'saturation')
   satellite_imagery = ee.Image.cat(huesat, gray).hsvToRgb()
```

STEP 39

Pansharpen the Landsat imagery. This is an intermediate data preparation step undertaken to enhance the resolution of the images. Pansharpening combines high resolution panchromatic images (black and white but sensitive to colors) with lower resolution multispectral band images.

```python
else:
    if int(year) < 2013:
        landsat_mission = 'LANDSAT/LE07/C01/T1' # Select Landsat 7
        LS_day_sat = "LS7"
    else:
        landsat_mission = 'LANDSAT/LC08/C01/T1' # Select Landsat 8
        LS_day_sat = "LS8"

    # Landsat 7 and 8 imageries are available starting January 1999 and April 2013 to present

    filtered_shp = ee.ImageCollection(landsat_mission)\
    .filterDate(start_date, end_date)\
    .filterBounds(bounding_box)

    # Use inbuilt Earth Engine function to create big composite image from the Landsat tiles
    composite = ee.Algorithms.Landsat.simpleComposite(filtered_shp).float();

    # Pansharpening
    ###########################
    if LS_day_sat == "LS7":
        rgb = composite.select('B3', 'B2', 'B1').unitScale(0, 255)
        # For information on Landsat 7 bands,
        # please visit https://developers.google.com/earth-engine/datasets/catalog/LANDSAT_LE07_C01_T1_SR#bands
    if LS_day_sat == "LS8":
        rgb = composite.select('B4', 'B3', 'B2').unitScale(0, 255)
        # For information on Landsat 7 bands,
        # please visit https://developers.google.com/earth-engine/datasets/catalog/LANDSAT_LC08_C01_T1_SR#bands
    gray = composite.select('B8').unitScale(0, 155)

    # Convert to HSV, swap in the pan band, and convert back to RGB.
    huesat = rgb.rgbToHsv().select('hue', 'saturation')
    satellite_imagery = ee.Image.cat(huesat, gray).hsvToRgb()
```

First, select the red, green, and blue (RGB) bands from the composite imagery generated. For Landsat 7, RGB bands are designated as B3, B2 and B1, while Landsat 8's RGB bands are designated as B4, B3 and B2.

```python
    # Pansharpening
    ###########################
    if LS day sat == "LS7":
        rgb = composite.select('B3', 'B2', 'B1').unitScale(0, 255)
        # For information on Landsat 7 bands,
        # please visit https://developers.google.com/earth-engine/datasets/catalog/LANDSAT_LE07_C01_T1_SR#bands
    if LS day sat == "LS8":
        rgb = composite.select('B4', 'B3', 'B2').unitScale(0, 255)
        # For information on Landsat 7 bands,
        # please visit https://developers.google.com/earth-engine/datasets/catalog/LANDSAT_LC08_C01_T1_SR#bands
    gray = composite.select('B8').unitScale(0, 155)

    # Convert to HSV, swap in the pan band, and convert back to RGB.
    huesat = rgb.rgbToHsv().select('hue', 'saturation')
    satellite_imagery = ee.Image.cat(huesat, gray).hsvToRgb()
```

Select the panchromatic band.

```
# Pansharpening
##########################
if LS_day_sat == "LS7":
  rgb = composite.select('B3', 'B2', 'B1').unitScale(0, 255)
  # For information on Landsat 7 bands,
  # please visit https://developers.google.com/earth-engine/datasets/catalog/LANDSAT_LE07_C01_T1_SR#bands
if LS_day_sat == "LS8":
  rgb = composite.select('B4', 'B3', 'B2').unitScale(0, 255)
  # For information on Landsat 7 bands,
  # please visit https://developers.google.com/earth-engine/datasets/catalog/LANDSAT_LC08_C01_T1_SR#bands
gray = composite.select('B8').unitScale(0, 155)

# Convert to HSV, swap in the pan band, and convert back to RGB.
huesat = rgb.rgbToHsv().select('hue', 'saturation')
satellite_imagery = ee.Image.cat(huesat, gray).hsvToRgb()
```

Convert the RGB image to Hue Saturation Value (HSV) and select only the hue and saturation bands.

```
# Pansharpening
##########################
if LS_day_sat == "LS7":
  rgb = composite.select('B3', 'B2', 'B1').unitScale(0, 255)
  # For information on Landsat 7 bands,
  # please visit https://developers.google.com/earth-engine/datasets/catalog/LANDSAT_LE07_C01_T1_SR#bands
if LS_day_sat == "LS8":
  rgb = composite.select('B4', 'B3', 'B2').unitScale(0, 255)
  # For information on Landsat 7 bands,
  # please visit https://developers.google.com/earth-engine/datasets/catalog/LANDSAT_LC08_C01_T1_SR#bands
gray = composite.select('B8').unitScale(0, 155)

# Convert to HSV, swap in the pan band, and convert back to RGB.
huesat = rgb.rgbToHsv().select('hue', 'saturation')
satellite_imagery = ee.Image.cat(huesat, gray).hsvToRgb()
```

Combine the hue, saturation and the panchromatic bands. Then convert it back into RGB to get the upscaled image.

```
# Pansharpening
##########################
if LS_day_sat == "LS7":
  rgb = composite.select('B3', 'B2', 'B1').unitScale(0, 255)
  # For information on Landsat 7 bands,
  # please visit https://developers.google.com/earth-engine/datasets/catalog/LANDSAT_LE07_C01_T1_SR#bands
if LS_day_sat == "LS8":
  rgb = composite.select('B4', 'B3', 'B2').unitScale(0, 255)
  # For information on Landsat 7 bands,
  # please visit https://developers.google.com/earth-engine/datasets/catalog/LANDSAT_LC08_C01_T1_SR#bands
gray = composite.select('B8').unitScale(0, 155)

# Convert to HSV, swap in the pan band, and convert back to RGB.
huesat = rgb.rgbToHsv().select('hue', 'saturation')
satellite_imagery = ee.Image.cat(huesat, gray).hsvToRgb()
```

STEP 40

Determine the x and y coordinates of the bounding box polygon's centroid.

```
#########
# Folium map visualization declarations
# get centroid coordinates of bounding box for map view centering
cen_x = bbox_poly.centroid.x[0]
cen_y = bbox_poly.centroid.y[0]

# create folium object
map = folium.Map(location=[cen_y, cen_x],
                 zoom_start=6,
                 width=1280,
                 height=766,
                 attr=day_sat)
```

STEP 41

Create a Folium map object. Use the centroid coordinates of the bounding box to indicate the location to display.

- **zoom_start** defines the initial zoom level of the map.
- **width and height** define the size of the map in pixel units.
- **attr** is the map tile attribution (optional) set to display the name of the satellite used as imagery source.

```
#########
# Folium map visualization declarations
# get centroid coordinates of bounding box for map view centering
cen_x = bbox_poly.centroid.x[0]
cen_y = bbox_poly.centroid.y[0]

# create folium object
map = folium.Map(location=[cen_y, cen_x],
                 zoom_start=6,
                 width=1280,
                 height=766,
                 attr=day_sat)
```

STEP 42

Get the **mapID** of the filtered satellite imagery.

```python
# get mapID of sat_imagery image from GEE
ee_image_map_id = ee.Image(satellite_imagery).getMapId()

# add sat_imagery to map
folium.raster_layers.TileLayer(
    tiles = ee_image_map_id['tile_fetcher'].url_format,
    attr = 'Google Earth Engine',
    name = 'Daytime Imagery',
    overlay = True,
    control = True,
    ).add_to(map)
```

STEP 43

Generate a new map layer to visualize the following parameters:

- **tiles** is the map data source. It uses the mapID to get the URL link of filtered satellite imagery from GEE.
- **attr** is the map tile attribution required if the URL link from Earth Engine is used.
- **name** is the layer name appearing in LayerControl.
- **overlay** is set to **True** to indicate that the imagery will be placed over the Folium default base map.
- **control** is set to **True** so that the layer will be included in the LayerControl.

```python
# get mapID of sat_imagery image from GEE
ee_image_map_id = ee.Image(satellite_imagery).getMapId()

# add sat_imagery to map
folium.raster_layers.TileLayer(
    tiles = ee_image_map_id['tile_fetcher'].url_format,
    attr = 'Google Earth Engine',
    name = 'Daytime Imagery',
    overlay = True,
    control = True,
    ).add_to(map)
```

STEP 44

Overlay the bounding box polygon.

```python
# add bounding box
folium.GeoJson(
    data = bounding_box.getInfo(),
    name = 'Bounding box',
    style_function=lambda feature: {
        'fillColor': '#FFFFFF00',
        'weight' : 3,
        'fillOpacity' : 0.5,
        },
    overlay = True,
    control = True,
    ).add_to(map)
```

STEP 45

Define the map title for Sentinel and Landsat imagery. Insert a reminder to check if the satellite imagery generated is complete.

```python
# add map title
if day_sat == "ST":
  map_title = "Sentinel-2 Imagery: Please check if composite image is complete"
else:
  map_title = "Landsat Imagery: Please check if composite image is complete"

title_html = '''
              <h3 align="center" style="font-size:16px"><b>{}</b></h3>
              '''.format(map_title)

map.get_root().html.add_child(folium.Element(title_html))
```

STEP 46

Add the **LayerControl** to the map object. Then instruct Python to display the map.

```
map.get_root().html.add_child(folium.Element(title_html))

# add layer control panel
map.add_child(folium.LayerControl())

# Display the map.
display(map)
```

Below is the output of the map visualization code cell.

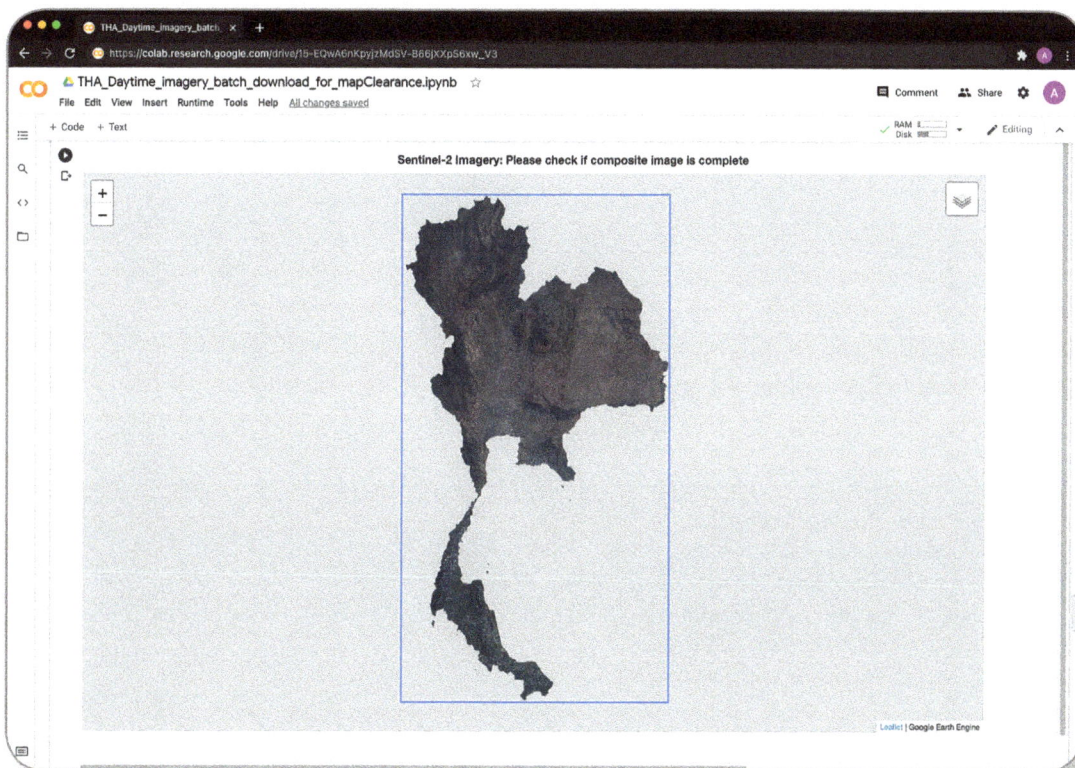

STEP 47

As the GEE is limited to only 3000 tasks, it is important to determine the number of tasks in queue to prevent errors.

Use the function **get_queued_tasks()** to identify the number of "Ready" and "Running" tasks from the GEE task list. This function is necessary to verify if there are fewer than 3000 tasks in queue.

```python
def get_queued_task():
  queued_task_count = 0
  for queued_task in ee.batch.Task.list():
    if queued_task.state in ["READY","RUNNING"]:
        queued_task_count += 1
  return queued_task_count

def get_queued_task_filenames():
  print("Fetching queued files")
  task_filenames = []
  for queued_task in ee.batch.Task.list():
    if queued_task.state in ["READY","RUNNING"]:
      print(queued_task.state+": "+queued_task.status()['description'])
      task_filenames.append(queued_task.status()['description'])
  print("---end fetch---\n")
  return  task_filenames
```

STEP 48

Implement the function **get_queued_task_filenames()** to obtain the filenames of the "Ready" and "Running" tasks on the GEE task list. This function is necessary to avoid file duplication.

```python
def get_queued_task():
  queued_task_count = 0
  for queued_task in ee.batch.Task.list():
    if queued_task.state in ["READY","RUNNING"]:
        queued_task_count += 1
  return queued_task_count

def get_queued_task_filenames():
  print("Fetching queued files")
  task_filenames = []
  for queued_task in ee.batch.Task.list():
    if queued_task.state in ["READY","RUNNING"]:
      print(queued_task.state+": "+queued_task.status()['description'])
      task_filenames.append(queued_task.status()['description'])
  print("---end fetch---\n")
  return  task_filenames
```

STEP 49

Define the function for downloading the satellite imagery.

```python
import os
def download_satellite_imagery(sat_imagery):
  next_batch_size = 10 # Set the number of new tasks to be added after reaching task limit
  target_count = 3000 - next_batch_size # Threshold before creating new tasks

  task_count = get_queued_task()
  queued_filenames = get_queued_task_filenames()
  print('Number of active tasks: {: }.'.format(task_count))

  for i in range(1,imagery_count):

    imagery_file = DIMG + '_{:06d}'.format(i)
    imagery_filepath = '/content/gdrive/MyDrive/' + drive_folder + '/' + imagery_file + '.tif'

    if task_count == 3000:  # Number of tasks has reached the limit

      # Loop until the task count has not reach the target_count
      while task_count > target_count:
        active_task = get_queued_task() # Get the number of tasks on the list

        if active_task < task_count: # Check if there are finished tasks
          task_count = active_task
          print("*********************")
          print('Number of current pending tasks in queue: {: }.'.format(task_count))
          print('Remaining tasks before starting new batch: {: }.'.format(task_count-target_count))
          #print(task.status())

    else:

      if (os.path.exists(imagery_filepath)==False):
        if (imagery_file not in queued_filenames):
          print("--------------------")
          print("Starting new task...")
          print("downloading " + imagery_file)

          c_lon = df['lon'][i]
          c_lat = df['lat'][i]
          geometry = ee.Geometry.Point([c_lon, c_lat]).buffer(1920) #Based imagery resolution of 25
          geometry = geometry.getInfo()['coordinates'][0]
```

First, import the operating system (**os**) library to enable Python to execute operating system commands. In this case, access the folders of the Colab virtual machine.

```python
import os
def download_satellite_imagery(sat_imagery):
  next_batch_size = 10 # Set the number of new tasks to be added after reaching task limit
  target_count = 3000 - next_batch_size # Threshold before creating new tasks

  task_count = get_queued_task()
  queued_filenames = get_queued_task_filenames()
  print('Number of active tasks: {: }.'.format(task_count))
```

Define the function ***download_satellite_imagery***, which requires a satellite imagery object (**sat_imagery**) as input.

```python
import os
def download_satellite_imagery(sat_imagery):
    next_batch_size = 10 # Set the number of new tasks to be added after reaching task limit
    target_count = 3000 - next_batch_size # Threshold before creating new tasks

    task_count = get_queued_task()
    queued_filenames = get_queued_task_filenames()
    print('Number of active tasks: {: }.'.format(task_count))
```

next_batch_size refers to the number of new imagery downloading tasks to be pooled.

target_count refers to the number of tasks in the task list to trigger pooling of new batch of tasks.

```python
import os
def download_satellite_imagery(sat_imagery):
    next_batch_size = 10 # Set the number of new tasks to be added after reaching task limit
    target_count = 3000 - next_batch_size # Threshold before creating new tasks

    task_count = get_queued_task()
    queued_filenames = get_queued_task_filenames()
    print('Number of active tasks: {: }.'.format(task_count))
```

Execute the function **get_queued_task()** to determine the number of "Ready" and "Running" tasks in the GEE task list, if any. Then store it in the ***task_count*** variable. Get the list of "Ready" and "Running" tasks' filenames, if any, by calling the function ***get_queued_task()*** and store it in ***queued_filenames*** variable. Lastly, print out the number of active tasks.

```python
import os
def download_satellite_imagery(sat_imagery):
    next_batch_size = 10 # Set the number of new tasks to be added after reaching task limit
    target_count = 3000 - next_batch_size # Threshold before creating new tasks

    task_count = get_queued_task()
    queued_filenames = get_queued_task_filenames()
    print('Number of active tasks: {: }.'.format(task_count))
```

STEP 50

Loop through the list of grid centroids and download the images. The for-loop range is the number of centroids in the CSV file.

```python
for i in range(1,imagery_count):

    imagery_file = DIMG + '_{:06d}'.format(i)
    imagery_filepath = '/content/gdrive/MyDrive/' + drive_folder + '/' + imagery_file + '.tif'

    if task_count == 3000:  # Number of tasks has reached the limit

        # Loop until the task count has not reach the target_count
        while task_count > target_count:
            active_task = get_queued_task() # Get the number of tasks on the list

            if active_task < task_count: # Check if there are finished tasks
                task_count = active_task
                print("**********************")
                print('Number of current pending tasks in queue: {: }.'.format(task_count))
                print('Remaining tasks before starting new batch: {: }.'.format(task_count-target_count))
```

Declare the imagery filename (**imagery_file**) to be used and its complete file path (**imagery_filepath**).

```python
for i in range(1,imagery_count):

    imagery_file = DIMG + '_{:06d}'.format(i)
    imagery_filepath = '/content/gdrive/MyDrive/' + drive_folder + '/' + imagery_file + '.tif'

    if task_count == 3000:  # Number of tasks has reached the limit

        # Loop until the task count has not reach the target_count
        while task_count > target_count:
            active_task = get_queued_task() # Get the number of tasks on the list

            if active_task < task_count: # Check if there are finished tasks
                task_count = active_task
                print("**********************")
                print('Number of current pending tasks in queue: {: }.'.format(task_count))
                print('Remaining tasks before starting new batch: {: }.'.format(task_count-target_count))
```

Implement an if-statement to limit the number of tasks in queue and to prevent errors. *If the **task_count** reaches 3000, it stops creating new tasks.*

```python
for i in range(1,imagery_count):

  imagery_file = DIMG + '_{:06d}'.format(i)
  imagery_filepath = '/content/gdrive/MyDrive/' + drive_folder + '/' + imagery_file + '.tif'

  if task_count == 3000:  # Number of tasks has reached the limit

    # Loop until the task count has not reach the target_count
    while task_count > target_count:
      active_task = get_queued_task() # Get the number of tasks on the list

      if active_task < task_count: # Check if there are finished tasks
        task_count = active_task
        print("**********************")
        print('Number of current pending tasks in queue: {: }.'.format(task_count))
        print('Remaining tasks before starting new batch: {: }.'.format(task_count-target_count))
```

The while-loop will check if the current **task_count** has reached the set threshold (**target_count**) before creating a new batch of tasks

```python
for i in range(1,imagery_count):

  imagery_file = DIMG + '_{:06d}'.format(i)
  imagery_filepath = '/content/gdrive/MyDrive/' + drive_folder + '/' + imagery_file + '.tif'

  if task_count == 3000:  # Number of tasks has reached the limit

    # Loop until the task count has not reach the target_count
    while task_count > target_count:
      active_task = get_queued_task() # Get the number of tasks on the list

      if active_task < task_count: # Check if there are finished tasks
        task_count = active_task
        print("**********************")
        print('Number of current pending tasks in queue: {: }.'.format(task_count))
        print('Remaining tasks before starting new batch: {: }.'.format(task_count-target_count))
```

The if-statement checks for finished tasks and prints out information on the number of tasks currently in queue and a countdown of when a new batch of tasks will be created.

```python
for i in range(1,imagery_count):

  imagery_file = DIMG + '_{:06d}'.format(i)
  imagery_filepath = '/content/gdrive/MyDrive/' + drive_folder + '/' + imagery_file + '.tif'

  if task_count == 3000:  # Number of tasks has reached the limit

    # Loop until the task count has not reach the target_count
    while task_count > target_count:
      active_task = get_queued_task() # Get the number of tasks on the list

      if active_task < task_count: # Check if there are finished tasks
        task_count = active_task
        print("**********************")
        print('Number of current pending tasks in queue: {: }.'.format(task_count))
        print('Remaining tasks before starting new batch: {: }.'.format(task_count-target_count))
```

STEP 51

If the number of tasks is fewer than 3000 or if the new batch of tasks needs to be created, first check whether the new imagery to be pooled is already in the Google Drive or in queue. *This verification will prevent duplication of tasks.*

```python
    else:

        if (os.path.exists(imagery_filepath)==False):
          if (imagery_file not in queued_filenames):
              print("--------------------")
              print("Starting new task...")
              print("downloading " + imagery_file)

            c_lon = df['lon'][i]
            c_lat = df['lat'][i]
            geometry = ee.Geometry.Point([c_lon, c_lat]).buffer(1920) #Based image
            geometry = geometry.getInfo()['coordinates'][0]

            if (day_sat == "ST"):
              scale = 10
            elif (day_sat == "LS"):
              scale = 15

            task_config = {
                'scale': scale,
                'region': geometry,
                'driveFolder': drive_folder,
            }

            task = ee.batch.Export.image(sat_imagery, imagery_file, task_config)

            task.start()

            task_count += 1

            if task_count % 1000 == 0:
              task_count = get_queued_task()

            print('Number of active tasks: {: }.'.format(task_count))
          else:
              print("On queue: " + imagery_file + ".tif")
        else:
          print("Downloaded: " + imagery_file + ".tif")
```

Print to determine whether the files are in the save path or if they are still in queue.

```
else:

  if (os.path.exists(imagery_filepath)==False):
    if (imagery_file not in queued_filenames):
        print("--------------------")
        print("Starting new task...")
        print("downloading " + imagery_file)

        c_lon = df['lon'][i]
        c_lat = df['lat'][i]
        geometry = ee.Geometry.Point([c_lon, c_lat]).buffer(1920) #Based image
        geometry = geometry.getInfo()['coordinates'][0]

        if (day_sat == "ST"):
          scale = 10
        elif (day_sat == "LS"):
          scale = 15

        task_config = {
            'scale': scale,
            'region': geometry,
            'driveFolder': drive_folder,
        }

        task = ee.batch.Export.image(sat_imagery, imagery_file, task_config)

        task.start()

        task_count += 1

        if task_count % 1000 == 0:
          task_count = get_queued_task()

        print('Number of active tasks: {: }.'.format(task_count))
    else:
        print("On queue: " + imagery_file + ".tif")
  else:
    print("Downloaded: " + imagery_file + ".tif")
```

Set **c_lon** and **c_lat** (i.e., longitude and latitude, respectively) to store the centroid coordinates obtained from the centroid CSV.

```
    else:

      if (os.path.exists(imagery_filepath)==False):
        if (imagery_file not in queued_filenames):
            print("-------------------")
            print("Starting new task...")
            print("downloading " + imagery_file)

            c_lon = df['lon'][i]
            c_lat = df['lat'][i]
            geometry = ee.Geometry.Point([c_lon, c_lat]).buffer(1920) #Based image
            geometry = geometry.getInfo()['coordinates'][0]

            if (day_sat == "ST"):
              scale = 10
            elif (day_sat == "LS"):
              scale = 15

            task_config = {
                'scale': scale,
                'region': geometry,
                'driveFolder': drive_folder,
            }

            task = ee.batch.Export.image(sat_imagery, imagery_file, task_config)

            task.start()

            task_count += 1

            if task_count % 1000 == 0:
              task_count = get_queued_task()

            print('Number of active tasks: {: }.'.format(task_count))
        else:
            print("On queue: " + imagery_file + ".tif")
      else:
        print("Downloaded: " + imagery_file + ".tif")
```

Employ the centroid coordinates to define a geospatial circle using a GEE point geometry with a buffer of 1920 meters. *This buffer value corresponds to half of the grid size measured from the centroid to the grid boundary.*

As illustrated in Step 6 of the section on Generating Centroids for Satellite imagery, buffer size is computed as follows:

256 pixel x 15 meters/pixel = 3840 meter grid size

3840 / 2 = 1920 meter buffer size

where: 15 meters/pixel is the Landsat resolution

```python
else:

    if (os.path.exists(imagery_filepath)==False):
      if (imagery_file not in queued_filenames):
          print("--------------------")
          print("Starting new task...")
          print("downloading " + imagery_file)

          c_lon = df['lon'][i]
          c_lat = df['lat'][i]
          geometry = ee.Geometry.Point([c_lon, c_lat]).buffer(1920) #Based image
          geometry = geometry.getInfo()['coordinates'][0]

          if (day_sat == "ST"):
            scale = 10
          elif (day_sat == "LS"):
            scale = 15

          task_config = {
              'scale': scale,
              'region': geometry,
              'driveFolder': drive_folder,
          }

          task = ee.batch.Export.image(sat_imagery, imagery_file, task_config)

          task.start()

          task_count += 1

          if task_count % 1000 == 0:
            task_count = get_queued_task()

          print('Number of active tasks: {: }.'.format(task_count))
      else:
          print("On queue: " + imagery_file + ".tif")
    else:
      print("Downloaded: " + imagery_file + ".tif")
```

Redefine the geometry variable using the coordinates of the circle as its value.

```
else:

    if (os.path.exists(imagery_filepath)==False):
        if (imagery_file not in queued_filenames):
            print("--------------------")
            print("Starting new task...")
            print("downloading " + imagery_file)

            c_lon = df['lon'][i]
            c_lat = df['lat'][i]
            geometry = ee.Geometry.Point([c_lon, c_lat]).buffer(1920) #Based imager
            geometry = geometry.getInfo()['coordinates'][0]

            if (day_sat == "ST"):
                scale = 10
            elif (day_sat == "LS"):
                scale = 15

            task_config = {
                'scale': scale,
                'region': geometry,
                'driveFolder': drive_folder,
            }

            task = ee.batch.Export.image(sat_imagery, imagery_file, task_config)

            task.start()

            task_count += 1

            if task_count % 1000 == 0:
                task_count = get_queued_task()

            print('Number of active tasks: {: }.'.format(task_count))
        else:
            print("On queue: " + imagery_file + ".tif")
    else:
        print("Downloaded: " + imagery_file + ".tif")
```

Next, define the export parameter using the task_config dictionary variable.

The **task_config** is composed of the following:

- **scale** – is the satellite resolution (10 meter/pixel – Sentinel; 15 meter/pixel – Landsat),
- **region** – is the area coverage to download, and
- **driveFolder** – is the folder path where the downloaded imagery will be stored.

```python
    else:

        if (os.path.exists(imagery_filepath)==False):
          if (imagery_file not in queued_filenames):
                print("--------------------")
                print("Starting new task...")
                print("downloading " + imagery_file)

                c_lon = df['lon'][i]
                c_lat = df['lat'][i]
                geometry = ee.Geometry.Point([c_lon, c_lat]).buffer(1920) #Based image:
                geometry = geometry.getInfo()['coordinates'][0]

                if (day_sat == "ST"):
                  scale = 10
                elif (day_sat == "LS"):
                  scale = 15

                task_config = {
                    'scale': scale,
                    'region': geometry,
                    'driveFolder': drive_folder,
                }

                task = ee.batch.Export.image(sat_imagery, imagery_file, task_config)

                task.start()

                task_count += 1

                if task_count % 1000 == 0:
                  task_count = get_queued_task()

                print('Number of active tasks: {: }.'.format(task_count))
            else:
                print("On queue: " + imagery_file + ".tif")
        else:
          print("Downloaded: " + imagery_file + ".tif")
```

Describe the image batch export object and name it as task. The image batch export object requires the following parameters:

- satellite imagery (**sat_imagery**),
- filename to be used (**imagery_file**), and
- export parameter (**task_config**).

Finally, pass the task to GEE using the command **task.start()** and add another task to the task counter variable **task_count**.

```python
    else:

        if (os.path.exists(imagery_filepath)==False):
          if (imagery_file not in queued_filenames):
             print("--------------------")
             print("Starting new task...")
             print("downloading " + imagery_file)

             c_lon = df['lon'][i]
             c_lat = df['lat'][i]
             geometry = ee.Geometry.Point([c_lon, c_lat]).buffer(1920) #Based image
             geometry = geometry.getInfo()['coordinates'][0]

             if (day_sat == "ST"):
               scale = 10
             elif (day_sat == "LS"):
               scale = 15

             task_config = {
                 'scale': scale,
                 'region': geometry,
                 'driveFolder': drive_folder,
             }

             task = ee.batch.Export.image(sat_imagery, imagery_file, task_config)

             task.start()

             task_count += 1

             if task_count % 1000 == 0:
               task_count = get_queued_task()

             print('Number of active tasks: {: }.'.format(task_count))
          else:
             print("On queue: " + imagery_file + ".tif")
        else:
          print("Downloaded: " + imagery_file + ".tif")
```

Provide printouts of the number of tasks being pooled. To speed up the task creation process, execute **get_queued_task()** only after every 1000 tasks to check the exact number of tasks in queue.

```python
        else:

            if (os.path.exists(imagery_filepath)==False):
                if (imagery_file not in queued_filenames):
                    print("--------------------")
                    print("Starting new task...")
                    print("downloading " + imagery_file)

                    c_lon = df['lon'][i]
                    c_lat = df['lat'][i]
                    geometry = ee.Geometry.Point([c_lon, c_lat]).buffer(1920) #Based imager
                    geometry = geometry.getInfo()['coordinates'][0]

                    if (day_sat == "ST"):
                      scale = 10
                    elif (day_sat == "LS"):
                      scale = 15

                    task_config = {
                        'scale': scale,
                        'region': geometry,
                        'driveFolder': drive_folder,
                    }

                    task = ee.batch.Export.image(sat_imagery, imagery_file, task_config)

                    task.start()

                    task_count += 1

                    if task_count % 1000 == 0:
                      task_count = get_queued_task()

                    print('Number of active tasks: {: }.'.format(task_count))
                else:
                    print("On queue: " + imagery_file + ".tif")
            else:
              print("Downloaded: " + imagery_file + ".tif")
```

STEP 52

Implement the function **download_satellite_imagery()** and pass it on to the filtered GEE imagery stored in the object **satellite_imagery** as the function's argument. *As the function runs, it prints out the task information.*

```
▾ Download satellite imagery

  ⏺ download_satellite_imagery(satellite_imagery)

  ... Fetching queued files
      ---end fetch---

      Number of active tasks:  0.
      --------------------
      Starting new task...
      downloading CNN_DIMG_THA_2015_ST_384_3840_000001
      Number of active tasks:  1.
      --------------------
      Starting new task...
      downloading CNN_DIMG_THA_2015_ST_384_3840_000002
      Number of active tasks:  2.
      --------------------
      Starting new task...
      downloading CNN_DIMG_THA_2015_ST_384_3840_000003
      Number of active tasks:  3.
      --------------------
      Starting new task...
      downloading CNN_DIMG_THA_2015_ST_384_3840_000004
      Number of active tasks:  4.
      --------------------
```

The following is the function printout when restarting the imagery download process, which displays all the files that are still in queue.

```
▾ Download satellite imagery

  ▶ download_satellite_imagery(satellite_imagery)

  ⤷ Fetching queued files
     READY: CNN_DIMG_THA_2015_ST_384_3840_000009
     RUNNING: CNN_DIMG_THA_2015_ST_384_3840_000008
     RUNNING: CNN_DIMG_THA_2015_ST_384_3840_000007
     RUNNING: CNN_DIMG_THA_2015_ST_384_3840_000006
     RUNNING: CNN_DIMG_THA_2015_ST_384_3840_000005
     RUNNING: CNN_DIMG_THA_2015_ST_384_3840_000004
     ---end fetch---

     Number of active tasks:  7.
     Downloaded: CNN_DIMG_THA_2015_ST_384_3840_000001.tif
     Downloaded: CNN_DIMG_THA_2015_ST_384_3840_000002.tif
     Downloaded: CNN_DIMG_THA_2015_ST_384_3840_000003.tif
     Downloaded: CNN_DIMG_THA_2015_ST_384_3840_000004.tif
     Downloaded: CNN_DIMG_THA_2015_ST_384_3840_000005.tif
     On queue: CNN_DIMG_THA_2015_ST_384_3840_000006.tif
     On queue: CNN_DIMG_THA_2015_ST_384_3840_000007.tif
     On queue: CNN_DIMG_THA_2015_ST_384_3840_000008.tif
     On queue: CNN_DIMG_THA_2015_ST_384_3840_000009.tif
     --------------------
     Starting new task...
     downloading CNN_DIMG_THA_2015_ST_384_3840_000010
     Number of active tasks:  8.
     --------------------
     Starting new task...
     downloading CNN_DIMG_THA_2015_ST_384_3840_000011
     Number of active tasks:  9.
     --------------------
     Starting new task...
     downloading CNN_DIMG_THA_2015_ST_384_3840_000012
     Number of active tasks:  10.
     --------------------
```

Below is the printout of the number of pending tasks and the downloaded and pending imagery, which were skipped to avoid duplication.

```
▼ Download satellite imagery

  ▶  download_satellite_imagery(satellite_imagery)

  ⤷  Fetching queued files
      READY: CNN_DIMG_THA_2015_ST_384_3840_000009
      RUNNING: CNN_DIMG_THA_2015_ST_384_3840_000008
      RUNNING: CNN_DIMG_THA_2015_ST_384_3840_000007
      RUNNING: CNN_DIMG_THA_2015_ST_384_3840_000006
      RUNNING: CNN_DIMG_THA_2015_ST_384_3840_000005
      RUNNING: CNN_DIMG_THA_2015_ST_384_3840_000004
      ---end fetch---

      Number of active tasks:  7.
      Downloaded: CNN_DIMG_THA_2015_ST_384_3840_000001.tif
      Downloaded: CNN_DIMG_THA_2015_ST_384_3840_000002.tif
      Downloaded: CNN_DIMG_THA_2015_ST_384_3840_000003.tif
      Downloaded: CNN_DIMG_THA_2015_ST_384_3840_000004.tif
      Downloaded: CNN_DIMG_THA_2015_ST_384_3840_000005.tif
      On queue: CNN_DIMG_THA_2015_ST_384_3840_000006.tif
      On queue: CNN_DIMG_THA_2015_ST_384_3840_000007.tif
      On queue: CNN_DIMG_THA_2015_ST_384_3840_000008.tif
      On queue: CNN_DIMG_THA_2015_ST_384_3840_000009.tif
      --------------------
      Starting new task...
      downloading CNN_DIMG_THA_2015_ST_384_3840_000010
      Number of active tasks:  8.
      --------------------
      Starting new task...
      downloading CNN_DIMG_THA_2015_ST_384_3840_000011
      Number of active tasks:  9.
      --------------------
      Starting new task...
      downloading CNN_DIMG_THA_2015_ST_384_3840_000012
      Number of active tasks:  10.
      --------------------
```

STEP 53

Saving of imagery from the GEE to Google Drive consumes some time. Depending on the quantity of imagery to download, the 12-hour Colab runtime may not suffice. Thus, it is necessary to re-run the code. In the browser, go back to Google Drive and verify if the files are downloaded.

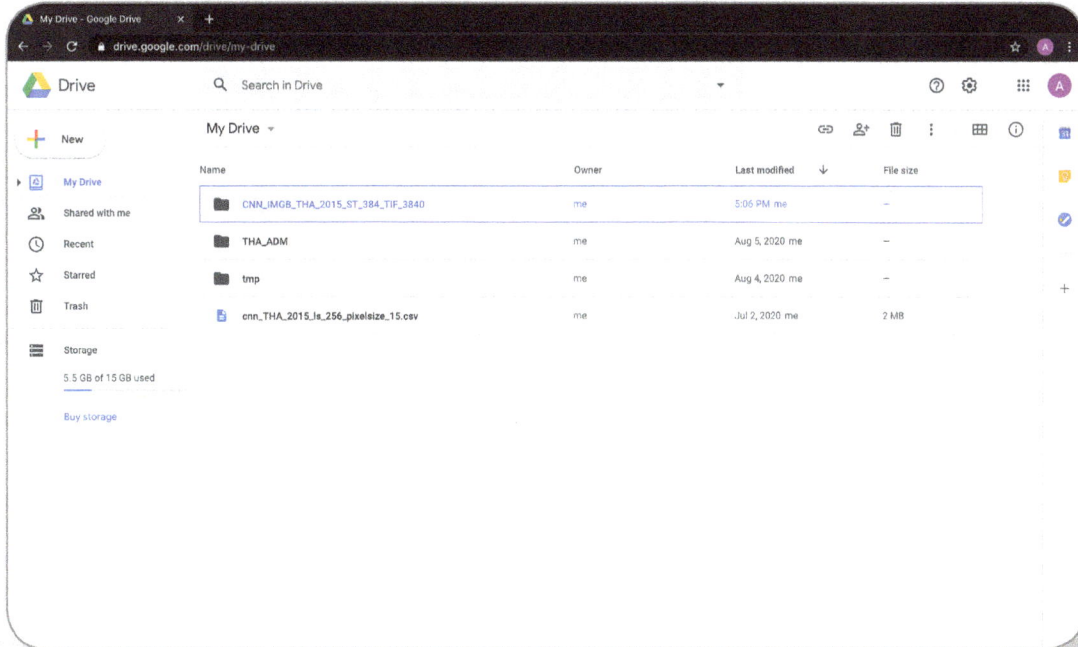

Click the folder name to verify if the files are downloaded.

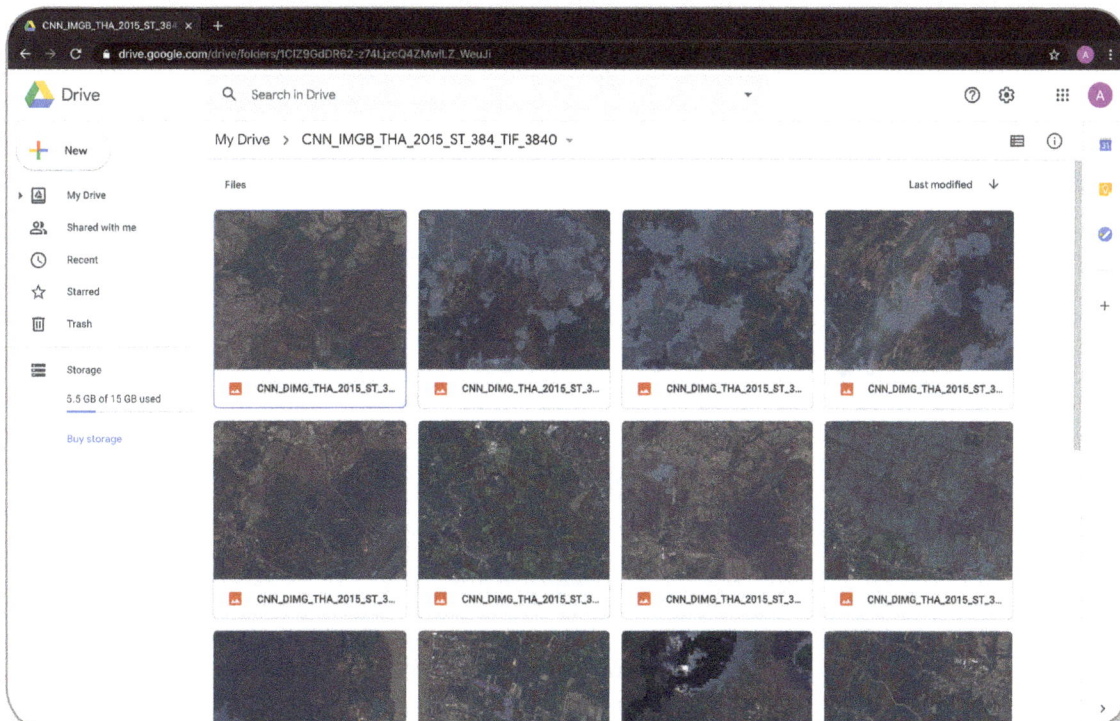

Download all images for specific country and year. Click the folder name to reveal folder options. Then press **Download**.

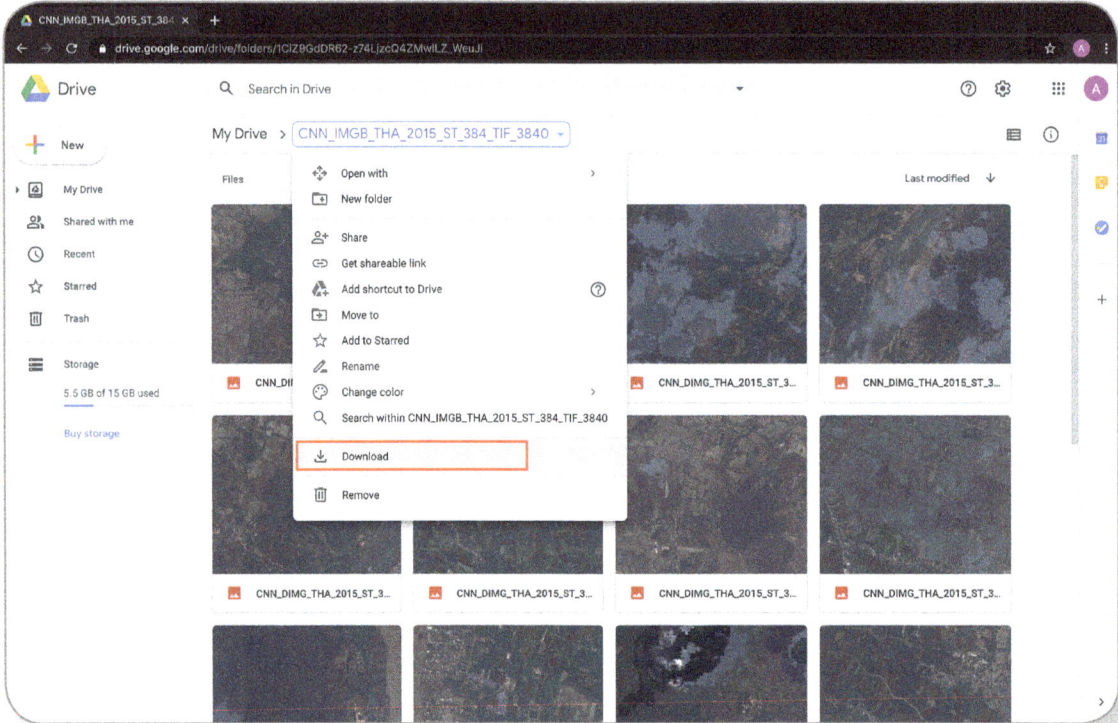

The download process starts after Google Drive has finished compressing the files.

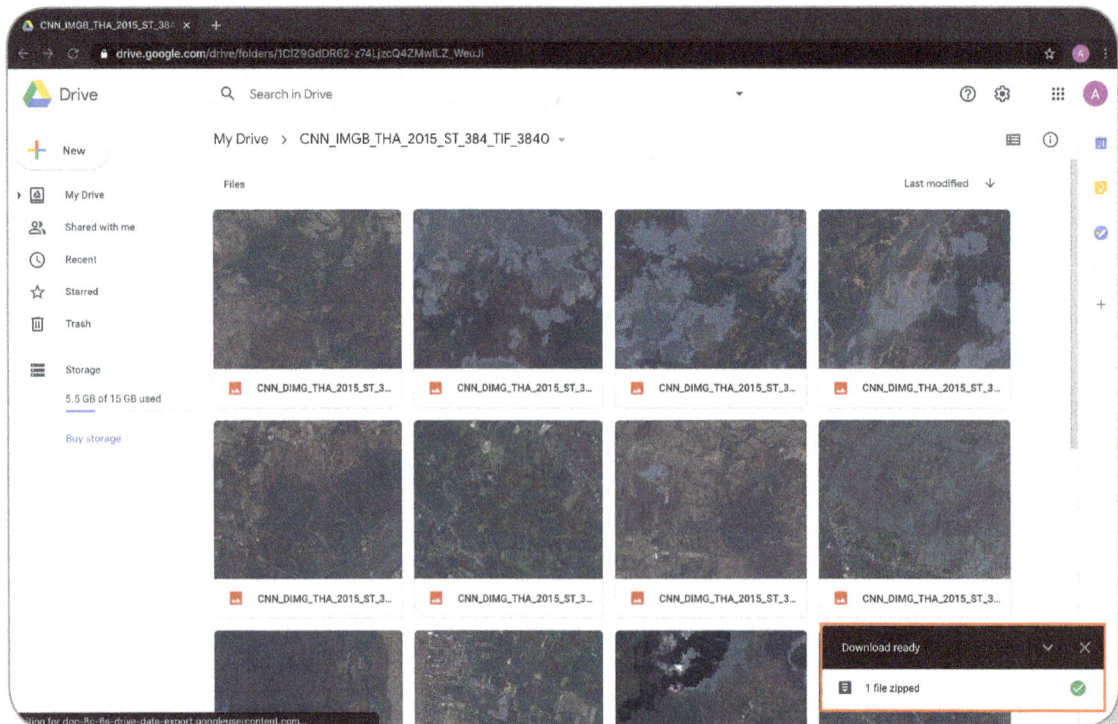

STEP 54

Save the ZIP file in the working folder and then **unzip the file**.

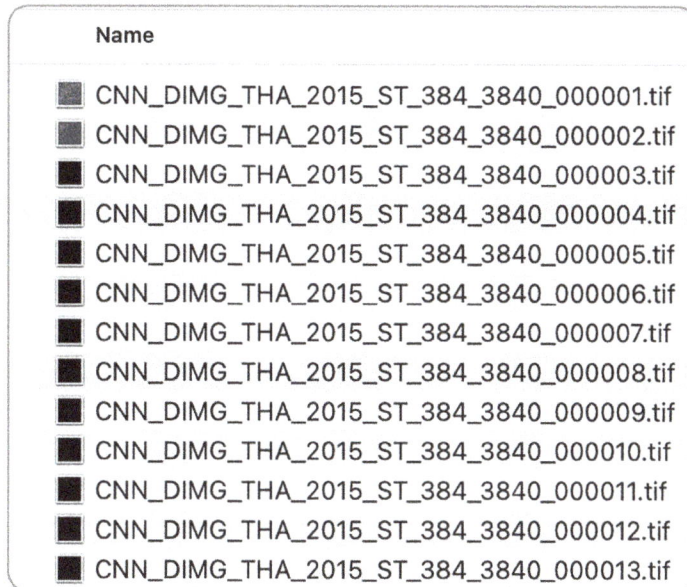

Name
CNN_DIMG_THA_2015_ST_384_3840_000001.tif
CNN_DIMG_THA_2015_ST_384_3840_000002.tif
CNN_DIMG_THA_2015_ST_384_3840_000003.tif
CNN_DIMG_THA_2015_ST_384_3840_000004.tif
CNN_DIMG_THA_2015_ST_384_3840_000005.tif
CNN_DIMG_THA_2015_ST_384_3840_000006.tif
CNN_DIMG_THA_2015_ST_384_3840_000007.tif
CNN_DIMG_THA_2015_ST_384_3840_000008.tif
CNN_DIMG_THA_2015_ST_384_3840_000009.tif
CNN_DIMG_THA_2015_ST_384_3840_000010.tif
CNN_DIMG_THA_2015_ST_384_3840_000011.tif
CNN_DIMG_THA_2015_ST_384_3840_000012.tif
CNN_DIMG_THA_2015_ST_384_3840_000013.tif

Converting Format of Satellite Imagery

Use the Geospatial Data Abstraction Library (GDAL) to convert images into geo-tagged image file format (geoTIFF). Crop the images to get the correct number of pixels. Prepare a *.tar.gz archive file of all input JPG images for easier handling in Colab.

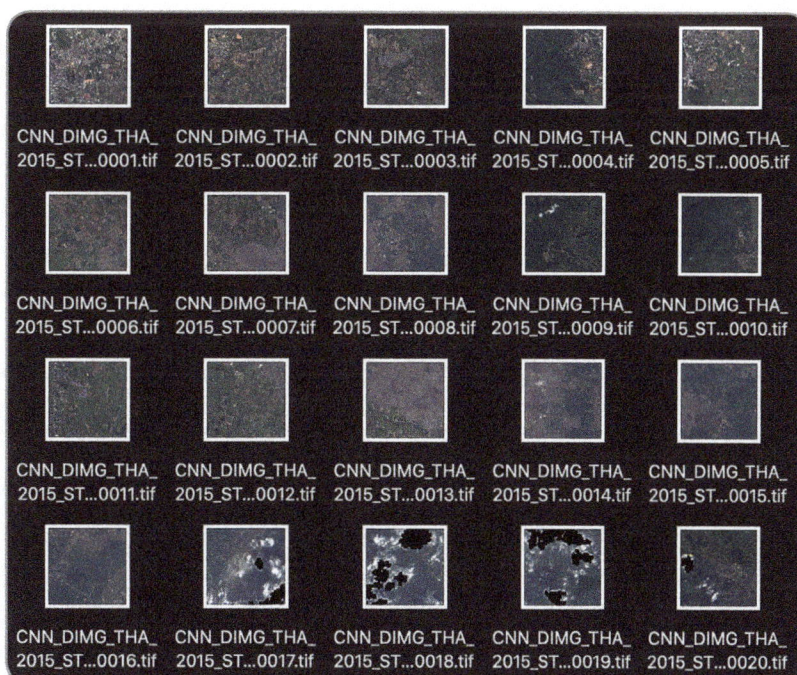

STEP 1

Use the R code: ***Daytime_imagery_format_conversion.R***.

```r
 7  #load packages
 8  library(gdalUtilities)
 9  library(tidyverse)
10
11  # Select location of satellite imagery----
12  # NOTE: Make sure to double click the folder to make the selection
13  sat_imagery_folder <- tcltk::tk_choose.dir(caption = "Select Directory Containing Daytime Satellite Imagery")
14
15  # set working directory using the directory holding satellite imagery folder
16  setwd(dirname(sat_imagery_folder))
17
18  # Load the centroid csv---
19  # select the csv path from the open dialog window
20  csv_path <- tcltk::tk_choose.files(filters = matrix(c("CSV",".csv","All files","*"),2,2,byrow = T),
21                                     caption = "Select Grid Centroid CSV")
22
23  # read centroid csv
24  df_centroid <- read.csv(csv_path, stringsAsFactors = F)
25
26  # Check if destination folders exists, otherwise create folders----
27  # create destination folder name
28  dest_path <-  paste0("./",str_replace(basename(sat_imagery_folder),"_TIF_","_JPG_"))
29
30  if (!dir.exists(dest_path)) {
31    dir.create(dest_path)
32  }
33
34  # Create new columns to hold the tif and jpg file paths----
35
36  df <- df_centroid %>%
37    mutate(tif_file=list.files(sat_imagery_folder,pattern = ".tif$",full.names = T)) %>%
38    mutate(jpg_file=paste0(dest_path,"/",
39                           str_replace(basename(tif_file),".tif",".jpg"))) %>%
40    mutate(filename=basename(jpg_file))
41
42  # Detect satellite imagery source embedded on folder name----
43  if (str_detect(sat_imagery_folder,"ST")) {
44    img_res = 384
45  }else if (str_detect(sat_imagery_folder,"LS")) {
46    img_res = 256
47  }
48
49  # Process images using gdalUtilities and create tar.gz----
50  process_imagery <- function(x){
51    print(paste0("processing: ", basename(x["tif_file"])," ---> ", basename(x["jpg_file"])))
52
53    gdal_translate(src_dataset = x["tif_file"],
54                   dst_dataset = x["jpg_file"],
55                   srcwin = c(0,0,img_res,img_res),
56                   of="JPEG",
57
```

Load the **tidyverse** and **gdalUtilities** packages.

```r
 6
 7  #load packages
 8  library(gdalUtilities)
 9  library(tidyverse)
10
```

STEP 2

Select the working directory using the function **tk_choose.dir()** from the package **tcltk**. This function opens a window for choosing the directory containing the daytime satellite imagery. Set the folder path to **sat_imagery_folder**.

```
11▾ # Select location of satellite imagery----
12  # NOTE: Make sure to double click the folder to make the selection
13  sat_imagery_folder <- tcltk::tk_choose.dir(caption = "Select Directory Containing Daytime Satellite Imagery")
14
15  # set working directory using the directory holding satellite imagery folder
16  setwd(dirname(sat_imagery_folder))
```

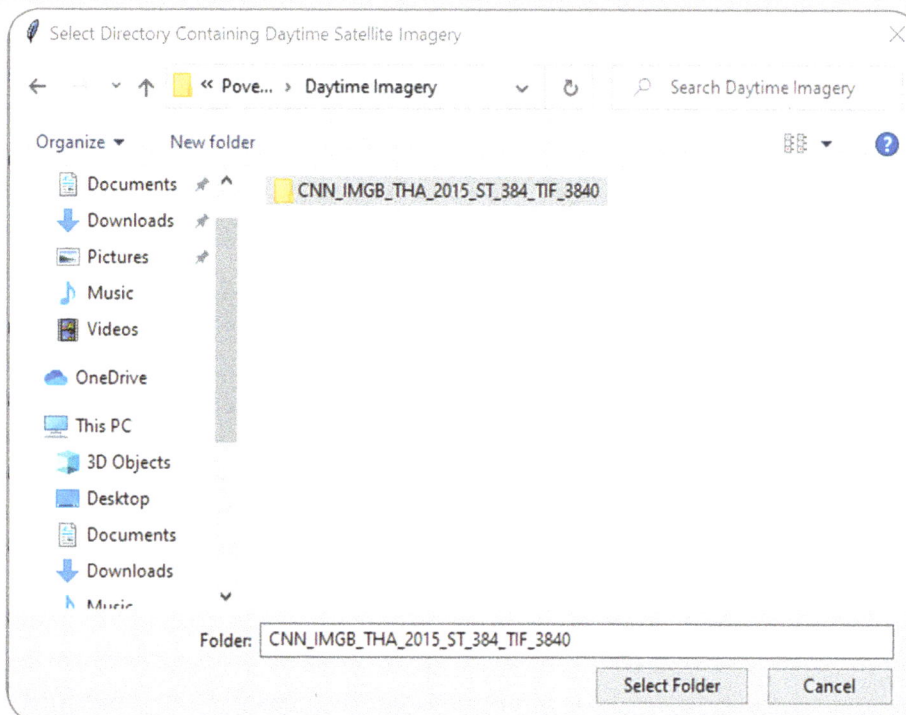

Using the **setwd()** command, set the previously assigned folder (i.e., **sat_imagery_folder** in this illustration) as the working directory.

```
11▾ # Select location of satellite imagery----
12  # NOTE: Make sure to double click the folder to make the selection
13  sat_imagery_folder <- tcltk::tk_choose.dir(caption = "Select Directory Containing Daytime Satellite Imagery")
14
15  # set working directory using the directory holding satellite imagery folder
16  setwd(dirname(sat_imagery_folder))
```

STEP 3

Use the function **tk_choose.dir()** from the package **tcltk** to open a window to select the CSV file containing the grid centroids used to download the satellite imagery.

```
18   # Load the centroid csv---
19   # select the csv path from the open dialog window
20   csv_path <- tcltk::tk_choose.files(filters = matrix(c("CSV",".csv","All files","*"),2,2,byrow = T),
21                                  caption = "Select Grid Centroid CSV")
22
23   # read centroid csv
24   df_centroid <- read.csv(csv_path, stringsAsFactors = F)
```

Load the CSV file as a **df_centroid** dataframe.

```
18   # Load the centroid csv---
19   # select the csv path from the open dialog window
20   csv_path <- tcltk::tk_choose.files(filters = matrix(c("CSV",".csv","All files","*"),2,2,byrow = T),
21                                  caption = "Select Grid Centroid CSV")
22
23   # read centroid csv
24   df_centroid <- read.csv(csv_path, stringsAsFactors = F)
```

STEP 4

Create a destination folder using the function **str_replace()** to change the character **TIF** from the variable **sat_imagery_folder** into **JPG**.

```
26 ▾ # Check if destination folders exists, otherwise create folders----
27   # create destination folder name
28   dest_path <-  paste0("./",str_replace(basename(sat_imagery_folder),"_TIF_","_JPG_"))
29
30 ▾ if (!dir.exists(dest_path)) {
31     dir.create(dest_path)
32 ▴ }
```

STEP 5

Create a new dataframe from **df_centroid**. In this dataframe, generate two columns containing the full path of the TIF and JPG filenames and a separate column containing only the filename of the JPG files without the file path.

```
34 ▾ # Create new columns to hold the tif and jpg file paths----
35
36   df <- df_centroid %>%
37     mutate(tif_file=list.files(sat_imagery_folder,pattern = ".tif$",full.names = T)) %>%
38     mutate(jpg_file=paste0(dest_path,"/",
39                            str_replace(basename(tif_file),".tif",".jpg"))) %>%
40     mutate(filename=basename(jpg_file))
```

STEP 6

Set the pixel resolution of each imagery based on the source satellite. Using the function **str_detect()**, check the satellite imagery folder name for the embedded satellite code name.

```
42 ▾  # Detect satellite imagery source embedded on folder name----
43 ▾  if (str_detect(sat_imagery_folder,"ST")) {
44       img_res = 384
45 ▾  }else if (str_detect(sat_imagery_folder,"LS")) {
46       img_res = 256
47 ▴  }
```

STEP 7

Define the function to crop and convert the TIF files into JPG files. *It takes the filename and path* of the TIF and JPG files as input. The function also prints out the TIF and JPG filename that are being processed.

```
49 ▾  # Process images using gdalUtilities and create tar.gz----
50 ▾  process_imagery <- function(x){
51       print(paste0("processing: ", basename(x["tif_file"]),"  ---> ", basename(x["jpg_file"])))
52
53       gdal_translate(src_dataset = x["tif_file"],
54                      dst_dataset = x["jpg_file"],
55                      srcwin = c(0,0,img_res,img_res),
56                      of="JPEG",
57                      ot="Byte", # for landsat
58                      scale="",
59                      co = "quality=100")
60 ▴  }
61
62   apply(df,1, process_imagery)
```

STEP 8

Employ the function **gdal_translate()** from the gdalUtilities package to execute this task through the following parameters:

- ▪ **src_dataset** – is the file path of the TIF input file.
- ▪ **dst_dataset** – is the file path of the JPG output file.
- ▪ **srcwin = c(xoff,yoff,xsize,ysize)** - selects a sub window from the source image for copying based on pixel/line location and specify pixel count based on the satellite imagery source.
- ▪ **of** – refers to the output format "JPEG".
- ▪ **scale** – is set to "" so that the input pixel values will not be changed.
- ▪ **co** - passes a creation option to the output format driver. This sets the JPEG output quality to 100% or no compression.

```
49 ▾ # Process images using gdalUtilities and create tar.gz----
50 ▾ process_imagery <- function(x){
51     print(paste0("processing: ", basename(x["tif_file"])," ---> ", basename(x["jpg_file"])))
52
53     gdal_translate(src_dataset = x["tif_file"],
54                    dst_dataset = x["jpg_file"],
55                    srcwin = c(0,0,img_res,img_res),
56                    of="JPEG",
57                    ot="Byte", # for landsat
58                    scale="",
59                    co = "quality=100")
60 ▴ }
61
62  apply(df,1, process_imagery)
```

STEP 9

Implement **apply()** function to go through each row of the TIF file listed in the dataframe and pass it on to the custom function **process_imagery()**.

```
49 ▾ # Process images using gdalUtilities and create tar.gz----
50 ▾ process_imagery <- function(x){
51     print(paste0("processing: ", basename(x["tif_file"])," ---> ", basename(x["jpg_file"])))
52
53     gdal_translate(src_dataset = x["tif_file"],
54                    dst_dataset = x["jpg_file"],
55                    srcwin = c(0,0,img_res,img_res),
56                    of="JPEG",
57                    ot="Byte", # for landsat
58                    scale="",
59                    co = "quality=100")
60 ▴ }
61
62  apply(df,1, process_imagery)
```

STEP 10

Remove the column containing TIF and JPG file path.

```
64   df <- df %>%
65      select(-c(tif_file,jpg_file))
```

STEP 11

Create a vector shapefile using the centroids coordinates. Load the package **sf**. Define the Coordinate Reference System (CRS) variable for the shapefile.

```
67 ▾ # Create multipoint vector shapefiles from the dataframe----
68   # This shall be use later in aggregating luminosity values in GEE
69
70   library(sf)
71
72 ▾ # Define crs variable ----
73   WGS84 <- "+proj=longlat +datum=WGS84 +no_defs +ellps=WGS84 +towgs84=0,0,0"
74
75   pt_shp <- df %>%
76     mutate(x = lon, y = lat) %>%
77     st_as_sf(coords = c("x","y"),crs = WGS84)
```

STEP 12

Generate a duplicate of the centroid coordinates to preserve the data inside the shapefile's attributes. Then using the sf function **st_as_sf()**, create the shapefile.

```
67 ▾ # Create multipoint vector shapefiles from the dataframe----
68   # This shall be use later in aggregating luminosity values in GEE
69
70   library(sf)
71
72 ▾ # Define crs variable ----
73   WGS84 <- "+proj=longlat +datum=WGS84 +no_defs +ellps=WGS84 +towgs84=0,0,0"
74
75   pt_shp <- df %>%
76     mutate(x = lon, y = lat) %>%
77     st_as_sf(coords = c("x","y"),crs = WGS84)
```

STEP 13

Generate the filename for the shapefile. Prefix the centroid's CSV filename with "shp" and change the file extension to ".shp". Then output the vector shapefile. *The shapefile is needed in for aggregating luminosity values of each grid in GEE in the subsequent steps.*

```
79 ▾ # generate filename ----
80   file_name <- paste("shp",
81                       str_replace(basename(csv_path),".csv$",".shp"),
82                       sep="_")
83 ▾ # Output SHP----
84   write_sf(pt_shp,
85            dsn = file_name)
```

```
> file_name
[1] "shp_THA_centroid_3840_grid.shp"
>
```

STEP 14

Create a gzip (.tar.gz) archive file containing the JPG files.

First, specify the filename of the archive file. Then use the **tar()** function to compress the JPG folder through the following parameters:

- **tarfile** – is the output filename,
- **file** – is the destination path, and
- **compression** – is the archive file type "gzip".

```
92 ▾ # Create tar.gz archive file----
93   tar_filename <- paste0(sub("^.+/","",dest_path),".tar.gz")
94
95   tar(tarfile = tar_filename,
96       files = dest_path,
97       compression = "gzip")
```

The JPG output folder and tar.gz file are saved in the same folder as the TIF folder.

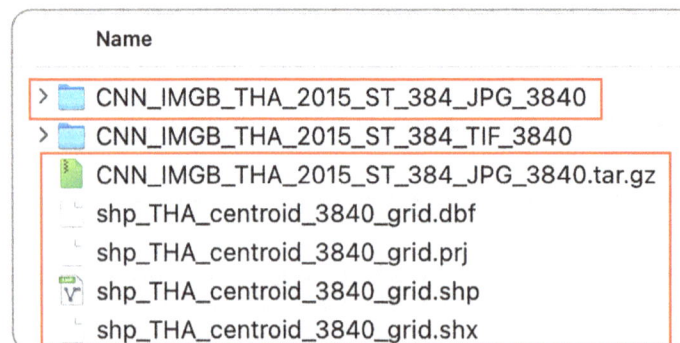

Name
> 📁 CNN_IMGB_THA_2015_ST_384_JPG_3840
> 📁 CNN_IMGB_THA_2015_ST_384_TIF_3840
📄 CNN_IMGB_THA_2015_ST_384_JPG_3840.tar.gz
shp_THA_centroid_3840_grid.dbf
shp_THA_centroid_3840_grid.prj
📄 shp_THA_centroid_3840_grid.shp
shp_THA_centroid_3840_grid.shx

STEP 15

On the Google Drive, click ➕ New .

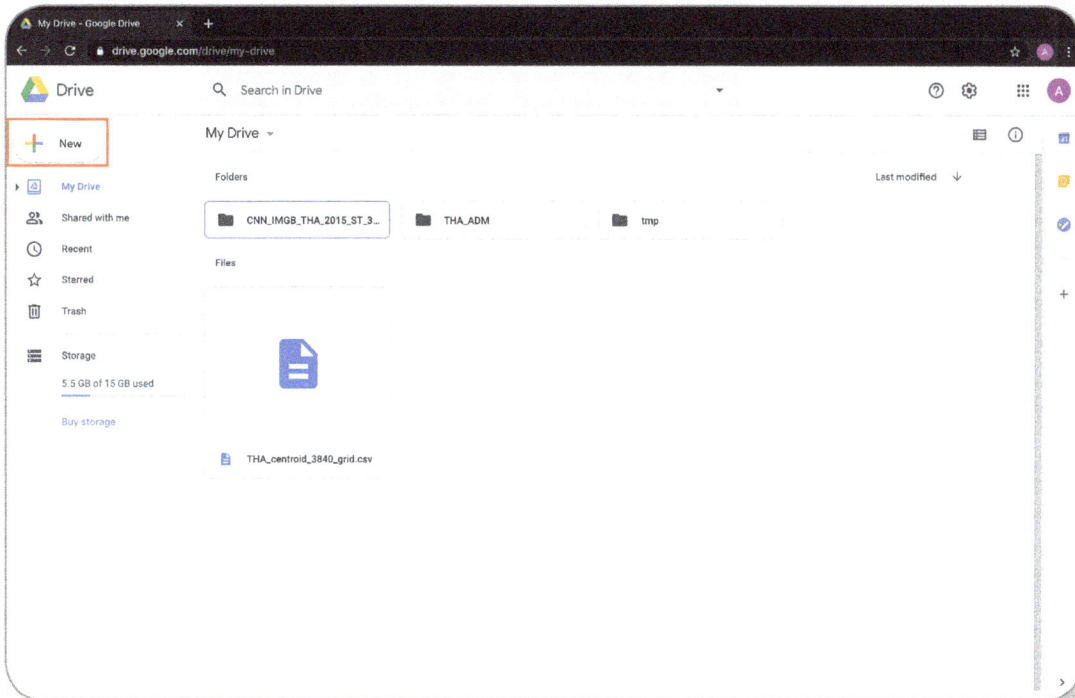

Then click **File upload**.

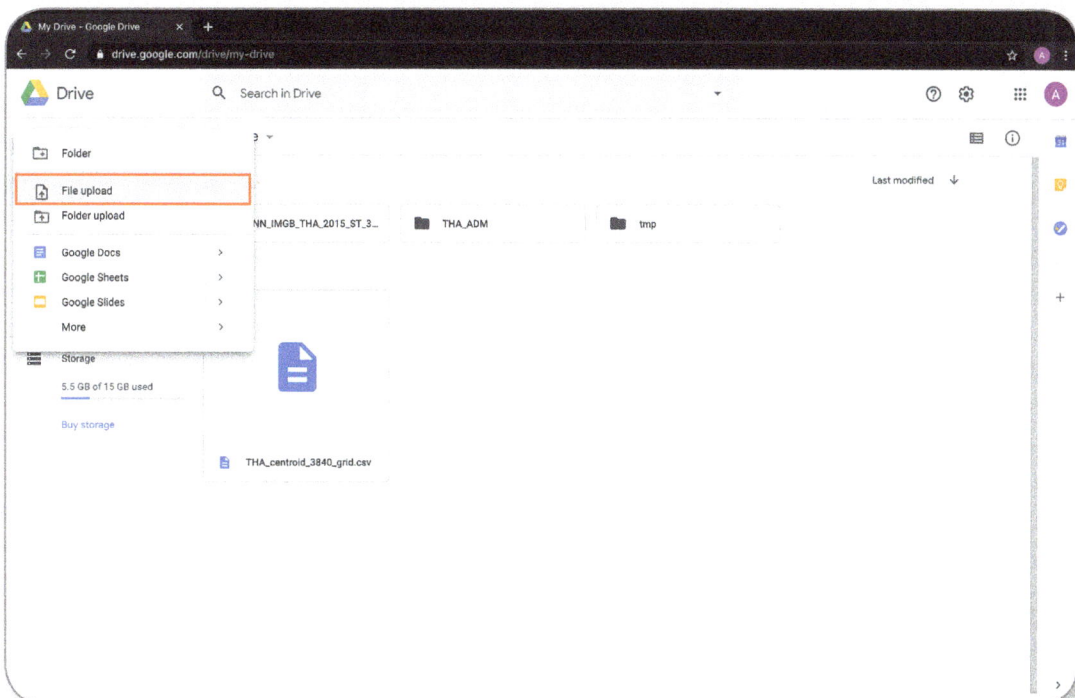

STEP 16

Locate and select the **tar.gz** archive file containing the JPG images.

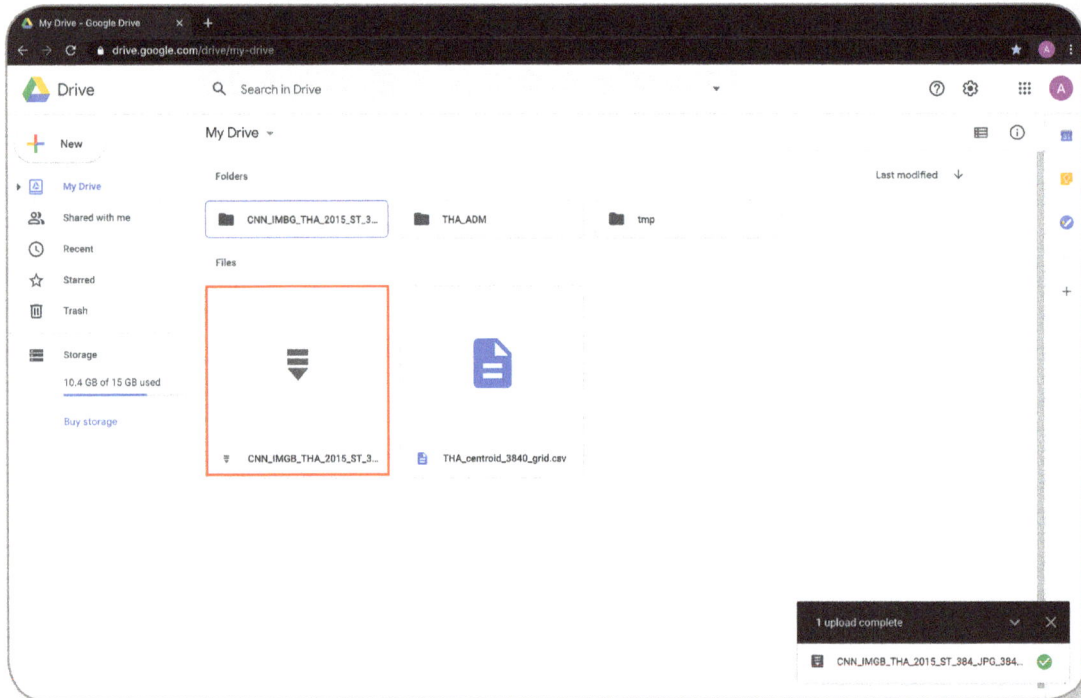

Nighttime Satellite Imagery Processing

Data Requirements
- DMSP-OLS/VIIRS annual composite nighttime lights

Tools
- Google Earth Engine

The following sections detail how to download nighttime satellite imagery and aggregating luminosity values.

Nighttime lights (NTL) imageries covering 1992 to 2013 are available from the Defense Meteorological Program (DMSP) Operational Line-Scan System (OLS) while NTL imageries covering 2012 to 2020 are available from the Visible Infrared Imaging Radiometer Suite (VIIRS). DMSP-OLS and VIIRS imagery are both hosted by the Earth Observation Group, Colorado School of Mines.

DMSP-OLS data are available as global coverage per year per image and can be downloaded from this link: *https://eogdata.mines.edu/dmsp/downloadV4composites.html.*

VIIRS imagery are published as daily mosaic and monthly and annual composite images. Unlike DMPS-OLS, VIIRS imagery is split into 6 tiles. Information on VIIRS NTL version 1 data is available from this link: https://eogdata.mines.edu/products/vnl/. When downloading, take note of the tile where the country of interest is covered.

For VIIRS, only 2015 and 2016 have annual composite images. Thus, GEE is used to create an annual composite for years other than those aforementioned using the monthly composite imagery.

STEP 1

Download VIIRS nightlight satellite imagery version 1 for years with available annual composite images.

In the browser, go to the VIIRS website https://eogdata.mines.edu/nighttime_light/annual/v10/. **Select**, and **click** the required year (e.g., "**2015**").

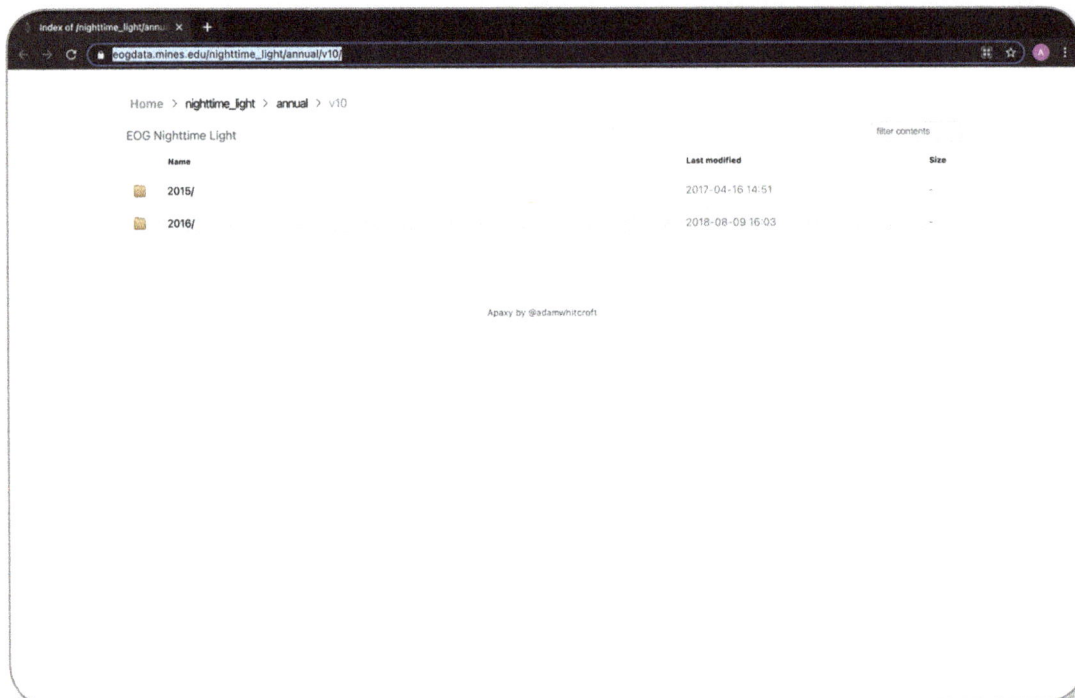

STEP 2

Select the tile **where the country of interest is located**. The tile information is the fourth group of characters from the right. **Save** the file in the working directory. Note that the file is a tar.gz archive with a size of approximately 4 GB.

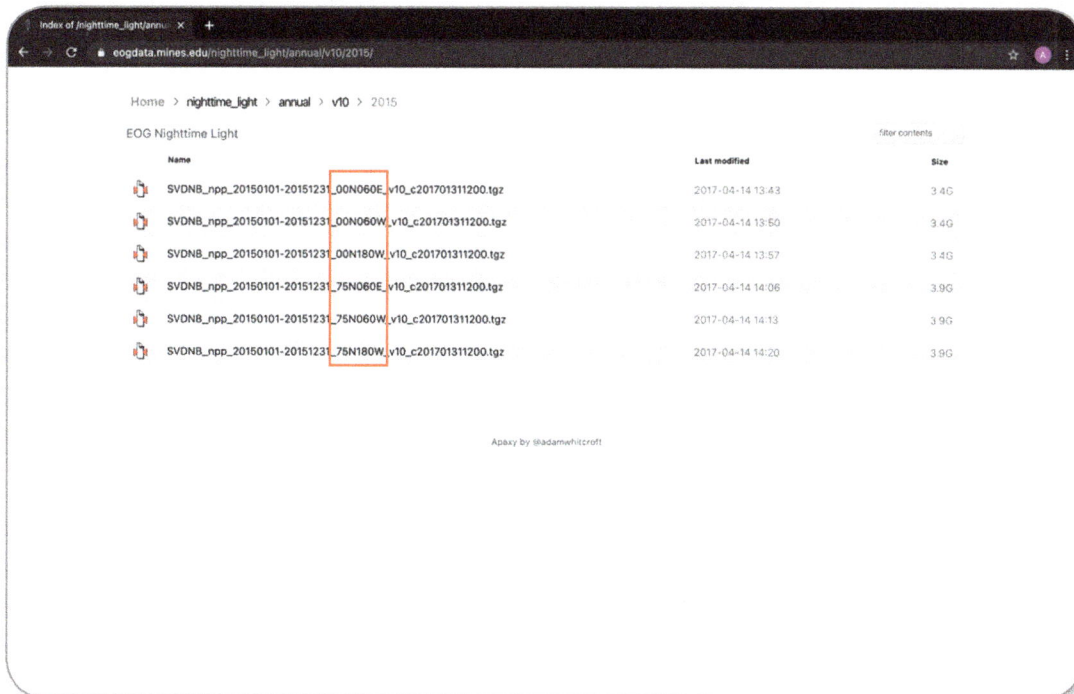

Once download has finished, **decompress** the archive file.

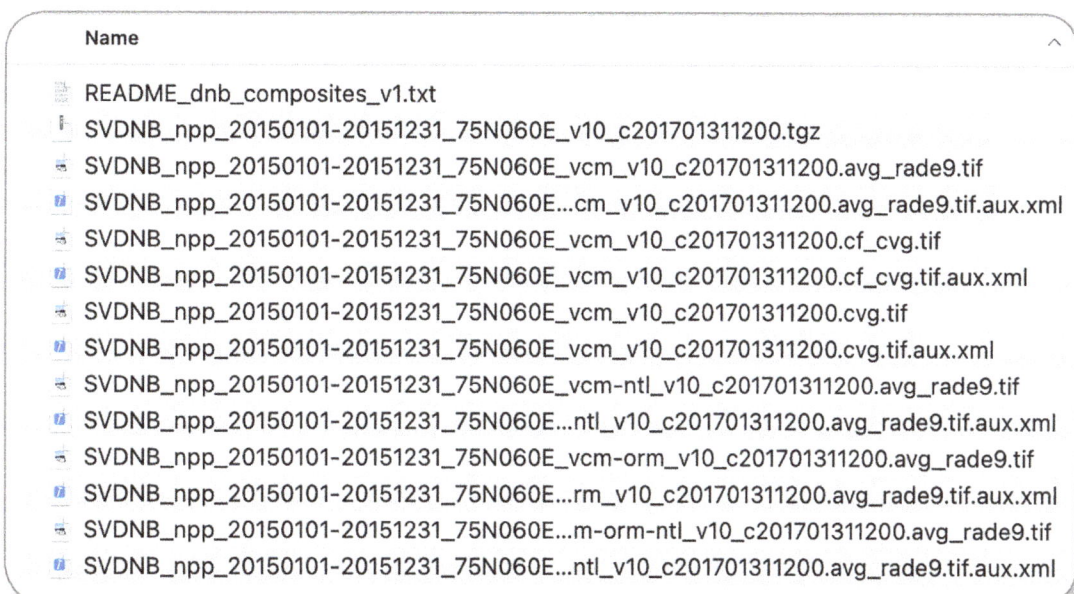

STEP 3

Crop out the nighttime imagery for the country of interest.

Open the Rcode ***Crop_NTL_imagery.R*** in Rstudio.

```
Crop_NTL_imagery.R ×

                                      Source on Save   Q   ⚡ ·                              → Run   ↱   → Source ·  ≡
 1   # Code for cropping Nighttime satellite imagery in preparation for upload to Google Earth Engine
 2
 3 ▾ # Load packages----
 4   library(tidyverse)
 5   library(sf)
 6   library(gdalUtilities)
 7
 8 ▾ # Opens a dialog box for selecting country shapefile----
 9   shapefile_path <- tcltk::tk_choose.files(filters = matrix(c("SHP",".shp","All files","*"),2,2,byrow = T),
10                                      caption = "Select Country Level Shapefile")
11   # read shapefile
12   shp <- read_sf(shapefile_path)
13
14   # extract bounding box and round up the values to add some buffer
15   xmin <- floor(st_bbox(shp)[[1]])
16   ymin <- floor(st_bbox(shp)[[2]])
17   xmax <- ceiling(st_bbox(shp)[[3]])
18   ymax <- ceiling(st_bbox(shp)[[4]])
19
20 ▾ # Opens a dialog box for selecting geoTIFF NTL data----
21   NTL_file_folder <- tcltk::tk_choose.dir(caption = "Select Directory Containing Nighttime Satellite Imagery")
22 ▾ # Get working directory from downloaded NTL data----
23   wd_path <- dirname(NTL_file_folder)
24   setwd(wd_path)
25
26 ▾ # Check if correct file is selected reselect if needed----
27   # Filter NTL data products:
28   #   for VIIRS: vcm-orm-ntl with extension avg_rade9.tif
29   #   for DMSP: web.stable_lights.avg_vis
30   NTL_file_list <- list.files(path = NTL_file_folder,
31                               pattern = ".tif$",
32                               full.names = T)
33
34 ▾ if (str_detect(NTL_file_folder,"SVDNB_npp")) {
35     # filter for VIIRS
36     NTL_file <- NTL_file_list[str_detect(NTL_file_list,"vcm-orm-ntl")]
37 ▾ } else{
38     # filter for DMPS
39     NTL_file <- NTL_file_list[str_detect(NTL_file_list,"web.stable_lights.avg_vis")]
40 ▴ }
41
42   print(basename(NTL_file))
43
44 ▾ # Generate destination folder and output file ----
45   dest_path <- paste0(wd_path,"/cropped_",basename(NTL_file_folder),"/")
46   output_file <- paste0(dest_path,"cropped_",basename(NTL_file))
47
48 ▾ # Check if destination folders exists, otherwise create folders----
49 ▾ if (!dir.exists(dest_path)) {
50     dir.create(dest_path)
51 ▴ }
1:1   (Top Level) ÷                                                                              R Script
```

Load the required packages.

```
3 ▾ # Load packages----
4   library(tidyverse)
5   library(sf)
6   library(gdalUtilities)
```

STEP 4

Use **tk_choose.files()** from the package **tcltk** to open a window for selecting and obtaining the country level shapefile path. *Please note that country level shapefiles are usually denoted as ADM0.*

```
8 ▾  # Opens a dialog box for selecting country shapefile----
9    shapefile_path <- tcltk::tk_choose.files(filters = matrix(c("SHP",".shp","All files","*"),2,2,byrow = T),
10                                        caption = "Select Country Level Shapefile")
11   # read shapefile
12   shp <- read_sf(shapefile_path)
13
14   # extract bounding box and round up the values to add some buffer
15   xmin <- floor(st_bbox(shp)[[1]])
16   ymin <- floor(st_bbox(shp)[[2]])
17   xmax <- ceiling(st_bbox(shp)[[3]])
18   ymax <- ceiling(st_bbox(shp)[[4]])
```

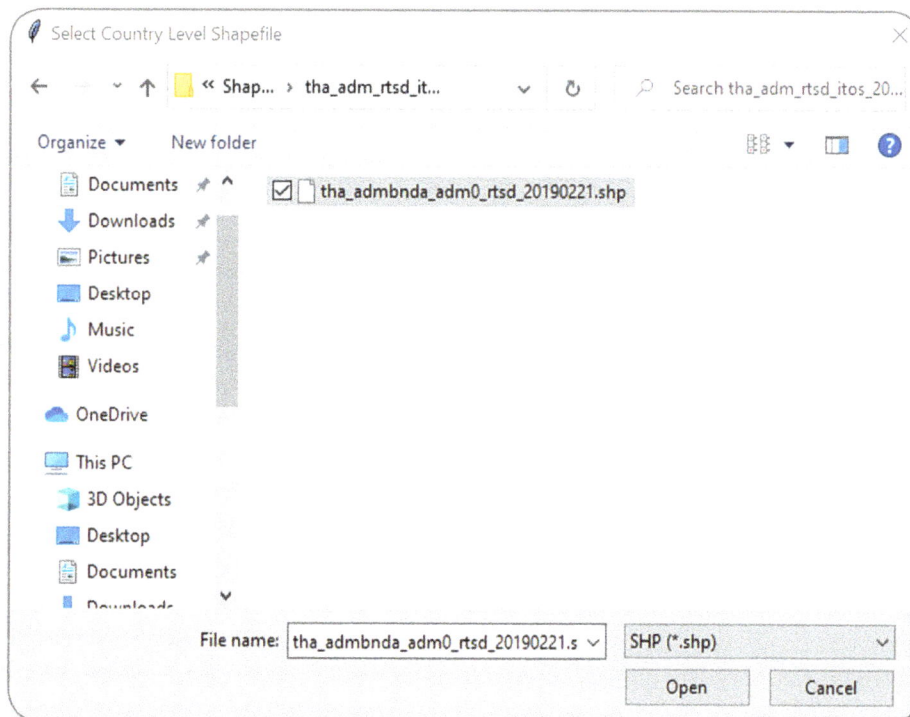

STEP 5

Load the shapefile using the sf function **read_sf()**.

```
 8 ▾ # Opens a dialog box for selecting country shapefile----
 9   shapefile_path <- tcltk::tk_choose.files(filters = matrix(c("SHP",".shp","All files","*"),2,2,byrow = T),
10                                            caption = "Select Country Level Shapefile")
11   # read shapefile
12   shp <- read_sf(shapefile_path)
13
14   # extract bounding box and round up the values to add some buffer
15   xmin <- floor(st_bbox(shp)[[1]])
16   ymin <- floor(st_bbox(shp)[[2]])
17   xmax <- ceiling(st_bbox(shp)[[3]])
18   ymax <- ceiling(st_bbox(shp)[[4]])
```

STEP 6

Extract the bounding box coordinates of the shapefile using the function **st_bbox()** from the **sf** package. Expand the bounding box to have some buffer. *This can be done by rounding down ymin and xmin, and rounding up ymax and xmax.*

```
 8 ▾ # Opens a dialog box for selecting country shapefile----
 9   shapefile_path <- tcltk::tk_choose.files(filters = matrix(c("SHP",".shp","All files","*"),2,2,byrow = T),
10                                            caption = "Select Country Level Shapefile")
11   # read shapefile
12   shp <- read_sf(shapefile_path)
13
14   # extract bounding box and round up the values to add some buffer
15   xmin <- floor(st_bbox(shp)[[1]])
16   ymin <- floor(st_bbox(shp)[[2]])
17   xmax <- ceiling(st_bbox(shp)[[3]])
18   ymax <- ceiling(st_bbox(shp)[[4]])
```

STEP 7

Select the directory containing the nighttime satellite imagery using the function **tk_choose.dir()** from the package **tcltk**.

```
20 ▾ # Opens a dialog box for selecting geoTIFF NTL data----
21   NTL_file_folder <- tcltk::tk_choose.dir(caption = "Select Directory Containing Nighttime Satellite Imagery")
22 ▾ # Get working directory from downloaded NTL data----
23   wd_path <- dirname(NTL_file_folder)
24   setwd(wd_path)
```

A window opens for selecting the directory containing the nighttime satellite imagery.

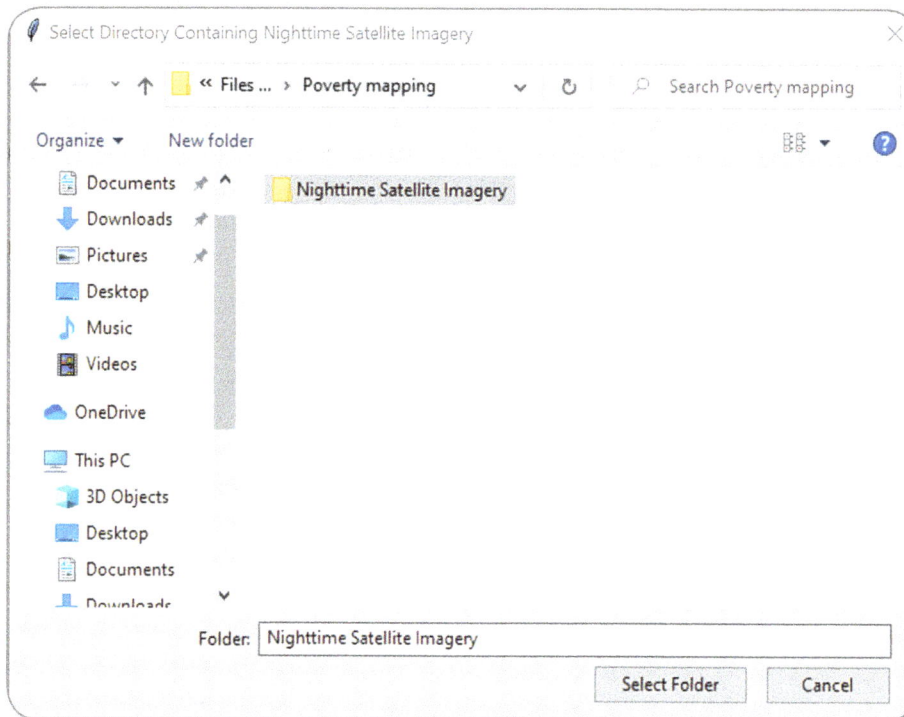

STEP 8

Extract the parent folder path of the nighttime satellite imagery and use it as the working directory through the **setwd()** command.

```
20 ▾ # Opens a dialog box for selecting geoTIFF NTL data----
21   NTL_file_folder <- tcltk::tk_choose.dir(caption = "Select Directory Containing Nighttime Satellite Imagery")
22 ▾ # Get working directory from downloaded NTL data----
23   wd_path <- dirname(NTL_file_folder)
24   setwd(wd_path)
```

STEP 9

Obtain the filenames of all nighttime satellite imagery files that are stored in the folder.

```
26▾ # Check if correct file is selected reselect if needed----
27  # Filter NTL data products:
28  #    for VIIRS: vcm-orm-ntl with extension avg_rade9.tif
29  #    for DMSP: web.stable_lights.avg_vis
30  NTL_file_list <- list.files(path = NTL_file_folder,
31                              pattern = ".tif$",
32                              full.names = T)
33
34▾ if (str_detect(NTL_file_folder,"SVDNB_npp")) {
35    # filter for VIIRS
36    NTL_file <- NTL_file_list[str_detect(NTL_file_list,"vcm-orm-ntl")]
37▾ } else{
38    # filter for DMPS
39    NTL_file <- NTL_file_list[str_detect(NTL_file_list,"web.stable_lights.avg_vis")]
40▴ }
41
42  print(basename(NTL_file))
```

STEP 10

Use an if-else statement to select the correct imagery product.

- For VIIRS, use the data product - ***vcm-orm-ntl*** with extension ***avg_rade9.tif***.
- For DMSP-OLS, use data product - ***web.stable_lights.avg_vis***.

```
26▾ # Check if correct file is selected reselect if needed----
27  # Filter NTL data products:
28  #    for VIIRS: vcm-orm-ntl with extension avg_rade9.tif
29  #    for DMSP: web.stable_lights.avg_vis
30  NTL_file_list <- list.files(path = NTL_file_folder,
31                              pattern = ".tif$",
32                              full.names = T)
33
34▾ if (str_detect(NTL_file_folder,"SVDNB_npp")) {
35    # filter for VIIRS
36    NTL_file <- NTL_file_list[str_detect(NTL_file_list,"vcm-orm-ntl")]
37▾ } else{
38    # filter for DMPS
39    NTL_file <- NTL_file_list[str_detect(NTL_file_list,"web.stable_lights.avg_vis")]
40▴ }
41
42  print(basename(NTL_file))
```

Print the filename to check.

```
> print(basename(NTL_file))
[1] "SVDNB_npp_20150101-20151231_75N060E_vcm-orm-ntl_v10_c201701311200.avg_rade9.tif"
>
```

STEP 11

Generate the destination path where the cropped nighttime imagery and base name for the output file will be saved.

```
44 ▾ # Generate destination folder and output file ----
45   dest_path <-  paste0(wd_path,"/cropped_",basename(NTL_file_folder),"/")
46   output_file <- paste0(dest_path,"cropped_",basename(NTL_file))
47
48 ▾ # Check if destination folders exists, otherwise create folders----
49 ▾ if (!dir.exists(dest_path)) {
50     dir.create(dest_path)
51 ▴ }
```

STEP 12

Check if the destination folder already exists. If the folder does not exist yet, create it.

```
44 ▾ # Generate destination folder and output file ----
45   dest_path <-  paste0(wd_path,"/cropped_",basename(NTL_file_folder),"/")
46   output_file <- paste0(dest_path,"cropped_",basename(NTL_file))
47
48 ▾ # Check if destination folders exists, otherwise create folders----
49 ▾ if (!dir.exists(dest_path)) {
50     dir.create(dest_path)
51 ▴ }
```

STEP 13

Run the **gdal_translate()** function from the **gdalUtilities** package to crop the nighttime satellite imagery.

```
53 ▾ # Crop the NTL image----
54
55   gdal_translate(NTL_file,output_file,projwin = c(xmin,ymax,xmax,ymin))
```

STEP 14

The code's output is stored in the folder with a prefix "cropped_". Likewise, the geoTIFF file is prefixed. It will later be uploaded to GEE for further processing.

Name	^
˅ 📁 cropped_SVDNB_npp_20150101-20151231_75N060E_v10_c201701311200	
🖼 cropped_SVDNB_npp_20150101-20151231...-orm-ntl_v10_c201701311200.avg_rade9.tif	
˃ 📁 SVDNB_npp_20150101-20151231_75N060E_v10_c201701311200	

STEP 15

Compute the aggregate average luminosity per area, where every pixel's night light intensity is considered.

Aggregation computation is done in GEE, where the shape for each area needs to be defined and nighttime imagery for corresponding year needs to be provided. The total sum is divided by the number of pixels.

Use the code in file: ***viirs_mean_luminosity.js***.

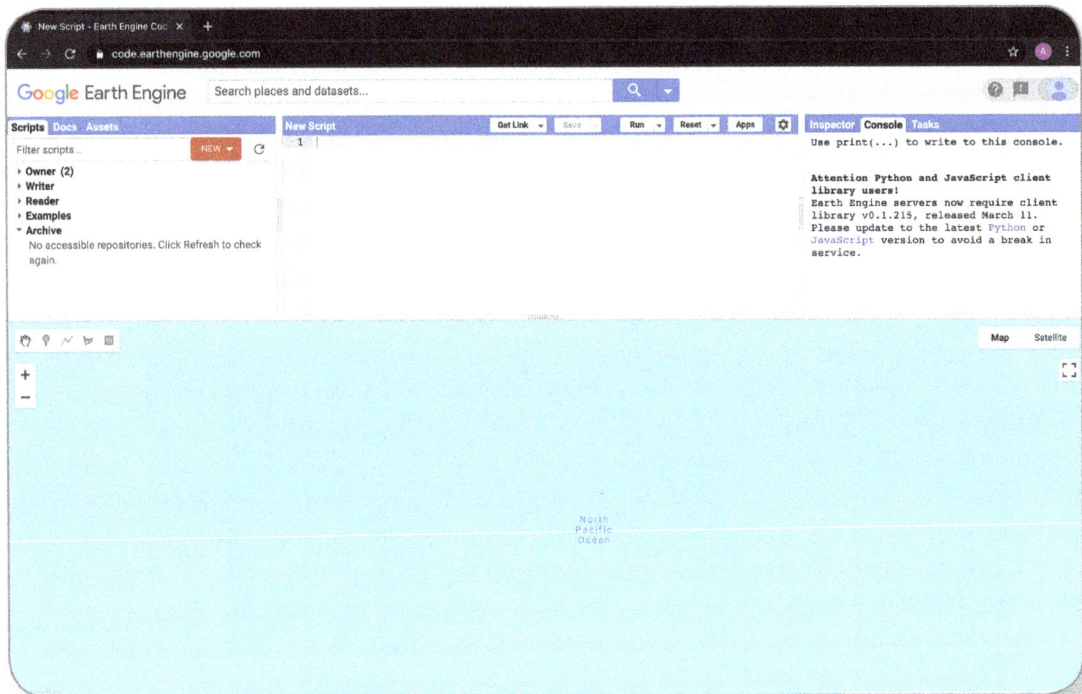

Upload the cropped nighttime lights imagery. Click **Assets.**

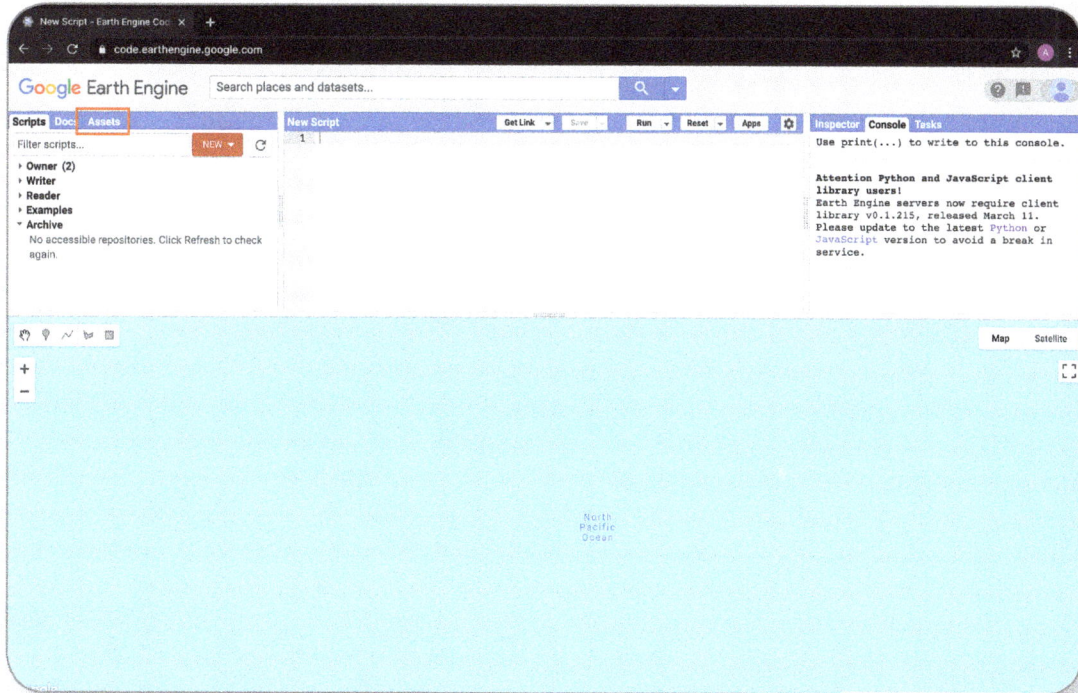

STEP 16

Click **New**.

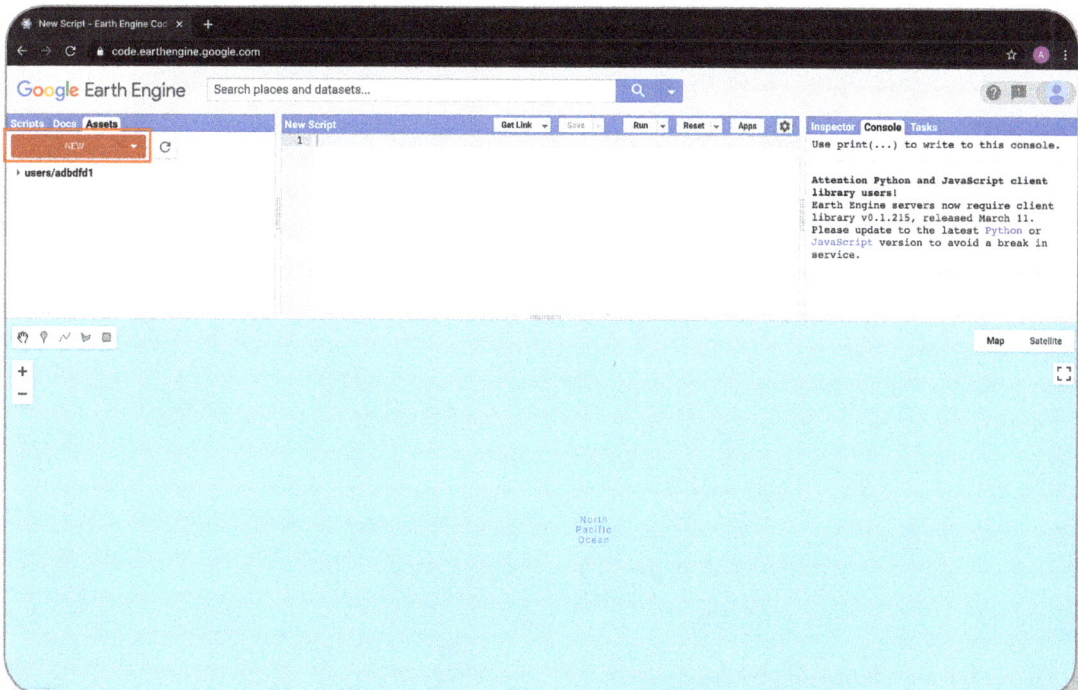

STEP 17

Click **GeoTIFF**.

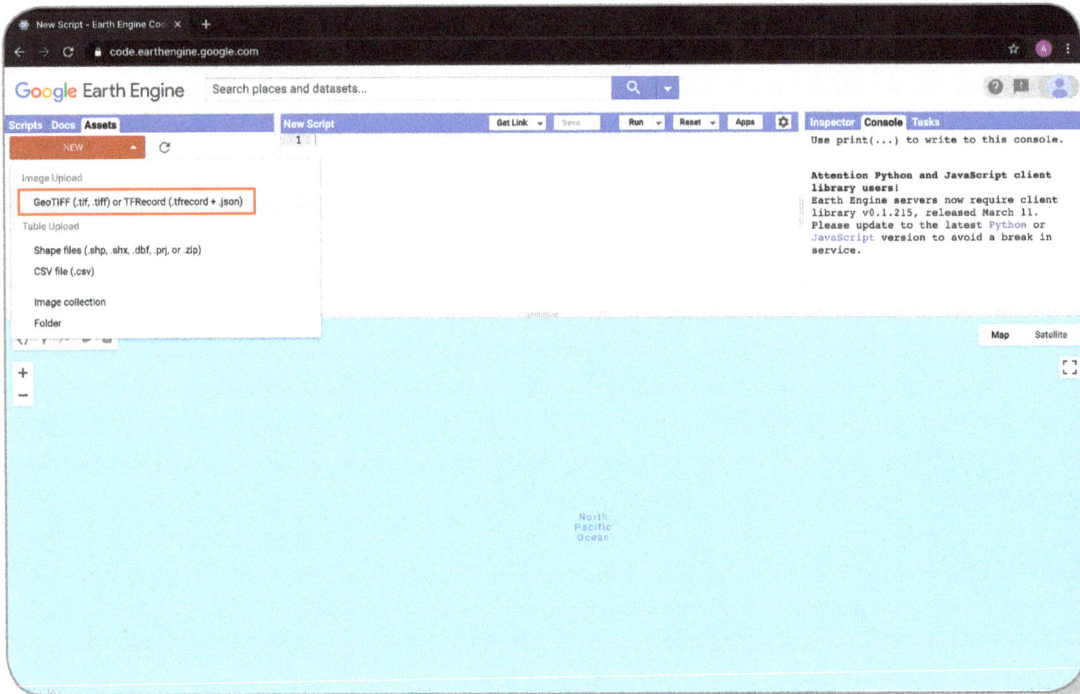

STEP 18

Click **Select** and locate the cropped nighttime lights imagery.

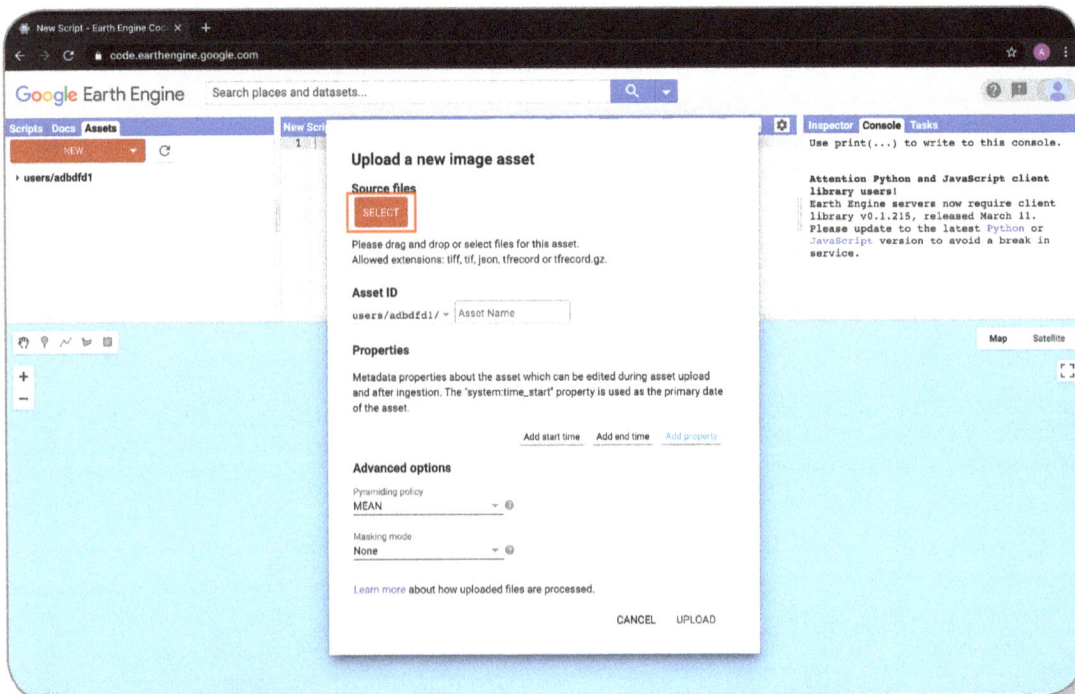

STEP 19

Change the **Asset ID**. Make sure that the ID only contains letters and numbers.

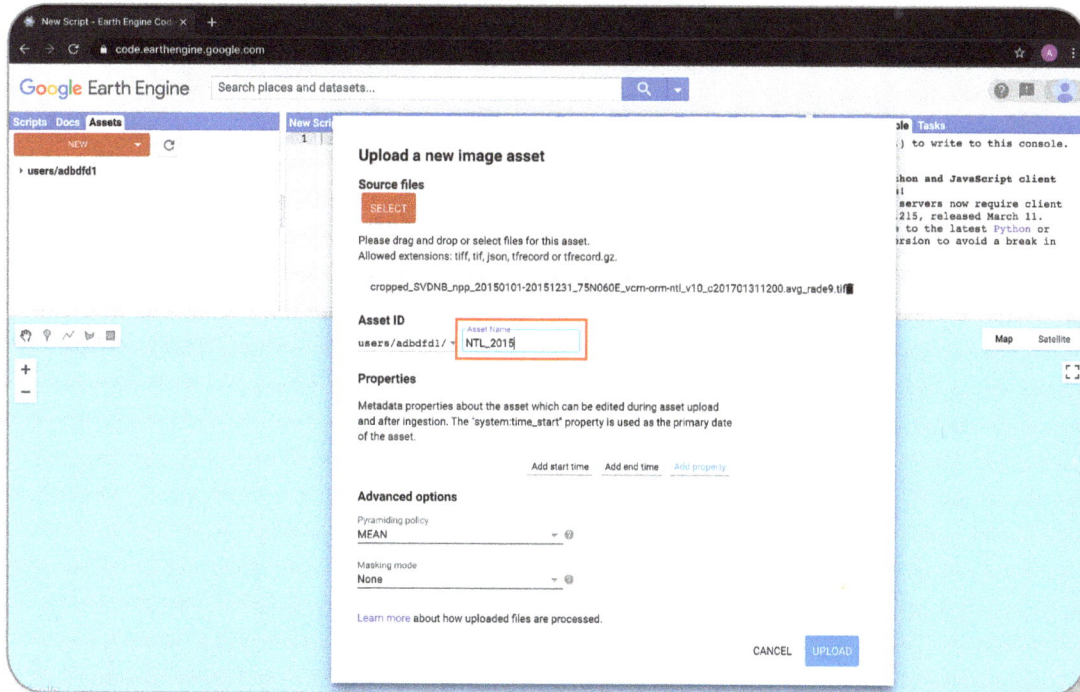

STEP 20

Click **Upload**.

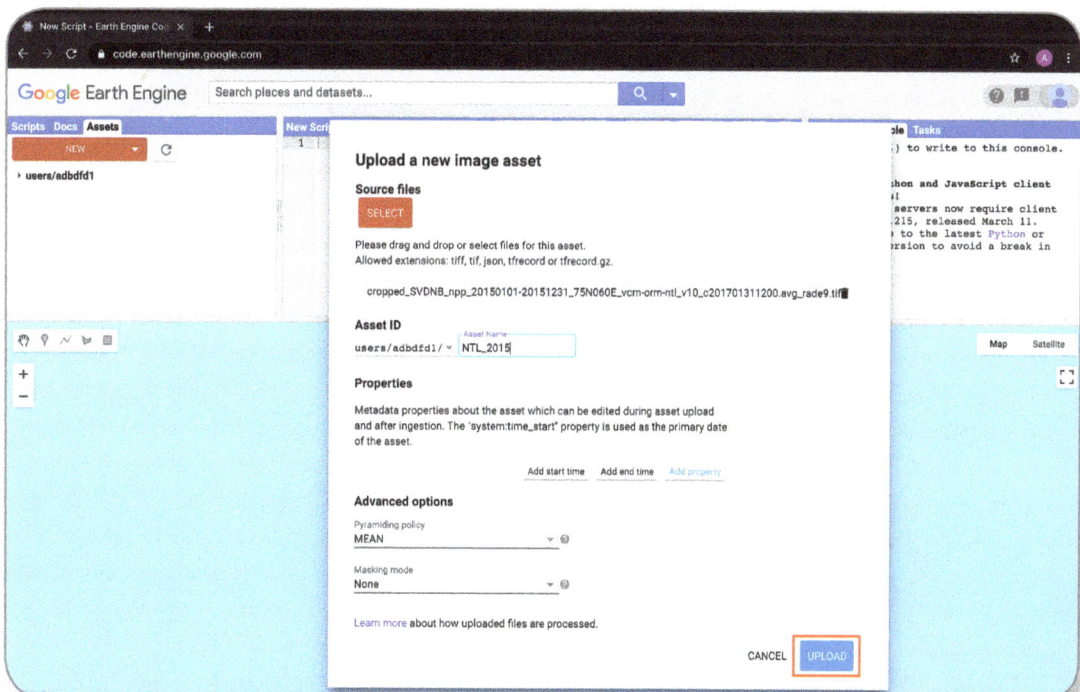

The uploaded nighttime lights data will appear as a new asset.

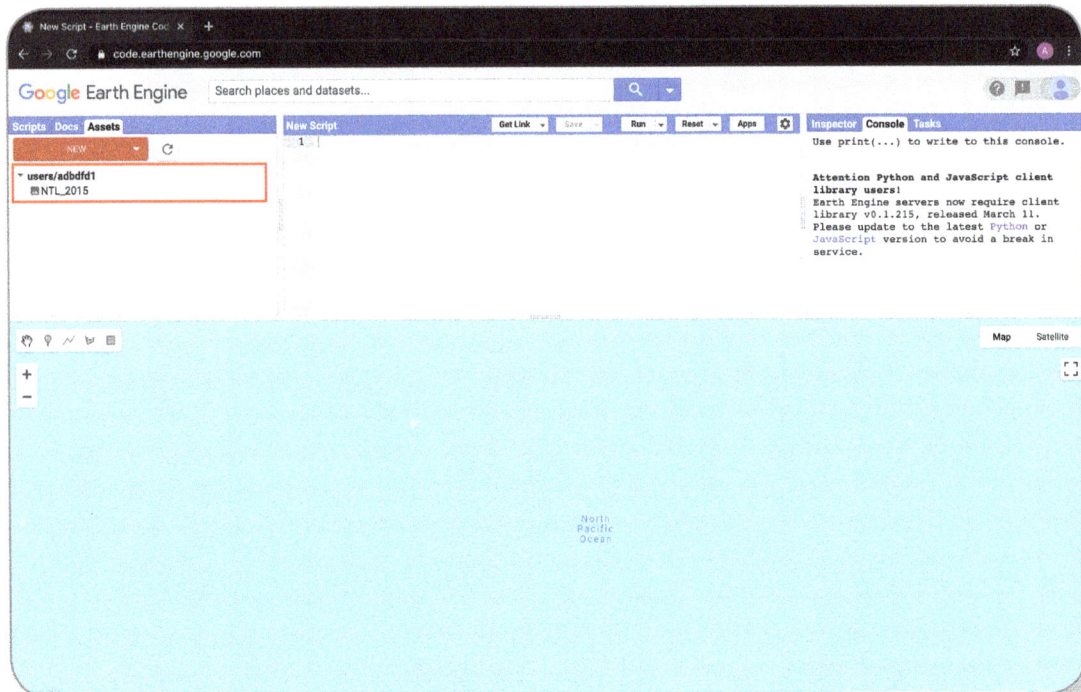

STEP 21

This time upload the point shapefile. Again click **New** and select **Shape files**.

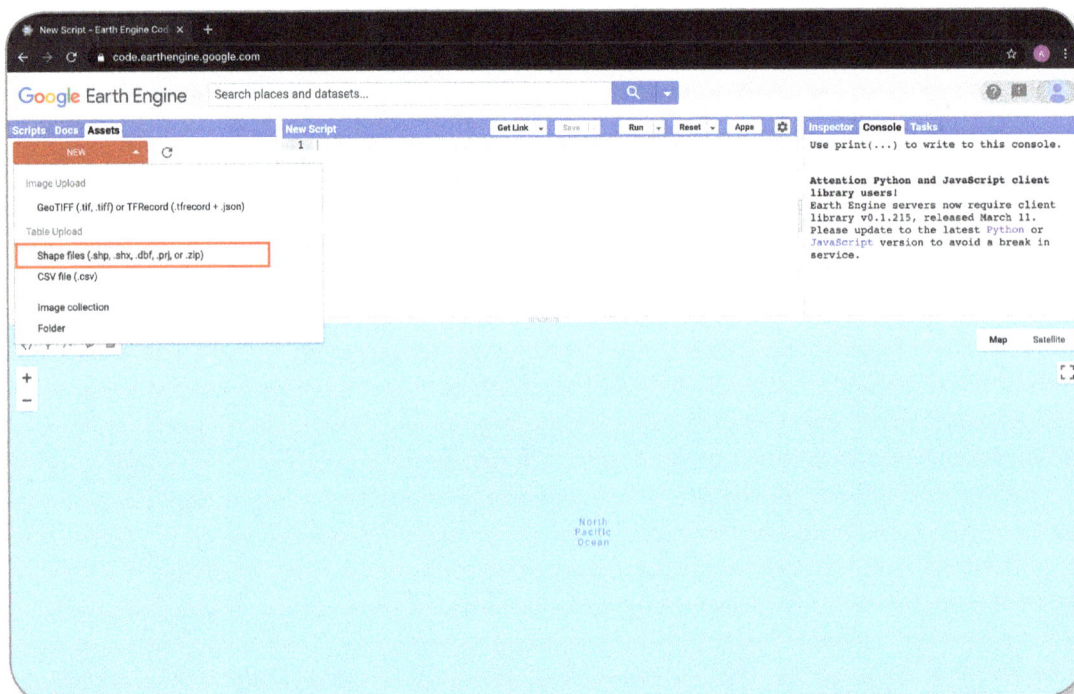

STEP 22

Click **Select**.

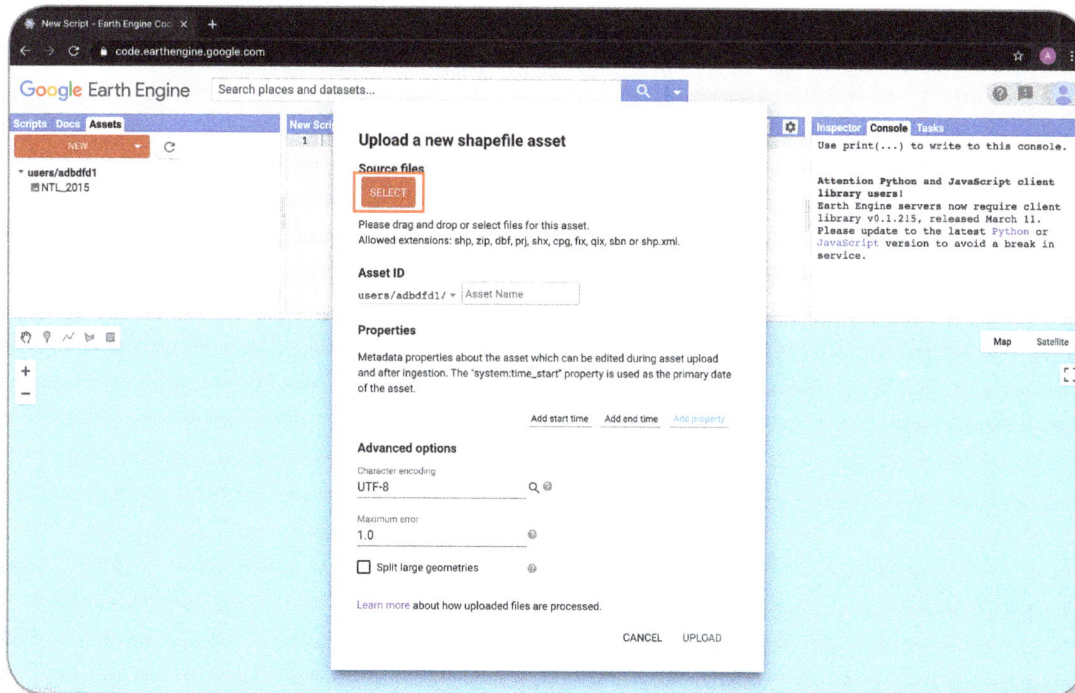

STEP 23

Locate the shapefile that was created from the code *Daytime_imagery_format_conversion.R*.

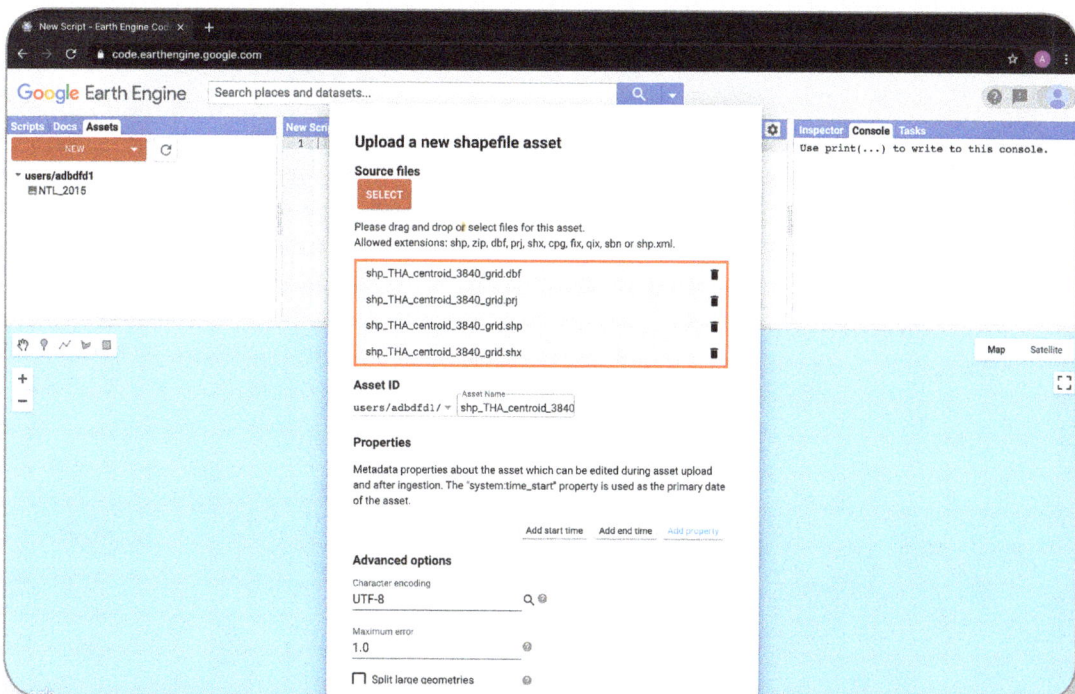

STEP 24

Click **Upload**.

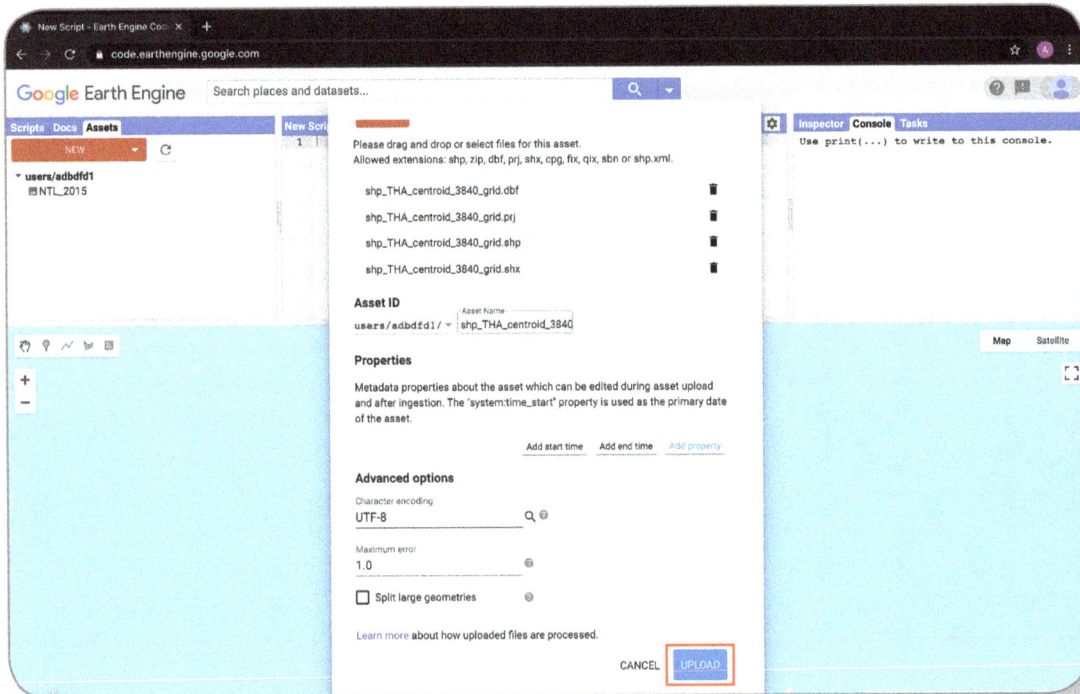

The uploaded shapefile will appear as a new asset.

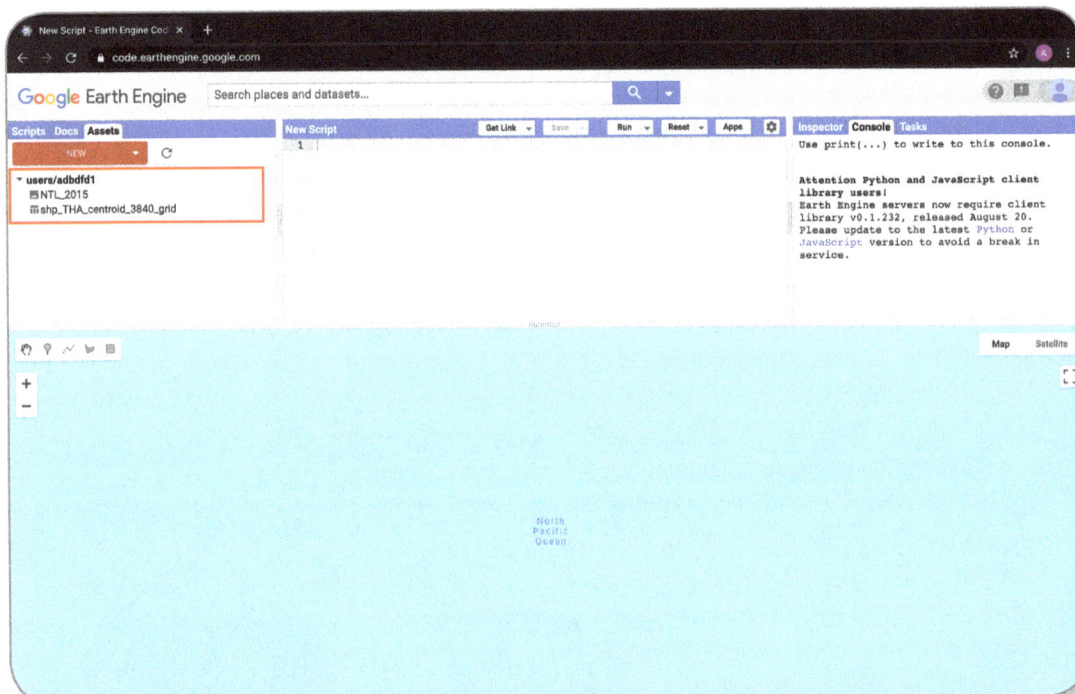

STEP 25

Open the JavaScript **ntl_mean_luminosity.js** using a text editing software (e.g., Windows Notepad).

```
                                    ntl_mean_luminosity.js

var annual_composite = viirs_annual
    .select('b1')//Average DNB radiance values
;

var nlVis = {
  min: 0.0,
  max: 1,
  bands: ['b1'],
};

Map.centerObject(pt_shp);
Map.addLayer(annual_composite,nlVis,"NTL annual composite");

// Aggregate mean of nightlight intensities for centroid regions of size 256px
var mappedFeatures = pt_shp.map(function(feature) {
  var geometry = ee.Geometry.Point([ee.Number(pt_shp.get('lon')), ee.Number(pt_shp.get('lat'))]).buffer(1920).bounds()
  return feature.set(annual_composite.reduceRegion({
    reducer: 'mean',
    geometry: feature.geometry(),
    scale: 100,
  })));
});

// Export the FeatureCollection.
Export.table.toDrive({
  collection: mappedFeatures,
  description: '',
  fileFormat: 'CSV'
});
```

Select "b1" band of viirs_annual raster and store it in the variable **annual_composite**.

```
                                    ntl_mean_luminosity.js

var annual_composite = viirs_annual
    .select('b1')//Average DNB radiance values
;

var nlVis = {
  min: 0.0,
  max: 1,
  bands: ['b1'],
};

Map.centerObject(pt_shp);
Map.addLayer(annual_composite,nlVis,"NTL annual composite");

// Aggregate mean of nightlight intensities for centroid regions of size 256px
var mappedFeatures = pt_shp.map(function(feature) {
  var geometry = ee.Geometry.Point([ee.Number(pt_shp.get('lon')), ee.Number(pt_shp.get('lat'))]).buffer(1920).bounds()
  return feature.set(annual_composite.reduceRegion({
    reducer: 'mean',
    geometry: feature.geometry(),
    scale: 100,
  })));
});

// Export the FeatureCollection.
Export.table.toDrive({
  collection: mappedFeatures,
  description: '',
  fileFormat: 'CSV'
});
```

Define variable **nlVis** to store the map visualization parameters.

```
                                    ntl_mean_luminosity.js

var annual_composite = viirs_annual
     .select('b1')//Average DNB radiance values
;

var nlVis = {
  min: 0.0,
  max: 1,
  bands: ['b1'],
};

Map.centerObject(pt_shp);
Map.addLayer(annual_composite,nlVis,"NTL annual composite");

// Aggregate mean of nightlight intensities for centroid regions of size 256px
var mappedFeatures = pt_shp.map(function(feature) {
  var geometry = ee.Geometry.Point([ee.Number(pt_shp.get('lon')), ee.Number(pt_shp.get('lat'))]).buffer(1920).bounds()
  return feature.set(annual_composite.reduceRegion({
    reducer: 'mean',
    geometry: feature.geometry(),
    scale: 100,
  }));
});

// Export the FeatureCollection.
Export.table.toDrive({
  collection: mappedFeatures,
  description: '',
  fileFormat: 'CSV'
});
```

Use the grid centroid shapefile, which will be imported later, to put the map view in the center.

```
                                    ntl_mean_luminosity.js

var annual_composite = viirs_annual
     .select('b1')//Average DNB radiance values
;

var nlVis = {
  min: 0.0,
  max: 1,
  bands: ['b1'],
};

Map.centerObject(pt_shp);
Map.addLayer(annual_composite,nlVis,"NTL annual composite");

// Aggregate mean of nightlight intensities for centroid regions of size 256px
var mappedFeatures = pt_shp.map(function(feature) {
  var geometry = ee.Geometry.Point([ee.Number(pt_shp.get('lon')), ee.Number(pt_shp.get('lat'))]).buffer(1920).bounds()
  return feature.set(annual_composite.reduceRegion({
    reducer: 'mean',
    geometry: feature.geometry(),
    scale: 100,
  }));
});

// Export the FeatureCollection.
Export.table.toDrive({
  collection: mappedFeatures,
  description: '',
  fileFormat: 'CSV'
});
```

Visualize b1 band of the viirs_annual raster using visualization parameters defined in nlVis through the command **Map.addLayer()**.

```
                                            ntl_mean_luminosity.js

var annual_composite = viirs_annual
      .select('b1')//Average DNB radiance values
;

var nlVis = {
  min: 0.0,
  max: 1,
  bands: ['b1'],
};

Map.centerObject(pt_shp);
Map.addLayer(annual_composite,nlVis,"NTL annual composite");

// Aggregate mean of nightlight intensities for centroid regions of size 256px
var mappedFeatures = pt_shp.map(function(feature) {
  var geometry = ee.Geometry.Point([ee.Number(pt_shp.get('lon')), ee.Number(pt_shp.get('lat'))]).buffer(1920).bounds()
  return feature.set(annual_composite.reduceRegion({
    reducer: 'mean',
    geometry: feature.geometry(),
    scale: 100,
  })));
});

// Export the FeatureCollection.
Export.table.toDrive({
  collection: mappedFeatures,
  description: '',
  fileFormat: 'CSV'
});
```

Define the luminosity aggregation function, which takes the centroid and creates a circle buffer around it with a radius that is half the grid size.

Get the average of the luminosity values within the buffer boundary using the **reduceRegion()** function. *The aggregated luminosity will be stored as a new column in the multipoint shapefile.*

```
                                            ntl_mean_luminosity.js

var annual_composite = viirs_annual
      .select('b1')//Average DNB radiance values
;

var nlVis = {
  min: 0.0,
  max: 1,
  bands: ['b1'],
};

Map.centerObject(pt_shp);
Map.addLayer(annual_composite,nlVis,"NTL annual composite");

// Aggregate mean of nightlight intensities for centroid regions of size 256px
var mappedFeatures = pt_shp.map(function(feature) {
  var geometry = ee.Geometry.Point([ee.Number(pt_shp.get('lon')), ee.Number(pt_shp.get('lat'))]).buffer(1920).bounds()
  return feature.set(annual_composite.reduceRegion({
    reducer: 'mean',
    geometry: feature.geometry(),
    scale: 100,
  })));
});

// Export the FeatureCollection.
Export.table.toDrive({
  collection: mappedFeatures,
  description: '',
  fileFormat: 'CSV'
});
```

Export the attribute table of the shapefile as CSV file into the Google Drive.

```
                              ntl_mean_luminosity.js

var annual_composite = viirs_annual
     .select('b1')//Average DNB radiance values
;

var nlVis = {
  min: 0.0,
  max: 1,
  bands: ['b1'],
};

Map.centerObject(pt_shp);
Map.addLayer(annual_composite,nlVis,"NTL annual composite");

// Aggregate mean of nightlight intensities for centroid regions of size 256px
var mappedFeatures = pt_shp.map(function(feature) {
  var geometry = ee.Geometry.Point([ee.Number(pt_shp.get('lon')), ee.Number(pt_shp.get('lat'))]).buffer(1920).bounds()
  return feature.set(annual_composite.reduceRegion({
    reducer: 'mean',
    geometry: feature.geometry(),
    scale: 100,
  }));
});

// Export the FeatureCollection.
Export.table.toDrive({
  collection: mappedFeatures,
  description: '',
  fileFormat: 'CSV'
});
```

Copy the codes from the script **ntl_mean_luminosity.js**. Paste the code into the GEE Code Editor, then click **Save**.

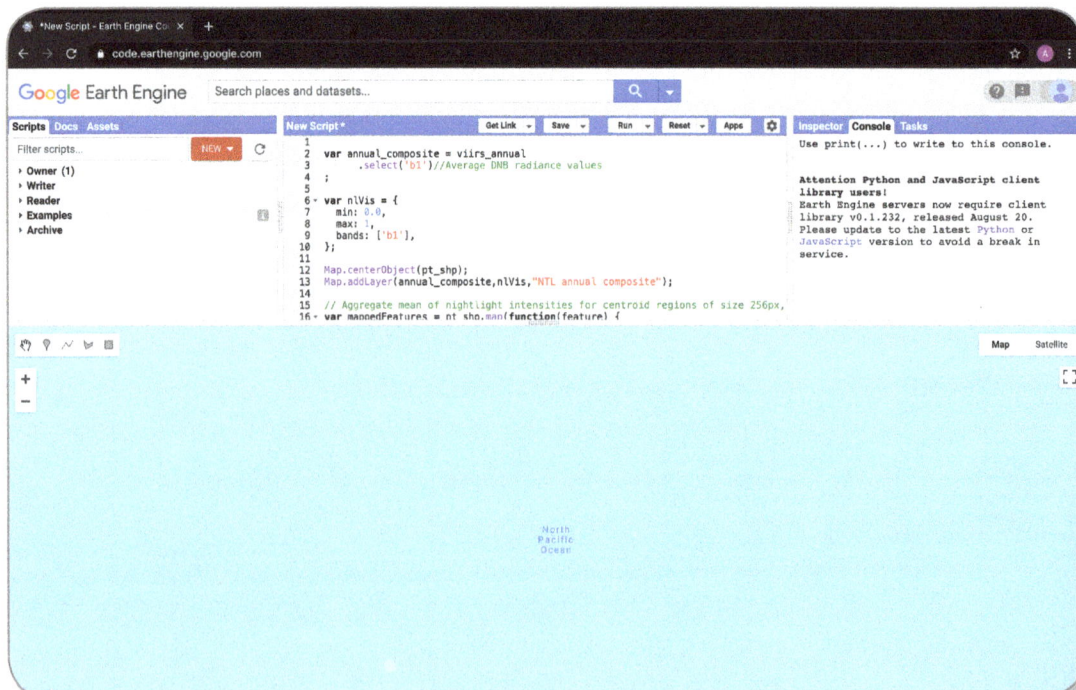

STEP 26

If a repository has not yet been created, GEE will prompt to provide a name for the new repository. Click **Create**.

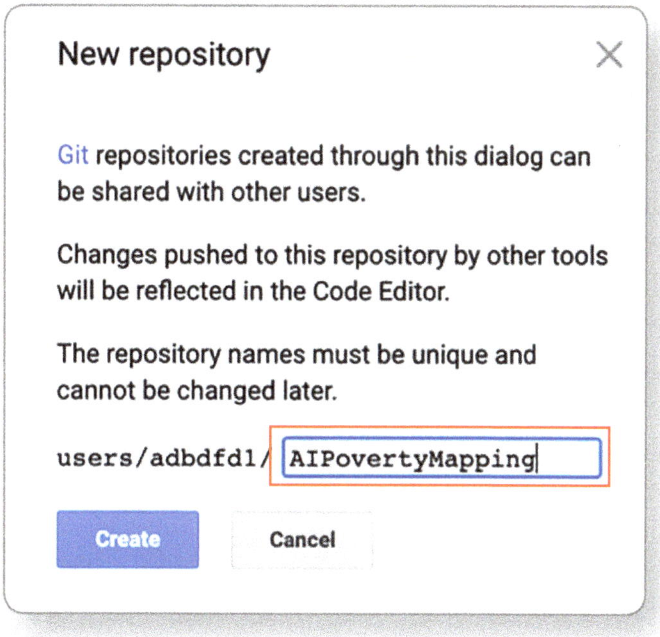

New repository ✕

Git repositories created through this dialog can be shared with other users.

Changes pushed to this repository by other tools will be reflected in the Code Editor.

The repository names must be unique and cannot be changed later.

users/adbdfd1/ `AIPovertyMapping`

[Create]   [Cancel]

STEP 27

GEE will then prompt to input the script's filename. A description of the script may be provided.

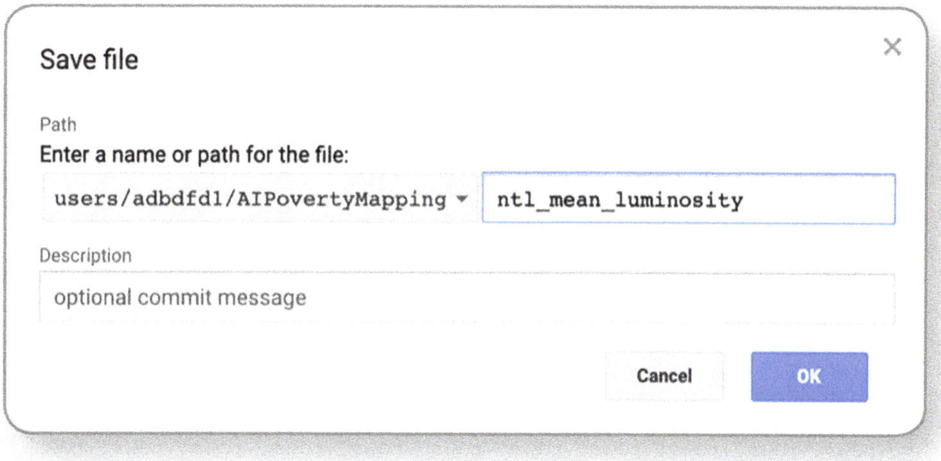

Save file ✕

Path
Enter a name or path for the file:

users/adbdfd1/AIPovertyMapping ▾   `ntl_mean_luminosity`

Description

optional commit message

[Cancel]   [OK]

The script will appear in the Script pane.

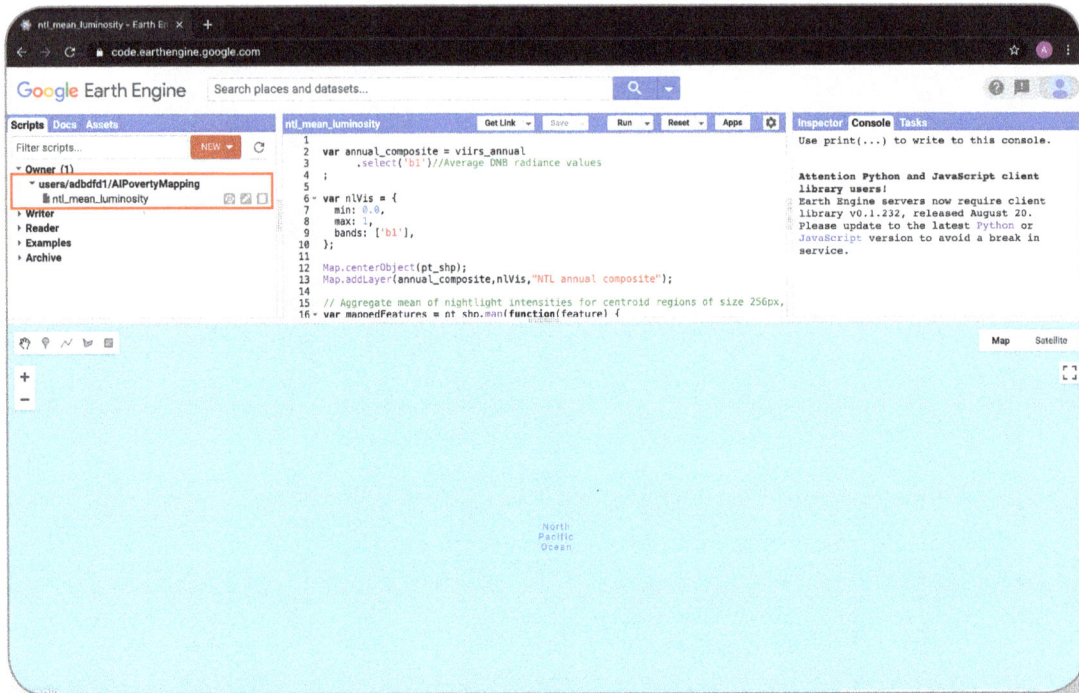

STEP 28

Click **Assets**.

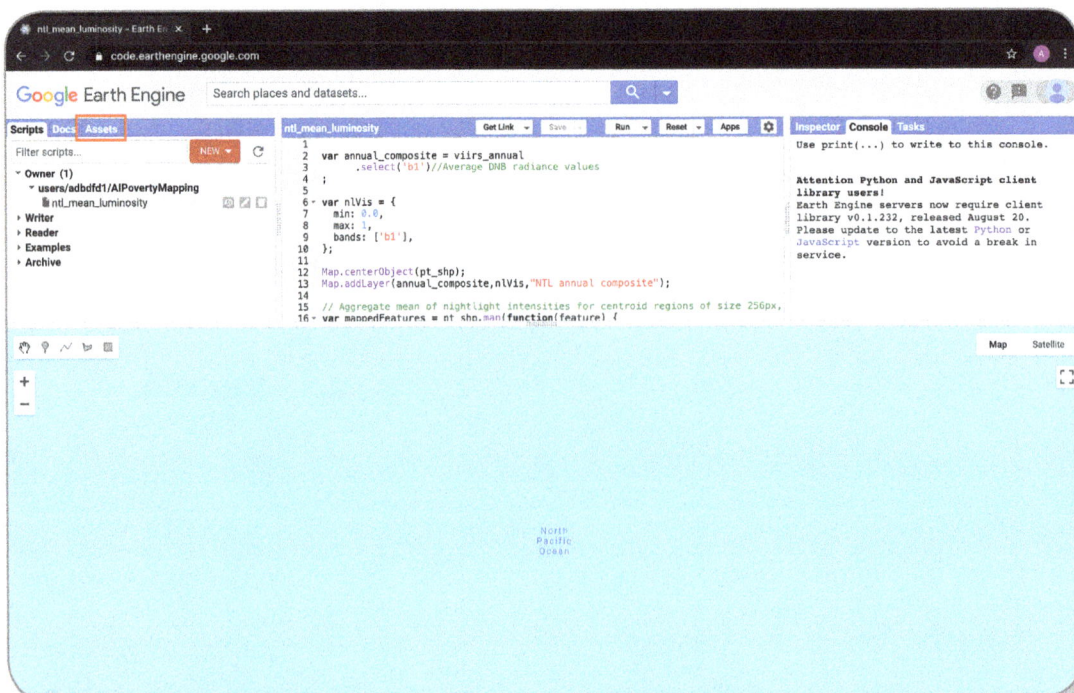

STEP 29

Click the **Import to script button** to place the NTL into the script.

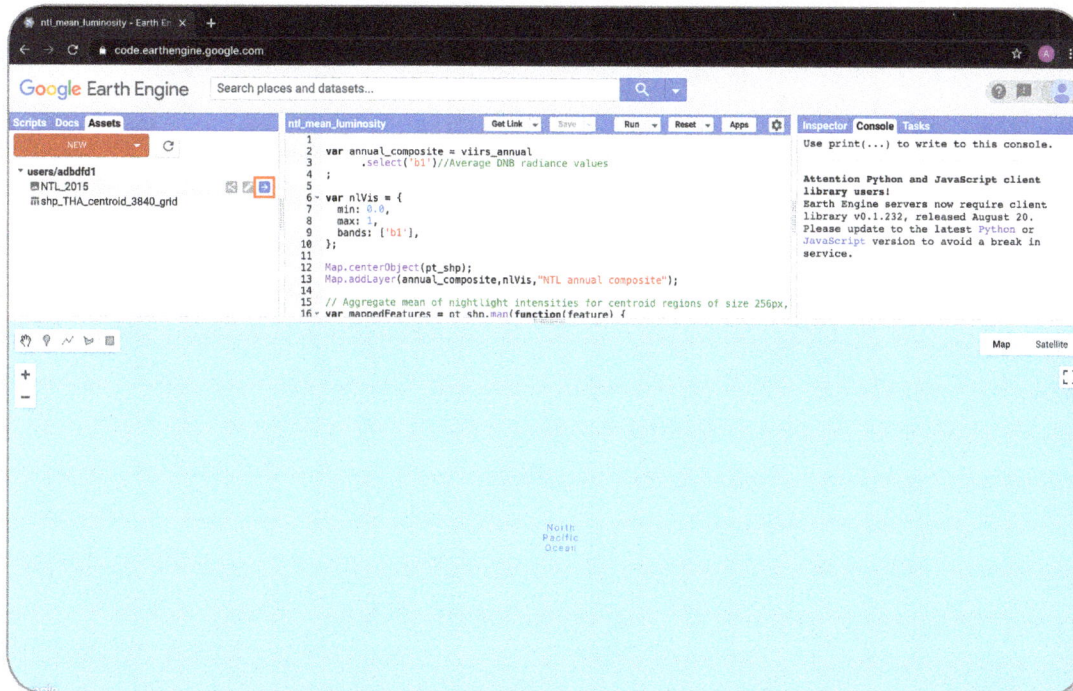

STEP 30

Rename the variable name from **image** to **viirs_annual**.

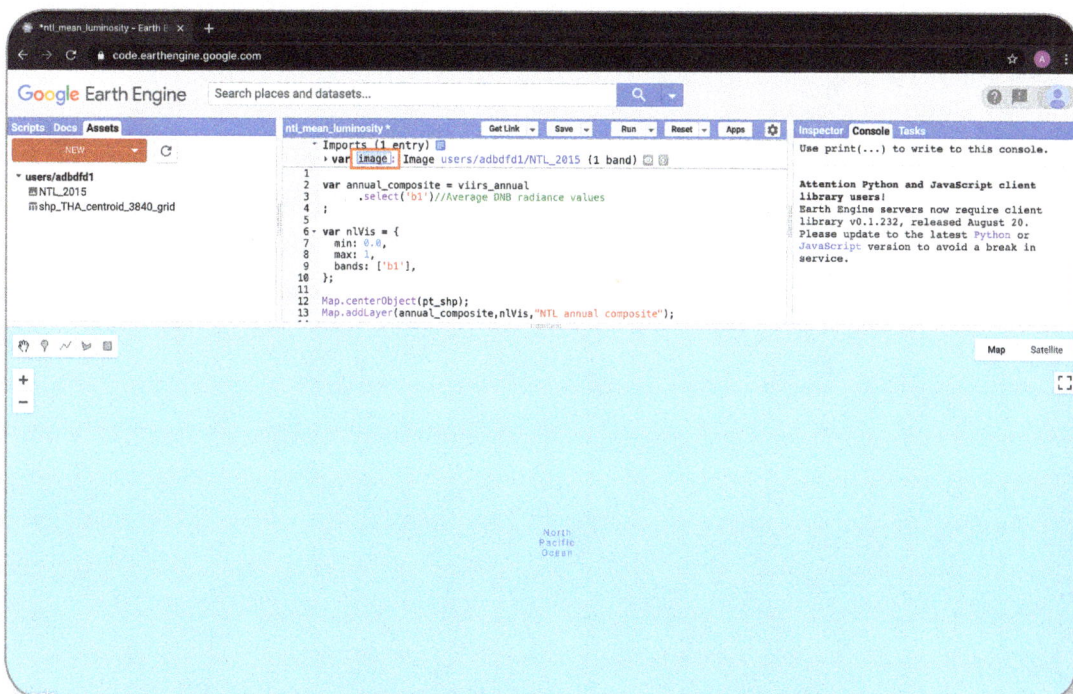

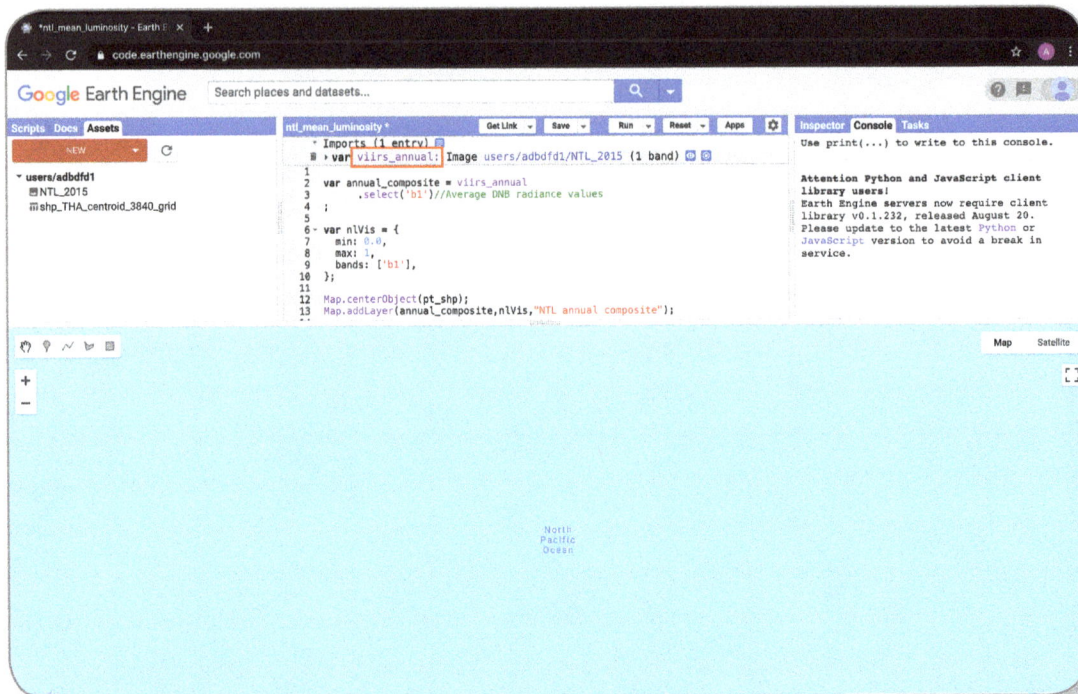

STEP 31

Click the **Import to script button** to place the shapefile into the script.

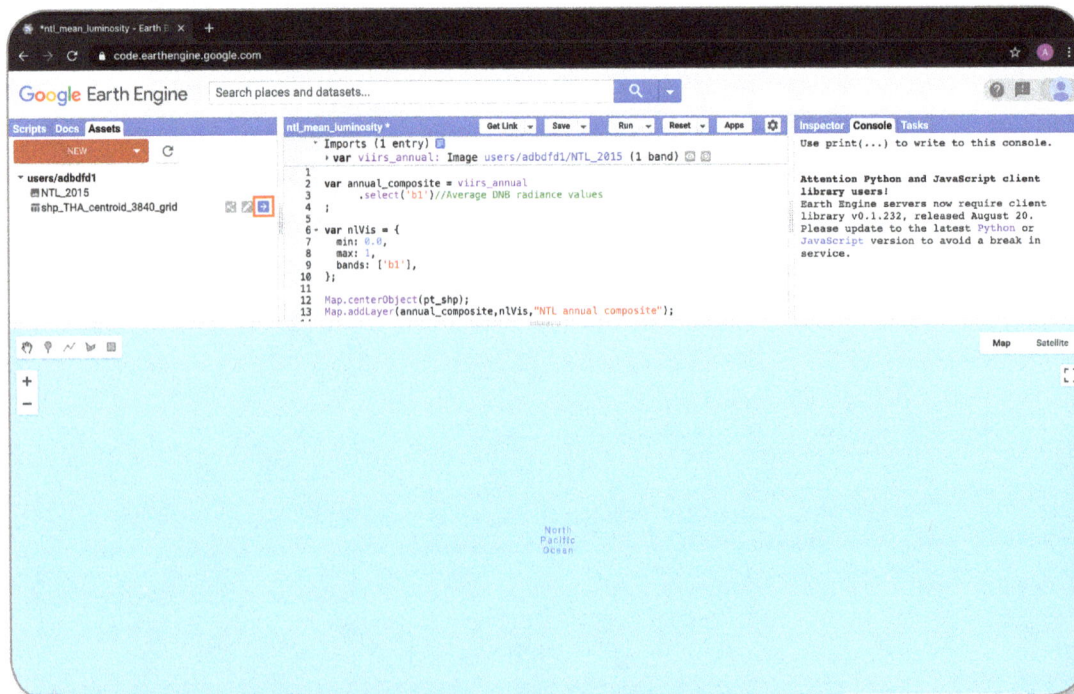

STEP 32

Rename the variable name from **table** to **pt_shp**.

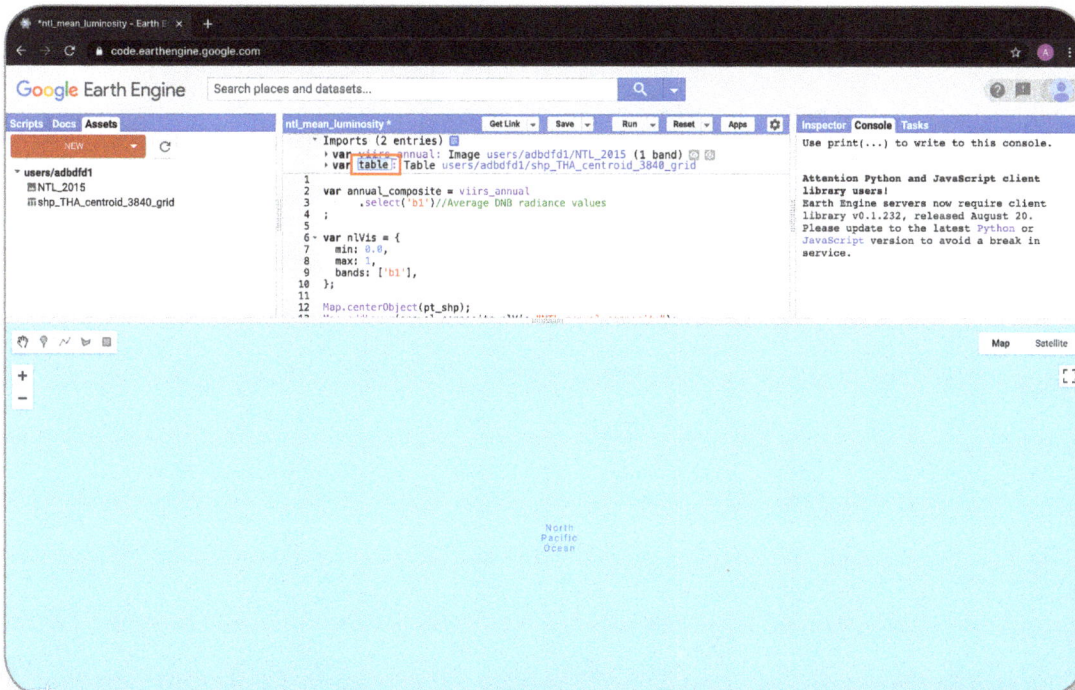

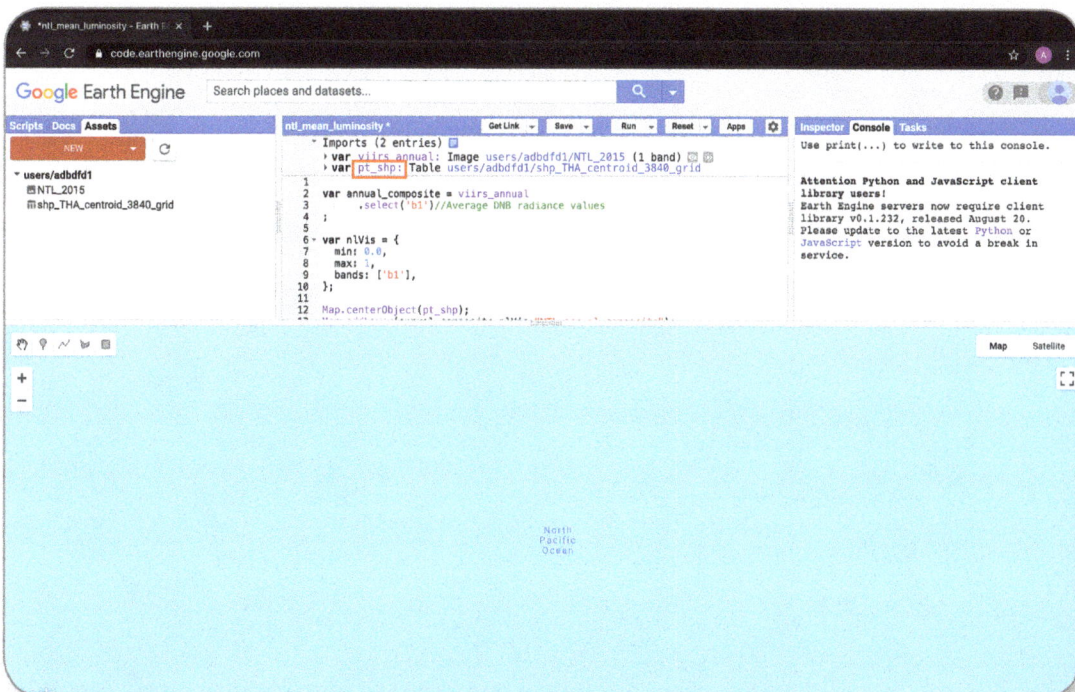

STEP 33

Scroll to the bottom of the script and locate the section labeled *"Export the FeatureCollection."*

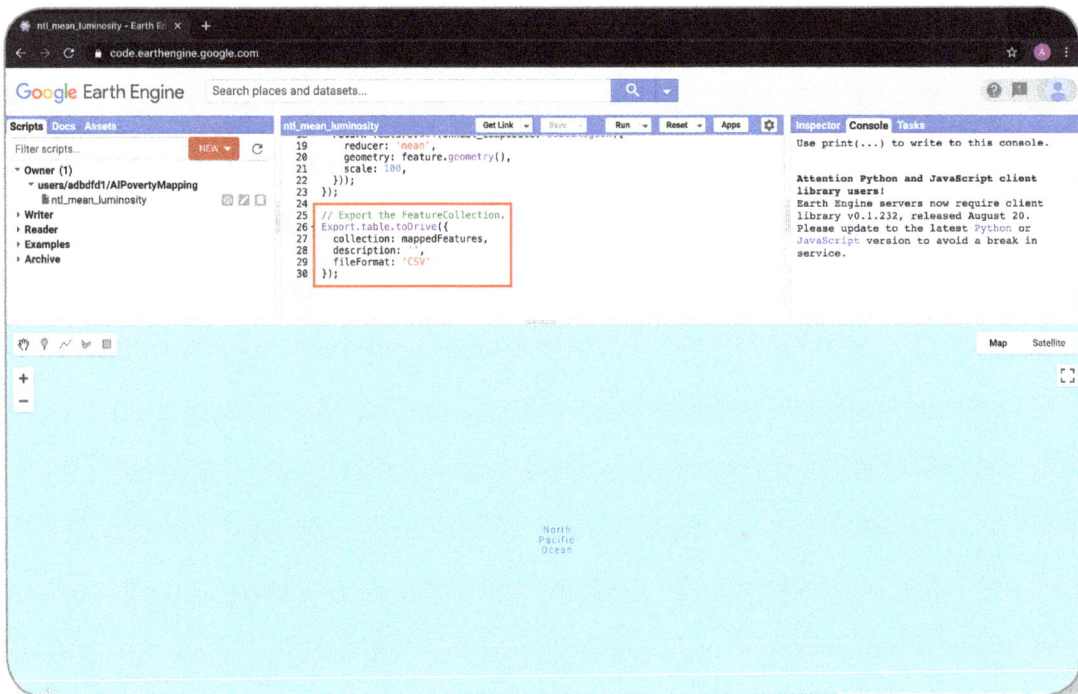

Indicate a filename beside *description*. Then click **Run**.

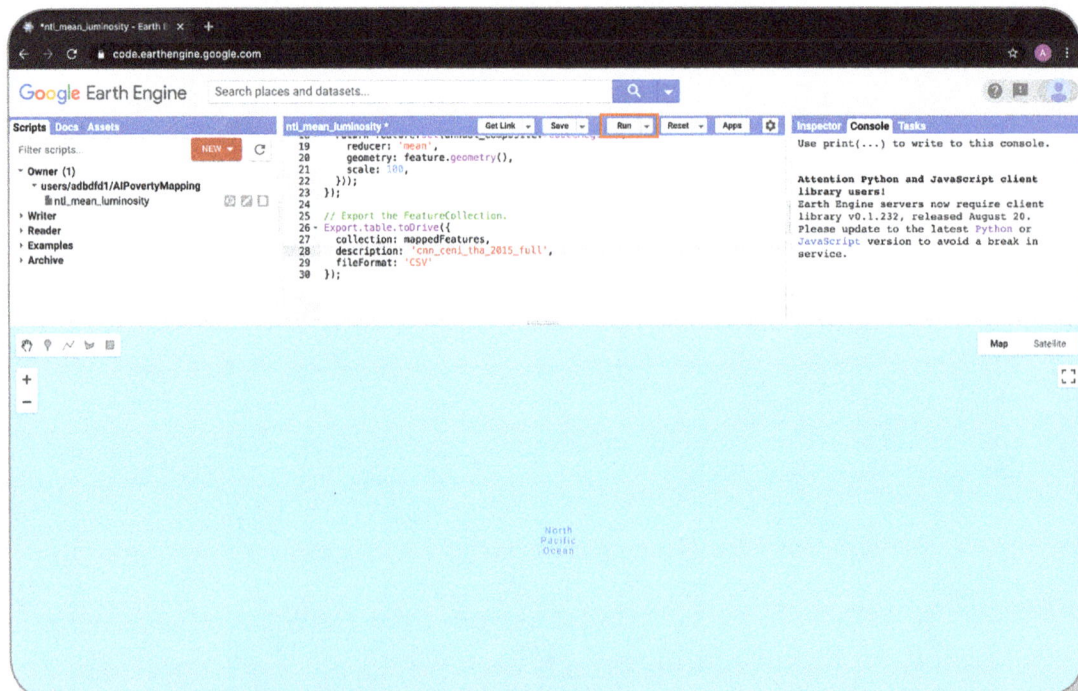

STEP 34

Click **Tasks**. Note that the task name is the same as the description provided in the output.

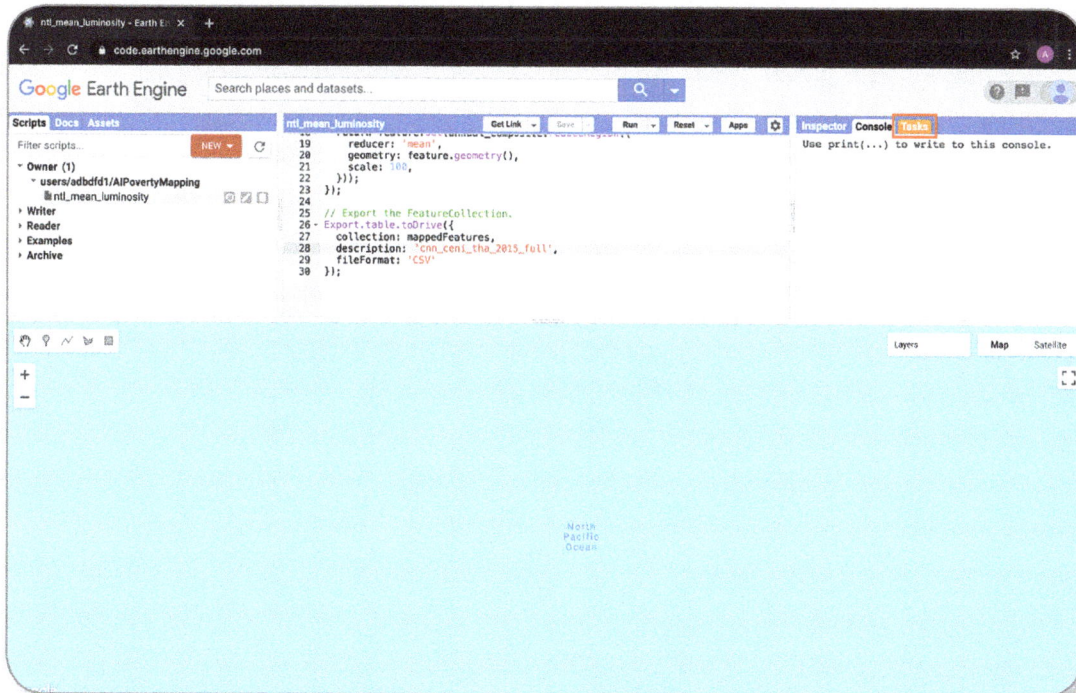

STEP 35

Click **Run** to begin processing the code's output.

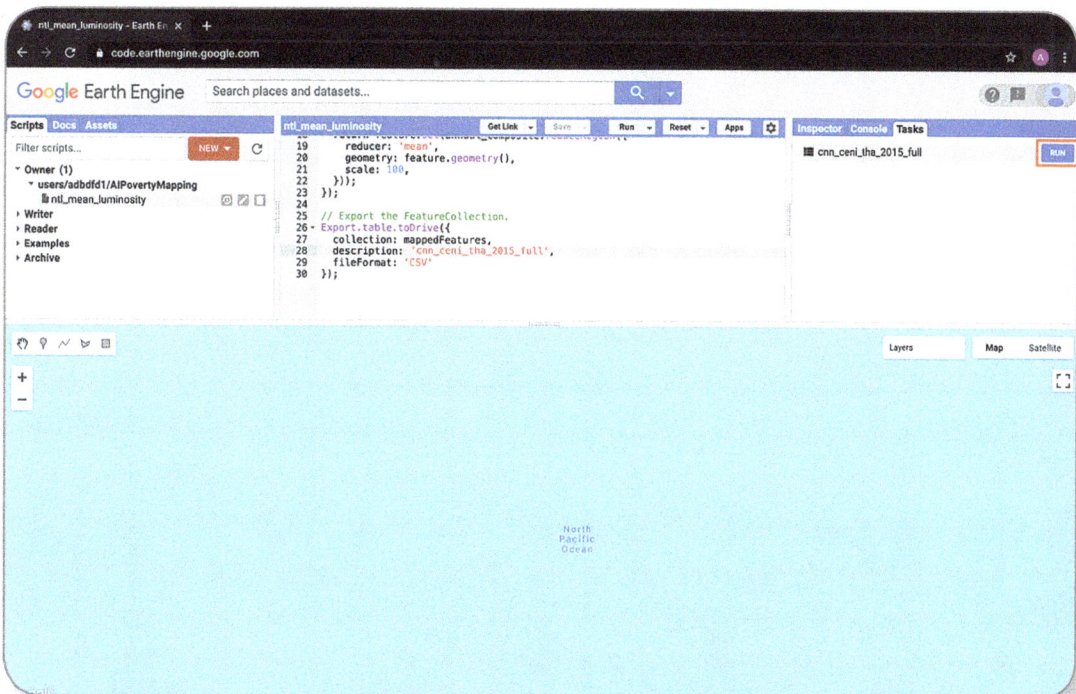

STEP 36

Verify all the information, including the filename and file format. Ensure that **Drive** is selected to save the output into the Google Drive. Click **Run**.

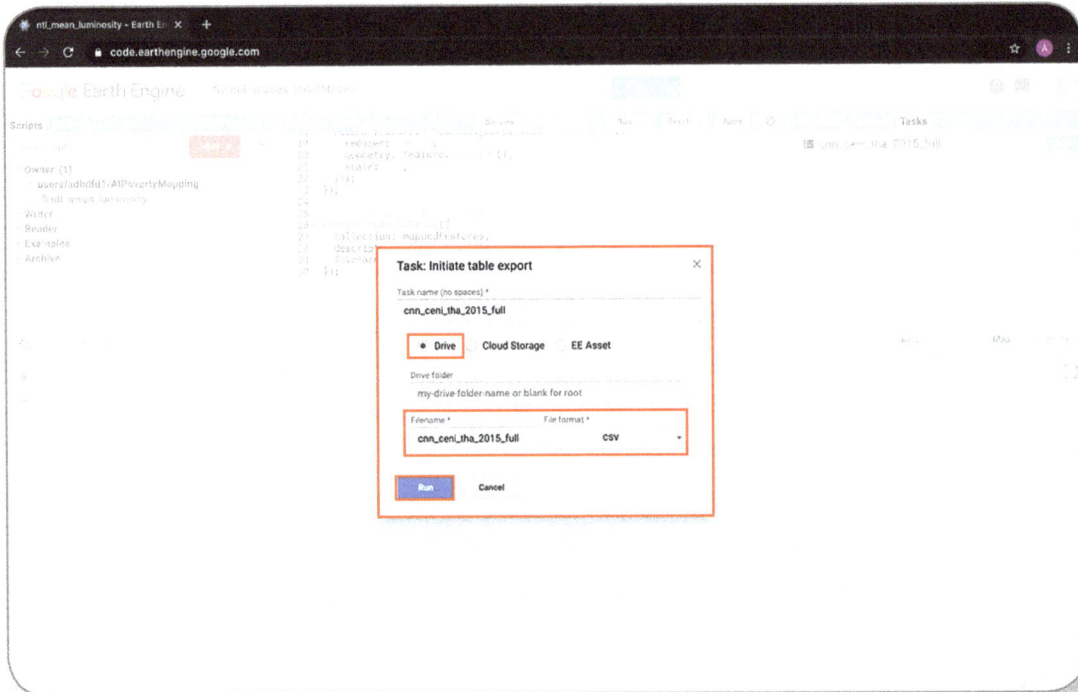

A check mark will appear to the right of the task name indicating that the task is completed. It may take some time to process.

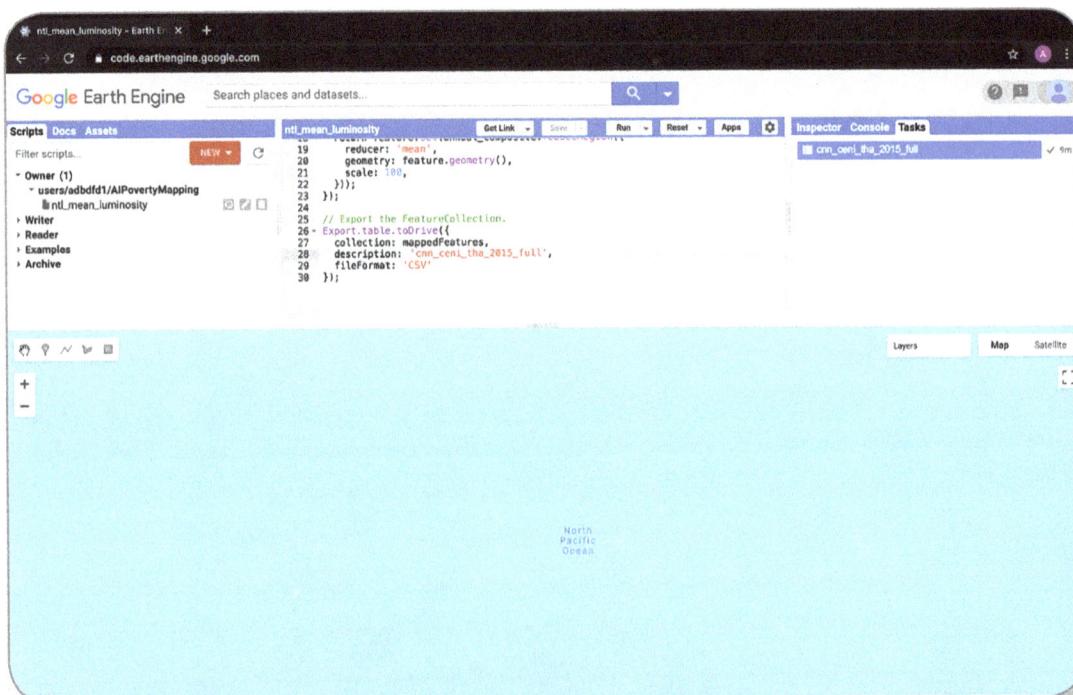

STEP 37

Go to Google Drive to check for the output CSV file. Download and save the CSV file to the working folder.

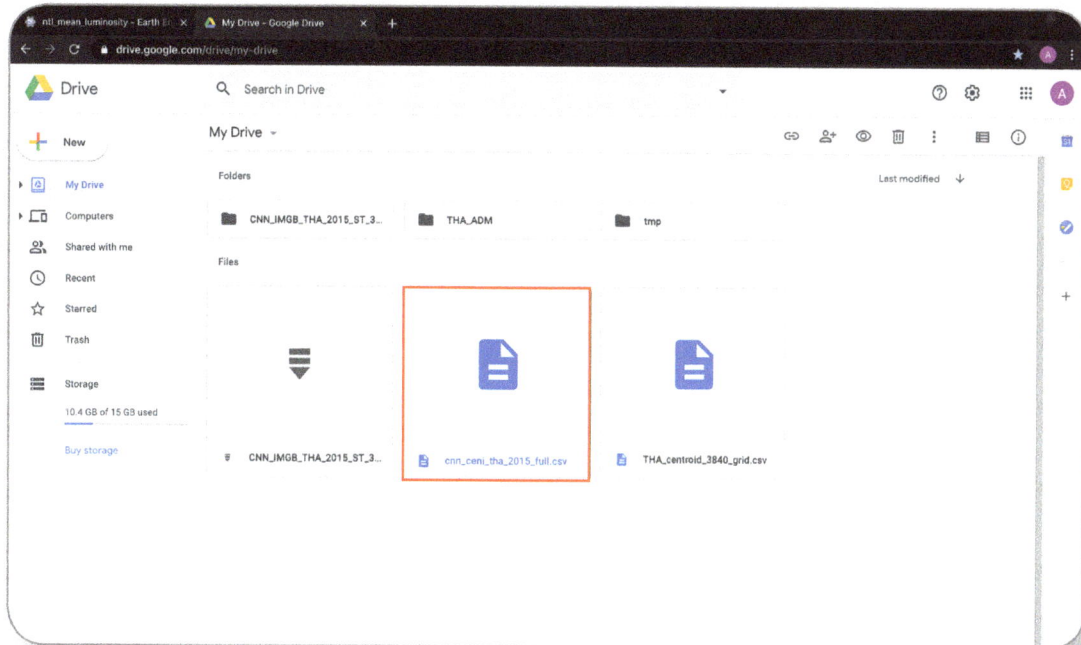

STEP 38

From this point, data from the Philippines will be used to illustrate the succeeding steps.

For years without available annual composite imagery, use the Google Earth Engine (GEE). To create the VIIRS annual composite imagery, use the script: ***custom_viirs_annual_composite.js***.

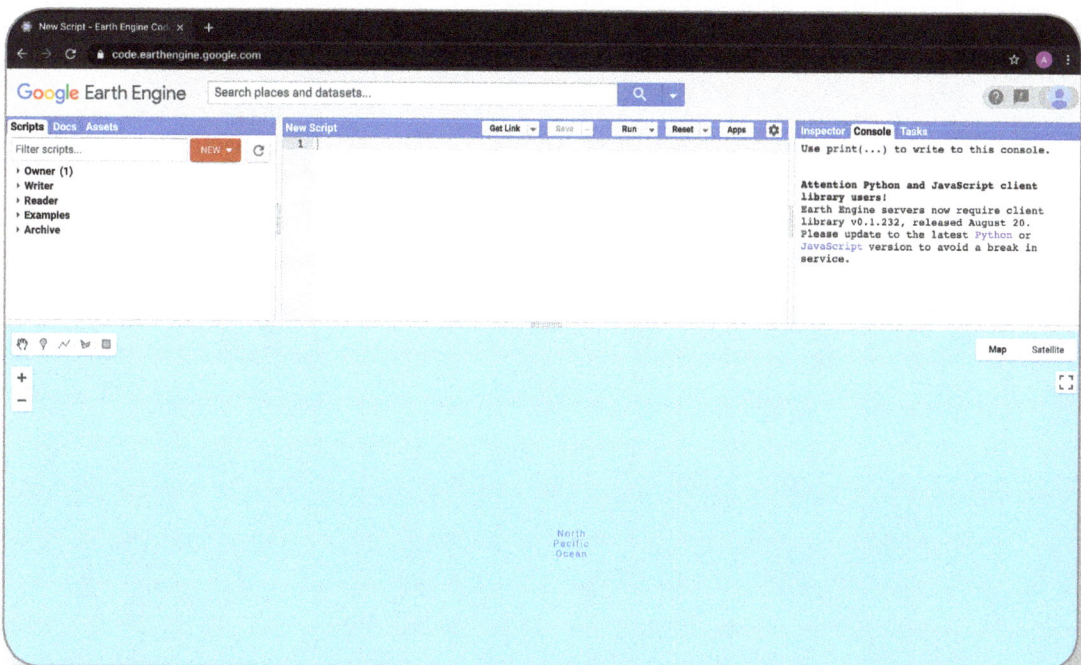

STEP 39

Open the JavaScript ***custom_viirs_annual_composite.js*** using a text editing software (e.g., Windows Notepad) and copy the code.

```
                            custom_viirs_annual_composite.js

var viirs_monthly = ee.ImageCollection("NOAA/VIIRS/DNB/MONTHLY_V1/VCMCFG");
var annual_composite = viirs_monthly
     .filterDate('', '')
     .select('avg_rad')
     .median()
;

var nlVis = {
  min: 0.0,
  max: 1,
  bands: ['avg_rad'],
};

Map.centerObject(pt_shp);
Map.addLayer(annual_composite,nlVis,"VIIRS annual composite");

// aggregate mean of nightlight intensities for centroid regions of size 256px
var mappedFeatures = pt_shp.map(function(feature) {
  var geometry = ee.Geometry.Point([ee.Number(pt_shp.get('lon')), ee.Number(pt_shp.get('lat'))]).buffer(1920).bounds()
  return feature.set(annual_composite.reduceRegion({
    reducer: 'mean',
    geometry: feature.geometry(),
    scale: 100,
  }));
});

// Export the FeatureCollection.
Export.table.toDrive({
  collection: mappedFeatures,
  description: '',
  fileFormat: 'CSV'
});
```

STEP 40

Paste the code into the GEE code editor then click **Save**.

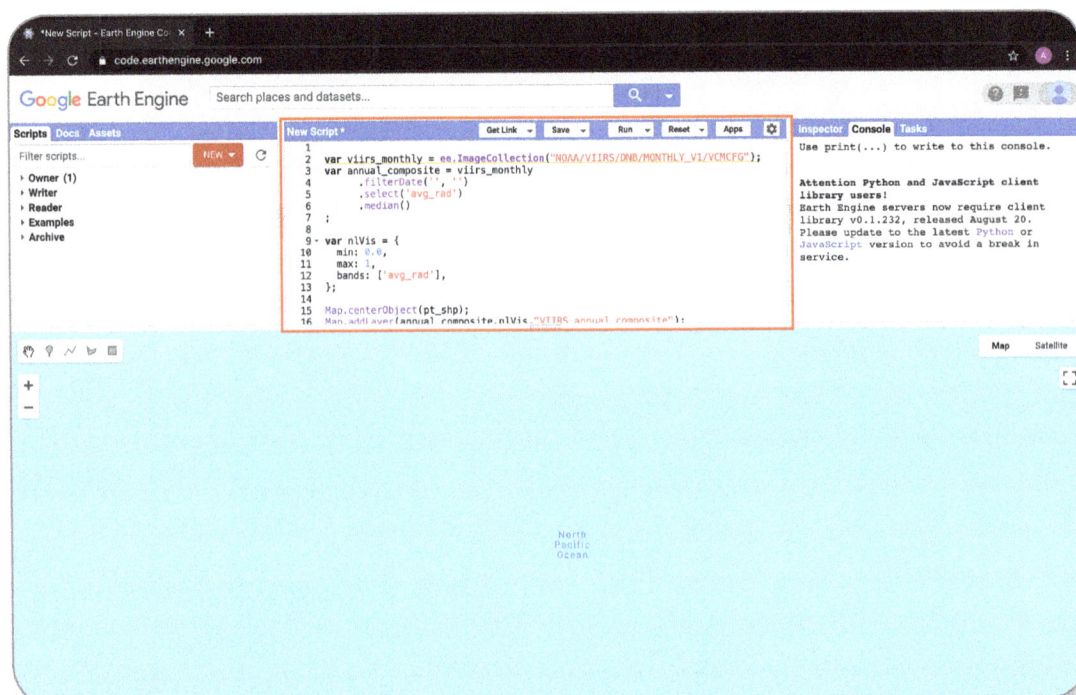

Change the filter date range and then click **Save**.

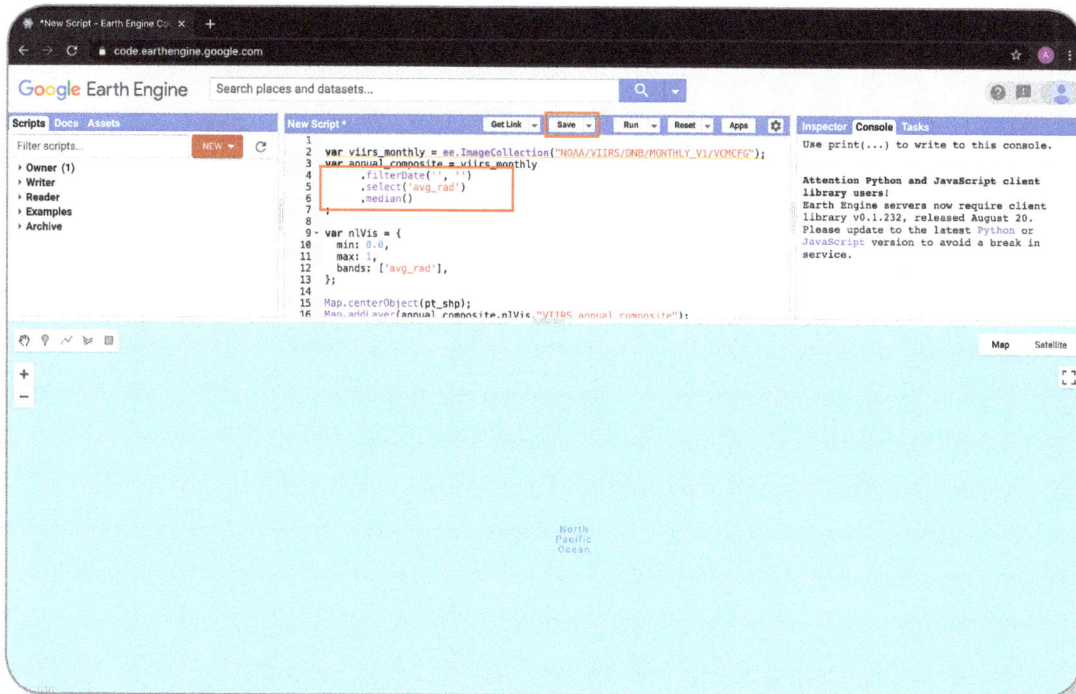

STEP 41

GEE will then prompt to input the script's filename. A description of the script may be provided.

The script will appear in the Script pane.

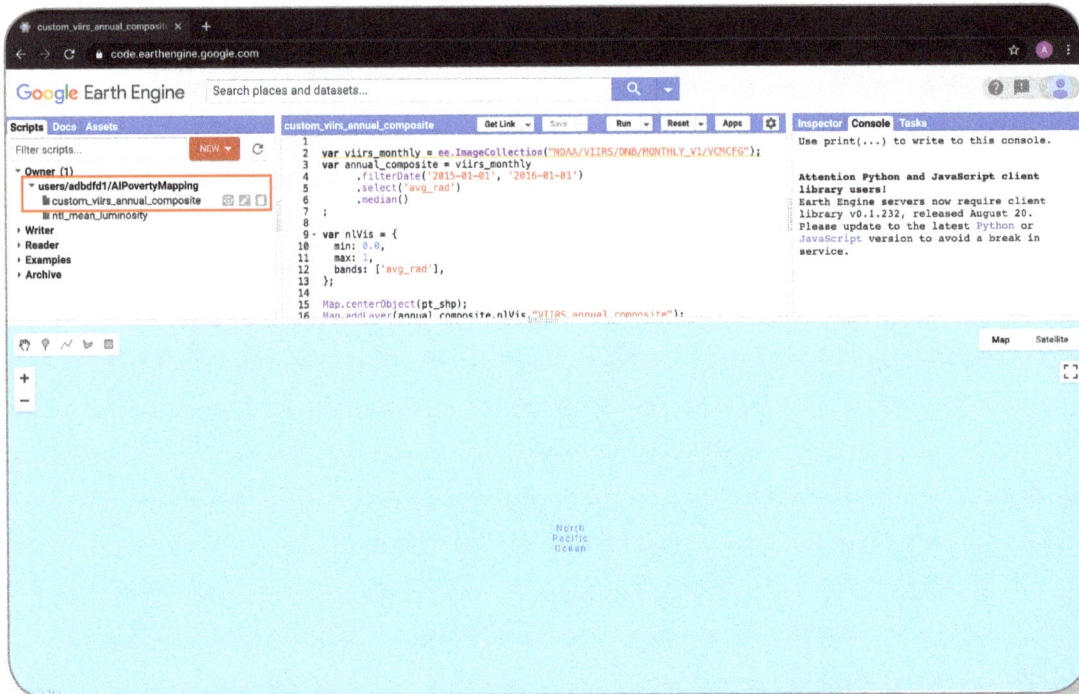

STEP 42

Go to Assets then click the **Import to script button** to place the shapefile into the script.

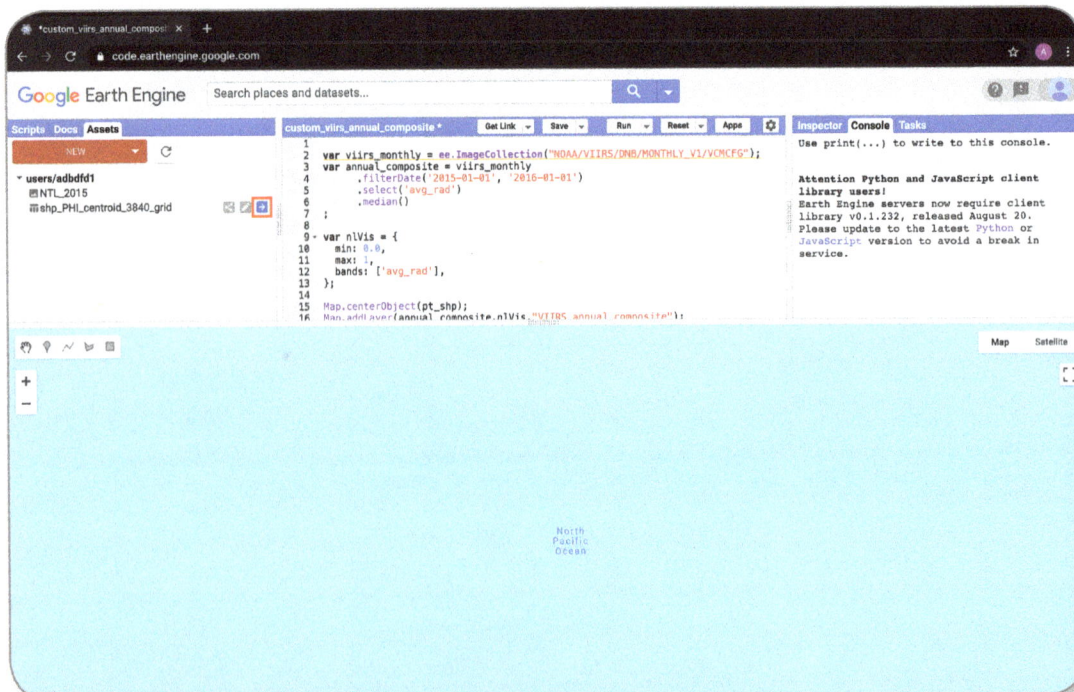

STEP 43

Rename the variable name from **table** to **pt_shp**.

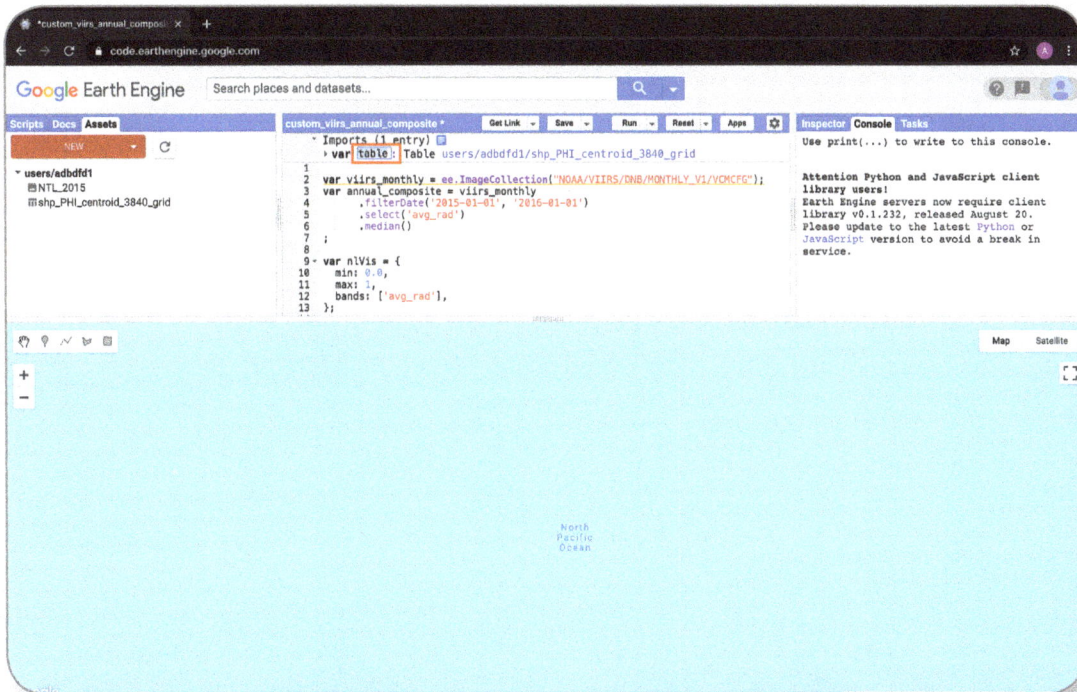

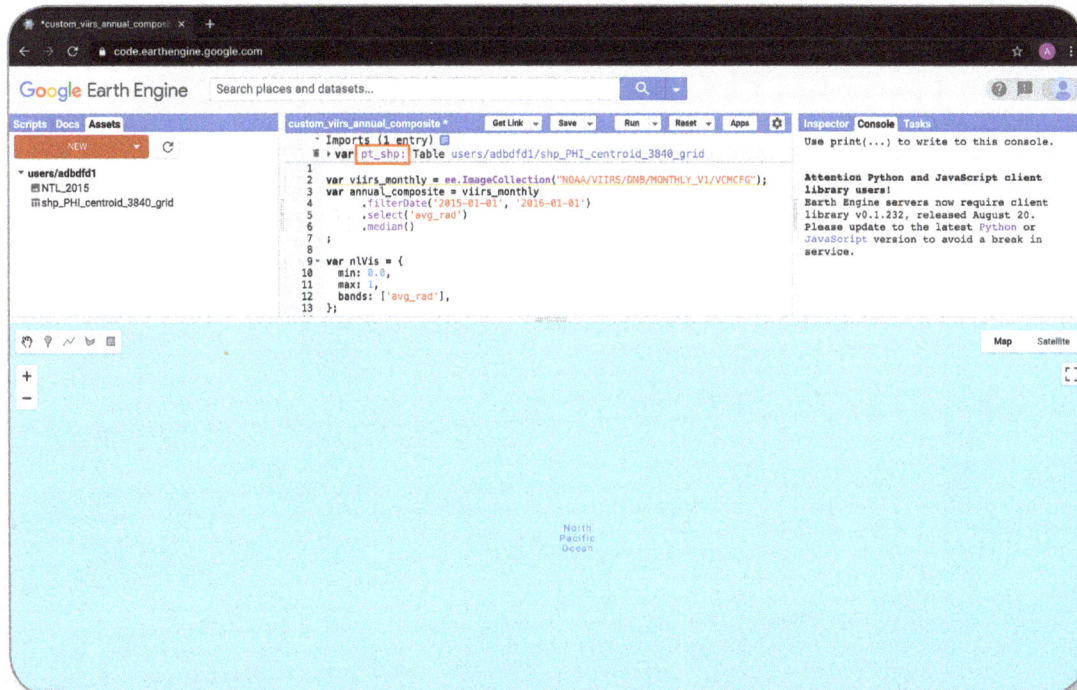

Step 44

Locate the section labeled **"Export the FeatureCollection"** at the bottom of the script. Indicate a filename beside description then click **Run**.

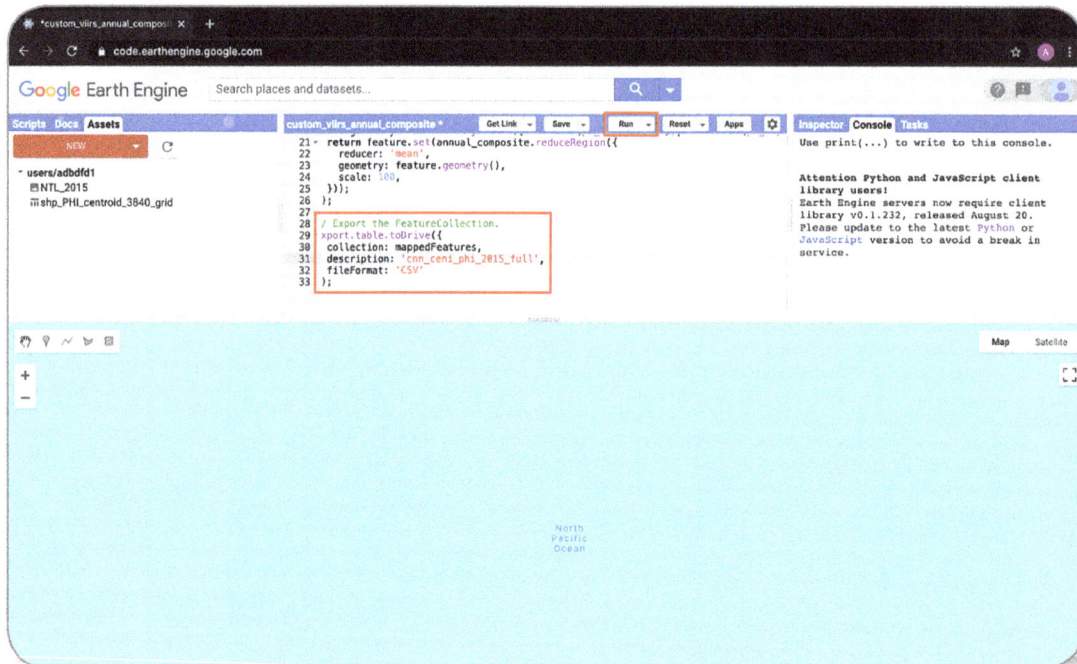

STEP 45

Go to **Tasks**. Note that the task name is the same as the description provided in the output. Click **Run** to begin processing the code's output.

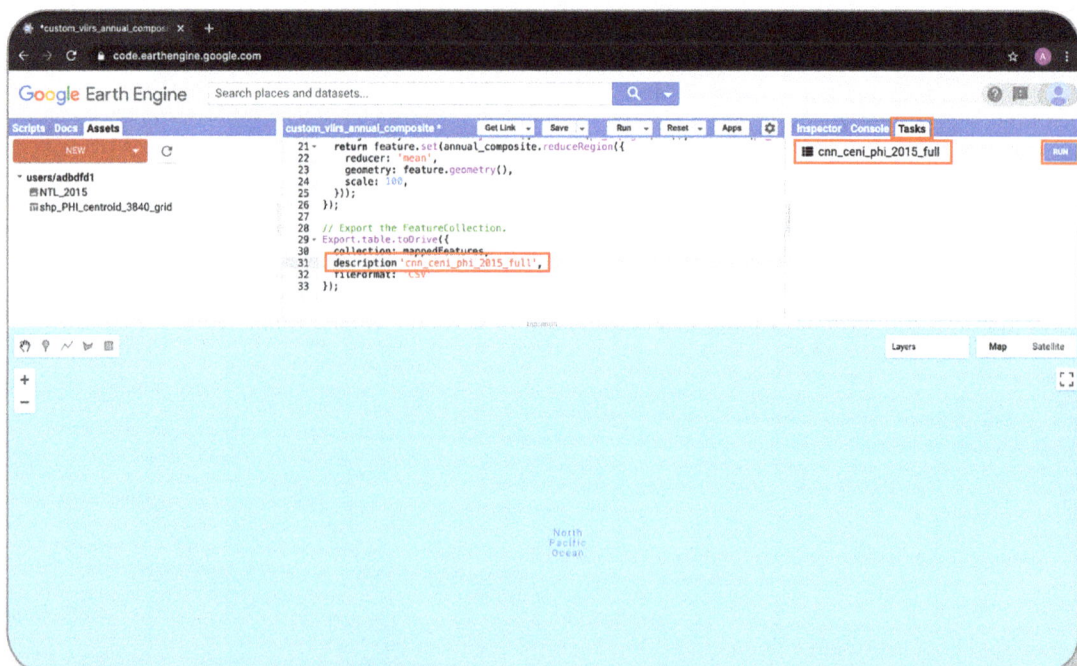

STEP 46

Verify all the information including the filename and file format. Ensure that **Drive** *is selected* to save the output into the Google Drive. Click **Run**.

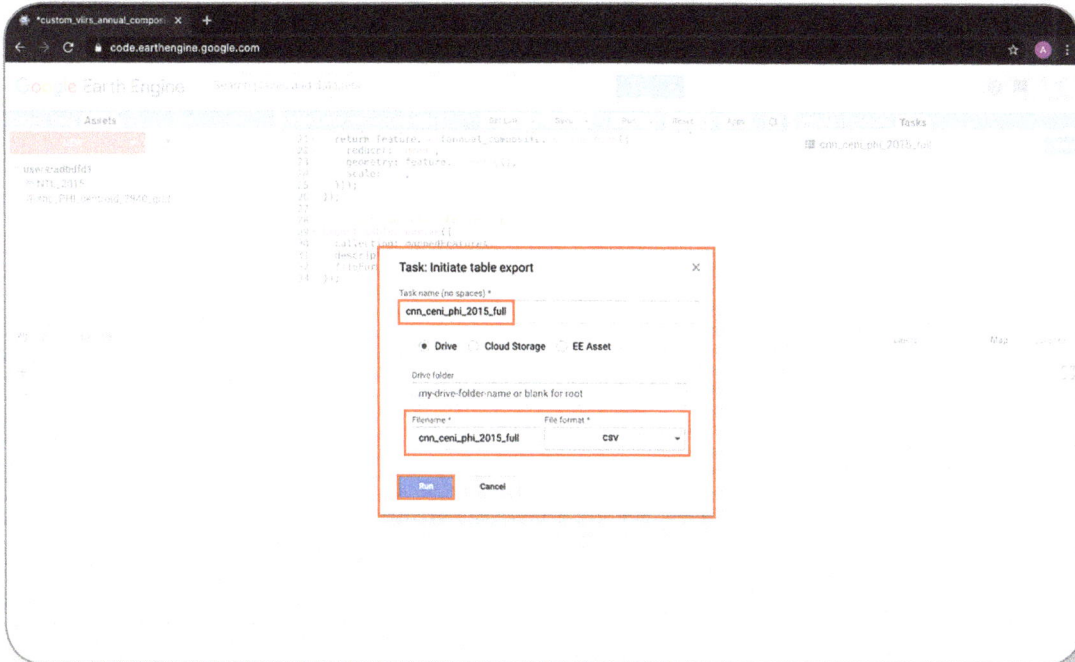

A check mark will appear to the right of the task name indicating that the task is completed. Note that it may take some time to process this task.

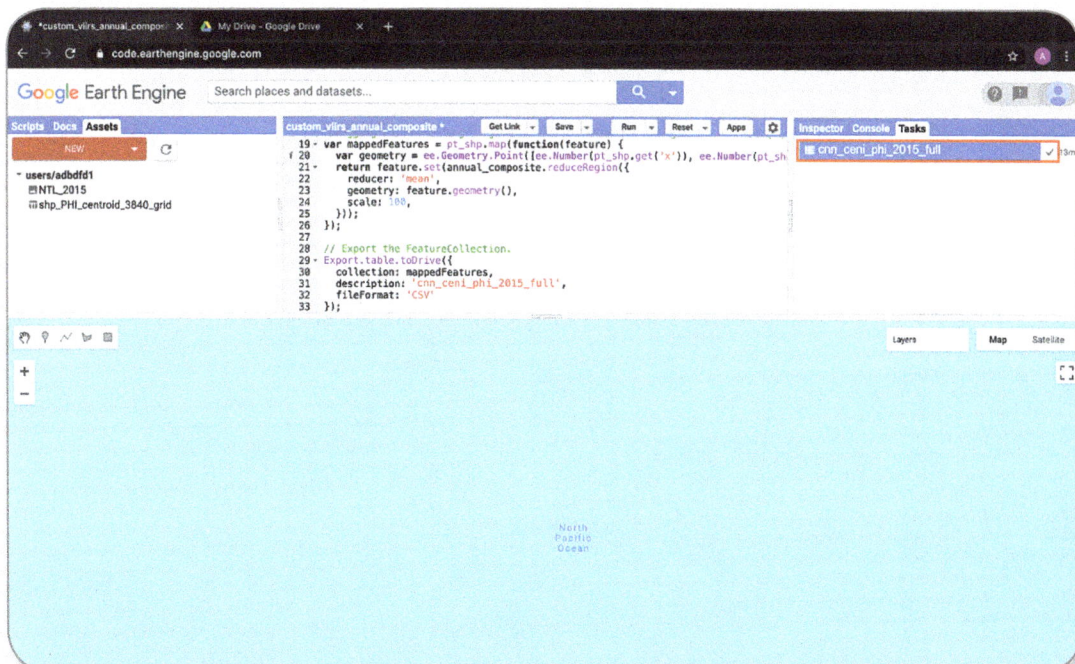

STEP 47

Go to Google Drive to verify the output file. Download and save the CSV file to the working folder.

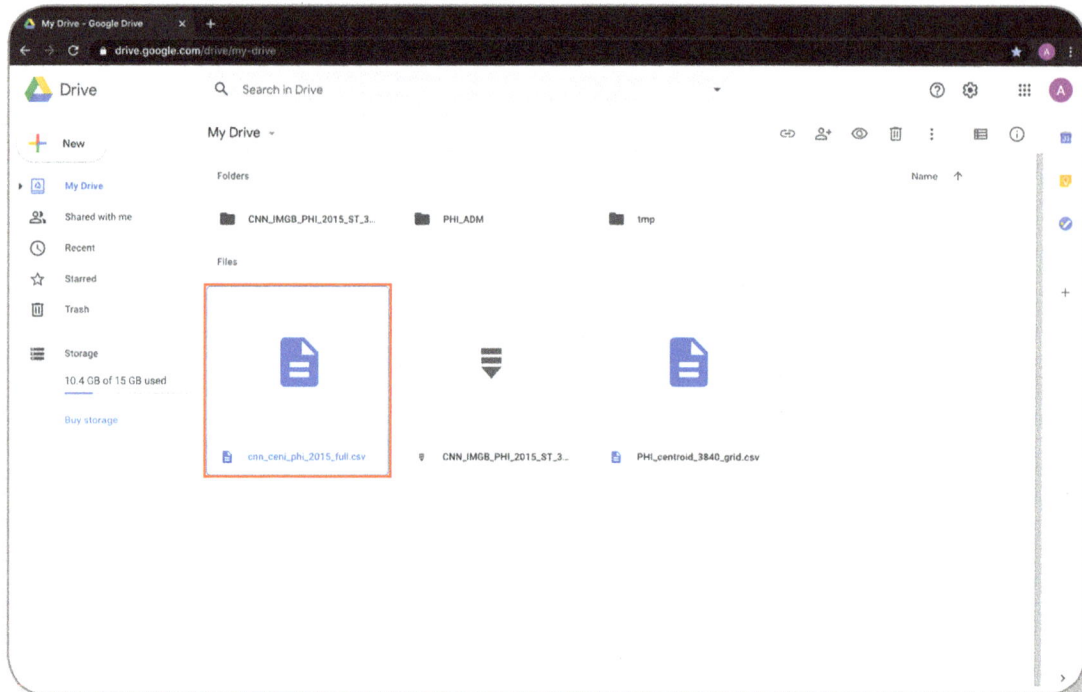

Binning Luminosity Values and Splitting Dataset

Actual nighttime luminosity values are binned into different levels or classes following the approach implemented in the study by Jean et al. (2016) (footnote 1). Binning is done to facilitate more effective training of CNN models. It is implemented using Gaussian mixture models (GMMs). GMMs assume that the distribution of univariate night light intensities comes from the mixture of k-underlying normal or Gaussian distributions and find the set of normal distributions that best fit the data. Based on these, the probability of each observation belonging to each group is derived.

Nighttime luminosity values are grouped into three classes which were found optimal based on experimentation. These are low class, medium class, and high class.

Splitting of datasets is done by performing random sampling within each luminosity bin to preserve overall class distribution. The result is a balanced split of the dataset.

STEP 1

Use the R script **Binning_and_splitting.R** to bin luminosity values.

```
Binning_and_splitting.R ×

    Source on Save                                                   Run        Source

1 ▾ # Gaussian Mixture Model----
2 ▾ # load packages----
3   library(mclust)
4   library(tidyverse)
5
6   # select csv file containing mean luminosity values
7   NTL_csv_path <- tcltk::tk_choose.files(filters = matrix(c("CSV",".csv","All files","*"),2,2,byrow = T),
8                                          caption = "Select Luminosity CSV")
9
10 ▾ # get working directory from csv file----
11  wd_path <- dirname(NTL_csv_path)
12  # set working directory
13  setwd(wd_path)
14
15 ▾ # load csv file to dataframe----
16  datapoints <- read.csv(NTL_csv_path,stringsAsFactors = F)
17
18 ▾ # check csv data----
19  # please take note of the name of the column containing the luminosity values
20  head(datapoints)
21
22 ▾ # based on the result of head(), specify the column name containing the average luminosity----
23  ntl_col = ""
24
25  # subset column containing the average luminosity
26  avector <- datapoints[,ntl_col]
27
28 ▾ #check if data type is numeric----
29  class(avector)
30
31 ▾ # run GMM----
32  fit=Mclust(avector, G=3, model="V") # request clustering into 3 clusters
33
34  # view summary of model---
35  summary(fit)
36
37 ▾ # Check if Mclust yields results----
38 ▾ if (is.null(fit)==FALSE) {
39
40    # view bins
41    fit$classification
42
43    # merge bin results to the original dataframe and select relevant columns
44    df_bin <- data.frame(datapoints, bin_GMM = fit$classification) %>%
45      select(id,                      #grid ID
46             lon,lat,                 #centroid coordinates
47             geocode,                 #geocode
48             avg_rad = all_of(ntl_col),  #luminosity values, change column name based on the input csv
49             bin_GMM,                 #bins
50             filename)                #jpeg filenames
51
1:29   Gaussian Mixture Model                                                    R Script
```

First, load the required packages.

```
1 ▾ # Gaussian Mixture Model----
2 ▾ # load packages----
3   library(mclust)
4   library(tidyverse)
5
```

STEP 2

Select the CSV file containing the average luminosity values.

```
Binning_and_splitting.R ×
      Source on Save
 1 ▾ # Gaussian Mixture Model----
 2 ▾ # load packages----
 3   library(mclust)
 4   library(tidyverse)
 5
 6   # select csv file containing mean luminosity values
 7   NTL_csv_path <- tcltk::tk_choose.files(filters = matrix(c("CSV",".csv","All files","*"),2,2,byrow = T),
 8                                          caption = "Select Luminosity CSV")
 9
10 ▾ # get working directory from csv file----
11   wd_path <- dirname(NTL_csv_path)
12   # set working directory
13   setwd(wd_path)
```

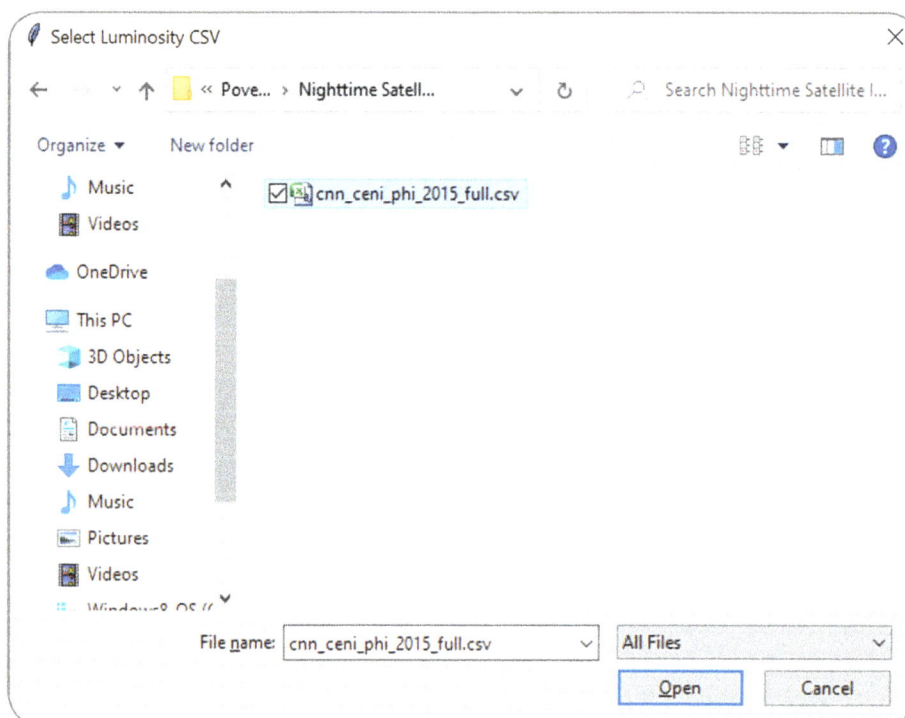

Select Luminosity CSV

« Pove... › Nighttime Satell...   Search Nighttime Satellite I...

Organize ▾   New folder

Music
Videos
OneDrive   ☑ ▣ cnn_ceni_phi_2015_full.csv
This PC
  3D Objects
  Desktop
  Documents
  Downloads
  Music
  Pictures
  Videos

File name: cnn_ceni_phi_2015_full.csv   All Files

                          Open   Cancel

STEP 3

Set the CSV file's folder path as the working directory.

```
10 ▾ # get working directory from csv file----
11   wd_path <- dirname(NTL_csv_path)
12   # set working directory
13   setwd(wd_path)
14
```

STEP 4

Load the CSV file as the dataframe – ***datapoints***.

```
15 ▾ # load csv file to dataframe----
16   datapoints <- read.csv(NTL_csv_path,stringsAsFactors = F)
17
```

STEP 5

Check the data using the ***head()*** function.

```
18 ▾ # check csv data----
19   # please take note of the name of the column containing the luminosity values
20   head(datapoints)
```

```
> # please take note of the name of the column containing the luminosity values
> head(datapoints)
        system.index b1                              filename  geocode  id      lon      lat
1 00000000000000001b0c  0 CNN_DIMG_PHI_2015_ST_384_3840_000313.jpg 148101000 313 121.0896 18.28221
2 00000000000000001b0d  0 CNN_DIMG_PHI_2015_ST_384_3840_000314.jpg 148101000 314 121.1245 18.28221
3 00000000000000001b0e  0 CNN_DIMG_PHI_2015_ST_384_3840_000315.jpg 148101000 315 121.1593 18.28221
4 00000000000000001b0f  0 CNN_DIMG_PHI_2015_ST_384_3840_000316.jpg 148101000 316 121.1942 18.28221
5 00000000000000001b10  0 CNN_DIMG_PHI_2015_ST_384_3840_000317.jpg 148105000 317 121.2290 18.28221
6 00000000000000001b11  0 CNN_DIMG_PHI_2015_ST_384_3840_000318.jpg 148105000 318 121.2638 18.28221
                                                          .geo
1  {"type":"Point","coordinates":[121.08963591257178,18.28220730070282]}
2  {"type":"Point","coordinates":[121.12447932820336,18.28220730070282]}
3   {"type":"Point","coordinates":[121.159322743835,18.28220730070282]}
4  {"type":"Point","coordinates":[121.19416615946663,18.28220730070282]}
5 {"type":"Point","coordinates":[121.22900511599723,18.282207300702822]}
6   {"type":"Point","coordinates":[121.26384853162884,18.28220730070282]}
>
```

STEP 6

Using the result of ***head()*** function, specify the name of the column values and assign it to variable ***ntl_col***.

```
22 ▾ # based on the result of head(), specify the column name containing the average luminosity----
23   ntl_col = "b1"
24
25   # subset column containing the average luminosity
26   avector <- datapoints[,ntl_col]
```

The luminosity column name that is used by GEE is based on the name of the raster's band, e.g., b1. Generate a subset of this column containing the average luminosity values and store it in the variable ***avector***.

```
> # please take note of the name of the column containing the luminosity values
> head(datapoints)
         system.index b1                                      filename  geocode  id      lon      lat
1 00000000000000001a40  0  CNN_DIMG_PHI_2015_ST_384_3840_000109.jpg 12801000 109 120.9154 18.49126
2 00000000000000001a41  0  CNN_DIMG_PHI_2015_ST_384_3840_000110.jpg 12801000 110 120.9503 18.49126
3 00000000000000001a5a  0  CNN_DIMG_PHI_2015_ST_384_3840_000135.jpg 12801000 135 120.9154 18.45642
4 00000000000000001a5b  0  CNN_DIMG_PHI_2015_ST_384_3840_000136.jpg 12801000 136 120.9503 18.45642
5 00000000000000001a75  0  CNN_DIMG_PHI_2015_ST_384_3840_000162.jpg 12801000 162 120.8806 18.42158
6 00000000000000001a76  0  CNN_DIMG_PHI_2015_ST_384_3840_000163.jpg 12801000 163 120.9154 18.42158
                                                                     .geo
1  {"type":"Point","coordinates":[120.91542329351466,18.49126333539152]}
2  {"type":"Point","coordinates":[120.95026670914629,18.49126333539152]}
3 {"type":"Point","coordinates":[120.91542329351466,18.456419919759895]}
4 {"type":"Point","coordinates":[120.95026670914629,18.456419919759895]}
5  {"type":"Point","coordinates":[120.88057987788305,18.42157650412827]}
6  {"type":"Point","coordinates":[120.91542329351466,18.42157650412827]}
> |
```

STEP 7

Use the ***class()*** function to examine if the extracted luminosity values are of numeric type.

```
27
28 ▾ #check if data type is numeric----
29   class(avector)
30
```

```
> #check if data type is numeric----
> class(avector)
[1] "numeric"
> |
```

STEP 8

Run the GMM model to produce 3 clusters.

```
30
31 ▾ # run GMM----
32   fit=Mclust(avector, G=3, model="V") # request clustering into 3 clusters
33
```

STEP 9

Display the model summary.

```
30
31 ▾ # run GMM----
32   fit=Mclust(avector, G=3, model="V") # request clustering into 3 clusters
33
```

```
> # view summary of model---
> summary(fit)
----------------------------------------------------
Gaussian finite mixture model fitted by EM algorithm
----------------------------------------------------

Mclust V (univariate, unequal variance) model with 3 components:

 log-likelihood      n df     BIC        ICL
        769.2522 35974  8 1454.58 -3717.266

Clustering table:
     1     2     3
 25301  8331  2342
>
```

Note that there are instances when GMM cannot cluster the data into 2, 3, 4, or 5 clusters because the corresponding cluster distribution is not found. These cases are assumed to be related to country-specific night lights.

```
> # view summary of model---
> summary(fit)
Length  Class    Mode
     0   NULL    NULL
>
```

STEP 10

Using an if-else statement, determine the course of action that should be taken from the result of the initial GMM calculation.

```
37 ▾ # Check if Mclust yields results----
38 ▾ if (is.null(fit)==FALSE) {
39
40     # view bins
41     fit$classification
42
43     # merge bin results to the original dataframe and select relevant columns
44     df_bin <- data.frame(datapoints, bin_GMM = fit$classification) %>%
45       select(id,                        #grid ID
46             lon,lat,                     #centroid coordinates
47             geocode,                     #geocode
48             avg_rad = all_of(ntl_col),   #luminosity values, change column name based on the input csv
49             bin_GMM,                     #bins
50             filename)                    #jpeg filenames
51
52 ▾ }else{ # if the resulting mclust is null
53
54     #filter luminosity less than or equal to zero
55     non_zero_datapoints <- datapoints %>%
56       filter(get(ntl_col)>0)
57
58     non_zero_avector <- non_zero_datapoints[,ntl_col]
59
60 ▾   # run GMM----
61     fit=Mclust(non_zero_avector, G=3, model="V") # request clustering into 3 clusters
62
63     # view summary of model---
64     print(summary(fit))
65
66     # merge the non-zero luminosity data with its bin classification
67     df_non_zero <- data.frame(non_zero_datapoints, bin_GMM = fit$classification) %>%
68       select(id, bin_GMM) #retain only the id and bin column for ease of merging
69
70     # merge the binned non-zero luminosity data with the rest of the data
71     df_bin <- left_join(datapoints,df_non_zero, by="id") %>%
72       mutate(bin_GMM = ifelse(is.na(bin_GMM),1,bin_GMM)) %>%  #classify zero luminosity values into bin category 1
73       select(id,                        #grid ID
74             lon,lat,                     #centroid coordinates
75             geocode,                     #geocode
76             avg_rad = all_of(ntl_col),   #luminosity values, change column name based on the input csv
77             bin_GMM,                     #bins
78             filename)                    #jpeg filenames
79 ▴ }
```

Display the bin classification to check if the initial calculation produced results.

```
37 ▾ # Check if Mclust yields results----
38 ▾ if (is.null(fit)==FALSE) {
39
40    # view bins
41    fit$classification
42
43    # merge bin results to the original dataframe and select relevant columns
44    df_bin <- data.frame(datapoints, bin_GMM = fit$classification) %>%
45      select(id,                        #grid ID
46             lon,lat,                   #centroid coordinates
47             geocode,                   #geocode
48             avg_rad = all_of(ntl_col), #luminosity values, change column name based on the input csv
49             bin_GMM,                   #bins
50             filename)                  #jpeg filenames
51
```

```
>    # view bins
>    fit$classification
  [1] 1 1 1 1 1 1 1 1 1 1 1 1 1 1 1 1 1 1 1 1 1 1 1 1 1 2 3 3 3 2 2 2 2 1 1 1 1 1 1 1 1 1 1 1 1 1 1 1 1 1 1 1 1 1 1 1 1 1 2 1 1 1 1 1 1 1 1 1 1
 [63] 1 1 1 1 1 1 1 1 1 1 1 1 1 2 1 1 1 1 1 1 1 1 1 2 2 3 2 2 1 1 1 1 1 1 1 1 1 1 1 1 1 1 1 1 1 1 1 1 1 1 1 1 1 1 1 1 1 1 2 2 1 2 2 2 1 1 1 1 1 1
[125] 1 1 1 1 1 1 1 1 1 1 1 1 1 3 2 2 1 1 1 1 1 1 1 1 1 1 1 1 1 1 1 1 1 1 1 1 1 1 1 2 2 2 1 1 2 2 1 1 1 1 1 1 1 1 1 1 1 1 1 1
[187] 1 1 1 1 1 1 1 2 2 2 1 1 2 1 1 1 1 1 1 1 1 1 1 1 1 1 1 1 1 1 1 1 2 3 3 2 2 1 1 1 1 1 2 1 1 1 1 1 1 1 2 1 1 1 1 1 1 1 1 1
[249] 1 1 1 1 1 1 1 1 1 1 1 2 1 1 2 3 3 3 2 2 1 1 1 2 2 2 1 1 2 1 1 2 1 1 1 1 1 1 1 1 1 1 1 1 1 1 2 1 1 2 2 2 2 1 1 2 2 1 1 1 1
[311] 1 3 1 1 1 1 1 1 1 1 1 1 1 1 1 1 2 1 2 2 3 2 2 1 1 1 1 1 1 1 1 1 1 1 1 1 1 1 1 1 1 1 1 1 1 3 1 1 1 2 2 2 2 1 1 1 1 1 1
[373] 1 1 1 1 1 1 1 1 1 1 1 1 1 1 1 1 1 2 2 1 1 1 3 1 1 1 1 1 1 1 1 1 1 1 2 2 2 1 1 1 1 1 1 2 2 2 1 1 1 1 1 1 1 1 1 1 1 1 1 1
[435] 1 1 1 1 1 1 2 2 1 1 1 1 1 1 1 1 1 1 1 1 1 1 1 1 1 1 1 2 2 1 2 1 1 1 1 2 1 1 1 1 1 1 1 1 1 1 1 1 1 1 1 2 3 1 1 1 1
[497] 1 1 1 1 1 1 1 1 1 1 2 2 2 2 2 2 1 1 1 1 2 1 1 1 1 1 1 1 1 1 1 1 1 1 1 1 2 3 2 1 1 1 1 1 1 1 1 1 1 1 1 1 1 1
[559] 1 1 1 2 2 1 1 1 1 1 1 1 2 1 1 1 1 1 1 1 1 1 1 1 1 1 1 1 1 1 1 1 2 2 1 2 1 2 1 1 1 1 1 1 1 2 1 1 1 1 2 1 1 1 2 1 2 1 1 1
[621] 1 2 2 1 1 1 1 1 1 1 1 1 1 1 1 1 1 1 1 1 1 1 1 1 2 1 1 1 1 1 1 1 1 1 1 1 1 1 1 1 1 1 1 2 1 2 2 2 2 1 1 2 1 1 1 2 1 1 1 1 1
[683] 1 1 1 1 1 1 1 1 1 1 1 2 2 2 1 2 1 1 1 1 1 1 1 1 1 1 1 1 2 2 2 2 2 1 1 1 2 2 1 1 1 1 1 1 1 1 2 2 1 1 1 1 1 1
[745] 1 1 1 1 1 1 1 1 1 1 2 1 1 1 1 1 1 1 1 1 1 1 1 2 2 2 1 1 1 1 1 2 1 1 1 1 1 1 1 1 1 1 1 1 1 1 2 1 1 1 1 1
[807] 1 1 1 1 1 1 1 3 1 1 1 2 1 1 1 1 1 1 1 1 1 1 1 1 1 1 1 1 1 1 2 1 1 1 1 1 1 1 1 1 2 2 2 2 3 1 1 1 1 1 1 1 1 1 1 1
[869] 1 1 1 1 1 1 1 1 1 1 1 1 1 1 1 1 1 1 1 1 2 3 2 3 1 1 1 1 1 1 1 1 1 1 1 1 1 1 1 1 1 1 1 1 1 1 1 1 1 1 1 1 1 1 1 1 1 1
[931] 1 1 1 1 2 1 1 1 1 1 2 1 1 1 1 1 1 1 1 1 1 1 1 1 1 1 3 2 1 1 1 1 1 1 1 1 1 1 2 1 1 1 1 1 1 1 1 1 2 3 1 2 1 1 2 1 1
[993] 1 1 1 1 1 1 1 1
[ reached getOption("max.print") -- omitted 19090 entries ]
>
```

STEP 11

Merge the cluster results with the original dataset. Then select the following relevant columns:

- **id** – grid ID,
- **lon, lat** – centroid coordinates,
- **geocode** – administrative boundary code,
- **avg_rad** – luminosity column (renamed to avg_rad),
- **bin_GMM** – bin column, and
- **filename** – imagery filename.

```
37 ▾  # Check if Mclust yields results----
38 ▾  if (is.null(fit)==FALSE) {
39
40       # view bins
41       fit$classification
42
43       # merge bin results to the original dataframe and select relevant columns
44       df_bin <- data.frame(datapoints, bin_GMM = fit$classification) %>%
45         select(id,                       #grid ID
46               lon,lat,                   #centroid coordinates
47               geocode,                   #geocode
48               avg_rad = all_of(ntl_col), #luminosity values, change column name based on the input csv
49               bin_GMM,                   #bins
50               filename)                  #jpeg filenames
51
```

STEP 12

If the initial calculation yields a null result, generate a subset of the original dataset to extract all positive non-zero luminosity values.

```
52 ▾  }else{ # if the resulting mclust is null
53
54       #filter luminosity less than or equal to zero
55       non_zero_datapoints <- datapoints %>%
56         filter(get(ntl_col)>0)
57
58       non_zero_avector <- non_zero_datapoints[,ntl_col]
59
60 ▾     # run GMM----
61       fit=Mclust(non_zero_avector, G=3, model="V") # request clustering into 3 clusters
62
63       # view summary of model---
64       print(summary(fit))
65
66       # merge the non-zero luminosity data with its bin classification
67       df_non_zero <- data.frame(non_zero_datapoints, bin_GMM = fit$classification) %>%
68         select(id, bin_GMM) #retain only the id and bin column for ease of merging
69
70       # merge the binned non-zero luminosity data with the rest of the data
71       df_bin <- left_join(datapoints,df_non_zero, by="id") %>%
72         mutate(bin_GMM = ifelse(is.na(bin_GMM),1,bin_GMM)) %>%  #classify zero luminosity values into bin category 1
73         select(id,                       #grid ID
74               lon,lat,                   #centroid coordinates
75               geocode,                   #geocode
76               avg_rad = all_of(ntl_col), #luminosity values, change column name based on the input csv
77               bin_GMM,                   #bins
78               filename)                  #jpeg filenames
79 ▴  }
```

STEP 13

Generate another subset of the column containing the average luminosity values and store it in the variable **non_zero_avector**.

```
52 ▾ }else{ # if the resulting mclust is null
53
54     #filter luminosity less than or equal to zero
55     non_zero_datapoints <- datapoints %>%
56       filter(get(ntl_col)>0)
57
58     non_zero_avector <- non_zero_datapoints[,ntl_col]
59
60 ▾   # run GMM----
61     fit=Mclust(non_zero_avector, G=3, model="V") # request clustering into 3 clusters
62
63     # view summary of model---
64     print(summary(fit))
65
66     # merge the non-zero luminosity data with its bin classification
67     df_non_zero <- data.frame(non_zero_datapoints, bin_GMM = fit$classification) %>%
68       select(id, bin_GMM) #retain only the id and bin column for ease of merging
69
70     # merge the binned non-zero luminosity data with the rest of the data
71     df_bin <- left_join(datapoints,df_non_zero, by="id") %>%
72       mutate(bin_GMM = ifelse(is.na(bin_GMM),1,bin_GMM)) %>%  #classify zero luminosity values into bin category 1
73       select(id,                        #grid ID
74              lon,lat,                   #centroid coordinates
75              geocode,                   #geocode
76              avg_rad = all_of(ntl_col), #luminosity values, change column name based on the input csv
77              bin_GMM,                   #bins
78              filename)                  #jpeg filenames
79 ▴ }
```

STEP 14

Re-run the GMM model to determine the 3 clusters.

```
52 ▾ }else{ # if the resulting mclust is null
53
54     #filter luminosity less than or equal to zero
55     non_zero_datapoints <- datapoints %>%
56       filter(get(ntl_col)>0)
57
58     non_zero_avector <- non_zero_datapoints[,ntl_col]
59
60 ▾   # run GMM----
61     fit=Mclust(non_zero_avector, G=3, model="V") # request clustering into 3 clusters
62
63     # view summary of model---
64     print(summary(fit))
65
66     # merge the non-zero luminosity data with its bin classification
67     df_non_zero <- data.frame(non_zero_datapoints, bin_GMM = fit$classification) %>%
68       select(id, bin_GMM) #retain only the id and bin column for ease of merging
69
70     # merge the binned non-zero luminosity data with the rest of the data
71     df_bin <- left_join(datapoints,df_non_zero, by="id") %>%
72       mutate(bin_GMM = ifelse(is.na(bin_GMM),1,bin_GMM)) %>%  #classify zero luminosity values into bin category 1
73       select(id,                        #grid ID
74              lon,lat,                   #centroid coordinates
75              geocode,                   #geocode
76              avg_rad = all_of(ntl_col), #luminosity values, change column name based on the input csv
77              bin_GMM,                   #bins
78              filename)                  #jpeg filenames
79 ▴ }
```

STEP 15

Print the summary of resulting clusters.

```
52  }else{ # if the resulting mclust is null
53
54    #filter luminosity less than or equal to zero
55    non_zero_datapoints <- datapoints %>%
56      filter(get(ntl_col)>0)
57
58    non_zero_avector <- non_zero_datapoints[,ntl_col]
59
60    # run GMM----
61    fit=Mclust(non_zero_avector, G=3, model="V") # request clustering into 3 clusters
62
63    # view summary of model---
64    print(summary(fit))
65
66    # merge the non-zero luminosity data with its bin classification
67    df_non_zero <- data.frame(non_zero_datapoints, bin_GMM = fit$classification) %>%
68      select(id, bin_GMM) #retain only the id and bin column for ease of merging
69
70    # merge the binned non-zero luminosity data with the rest of the data
71    df_bin <- left_join(datapoints,df_non_zero, by="id") %>%
72      mutate(bin_GMM = ifelse(is.na(bin_GMM),1,bin_GMM)) %>%  #classify zero luminosity values into bin category 1
73      select(id,                            #grid ID
74             lon,lat,                       #centroid coordinates
75             geocode,                       #geocode
76             avg_rad = all_of(ntl_col),     #luminosity values, change column name based on the input csv
77             bin_GMM,                       #bins
78             filename)                      #jpeg filenames
79  }
```

```
----------------------------------------------------
Gaussian finite mixture model fitted by EM algorithm
----------------------------------------------------

Mclust V (univariate, unequal variance) model with 3 components:

 log-likelihood    n df      BIC      ICL
      -2867.409 2146  8 -5796.19 -6198.36

Clustering table:
    1    2    3
 1341  581  224
>
```

STEP 16

Merge the resulting clusters with the non-zero subset and retain only the id and bin_GMM columns.

```
52 ▾ }else{ # if the resulting mclust is null
53
54     #filter luminosity less than or equal to zero
55     non_zero_datapoints <- datapoints %>%
56       filter(get(ntl_col)>0)
57
58     non_zero_avector <- non_zero_datapoints[,ntl_col]
59
60 ▾   # run GMM----
61     fit=Mclust(non_zero_avector, G=3, model="V") # request clustering into 3 clusters
62
63     # view summary of model---
64     print(summary(fit))
65
66     # merge the non-zero luminosity data with its bin classification
67     df_non_zero <- data.frame(non_zero_datapoints, bin_GMM = fit$classification) %>%
68       select(id, bin_GMM) #retain only the id and bin column for ease of merging
69
70     # merge the binned non-zero luminosity data with the rest of the data
71     df_bin <- left_join(datapoints,df_non_zero, by="id") %>%
72       mutate(bin_GMM = ifelse(is.na(bin_GMM),1,bin_GMM)) %>%  #classify zero luminosity values into bin category 1
73       select(id,                       #grid ID
74             lon,lat,                   #centroid coordinates
75             geocode,                   #geocode
76             avg_rad = all_of(ntl_col), #luminosity values, change column name based on the input csv
77             bin_GMM,                   #bins
78             filename)                  #jpeg filenames
79 ▴ }
```

STEP 17

Merge the binned non-zero dataset with the original dataset using the **left_join()** function.

```
52 ▾ }else{ # if the resulting mclust is null
53
54     #filter luminosity less than or equal to zero
55     non_zero_datapoints <- datapoints %>%
56       filter(get(ntl_col)>0)
57
58     non_zero_avector <- non_zero_datapoints[,ntl_col]
59
60 ▾   # run GMM----
61     fit=Mclust(non_zero_avector, G=3, model="V") # request clustering into 3 clusters
62
63     # view summary of model---
64     print(summary(fit))
65
66     # merge the non-zero luminosity data with its bin classification
67     df_non_zero <- data.frame(non_zero_datapoints, bin_GMM = fit$classification) %>%
68       select(id, bin_GMM) #retain only the id and bin column for ease of merging
69
70     # merge the binned non-zero luminosity data with the rest of the data
71     df_bin <- left_join(datapoints,df_non_zero, by="id") %>%
72       mutate(bin_GMM = ifelse(is.na(bin_GMM),1,bin_GMM)) %>%  #classify zero luminosity values into bin category 1
73       select(id,                       #grid ID
74             lon,lat,                   #centroid coordinates
75             geocode,                   #geocode
76             avg_rad = all_of(ntl_col), #luminosity values, change column name based on the input csv
77             bin_GMM,                   #bins
78             filename)                  #jpeg filenames
79 ▴ }
```

STEP 18

Classify all zero luminosity values in cluster 1.

```
52 ▾ }else{ # if the resulting mclust is null
53
54    #filter luminosity less than or equal to zero
55    non_zero_datapoints <- datapoints %>%
56      filter(get(ntl_col)>0)
57
58    non_zero_avector <- non_zero_datapoints[,ntl_col]
59
60 ▾  # run GMM----
61    fit=Mclust(non_zero_avector, G=3, model="V") # request clustering into 3 clusters
62
63    # view summary of model---
64    print(summary(fit))
65
66    # merge the non-zero luminosity data with its bin classification
67    df_non_zero <- data.frame(non_zero_datapoints, bin_GMM = fit$classification) %>%
68      select(id, bin_GMM) #retain only the id and bin column for ease of merging
69
70    # merge the binned non-zero luminosity data with the rest of the data
71    df_bin <- left_join(datapoints,df_non_zero, by="id") %>%
72      mutate(bin_GMM = ifelse(is.na(bin_GMM),1,bin_GMM)) %>%  #classify zero luminosity values into bin category 1
73      select(id,                    #grid ID
74             lon,lat,               #centroid coordinates
75             geocode,               #geocode
76             avg_rad = all_of(ntl_col),  #luminosity values, change column name based on the input csv
77             bin_GMM,               #bins
78             filename)              #jpeg filenames
79 ▴ }
```

STEP 19

Select the relevant columns.

```
52 ▾ }else{ # if the resulting mclust is null
53
54    #filter luminosity less than or equal to zero
55    non_zero_datapoints <- datapoints %>%
56      filter(get(ntl_col)>0)
57
58    non_zero_avector <- non_zero_datapoints[,ntl_col]
59
60 ▾  # run GMM----
61    fit=Mclust(non_zero_avector, G=3, model="V") # request clustering into 3 clusters
62
63    # view summary of model---
64    print(summary(fit))
65
66    # merge the non-zero luminosity data with its bin classification
67    df_non_zero <- data.frame(non_zero_datapoints, bin_GMM = fit$classification) %>%
68      select(id, bin_GMM) #retain only the id and bin column for ease of merging
69
70    # merge the binned non-zero luminosity data with the rest of the data
71    df_bin <- left_join(datapoints,df_non_zero, by="id") %>%
72      mutate(bin_GMM = ifelse(is.na(bin_GMM),1,bin_GMM)) %>%  #classify zero luminosity values into bin category 1
73      select(id,                    #grid ID
74             lon,lat,               #centroid coordinates
75             geocode,               #geocode
76             avg_rad = all_of(ntl_col),  #luminosity values, change column name based on the input csv
77             bin_GMM,               #bins
78             filename)              #jpeg filenames
79 ▴ }
```

STEP 20

Determine the cutoff values for each bin.

```
81 ▾ # Determine the cutoff values for the each bins----
82   df_cutoff <- df_bin %>%
83     group_by(bin_GMM) %>%
84     summarize(min_cutoff = min(avg_rad),
85               max_cutoff = max(avg_rad),
86               n_samples = n())
87
88   # view cutoff table
89   view(df_cutoff)
```

	bin_GMM	min_cutoff	max_cutoff	n_samples
1	1	0.0000000	0.6730738	19222
2	2	0.6746415	3.6485722	631
3	3	3.6580737	104.2493210	237

Alternatively, one can use heuristic methods if the GMMs do not provide optimal clusters.

STEP 21

Merge the government-published poverty and population data with the dataset in preparation for machine learning.

Select the government-published dataset.

```
91 ▾ # Merge published poverty and population data----
92
93   # select csv file containing published population and poverty data
94   SAE_csv_path <- tcltk::tk_choose.files(filters = matrix(c("CSV",".csv","All files","*"),2,2,byrow = T),
95                             caption = "Select Published Population and Poverty CSV")
96   #load csv file as dataframe
97   df_sae <- read.csv(SAE_csv_path)
98
99   # check csv data
100  head(df_sae)
101
102  # merge the dataframe containing binned NTL and published poverty data
103  df <- left_join(df_bin,df_sae, by = c('geocode'='PSGC_code'))
104
105  # view merged dataframe
106  head(df)
107
```

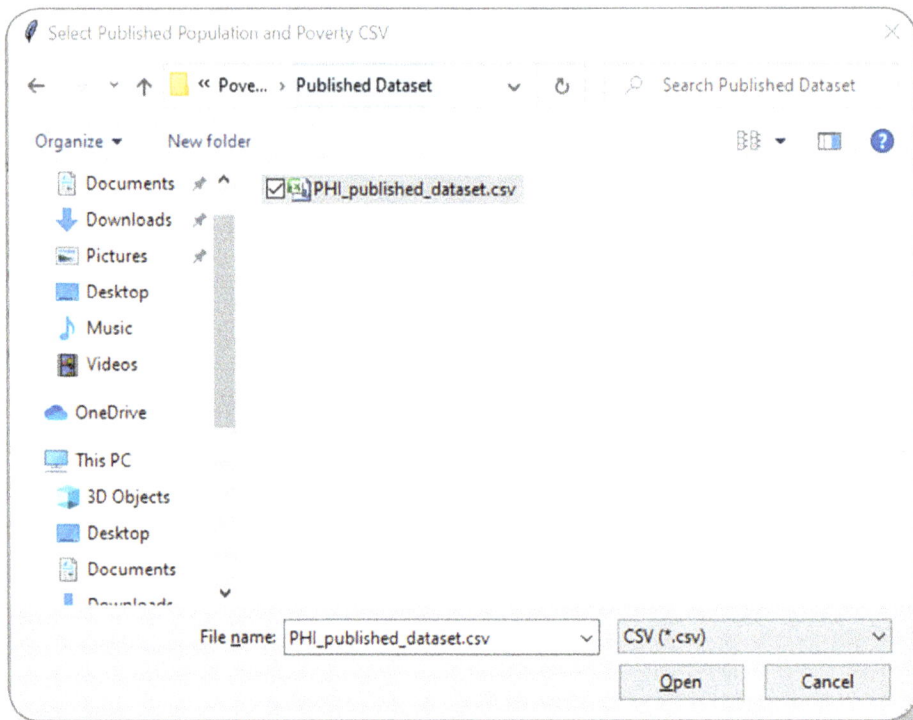

STEP 22

Load the CSV file as a dataframe.

```
91 ▾ # Merge published poverty and population data----
92
93    # select csv file containing published population and poverty data
94    SAE_csv_path <- tcltk::tk_choose.files(filters = matrix(c("CSV",".csv","All files","*"),2,2,byrow = T),
95                                          caption = "Select Published Population and Poverty CSV")
96    #load csv file as dataframe
97    df_sae <- read.csv(SAE_csv_path)
98
99    # check csv data
100   head(df_sae)
101
102   # merge the dataframe containing binned NTL and published poverty data
103   df <- left_join(df_bin,df_sae, by = c('geocode'='PSGC_code'))
104
105   # view merged dataframe
106   head(df)
107
```

STEP 23

Assess the structure of the datasets and identify the common variable for joining the two datasets.

```
91 ▾ # Merge published poverty and population data----
92
93    # select csv file containing published population and poverty data
94    SAE_csv_path <- tcltk::tk_choose.files(filters = matrix(c("CSV",".csv","All files","*"),2,2,byrow = T),
95                                    caption = "Select Published Population and Poverty CSV")
96    #load csv file as dataframe
97    df_sae <- read.csv(SAE_csv_path)
98
99    # check csv data
100   head(df_sae)
101
102   # merge the dataframe containing binned NTL and published poverty data
103   df <- left_join(df_bin,df_sae, by = c('geocode'='PSGC_code'))
104
105   # view merged dataframe
106   head(df)
107
```

```
> # check csv data
> head(df_sae)
  City_Municipality City_Municipality_PCODE      Province Province_PCODE   Region Region_PCODE POCEN2010 POPCEN2015 POV_2009
1            Adams           PH012801000 Ilocos Norte   PH012800000 Region I  PH010000000     1785       1792    29.44
2          Bacarra           PH012802000 Ilocos Norte   PH012800000 Region I  PH010000000    31648      32215    13.20
3            Badoc           PH012803000 Ilocos Norte   PH012800000 Region I  PH010000000    30708      31616    19.55
4           Bangui           PH012804000 Ilocos Norte   PH012800000 Region I  PH010000000    15025      14672    12.63
5     City of Batac         PH012805000 Ilocos Norte   PH012800000 Region I  PH010000000    53542      55201    15.26
6           Carasi          PH012807000 Ilocos Norte   PH012800000 Region I  PH010000000     1473       1567    22.63
  POV_2012 POV_2015 PSGC_code Highly_Urbanized Is.City
1    17.09    16.46  12801000            FALSE   FALSE
2     4.45     7.48  12802000            FALSE   FALSE
3    17.51    10.70  12803000            FALSE   FALSE
4    10.61     8.52  12804000            FALSE   FALSE
5    10.90     7.75  12805000            FALSE    TRUE
6    16.07    20.34  12807000            FALSE   FALSE
>
```

STEP 24

Merge the binned luminosity and government-published datasets using the **left_join()** function with the geocode and PSGC_code as the join variable.

```
91 ▾ # Merge published poverty and population data----
92
93    # select csv file containing published population and poverty data
94    SAE_csv_path <- tcltk::tk_choose.files(filters = matrix(c("CSV",".csv","All files","*"),2,2,byrow = T),
95                                    caption = "Select Published Population and Poverty CSV")
96    #load csv file as dataframe
97    df_sae <- read.csv(SAE_csv_path)
98
99    # check csv data
100   head(df_sae)
101
102   # merge the dataframe containing binned NTL and published poverty data
103   df <- left_join(df_bin,df_sae, by = c('geocode'='PSGC_code'))
104
105   # view merged dataframe
106   head(df)
107
```

```
> # please take note of the name of the column containing the luminosity values
> head(datapoints)
        system.index b1                              filename  geocode  id    lon      lat
1 00000000000000001a40  0 CNN_DIMG_PHI_2015_ST_384_3840_000109.jpg 12801000 109 120.9154 18.49126
2 00000000000000001a41  0 CNN_DIMG_PHI_2015_ST_384_3840_000110.jpg 12801000 110 120.9503 18.49126
3 00000000000000001a5a  0 CNN_DIMG_PHI_2015_ST_384_3840_000135.jpg 12801000 135 120.9154 18.45642
4 00000000000000001a5b  0 CNN_DIMG_PHI_2015_ST_384_3840_000136.jpg 12801000 136 120.9503 18.45642
5 00000000000000001a75  0 CNN_DIMG_PHI_2015_ST_384_3840_000162.jpg 12801000 162 120.8806 18.42158
6 00000000000000001a76  0 CNN_DIMG_PHI_2015_ST_384_3840_000163.jpg 12801000 163 120.9154 18.42158
                                                        .geo
1  {"type":"Point","coordinates":[120.91542329351466,18.49126333539152]}
2  {"type":"Point","coordinates":[120.95026670914629,18.49126333539152]}
3  {"type":"Point","coordinates":[120.91542329351466,18.456419919759895]}
4  {"type":"Point","coordinates":[120.95026670914629,18.456419919759895]}
5  {"type":"Point","coordinates":[120.88057987788305,18.42157650412827]}
6  {"type":"Point","coordinates":[120.91542329351466,18.42157650412827]}
> |
```

```
> # check csv data
> head(df_sae)
  City_Municipality City_Municipality_PCODE     Province Province_PCODE   Region Region_PCODE POCEN2010 POPCEN2015 POV_2009
1            Adams          PH012801000 Ilocos Norte    PH012800000 Region I  PH010000000      1785       1792    29.44
2          Bacarra          PH012802000 Ilocos Norte    PH012800000 Region I  PH010000000     31648      32215    13.20
3            Badoc          PH012803000 Ilocos Norte    PH012800000 Region I  PH010000000     30708      31616    19.55
4           Bangui          PH012804000 Ilocos Norte    PH012800000 Region I  PH010000000     15025      14672    12.63
5    City of Batac          PH012805000 Ilocos Norte    PH012800000 Region I  PH010000000     53542      55201    15.26
6           Carasi          PH012807000 Ilocos Norte    PH012800000 Region I  PH010000000      1473       1567    22.63
  POV_2012 POV_2015 PSGC_code Highly_Urbanized Is.City
1    17.09    16.46  12801000            FALSE   FALSE
2     4.45     7.48  12802000            FALSE   FALSE
3    17.51    10.70  12803000            FALSE   FALSE
4    10.61     8.52  12804000            FALSE   FALSE
5    10.90     7.75  12805000            FALSE    TRUE
6    16.07    20.34  12807000            FALSE   FALSE
> |
```

STEP 25

Check the structure of the new dataset structure to ensure that the two datasets are merged.

```
 91 ▾ # Merge published poverty and population data----
 92
 93    # select csv file containing published population and poverty data
 94    SAE_csv_path <- tcltk::tk_choose.files(filters = matrix(c("CSV",".csv","All files","*"),2,2,byrow = T),
 95                              caption = "Select Published Population and Poverty CSV")
 96    #load csv file as dataframe
 97    df_sae <- read.csv(SAE_csv_path)
 98
 99    # check csv data
100    head(df_sae)
101
102    # merge the dataframe containing binned NTL and published poverty data
103    df <- left_join(df_bin,df_sae, by = c('geocode'='PSGC_code'))
104
105    # view merged dataframe
106    head(df)
107
```

```
> # view merged dataframe
> head(df)
   id      lon      lat geocode avg_rad bin_GMM                          filename City_Municipality
1 109 120.9154 18.49126 12801000       0       1 CNN_DIMG_PHI_2015_ST_384_3840_000109.jpg      Adams
2 110 120.9503 18.49126 12801000       0       1 CNN_DIMG_PHI_2015_ST_384_3840_000110.jpg      Adams
3 135 120.9154 18.45642 12801000       0       1 CNN_DIMG_PHI_2015_ST_384_3840_000135.jpg      Adams
4 136 120.9503 18.45642 12801000       0       1 CNN_DIMG_PHI_2015_ST_384_3840_000136.jpg      Adams
5 162 120.8806 18.42158 12801000       0       1 CNN_DIMG_PHI_2015_ST_384_3840_000162.jpg      Adams
6 163 120.9154 18.42158 12801000       0       1 CNN_DIMG_PHI_2015_ST_384_3840_000163.jpg      Adams
  City_Municipality_PCODE     Province    Region POCEN2010 POPCEN2015 POV_2009 POV_2012 POV_2015 Highly_Urbanized Is.City
1             PH012801000 Ilocos Norte Region I      1785       1792    29.44    17.09    16.46            FALSE   FALSE
2             PH012801000 Ilocos Norte Region I      1785       1792    29.44    17.09    16.46            FALSE   FALSE
3             PH012801000 Ilocos Norte Region I      1785       1792    29.44    17.09    16.46            FALSE   FALSE
4             PH012801000 Ilocos Norte Region I      1785       1792    29.44    17.09    16.46            FALSE   FALSE
5             PH012801000 Ilocos Norte Region I      1785       1792    29.44    17.09    16.46            FALSE   FALSE
6             PH012801000 Ilocos Norte Region I      1785       1792    29.44    17.09    16.46            FALSE   FALSE
>
```

STEP 26

Split the dataset into training and test sets. It is up to the user to decide on an optimal splitting strategy. In the ADB study (footnote 2), the dataset was split into two: 90% for training and 10% for test. The training dataset will be used for training the CNN model. This dataset is further split into 80% for training and 20% for validation through fastai. After developing the trained model, the test dataset will be used to validate its accuracy.

First, load the package caret. This package contains the function **createDataPartition()** that will enable the generation of a balanced split in the dataset. **createDataPartition()** returns the row index of the dataset belonging to the specified split.

```
108 ▾ # Dataset Splitting-----
109   # Data shall be split into 90% for training and validation and 10% holdout dataset
110   library(caret)
111
112   #generate index of the 90% training and validation dataset
113   splitIndex <- createDataPartition(df$bin_GMM,       #specify column for basis of split
114                                     times = 1,        #number of split
115                                     p = 0.9,          #percent split
116                                     list=FALSE)       #outputs the data as a matrix
117
118   #subset dataset to extract the training and validation dataset
119   df_Train <- df[ splitIndex,]
120   #subset dataset to extract the holdout dataset
121   df_Test  <- df[-splitIndex,]
122
123   #check the resulting datasets
124   head(df_Train)
125   head(df_Test)
126
127   nrow(df_Train)
128   nrow(df_Test)
```

STEP 27

createDataPartition() requires the following parameters:

- column of dataset for the basis of the split,
- **times** – number of split to perform, in our case only one,
- **p** – split ratio in our case 0.9 or 90%, and
- **list = FALSE** – to output the data as a matrix. This will be used when subsetting the dataset.

```
108 ▾  # Dataset Splitting-----
109    # Data shall be split into 90% for training and validation and 10% holdout dataset
110    library(caret)
111
112    #generate index of the 90% training and validation dataset
113    splitIndex <- createDataPartition(df$bin_GMM,        #specify column for basis of split
114                                       times = 1,         #number of split
115                                       p = 0.9,           #percent split
116                                       list=FALSE)        #outputs the data as a matrix
117
118    #subset dataset to extract the training and validation dataset
119    df_Train <- df[ splitIndex,]
120    #subset dataset to extract the holdout dataset
121    df_Test  <- df[-splitIndex,]
122
123    #check the resulting datasets
124    head(df_Train)
125    head(df_Test)
126
127    nrow(df_Train)
128    nrow(df_Test)
```

STEP 28

Extract the training and test datasets from the subset of the dataset.

```
108 ▾  # Dataset Splitting-----
109    # Data shall be split into 90% for training and validation and 10% holdout dataset
110    library(caret)
111
112    #generate index of the 90% training and validation dataset
113    splitIndex <- createDataPartition(df$bin_GMM,        #specify column for basis of split
114                                       times = 1,         #number of split
115                                       p = 0.9,           #percent split
116                                       list=FALSE)        #outputs the data as a matrix
117
118    #subset dataset to extract the training and validation dataset
119    df_Train <- df[ splitIndex,]
120    #subset dataset to extract the holdout dataset
121    df_Test  <- df[-splitIndex,]
122
123    #check the resulting datasets
124    head(df_Train)
125    head(df_Test)
126
127    nrow(df_Train)
128    nrow(df_Test)
```

STEP 29

Check the dataset's structure.

```
108 ▾ # Dataset Splitting-----
109   # Data shall be split into 90% for training and validation and 10% holdout dataset
110   library(caret)
111
112   #generate index of the 90% training and validation dataset
113   splitIndex <- createDataPartition(df$bin_GMM,      #specify column for basis of split
114                                     times = 1,        #number of split
115                                     p = 0.9,          #percent split
116                                     list=FALSE)       #outputs the data as a matrix
117
118   #subset dataset to extract the training and validation dataset
119   df_Train <- df[ splitIndex,]
120   #subset dataset to extract the holdout dataset
121   df_Test  <- df[-splitIndex,]
122
123   #check the resulting datasets
124   head(df_Train)
125   head(df_Test)
126
127   nrow(df_Train)
128   nrow(df_Test)
```

```
> #check the resulting datasets
> head(df_Train)
    id       x       y  geocode avg_rad bin_GMM filename City_Municipality City_Municipality_PCODE       Province Province_PCODE
1 6748 123.5286 13.7875 51717000       0       1       NA           Lagonoy            PH051717000 Camarines Sur   PH051700000
2 6749 123.5635 13.7875 51717000       0       1       NA           Lagonoy            PH051717000 Camarines Sur   PH051700000
3 6750 123.5983 13.7875 51717000       0       1       NA           Lagonoy            PH051717000 Camarines Sur   PH051700000
4 6751 123.6332 13.7875 51714000       0       1       NA       Garchitorena            PH051714000 Camarines Sur   PH051700000
5 6752 123.6680 13.7875 51729000       0       1       NA       Presentacion           PH051729000 Camarines Sur   PH051700000
6 6753 123.7028 13.7875 51729000       0       1       NA       Presentacion           PH051729000 Camarines Sur   PH051700000
    Region Region_PCODE POCEN2010 POPCEN2015 POV_2009 POV_2012 POV_2015 Highly_Urbanized Is.City
1 Region V  PH050000000     51814      55465    46.73    37.56 41.25886            FALSE   FALSE
2 Region V  PH050000000     51814      55465    46.73    37.56 41.25886            FALSE   FALSE
3 Region V  PH050000000     51814      55465    46.73    37.56 41.25886            FALSE   FALSE
4 Region V  PH050000000     25204      27010    58.97    56.06 59.74208            FALSE   FALSE
5 Region V  PH050000000     20023      20996    50.22    48.81 52.79054            FALSE   FALSE
6 Region V  PH050000000     20023      20996    50.22    48.81 52.79054            FALSE   FALSE
>
```

```
> head(df_Test)
    id       x        y  geocode    avg_rad bin_GMM filename City_Municipality City_Municipality_PCODE    Province
30 6777 121.1942 13.75266 41032000 0.44603384       1       NA            Taysan            PH041032000    Batangas
37 6784 122.1349 13.75266 45625000 0.07993966       1       NA          Macalelon            PH045625000      Quezon
48 6795 122.8318 13.75266 51719000 0.00000000       1       NA              Lupi            PH051719000 Camarines Sur
49 6796 122.8666 13.75266 51719000 0.00000000       1       NA              Lupi            PH051719000 Camarines Sur
50 6797 122.9015 13.75266 51734000 0.00000000       1       NA           Sipocot            PH051734000 Camarines Sur
66 6813 123.6332 13.75266 51717000 0.00000000       1       NA           Lagonoy            PH051717000 Camarines Sur
   Province_PCODE      Region Region_PCODE POCEN2010 POPCEN2015 POV_2009 POV_2012 POV_2015 Highly_Urbanized Is.City
30   PH041000000 Region IV-A  PH040000000     35357      38007    16.62    14.94 13.00000            FALSE   FALSE
37   PH045600000 Region IV-A  PH040000000     26419      28188    29.47    30.03 28.90000            FALSE   FALSE
48   PH051700000    Region V  PH050000000     30118      32167    49.89    36.97 44.39134            FALSE   FALSE
49   PH051700000    Region V  PH050000000     30118      32167    49.89    36.97 44.39134            FALSE   FALSE
50   PH051700000    Region V  PH050000000     64042      64855    43.83    33.62 41.79626            FALSE   FALSE
66   PH051700000    Region V  PH050000000     51814      55465    46.73    37.56 41.25886            FALSE   FALSE
```

STEP 30

Check the number of observations per dataset by displaying the number of rows.

```
108 ▾ # Dataset Splitting-----
109    # Data shall be split into 90% for training and validation and 10% holdout dataset
110    library(caret)
111
112    #generate index of the 90% training and validation dataset
113    splitIndex <- createDataPartition(df$bin_GMM,        #specify column for basis of split
114                                      times = 1,         #number of split
115                                      p = 0.9,           #percent split
116                                      list=FALSE)        #outputs the data as a matrix
117
118    #subset dataset to extract the training and validation dataset
119    df_Train <- df[ splitIndex,]
120    #subset dataset to extract the holdout dataset
121    df_Test   <- df[-splitIndex,]
122
123    #check the resulting datasets
124    head(df_Train)
125    head(df_Test)
126
127    nrow(df_Train)
128    nrow(df_Test)
```

```
> nrow(df_Train)
[1] 18081
> nrow(df_Test)
[1] 2009
>
```

STEP 31

Output the two datasets as CSV files.

```
130 ▾ # output results to as csv files----
131    # generate filename
132    train_file_name <- str_replace(basename(NTL_csv_path), "full","train90")
133    test_file_name <- str_replace(basename(NTL_csv_path), "full","test10")
134
135    write.csv(df_Train, train_file_name, row.names = F)
136    write.csv(df_Test, test_file_name, row.names = F)
```

STEP 32

Upload the files in Google Drive. This will be used for training the CNN model.

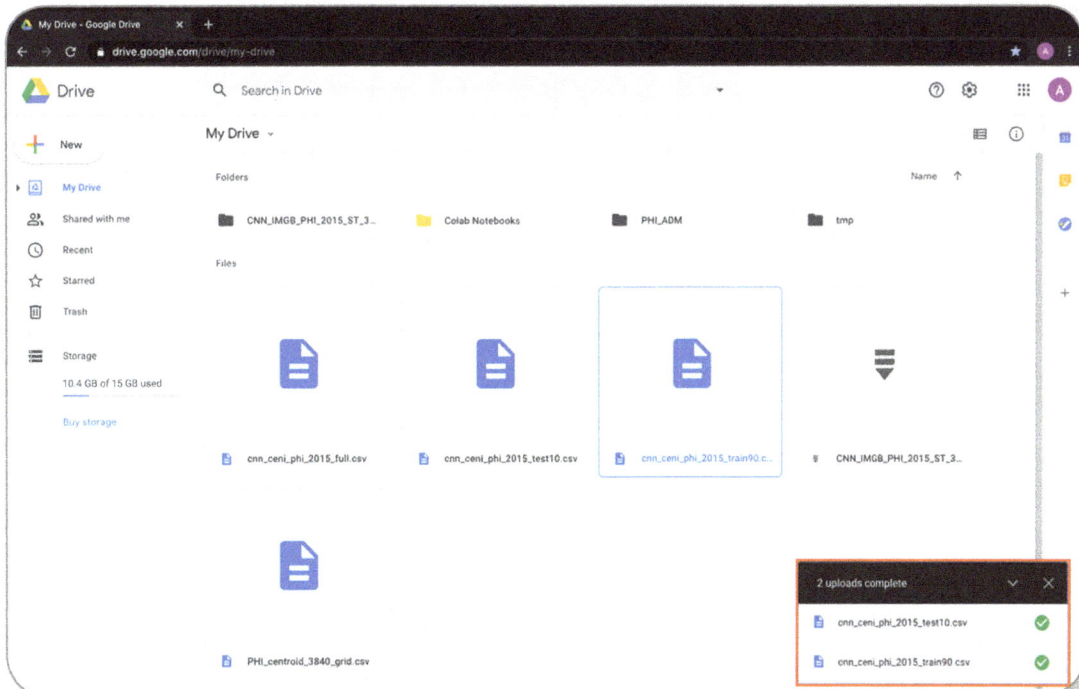

4 TRAINING OF CONVOLUTIONAL NEURAL NETWORK

A convolutional neural network (CNN) is a subclass of artificial neural networks that is primarily used in computer vision (e.g., classification, recognition). It is designed to cope with a large amount of unstructured and pixelated data from digital images. In this context, a CNN is trained to extract features in daytime images using intensity of night lights as labels. These extracted features are then used to predict poverty.

Data Requirements

- Archive file containing daytime satellite imagery (JPG)
- CSV file containing binned luminosity

Tools

- Google Colaboratory (CNN_training_template.ipynb)

STEP 1

In the browser address bar, input the Google Colab (footnote 7) web address https://colab.research.google.com/ and press **Enter** from the keyboard. *Make sure to log in to Google account.* Then click **Upload**.

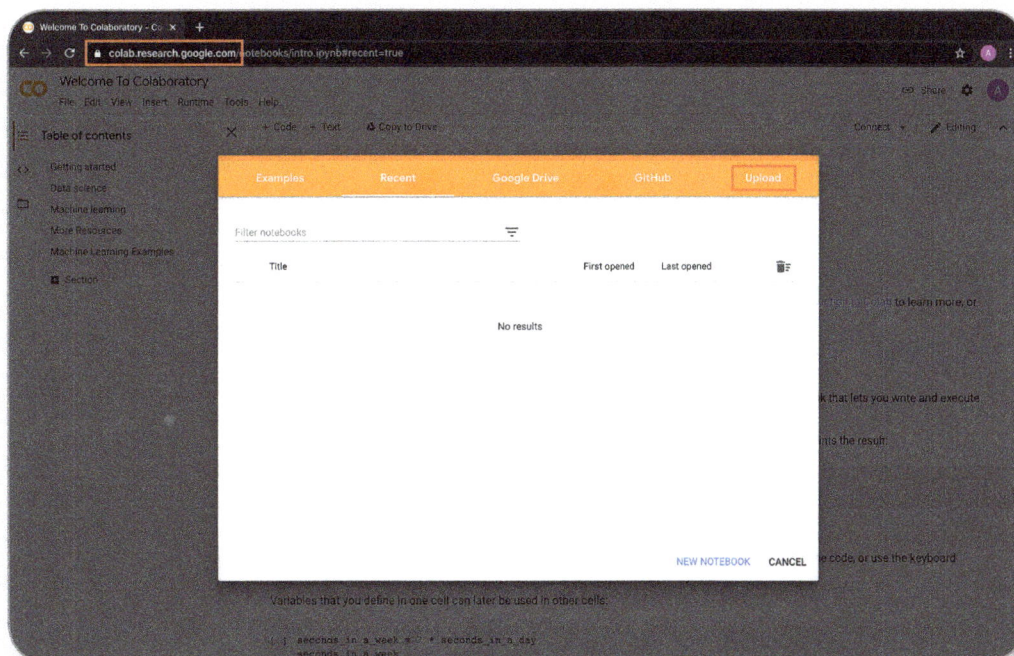

STEP 2

Click **Choose File**.

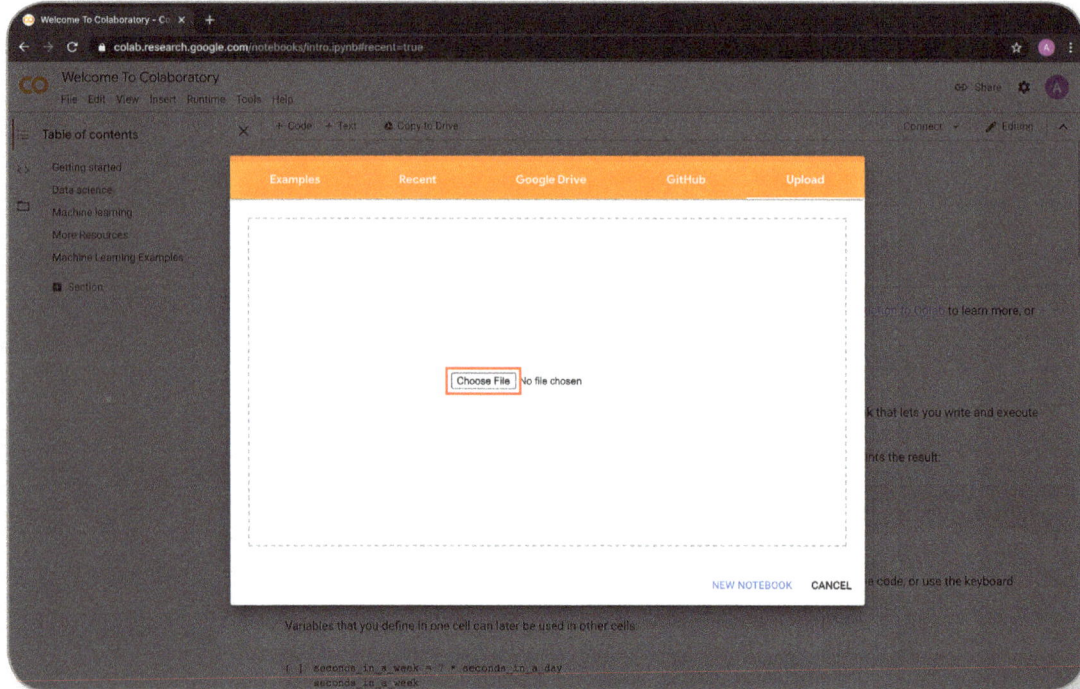

Locate the Jupyter Notebook file from the computer. Use **CNN_training_template.ipynb**. Click **Open**.

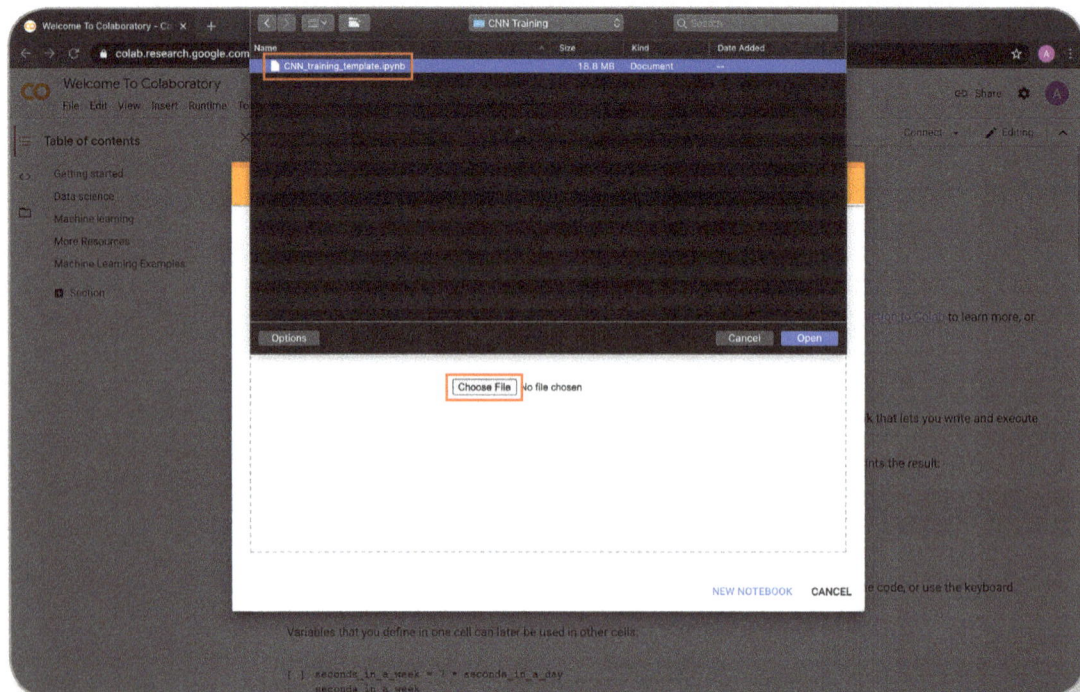

STEP 3

Setup the runtime type once the file has loaded. Click **Runtime** on the menu bar.

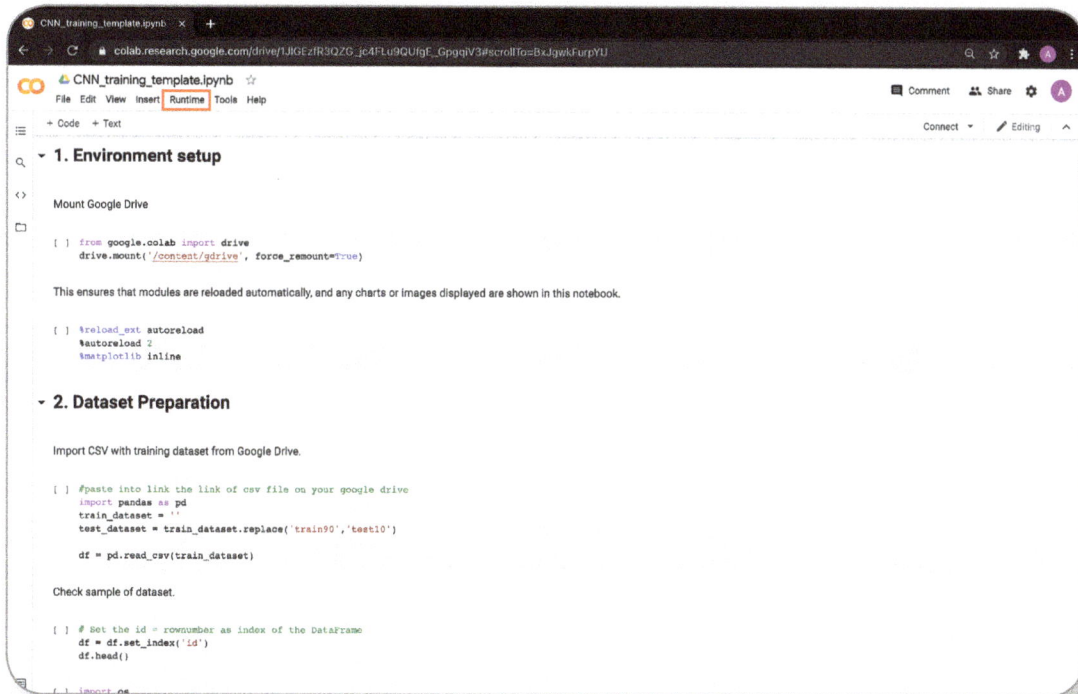

Then click **Change runtime type**.

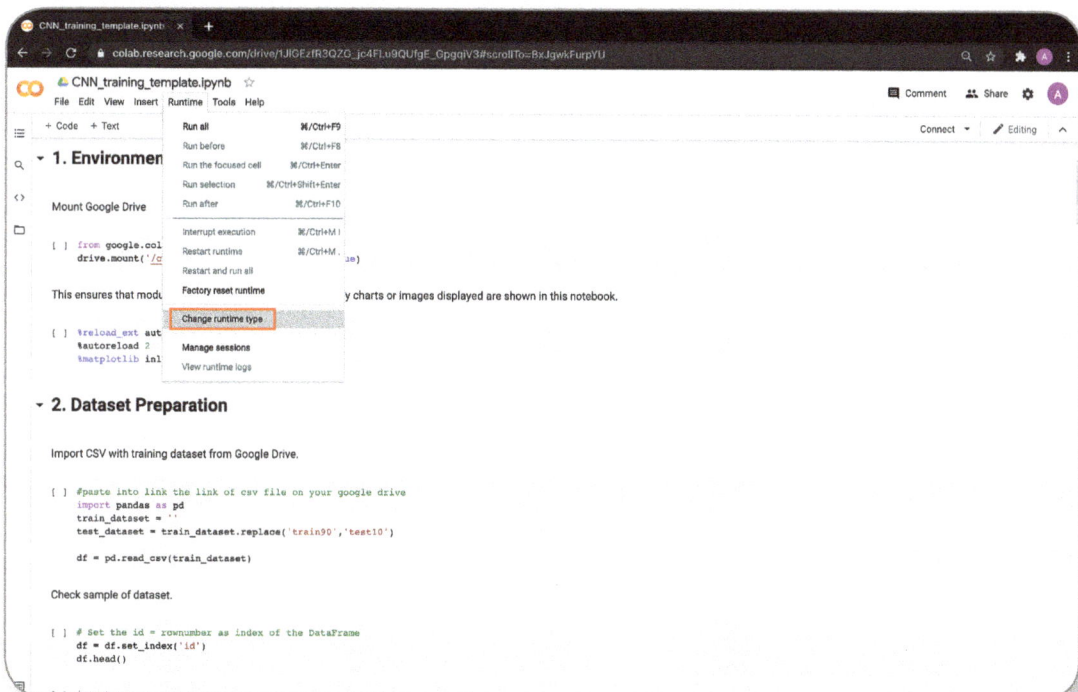

STEP 4

On the Notebook settings, change **Hardware accelerator** into **GPU**. Then click **Save**.

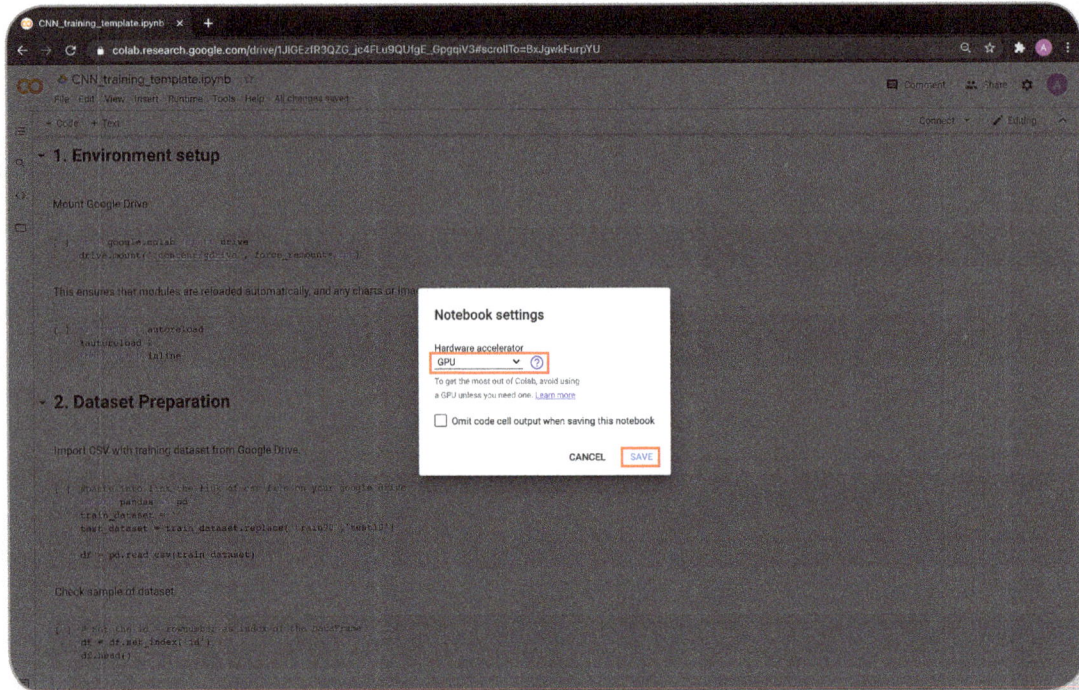

STEP 5

Click **Connect**.

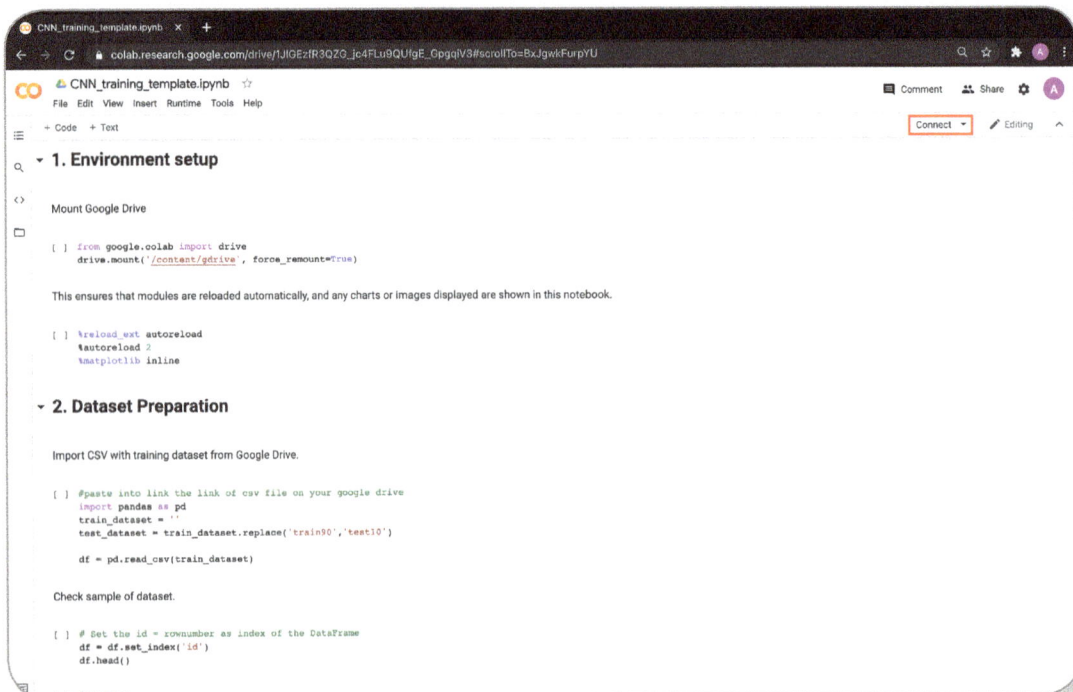

This will initialize the Colab's environment.

STEP 6

To execute, click each code cell and click ▶ button at the beginning of each cell.

Setup and mount the Google Drive (footnote 6).

```
from google.colab import drive
drive.mount('/content/gdrive', force_remount=True)
```

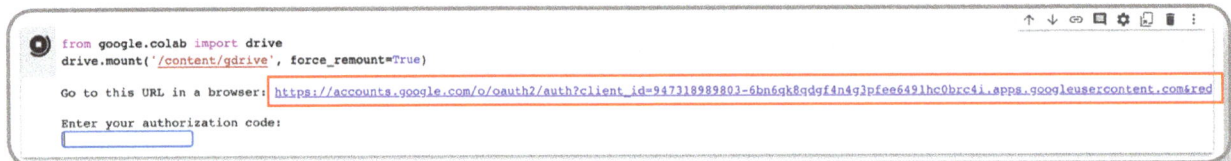

```
from google.colab import drive
drive.mount('/content/gdrive', force_remount=True)

Go to this URL in a browser: https://accounts.google.com/o/oauth2/auth?client_id=947318989803-6bn6qk8qdgf4n4g3pfee6491hc0brc4i.apps.googleusercontent.com&red

Enter your authorization code:
```

STEP 7

In the browser, sign in to your Google account.

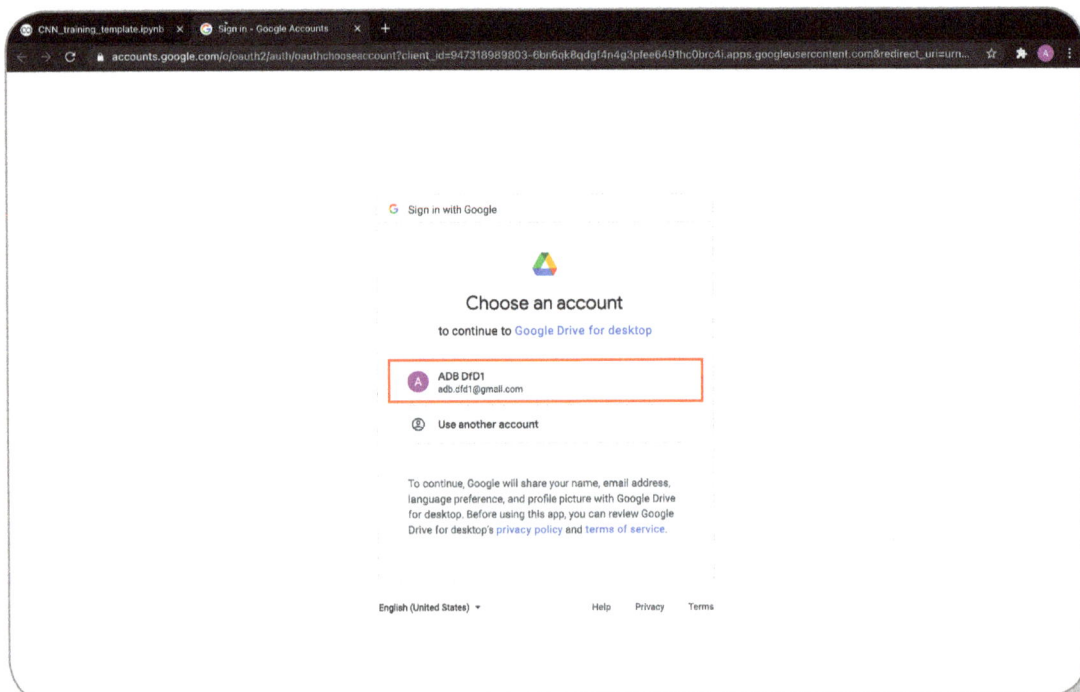

Click **Allow**.

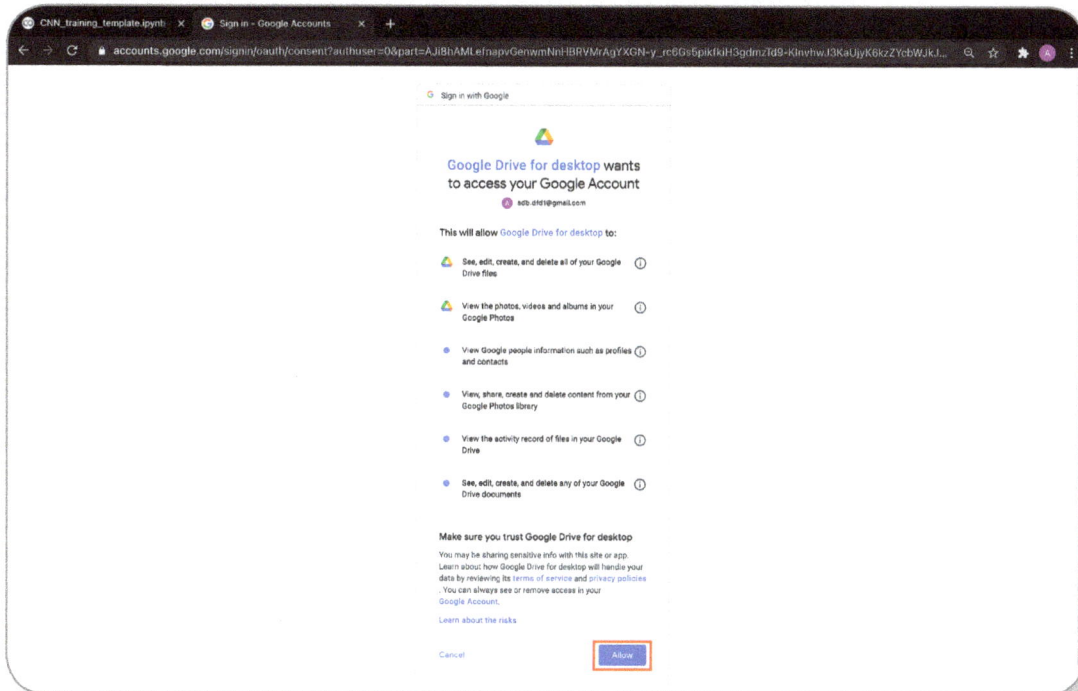

Click the **Copy** icon to copy the code.

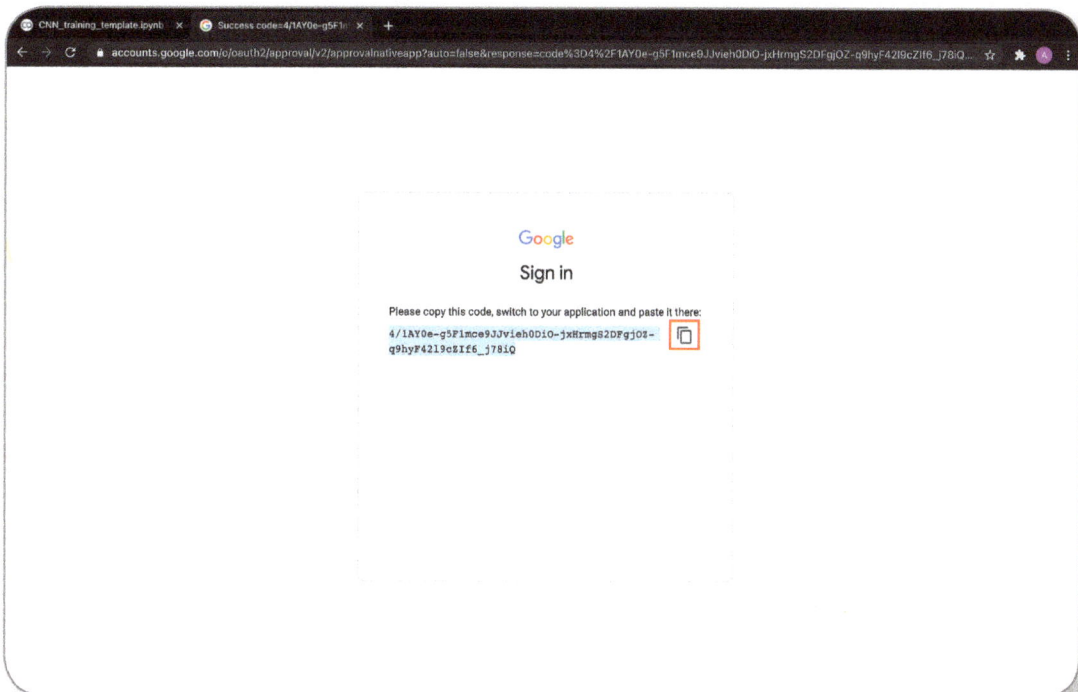

STEP 8

Return to the Colab browser tab. **Paste** the code in the text box. Then press **Enter**.

```
from google.colab import drive
drive.mount('/content/gdrive', force_remount=True)

... Go to this URL in a browser: https://accounts.google.com/o/oauth2/auth?client_id=947318989803-6bn6qk8qdgf4n4g3pfee6491hc0brc4i.apps.googleusercontent.com&red

Enter your authorization code:
J2ozLZusV5BJwbaezG8
```

A status will show the path where Google Drive is mounted.

```
from google.colab import drive
drive.mount('/content/gdrive', force_remount=True)

Mounted at /content/gdrive
```

STEP 9

Ensure that modules are reloaded automatically and any charts or images displayed are shown in this notebook.

```
%reload_ext autoreload
%autoreload 2
%matplotlib inline
```

STEP 10

Locate the path to the CSV file containing the binned luminosity values that was previously uploaded in Google Drive.

```
#paste into link the link of csv file on your google drive
import pandas as pd
train_dataset = ''
test_dataset = train_dataset.replace('train90','test10')

df = pd.read_csv(train_dataset)
```

STEP 11

Click **Files** icon ⬜ to show the **Files section**.

STEP 12

Click **gdrive** from the list of folders and expand the file directory tree to find the CSV file location.

STEP 13

Click the vertical ellipsis to show more file options.

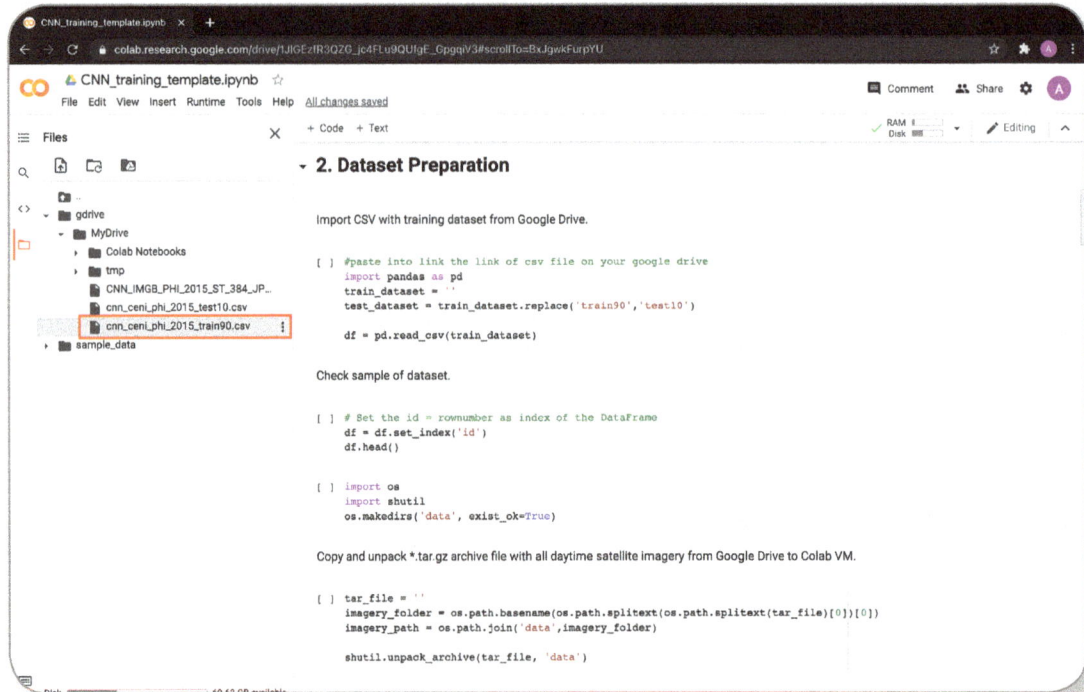

STEP 14

Click **Copy path**.

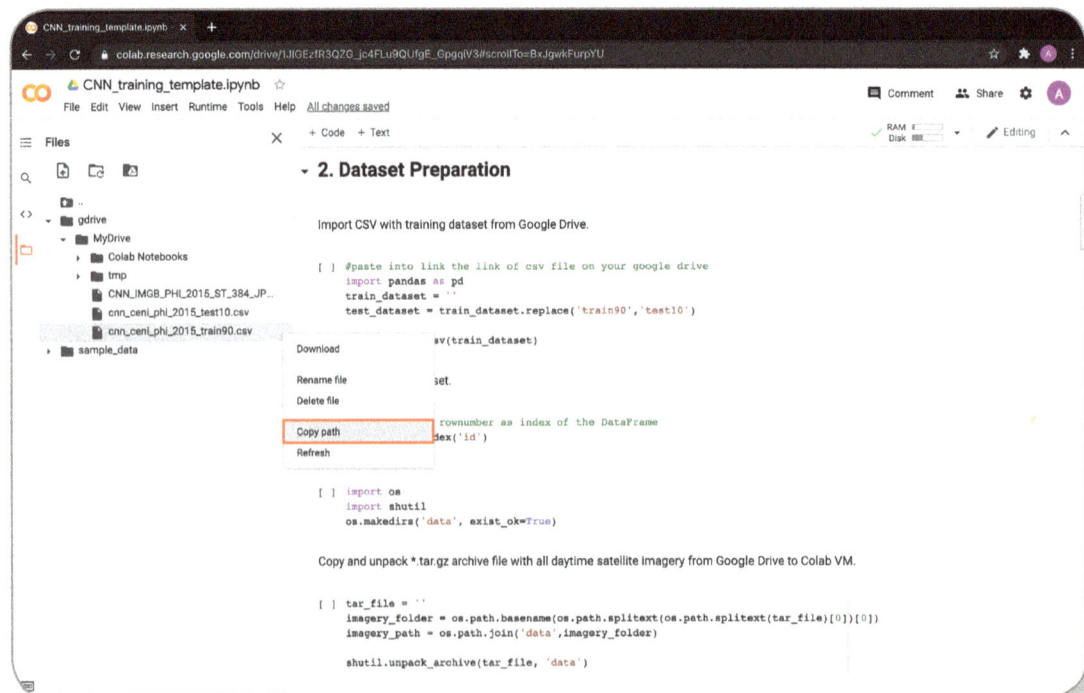

STEP 15

Paste the link on the blank space after the variable **csv_path** and enclose in apostrophes.

```python
#paste into link the link of csv file on your google drive
import pandas as pd
train_dataset = ''
test_dataset = train_dataset.replace('train90','test10')

df = pd.read_csv(train_dataset)
```

```python
#paste into link the link of csv file on your google drive
import pandas as pd
train_dataset = '/content/gdrive/MyDrive/cnn_ceni_phi_2015_train90.csv'
test_dataset = train_dataset.replace('train90','test10')

df = pd.read_csv(train_dataset)
```

STEP 16

Execute the code cell to check the contents of the first five rows of the CSV file.

```python
# Set the id = rownumber as index of the DataFrame
df = df.set_index('id')
df.head()
```

The information on the column contents will be used later in building the ImageDataBunch object, particularly the binned luminosity and filename column.

```python
# Set the id = rownumber as index of the DataFrame
df = df.set_index('id')
df.head()
```

id	x	y	geocode	avg_rad	bin_GMM	filename	City_Municipality	City_Municipality_PCODE	Province	Region
313	121.089636	18.282207	148101000	0.0	1	CNN_DIMG_PHI_2015_ST_384_3840_000313.jpg	Calanasan	PH148101000	Apayao	Cordillera Administrative Region
315	121.159321	18.282207	148101000	0.0	1	CNN_DIMG_PHI_2015_ST_384_3840_000315.jpg	Calanasan	PH148101000	Apayao	Cordillera Administrative Region
316	121.194164	18.282207	148101000	0.0	1	CNN_DIMG_PHI_2015_ST_384_3840_000316.jpg	Calanasan	PH148101000	Apayao	Cordillera Administrative Region
317	121.229007	18.282207	148105000	0.0	1	CNN_DIMG_PHI_2015_ST_384_3840_000317.jpg	Luna	PH148105000	Apayao	Cordillera Administrative Region
318	121.263850	18.282207	148105000	0.0	1	CNN_DIMG_PHI_2015_ST_384_3840_000318.jpg	Luna	PH148105000	Apayao	Cordillera Administrative Region

STEP 17

Import **os** and **shutil** python modules and create folder **data** in the Colab virtual machine's drive.

```
import os
import shutil
os.makedirs('data', exist_ok=True)
```

STEP 18

Click **Files** icon 🗀 to show the **Files section**.

STEP 19

From the list of folders, click *gdrive*.

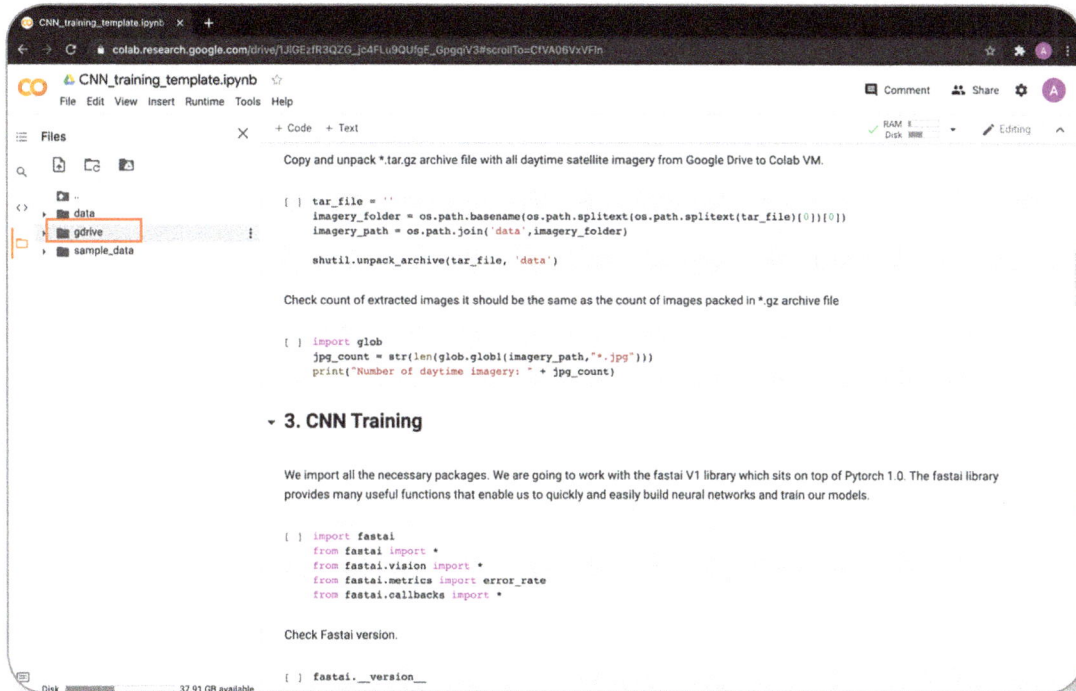

Expand the file directory tree to find the location of the *tar.gz* file.

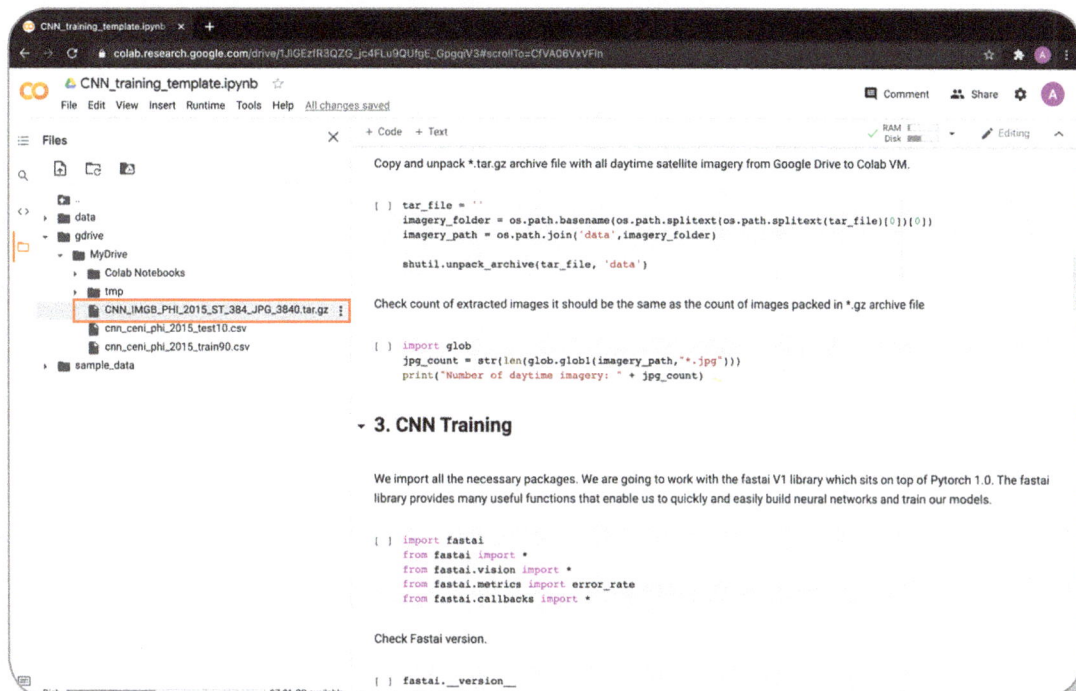

STEP 20

Click the vertical ellipsis to show more file options.

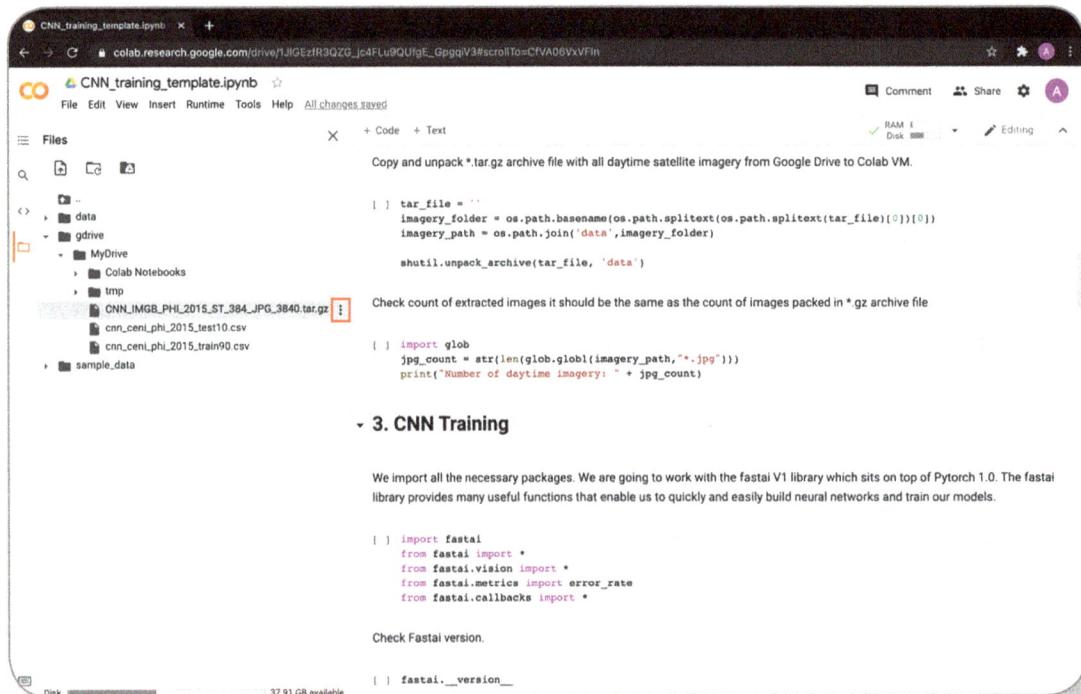

STEP 21

Click **Copy path**.

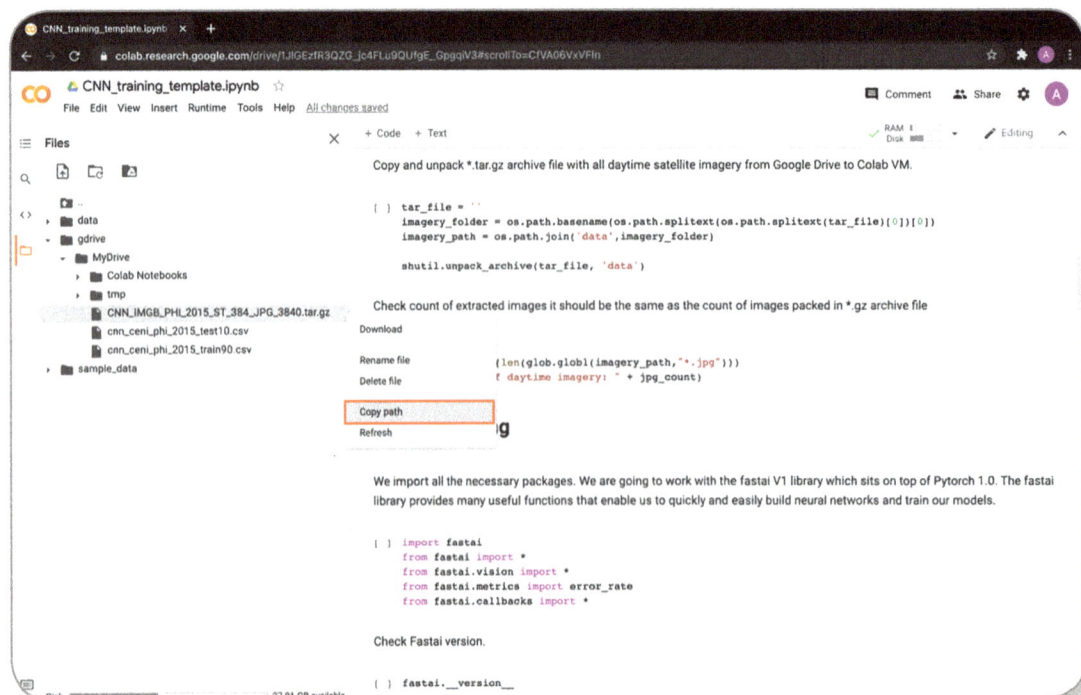

STEP 22

Paste the link beside the variable **tar_file** and enclose it in apostrophes.

```
tar_file = ''
imagery_folder = os.path.basename(os.path.splitext(os.path.splitext(tar_file)[0])[0])
imagery_path = os.path.join('data',imagery_folder)

shutil.unpack_archive(tar_file, 'data')
```

```
tar_file = '/content/gdrive/MyDrive/CNN_IMGB_PHI_2015_ST_384_JPG_3840.tar.gz'
imagery_folder = os.path.basename(os.path.splitext(os.path.splitext(tar_file)[0])[0])
imagery_path = os.path.join('data',imagery_folder)

shutil.unpack_archive(tar_file, 'data')
```

STEP 23

Count the number of daytime imagery files extracted.

```
import glob
jpg_count = str(len(glob.glob1(imagery_path,"*.jpg")))
print("Number of daytime imagery: " + jpg_count)
```

STEP 24

The CNN training process starts in this step.

Import all the necessary packages in fastai.

```
import fastai
from fastai import *
from fastai.vision import *
from fastai.metrics import error_rate
from fastai.callbacks import *
```

STEP 25

Check the fastai version to determine if the latest version is running.

```
fastai.__version__

'1.0.61'
```

STEP 26

Define all the parameter variables needed to create the ImageDataBunch. Load **re** library to be used for string manipulation.

```
import re

root_col = '/content/'
val_pct = 0.2            # percentage of dataset to be used for validation
label_col = 'bin_GMM'    # names of column containing the binned luminosity in dataset
filename_col = 'filename' # names of column containing the imagery filenamesin dataset

# extract country code, year, daytime satellite imagery source and imagery file resolution from tar filename
country, year, day_sat, img_res = re.search("[A-Z]{3}_[0-9]{4}_[A-Z]{2}_[0-9]{3}",tar_file).group().split("_")

# assemble learner and CNN model filenames
learner_filename = "_".join(["CNN_LRNR_RES34",country,year,day_sat,str(img_res)]) + ".pkl"
modelWt_filename = "_".join(["CNN_TCNN_RES34",country,year,day_sat,str(img_res)])

print(learner_filename)
print(modelWt_filename)
```

STEP 27

The **root_col** variable stores the root directory path containing the daytime satellite images. The **valid_pct** command stores the percentage of dataset used for validation.

```python
import re

root_col = '/content/'
val_pct = 0.2                # percentage of dataset to be used for validation
label_col = 'bin_GMM'        # names of column containing the binned luminosity in dataset
filename_col = 'filename'    # names of column containing the imagery filenamesin dataset

# extract country code, year, daytime satellite imagery source and imagery file resolution from tar filename
country, year, day_sat, img_res = re.search("[A-Z]{3}_[0-9]{4}_[A-Z]{2}_[0-9]{3}",tar_file).group().split("_")

# assemble learner and CNN model filenames
learner_filename = "_".join(["CNN_LRNR_RES34",country,year,day_sat,str(img_res)]) + ".pkl"
modelWt_filename = "_".join(["CNN_TCNN_RES34",country,year,day_sat,str(img_res)])

print(learner_filename)
print(modelWt_filename)
```

From the previous code, check the data contained in the CSV file, particularly the **bin_GMM** and **filename**.

```python
# Set the id = rownumber as index of the DataFrame
df = df.set_index('id')
df.head()
```

id	lon	lat	geocode	avg_rad	bin_GMM	filename
109	120.915423	18.491263	12801000	0.0	1	CNN_DIMG_PHI_2015_ST_384_3840_000109.jpg
110	120.950265	18.491263	12801000	0.0	1	CNN_DIMG_PHI_2015_ST_384_3840_000110.jpg
162	120.880580	18.421578	12801000	0.0	1	CNN_DIMG_PHI_2015_ST_384_3840_000162.jpg
163	120.915423	18.421578	12801000	0.0	1	CNN_DIMG_PHI_2015_ST_384_3840_000163.jpg
194	120.915423	18.386735	12801000	0.0	1	CNN_DIMG_PHI_2015_ST_384_3840_000194.jpg

STEP 28

The **label_col** command stores the name of binned-luminosity-containing column. The **filename_col** command stores the name of the filename-containing column.

```
import re

root_col = '/content/'
val_pct = 0.2              # percentage of dataset to be used for validation
label_col = 'bin_GMM'      # names of column containing the binned luminosity in dataset
filename_col = 'filename'  # names of column containing the imagery filenamesin dataset

# extract country code, year, daytime satellite imagery source and imagery file resolution from tar filename
country, year, day_sat, img_res = re.search("[A-Z]{3}_[0-9]{4}_[A-Z]{2}_[0-9]{3}",tar_file).group().split("_")

# assemble learner and CNN model filenames
learner_filename = "_".join(["CNN_LRNR_RES34",country,year,day_sat,str(img_res)]) + ".pkl"
modelWt_filename = "_".join(["CNN_TCNN_RES34",country,year,day_sat,str(img_res)])

print(learner_filename)
print(modelWt_filename)
```

STEP 29

Extract the country code, year, daytime satellite imagery code, and imagery file resolution from the **tar.gz** filename. Then store them in variables **country, year, day_sat**, and **img_res**, respectively.

```
import re

root_col = '/content/'
val_pct = 0.2              # percentage of dataset to be used for validation
label_col = 'bin_GMM'      # names of column containing the binned luminosity in dataset
filename_col = 'filename'  # names of column containing the imagery filenamesin dataset

# extract country code, year, daytime satellite imagery source and imagery file resolution from tar filename
country, year, day_sat, img_res = re.search("[A-Z]{3}_[0-9]{4}_[A-Z]{2}_[0-9]{3}",tar_file).group().split("_")

# assemble learner and CNN model filenames
learner_filename = "_".join(["CNN_LRNR_RES34",country,year,day_sat,str(img_res)]) + ".pkl"
modelWt_filename = "_".join(["CNN_TCNN_RES34",country,year,day_sat,str(img_res)])

print(learner_filename)
print(modelWt_filename)
```

STEP 30

Generate and print the filename to be used when saving the learner and model objects.

```
import re

root_col = '/content/'
val_pct = 0.2              # percentage of dataset to be used for validation
label_col = 'bin_GMM'      # names of column containing the binned luminosity in dataset
filename_col = 'filename'  # names of column containing the imagery filenamesin dataset

# extract country code, year, daytime satellite imagery source and imagery file resolution from tar filename
country, year, day_sat, img_res = re.search("[A-Z]{3}_[0-9]{4}_[A-Z]{2}_[0-9]{3}",tar_file).group().split("_")

# assemble learner and CNN model filenames
learner_filename = "_".join(["CNN_LRNR_RES34",country,year,day_sat,str(img_res)]) + ".pkl"
modelWt_filename = "_".join(["CNN_TCNN_RES34",country,year,day_sat,str(img_res)])

print(learner_filename)
print(modelWt_filename)
```

STEP 31

Define the image transformation to be applied to the daytime images, like vertical flipping, random lighting and contrast change with 10% probability, dihedral and symmetric warp. *This is called data augmentation. Data augmentation is used to increase the number of samples in the training dataset, to get the model to generalize better, and to mitigate imbalanced classes in dataset. It also prevents the model from overfitting. In effect, it increases the accuracy of the model.*

```
# by default Fastai uses horizontal flipping augmentation, we add some more
aug_tfms = [contrast(scale = (0.9, 1.11),p = 0.9)
           ,dihedral()
           ,symmetric_warp(magnitude = (-0.2,0.2))
           ]

tfms = get_transforms(flip_vert = True,
                      max_lighting = 0.1,
                      xtra_tfms = aug_tfms,
                      )

data = ImageDataBunch.from_df(df = df,               # using df to define training dataset
                             path = root_col,        # root directory
                             folder = imagery_path,  # imagery folder path
                             valid_pct = val_pct,    # 20% of data will be used for validation
                             fn_col = filename_col,  # filename column in dataset
                             label_col = label_col,  # classes column in dataset
                             ds_tfms = tfms,         # use transformations defined above
                             size = int(img_res)     # image size
                              ).normalize(imagenet_stats) # use the normalization that was used to train the pretrained model
```

STEP 32

Define the ImageDataBunch.

ImageDataBunch is a fastai object, which stores the path to the image folder, training dataset, augmentation, and other settings of the training.

```
# by default Fastai uses horizontal flipping augmentation, we add some more
aug_tfms = [contrast(scale = (0.9, 1.11),p = 0.9)
            ,dihedral()
            ,symmetric_warp(magnitude = (-0.2,0.2))
            ]

tfms = get_transforms(flip_vert = True,
                      max_lighting = 0.1,
                      xtra_tfms = aug_tfms,
                      )

data = ImageDataBunch.from_df(df = df,                      # using df to define training dataset
                              path = root_col,              # root directory
                              folder = imagery_path,        # imagery folder path
                              valid_pct = val_pct,          # 20% of data will be used for validation
                              fn_col = filename_col,        # filename column in dataset
                              label_col = label_col,        # classes column in dataset
                              ds_tfms = tfms,               # use transformations defined above
                              size = int(img_res)           # image size
                              ).normalize(imagenet_stats)   # use the normalization that was used to train the pretrained model
```

STEP 33

View the first 25 images of the training dataset.

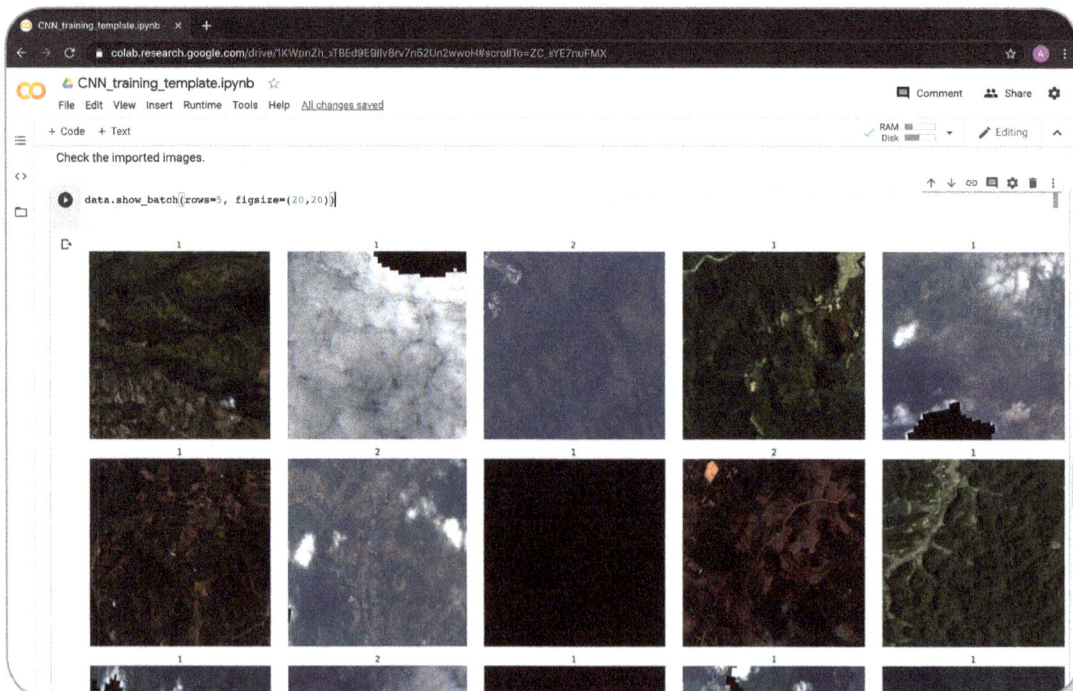

STEP 34

Create a CNN learner object with the pre-trained model, training and validation datasets, metrics, and loss function as arguments. A **model** is the combination of mathematical functions and parameters or weights. Both **metrics** and **loss** functions measure the model's performance, but they differ in use. **Metrics** are used by researchers to define the performance of their models, while **loss** functions are used by the deep learning platform to update the model's weights during training.[9]

Set the CNN model parameter to ResNet-34 and metrics to **error_rate**. Resnet models have been trained on an image-net database of over 14 million images, with 1.2 million of them assigned to one of a thousand categories. It has different variants like ResNet-18, ResNet-34, ResNet-50, ResNet-101, and ResNet-152, which differ in the number of layers. According to PyTorch documentation (https://pytorch.org/vision/stable/models.html), ResNet-34 has higher accuracy and six times fewer parameters compared to the pre-trained model VGG. The reduced file size of ResNet-34 is important since no dedicated stand-alone hardware is used for training the model. Though ResNet-18 has smaller number of parameters and smaller file size, ResNet-34 performs better.

The learner also uses a **weighted Cross Entropy loss** function to mitigate imbalanced prediction classes. It penalizes the model for wrong prediction of low frequency class (i.e., 3- high nightlight) based on weight. It also prevents the model from tending to predict more of low nightlight classes 1 and 2 because these classes have the most samples. Weights [0.7,1.0,1.1] are chosen based on experiments. In general, however, users may define other weights as deem suitable (see Box 1).

```
w = torch.cuda.FloatTensor([0.7, 1.0, 1.1])
learn = cnn_learner(data, models.resnet34, metrics = error_rate, loss_func=torch.nn.CrossEntropyLoss(weight=w))

Downloading: "https://download.pytorch.org/models/resnet34-333f7ec4.pth" to /root/.cache/torch/hub/checkpoints/resnet34-333f7ec4.pth
100%                                          83.3M/83.3M [00:00<00:00, 240MB/s]
```

STEP 35

Define the callbacks. In fastai, **callbacks** are functions that are executed when an "event" occurs during the training process.

```
callbacks = [SaveModelCallback(learn, monitor='error_rate', mode='min', name=modelWt_filename),
             ShowGraph(learn),
             EarlyStoppingCallback(learn, min_delta=0.0001, patience=3)
             ]

learn.callbacks = callbacks
```

---

[9] "Lesson 2 - Deep Learning for Coders (2020)", Youtube video, 1:31:04, posted by Jeremy Howard on 22 August 2020. https://www.youtube.com/watch?v=BvHmRx14HQ8.

The first callback function saves the weights of the best training cycle in the batch into a **.pth** file with specified filename.

```
callbacks = [SaveModelCallback(learn, monitor='error_rate', mode='min', name=modelWt_filename),
             ShowGraph(learn),
             EarlyStoppingCallback(learn, min_delta=0.0001, patience=3)
             ]

learn.callbacks = callbacks
```

The second callback function displays a graph of training and validation dataset loss during training.

```
callbacks = [SaveModelCallback(learn, monitor='error_rate', mode='min', name=modelWt_filename),
             ShowGraph(learn),
             EarlyStoppingCallback(learn, min_delta=0.0001, patience=3)
             ]

learn.callbacks = callbacks
```

The last callback function stops the training batch when there are three consecutive training cycles that did not improve the model.

```
callbacks = [SaveModelCallback(learn, monitor='error_rate', mode='min', name=modelWt_filename),
             ShowGraph(learn),
             EarlyStoppingCallback(learn, min_delta=0.0001, patience=3)
             ]

learn.callbacks = callbacks
```

STEP 36

Execute the code to train the model using the dataset. Since the pre-trained CNN is used, the weights are already in place and thus the number of training epochs can be lower. An **epoch** is equal to one cycle of training through all the training dataset.

Unfreeze the last layer group and train it for 14 epochs. The layer group being trained will determine the final predictions. This will create new weights for the layer group that will identify what an image looks like if it belongs to either of the three luminosity intensity classes (i.e., 1=low, 2=medium, 3=high).

A higher epoch can be used, however, a point will be reached when the errors no longer change. Even if the training continues further, the last best model will still be saved through the first callback function. Also, as specified in the third callback function, the training stops after three consecutive cycles without the model improving. This will save time and computing resources.

A weight decay of 0.1 is also used, following the best practice for fastai as suggested by its developers. **Weight decay** is a model regularization technique where it penalizes parameters (weights) to prevent overfitting. Too large a weight decay could prevent the model from fitting well, in other words, the model is not "learning". Too small a weight will make the model over-fit earlier.[10]

```
learn.fit_one_cycle(14,wd=0.1)
```

Upon execution, the following will be displayed:

- tabulated training, validation loss, and error rate per training cycle (epoch),

```
learn.fit_one_cycle(14,wd=0.1)
```

epoch	train_loss	valid_loss	error_rate	time
0	1.305557	0.805994	0.299501	07:24
1	0.562724	0.354175	0.111065	07:20
2	0.363034	0.310001	0.091930	07:23
3	0.310701	0.324480	0.113561	07:29
4	0.288004	0.338272	0.135607	07:26
5	0.276277	0.282223	0.094426	07:19
6	0.255962	0.280579	0.094842	07:14
7	0.257208	0.258113	0.084027	07:07
8	0.217977	0.255525	0.083611	07:09
9	0.221811	0.249395	0.081531	07:19
10	0.208625	0.250966	0.084859	07:10
11	0.205244	0.243462	0.080283	07:10
12	0.208900	0.242800	0.079451	07:15
13	0.204030	0.242547	0.079451	07:12

```
Better model found at epoch 0 with error_rate value: 0.29950082302093506.
```

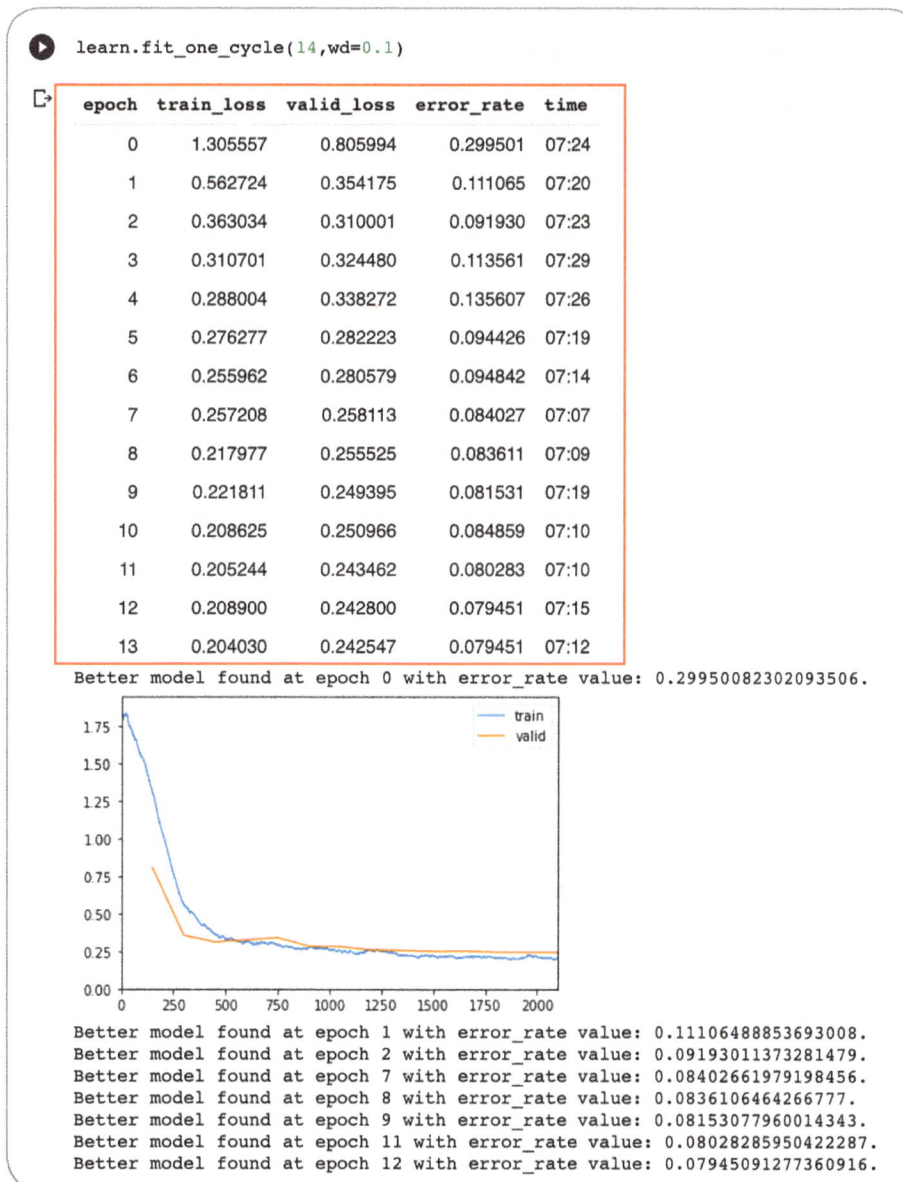

```
Better model found at epoch 1 with error_rate value: 0.11106488853693008.
Better model found at epoch 2 with error_rate value: 0.09193011373281479.
Better model found at epoch 7 with error_rate value: 0.08402661979198456.
Better model found at epoch 8 with error_rate value: 0.0836106464266777.
Better model found at epoch 9 with error_rate value: 0.08153077960014343.
Better model found at epoch 11 with error_rate value: 0.08028285950422287.
Better model found at epoch 12 with error_rate value: 0.07945091277360916.
```

---

[10] "Lesson 5: Deep Learning 2019 – Back propagation; Accelerated SGD; Neural net from scratch", Youtube video, 2:13:33, posted by Jeremy Howard on 26 January 2019. https://www.youtube.com/watch?v=CJKnDu2dxOE.

■ training and validation loss graph, which is the second callback function, and

```
learn.fit_one_cycle(14,wd=0.1)
```

epoch	train_loss	valid_loss	error_rate	time
0	1.305557	0.805994	0.299501	07:24
1	0.562724	0.354175	0.111065	07:20
2	0.363034	0.310001	0.091930	07:23
3	0.310701	0.324480	0.113561	07:29
4	0.288004	0.338272	0.135607	07:26
5	0.276277	0.282223	0.094426	07:19
6	0.255962	0.280579	0.094842	07:14
7	0.257208	0.258113	0.084027	07:07
8	0.217977	0.255525	0.083611	07:09
9	0.221811	0.249395	0.081531	07:19
10	0.208625	0.250966	0.084859	07:10
11	0.205244	0.243462	0.080283	07:10
12	0.208900	0.242800	0.079451	07:15
13	0.204030	0.242547	0.079451	07:12

```
Better model found at epoch 0 with error_rate value: 0.29950082302093506.
```

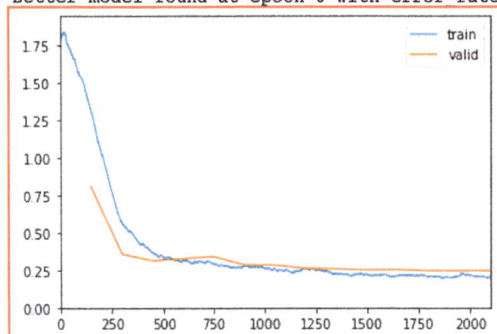

```
Better model found at epoch 1 with error_rate value: 0.11106488853693008.
Better model found at epoch 2 with error_rate value: 0.09193011373281479.
Better model found at epoch 7 with error_rate value: 0.08402661979198456.
Better model found at epoch 8 with error_rate value: 0.0836106464266777.
Better model found at epoch 9 with error_rate value: 0.08153077960014343.
Better model found at epoch 11 with error_rate value: 0.08028285950422287.
Better model found at epoch 12 with error_rate value: 0.07945091277360916.
```

■ resulting models with better error_rate from each epoch.

```
learn.fit_one_cycle(14,wd=0.1)
```

epoch	train_loss	valid_loss	error_rate	time
0	1.305557	0.805994	0.299501	07:24
1	0.562724	0.354175	0.111065	07:20
2	0.363034	0.310001	0.091930	07:23
3	0.310701	0.324480	0.113561	07:29
4	0.288004	0.338272	0.135607	07:26
5	0.276277	0.282223	0.094426	07:19
6	0.255962	0.280579	0.094842	07:14
7	0.257208	0.258113	0.084027	07:07
8	0.217977	0.255525	0.083611	07:09
9	0.221811	0.249395	0.081531	07:19
10	0.208625	0.250966	0.084859	07:10
11	0.205244	0.243462	0.080283	07:10
12	0.208900	0.242800	0.079451	07:15
13	0.204030	0.242547	0.079451	07:12

Better model found at epoch 0 with error_rate value: 0.29950082302093506.

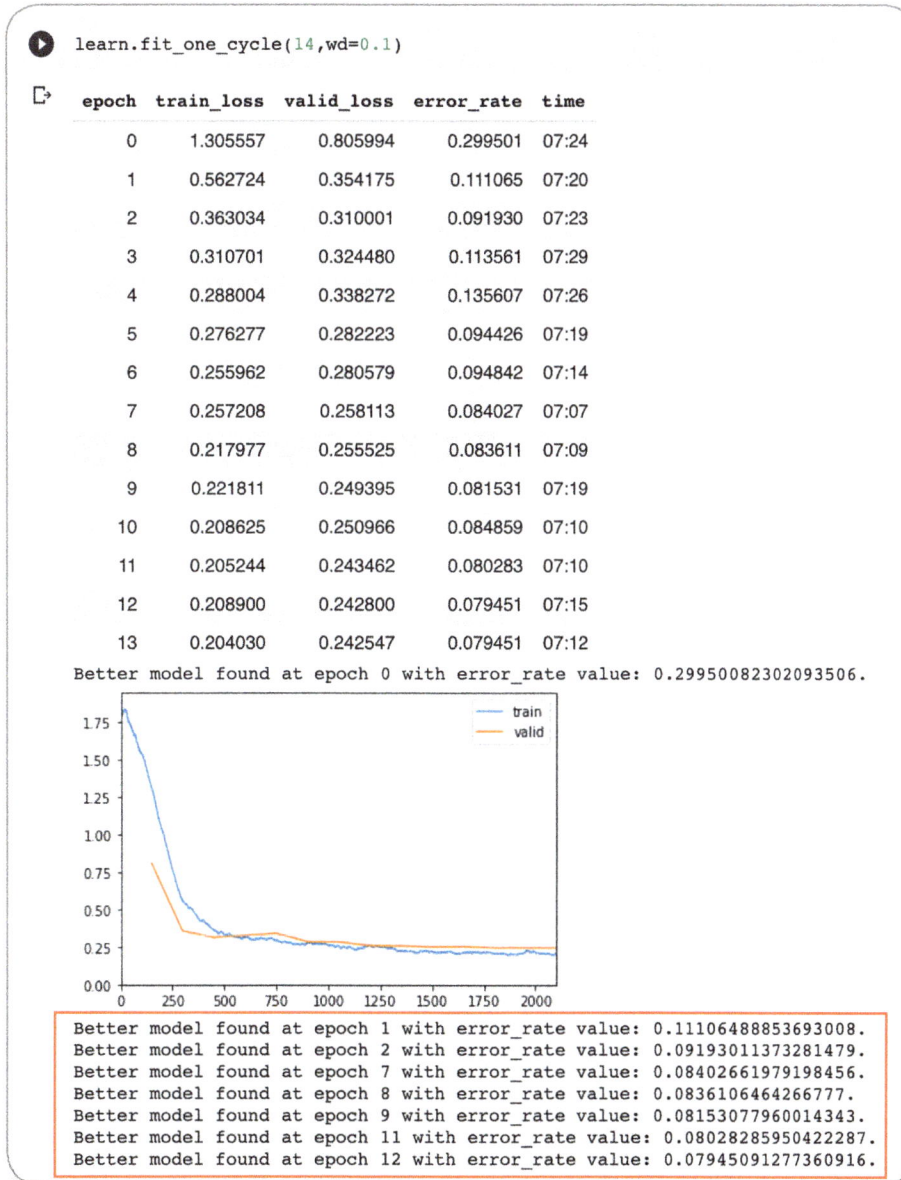

```
Better model found at epoch 1 with error_rate value: 0.11106488853693008.
Better model found at epoch 2 with error_rate value: 0.09193011373281479.
Better model found at epoch 7 with error_rate value: 0.08402661979198456.
Better model found at epoch 8 with error_rate value: 0.0836106464266777.
Better model found at epoch 9 with error_rate value: 0.08153077960014343.
Better model found at epoch 11 with error_rate value: 0.08028285950422287.
Better model found at epoch 12 with error_rate value: 0.07945091277360916.
```

STEP 37

Unfreeze the last two layer groups of the model.

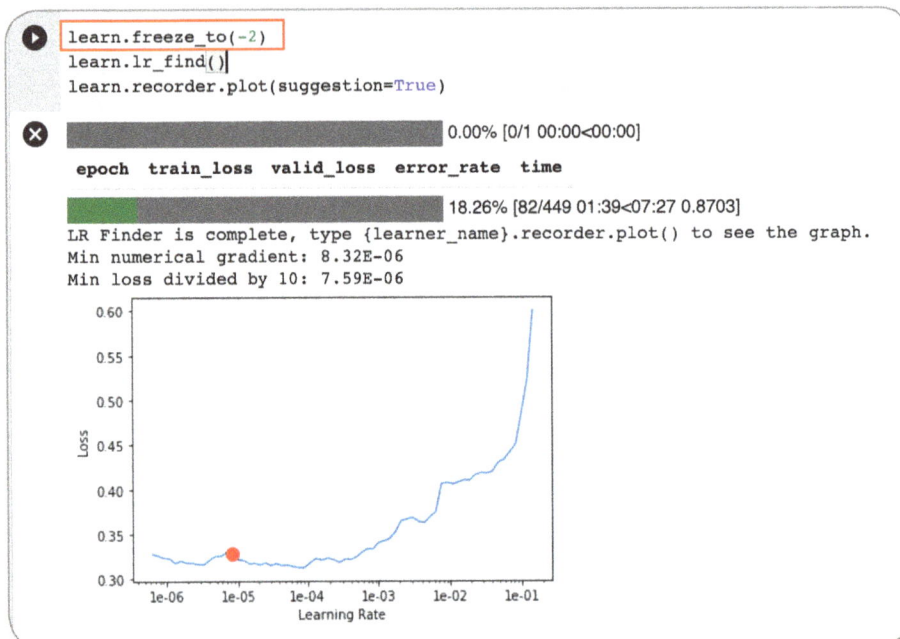

Find the best learning rate. The **learning rate** specifies the degree of change of the parameters. The parameters are adjusted based on the gradient to decrease the loss function. A **cyclical learning rate** approach eliminates the need to experimentally find the best values and schedule for the global learning rates. Instead of monotonously decreasing the learning rate, this method lets the learning rate cyclically vary between reasonable boundary values. Training with cyclical learning rates instead of fixed values achieves improved classification accuracy without the need to fine-tune and iterate.

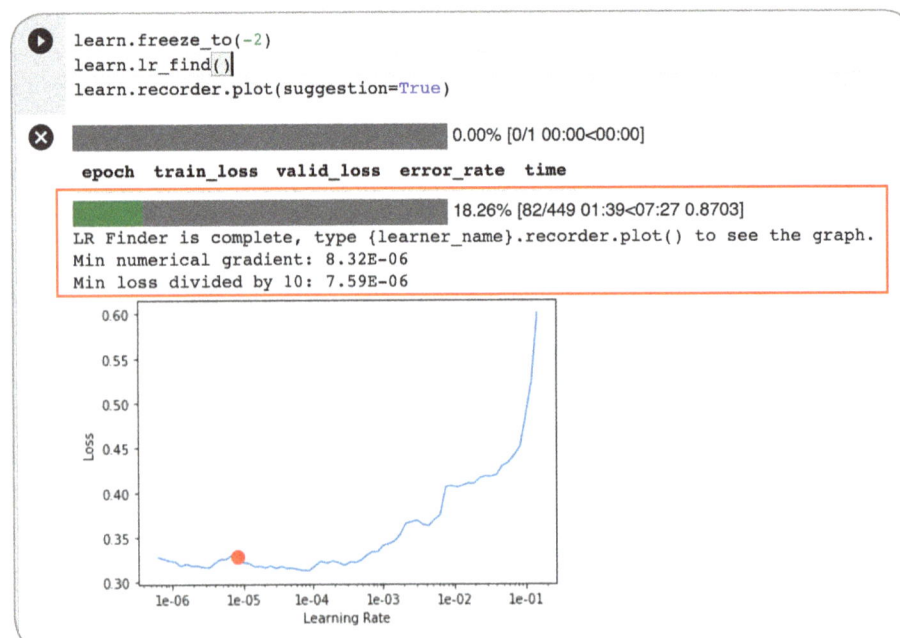

Plot the best learning rate.

```
learn.freeze_to(-2)
learn.lr_find()
learn.recorder.plot(suggestion=True)
```

0.00% [0/1 00:00<00:00]

epoch	train_loss	valid_loss	error_rate	time

18.26% [82/449 01:39<07:27 0.8703]

```
LR Finder is complete, type {learner_name}.recorder.plot() to see the graph.
Min numerical gradient: 8.32E-06
Min loss divided by 10: 7.59E-06
```

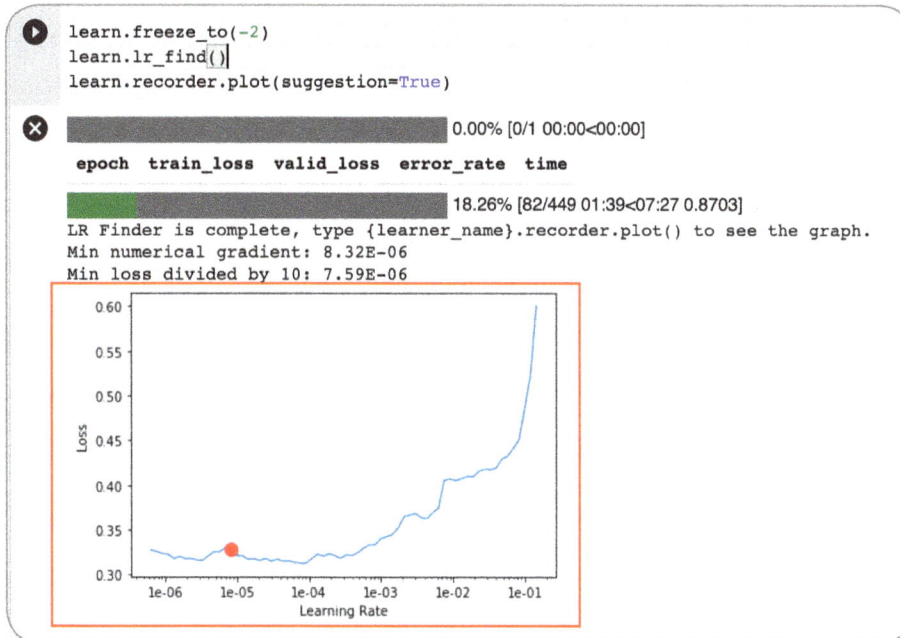

Take note of the range of learning rate before the loss starts to rise.

```
learn.freeze_to(-2)
learn.lr_find()
learn.recorder.plot(suggestion=True)
```

0.00% [0/1 00:00<00:00]

epoch	train_loss	valid_loss	error_rate	time

18.26% [82/449 01:39<07:27 0.8703]

```
LR Finder is complete, type {learner_name}.recorder.plot() to see the graph.
Min numerical gradient: 8.32E-06
Min loss divided by 10: 7.59E-06
```

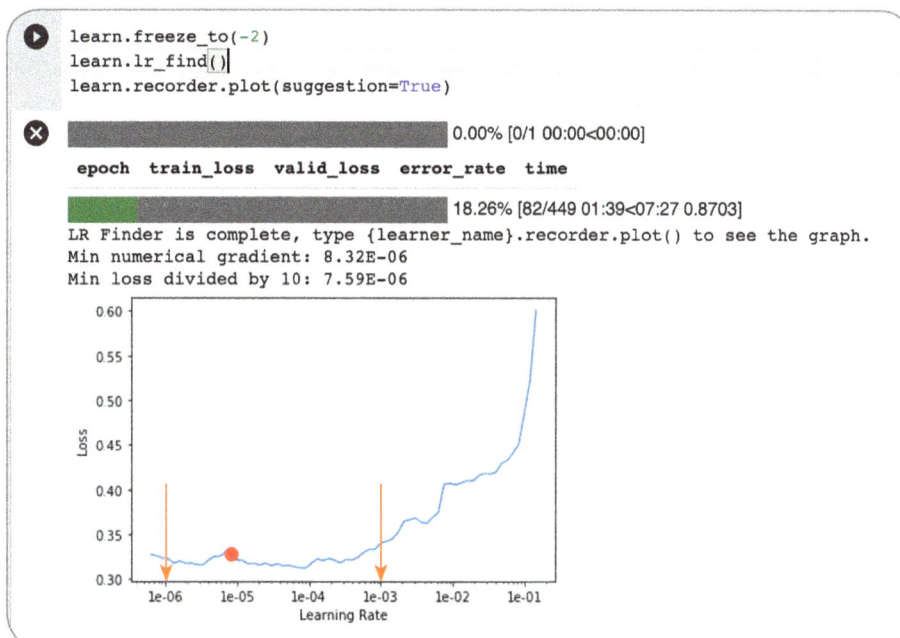

STEP 38

Unfreeze the last two layer groups.

```
learn.freeze_to(-2)
learn.fit_one_cycle(6,max_lr=slice(1e-6, 1e-3),wd=0.1)
```

epoch	train_loss	valid_loss	error_rate	time
0	0.410242	0.498959	0.153333	00:39
1	0.418009	0.522044	0.173333	00:39
2	0.430769	0.475751	0.166667	00:40
3	0.417897	0.493684	0.168333	00:40
4	0.393658	0.455786	0.153333	00:40
5	0.378205	0.455251	0.153333	00:40

Better model found at epoch 0 with error_rate value: 0.15333333611488342.

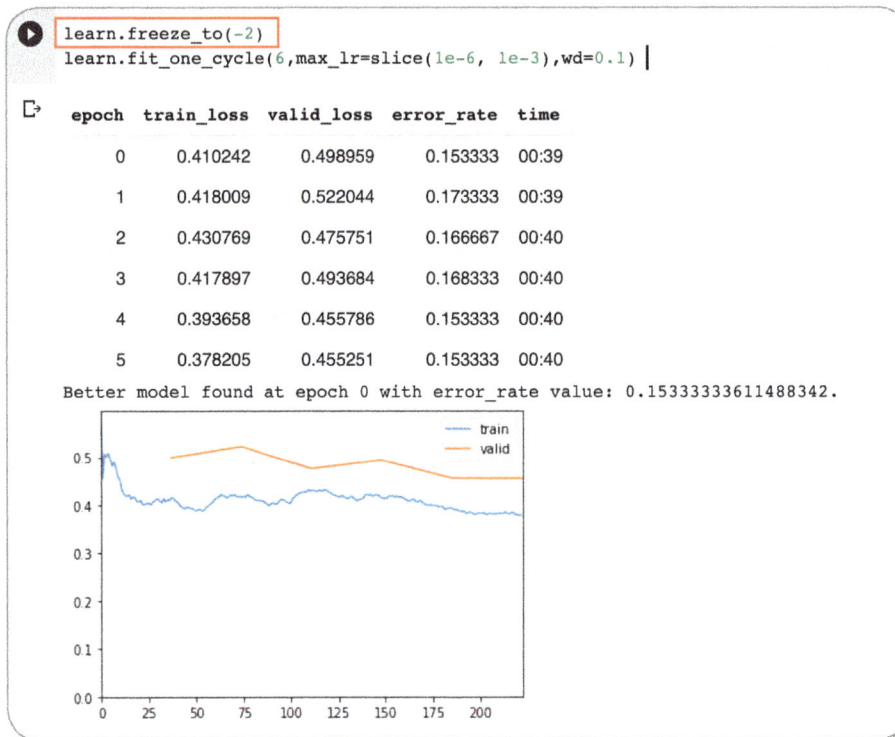

Train for six more epochs.

```
learn.freeze_to(-2)
learn.fit_one_cycle(6,max_lr=slice(1e-6, 1e-3),wd=0.1)
```

epoch	train_loss	valid_loss	error_rate	time
0	0.410242	0.498959	0.153333	00:39
1	0.418009	0.522044	0.173333	00:39
2	0.430769	0.475751	0.166667	00:40
3	0.417897	0.493684	0.168333	00:40
4	0.393658	0.455786	0.153333	00:40
5	0.378205	0.455251	0.153333	00:40

Better model found at epoch 0 with error_rate value: 0.15333333611488342.

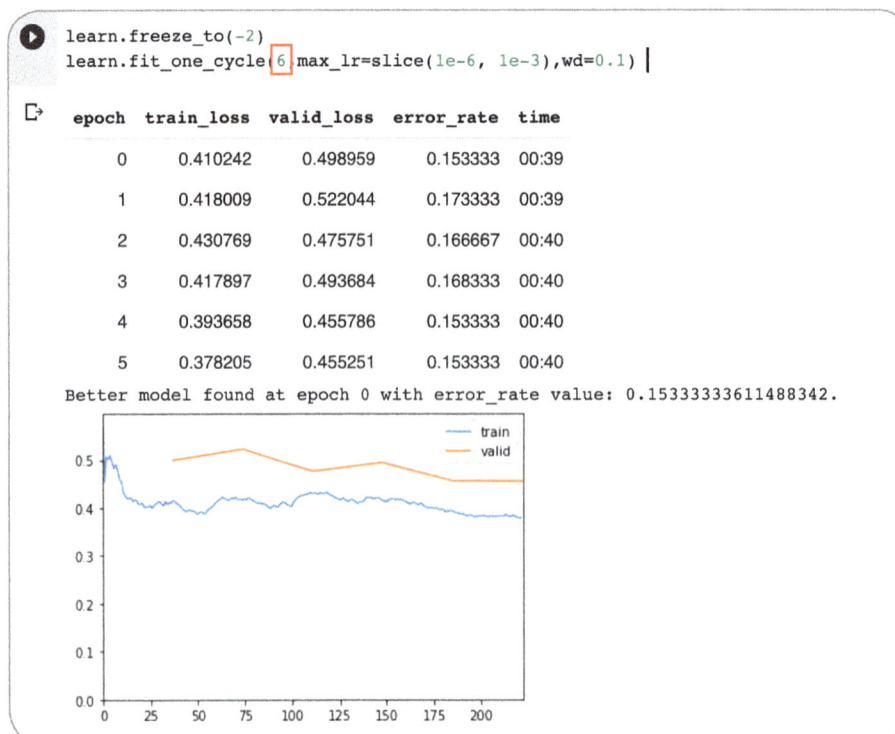

Specify the learning rate range generated from the previous graph.

```
learn.freeze_to(-2)
learn.fit_one_cycle(6,max_lr=slice(1e-6, 1e-3),wd=0.1)
```

epoch	train_loss	valid_loss	error_rate	time
0	0.410242	0.498959	0.153333	00:39
1	0.418009	0.522044	0.173333	00:39
2	0.430769	0.475751	0.166667	00:40
3	0.417897	0.493684	0.168333	00:40
4	0.393658	0.455786	0.153333	00:40
5	0.378205	0.455251	0.153333	00:40

```
Better model found at epoch 0 with error_rate value: 0.15333333611488342.
```

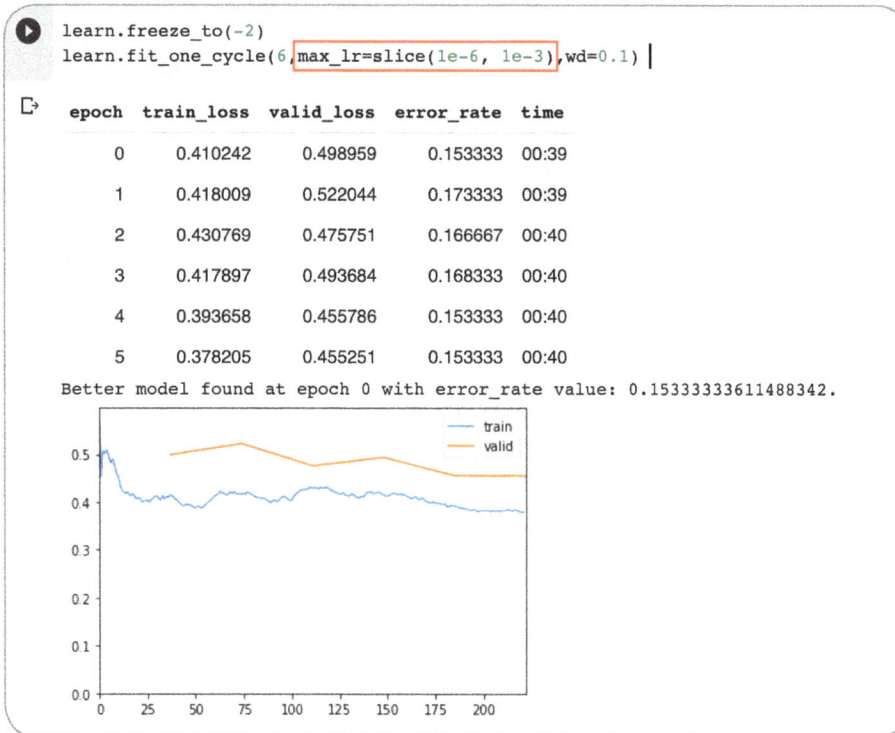

STEP 39

Define the interpretation methods for classification models. Generate a confusion matrix and visualization of the images with inconsistencies. *A **confusion matrix or error matrix** can validate and enhance the performance of the machine learning classification-related tasks by comparing the number of correct and incorrect predicted images and employing a particular loss function to minimize imbalanced prediction losses.*

```
interp = ClassificationInterpretation.from_learner(learn)

losses,idxs = interp.top_losses()

len(data.valid_ds)==len(losses)==len(idxs)
```
```
True
```

Extract the top losses and the corresponding image ID.

```
interp = ClassificationInterpretation.from_learner(learn)

losses,idxs = interp.top_losses()

len(data.valid_ds)==len(losses)==len(idxs)
```
```
True
```

Check if the validation dataset, losses, and image IDs (idx) are of the same number.

```
interp = ClassificationInterpretation.from_learner(learn)

losses,idxs = interp.top_losses()

len(data.valid_ds)==len(losses)==len(idxs)

True
```

STEP 40

Plot the satellite images with highest training losses or with inconsistencies.

Take note of any inconsistences between the input data and the output class (e.g., low-quality day images, high percentage of cloud cover, or illogical nightlight category).

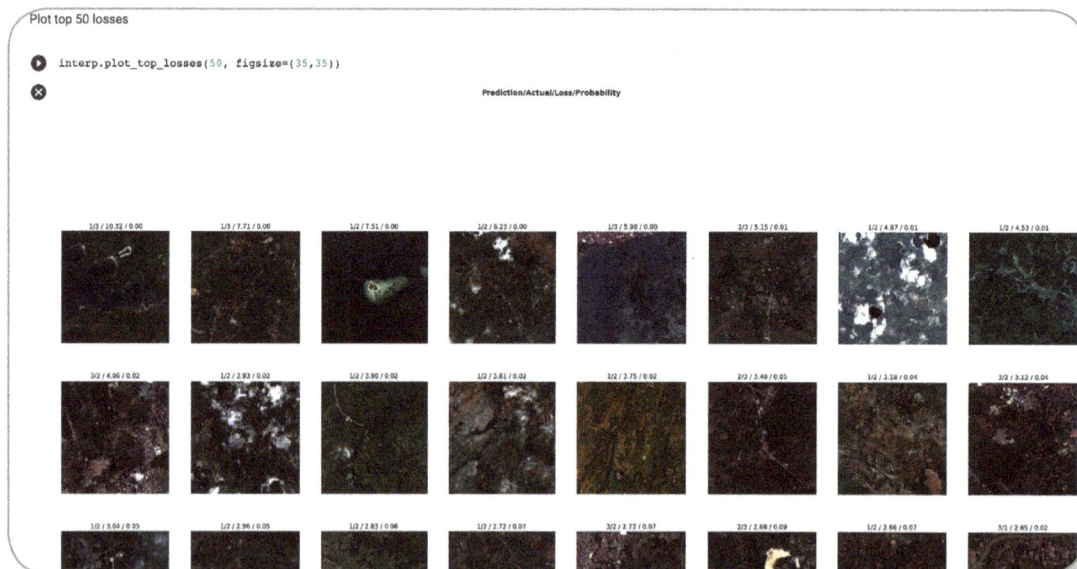

```
Plot top 50 losses

interp.plot_top_losses(50, figsize=(35,35))
```

STEP 41

Print the corresponding image filenames of satellite images with high loss function values. In this example, the filenames of the top 50 satellite images with high loss function values are displayed.

```
##to display filenames##
losses,idxs = interp.top_losses(50)
for p in data.valid_ds.x.items[idxs]:
    print(p)
```

```
/content/data/CNN_IMGB_PHI_2015_ST_384_JPG_3840CNN_DIMG_PHI_2015_ST_384_3840_010484.jpg
/content/data/CNN_IMGB_PHI_2015_ST_384_JPG_3840CNN_DIMG_PHI_2015_ST_384_3840_002647.jpg
/content/data/CNN_IMGB_PHI_2015_ST_384_JPG_3840CNN_DIMG_PHI_2015_ST_384_3840_003036.jpg
/content/data/CNN_IMGB_PHI_2015_ST_384_JPG_3840CNN_DIMG_PHI_2015_ST_384_3840_000653.jpg
/content/data/CNN_IMGB_PHI_2015_ST_384_JPG_3840CNN_DIMG_PHI_2015_ST_384_3840_002251.jpg
/content/data/CNN_IMGB_PHI_2015_ST_384_JPG_3840CNN_DIMG_PHI_2015_ST_384_3840_009706.jpg
/content/data/CNN_IMGB_PHI_2015_ST_384_JPG_3840CNN_DIMG_PHI_2015_ST_384_3840_000648.jpg
/content/data/CNN_IMGB_PHI_2015_ST_384_JPG_3840CNN_DIMG_PHI_2015_ST_384_3840_011642.jpg
/content/data/CNN_IMGB_PHI_2015_ST_384_JPG_3840CNN_DIMG_PHI_2015_ST_384_3840_011722.jpg
/content/data/CNN_IMGB_PHI_2015_ST_384_JPG_3840CNN_DIMG_PHI_2015_ST_384_3840_002665.jpg
/content/data/CNN_IMGB_PHI_2015_ST_384_JPG_3840CNN_DIMG_PHI_2015_ST_384_3840_008599.jpg
/content/data/CNN_IMGB_PHI_2015_ST_384_JPG_3840CNN_DIMG_PHI_2015_ST_384_3840_008808.jpg
/content/data/CNN_IMGB_PHI_2015_ST_384_JPG_3840CNN_DIMG_PHI_2015_ST_384_3840_001420.jpg
/content/data/CNN_IMGB_PHI_2015_ST_384_JPG_3840CNN_DIMG_PHI_2015_ST_384_3840_011988.jpg
/content/data/CNN_IMGB_PHI_2015_ST_384_JPG_3840CNN_DIMG_PHI_2015_ST_384_3840_002490.jpg
/content/data/CNN_IMGB_PHI_2015_ST_384_JPG_3840CNN_DIMG_PHI_2015_ST_384_3840_010928.jpg
/content/data/CNN_IMGB_PHI_2015_ST_384_JPG_3840CNN_DIMG_PHI_2015_ST_384_3840_002749.jpg
/content/data/CNN_IMGB_PHI_2015_ST_384_JPG_3840CNN_DIMG_PHI_2015_ST_384_3840_012435.jpg
/content/data/CNN_IMGB_PHI_2015_ST_384_JPG_3840CNN_DIMG_PHI_2015_ST_384_3840_012966.jpg
/content/data/CNN_IMGB_PHI_2015_ST_384_JPG_3840CNN_DIMG_PHI_2015_ST_384_3840_009504.jpg
/content/data/CNN_IMGB_PHI_2015_ST_384_JPG_3840CNN_DIMG_PHI_2015_ST_384_3840_003067.jpg
/content/data/CNN_IMGB_PHI_2015_ST_384_JPG_3840CNN_DIMG_PHI_2015_ST_384_3840_007332.jpg
/content/data/CNN_IMGB_PHI_2015_ST_384_JPG_3840CNN_DIMG_PHI_2015_ST_384_3840_005578.jpg
/content/data/CNN_IMGB_PHI_2015_ST_384_JPG_3840CNN_DIMG_PHI_2015_ST_384_3840_003382.jpg
/content/data/CNN_IMGB_PHI_2015_ST_384_JPG_3840CNN_DIMG_PHI_2015_ST_384_3840_011383.jpg
/content/data/CNN_IMGB_PHI_2015_ST_384_JPG_3840CNN_DIMG_PHI_2015_ST_384_3840_007798.jpg
/content/data/CNN_IMGB_PHI_2015_ST_384_JPG_3840CNN_DIMG_PHI_2015_ST_384_3840_008592.jpg
/content/data/CNN_IMGB_PHI_2015_ST_384_JPG_3840CNN_DIMG_PHI_2015_ST_384_3840_001820.jpg
```

Plot the confusion matrix to further validate the training process. On the vertical axis, list the known classes for each image, in this case the nighttime light intensity. On the horizontal axis, list the predictions from the CNN. Each cell contains the number of images for true and predictive classes. Correctly predicted images lie on the main diagonal and every other image lies on the off diagonal. As the classes are ordinal (class1 < class2 < class3: low < middle < high intensity), it holds that the farther away the values are from the main diagonal, the larger the error. (Note: Other projects might have non-ordered classes like "cats versus dogs", hence, the distance to the diagonal is irrelevant.) These values should be as small as possible to avoid "big mistakes" during prediction.

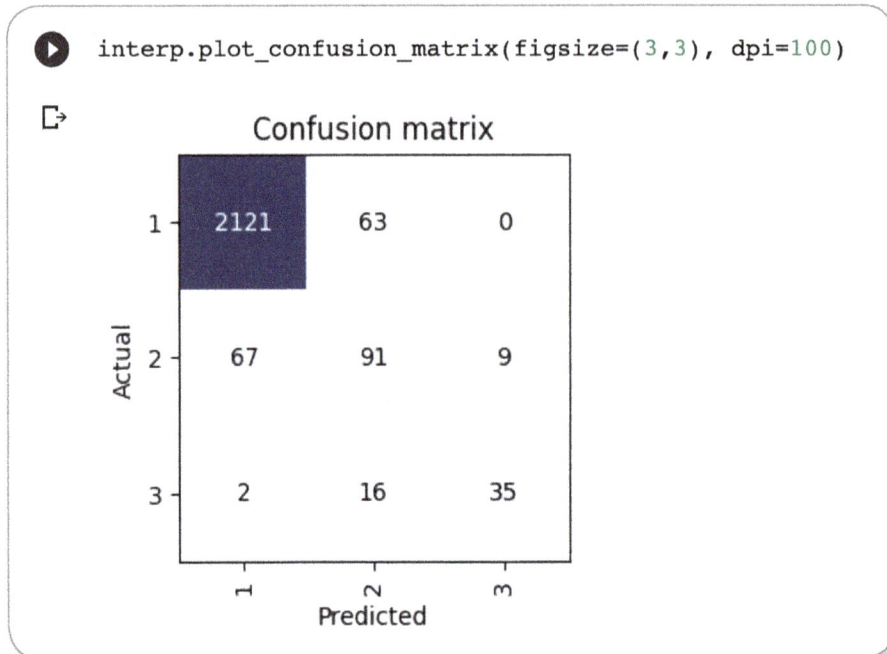

```
interp.plot_confusion_matrix(figsize=(3,3), dpi=100)
```

Confusion matrix

	Predicted 1	Predicted 2	Predicted 3
Actual 1	2121	63	0
Actual 2	67	91	9
Actual 3	2	16	35

STEP 42

Present the list of largest non-diagonal entries of the confusion matrix. *This refers to actual, predicted, and number of occurrences.*

```
interp.most_confused(min_val=2)
[(2, 1, 91), (1, 2, 54), (2, 3, 16), (3, 2, 12), (3, 1, 4), (1, 3, 2)]
```

One cell of confusion matrix

Number of occurrences

Predicted

Actual

Box 1. Steps in Adjusting Weights of Cross Entropy Loss Function

1. Start with equal weights of [1.0, 1.0, 1.0].

2. Unfreeze the last layer and train for 14 epochs.

3. Plot and check the confusion matrix results.

Try to achieve a relatively balanced matrix.

- In Figure A, the equal weights created a confusion matrix with more predictions below the diagonal.

- In Figure B, the extreme low and extreme high 1st and 3rd weights are tried, respectively. This resulted in a higher prediction above the diagonal.

- In Figure C, a relatively balanced matrix is achieved.

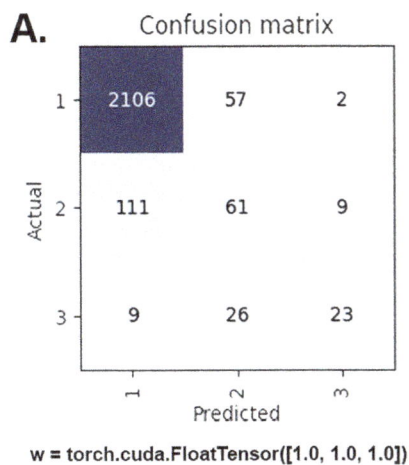

A. Confusion matrix

w = torch.cuda.FloatTensor([1.0, 1.0, 1.0])

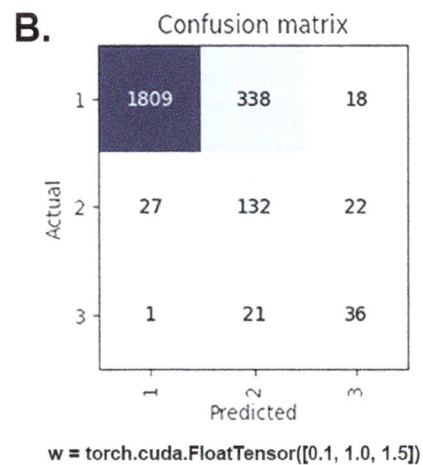

B. Confusion matrix

w = torch.cuda.FloatTensor([0.1, 1.0, 1.5])

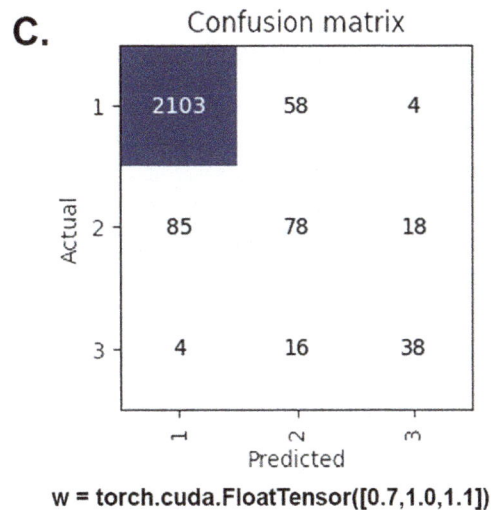

C. Confusion matrix

w = torch.cuda.FloatTensor([0.7,1.0,1.1])

STEP 43

Define the function for removing "anomalous" images from the training and validation dataframe.

If there is a significant number of inconsistencies between input data and output class (e.g., low-quality daytime images, too cloudy images), remove these instances from the original dataframe. *Since the ImageDataBunch contains labels and image file path, remove these images using their filenames as subset parameters for the dataframe.*

```python
#Function for dropping images from dataframe
def drop_image(loss_index):
    filename_list = [os.path.basename(data.valid_ds.x.items[i]) for i in loss_index]
    # view data to be dropped
    print(df.loc[df['filename'].isin(filename_list)])
    # get filename and index of rows to be dropped from dataframe
    df_filenames = df['filename'].loc[df['filename'].isin(filename_list)]
    index_names = df.loc[df['filename'].isin(filename_list)].index
    df.drop(index_names, inplace = True)
    print("Image filenames dropped from dataframe:")
    for f in df_filenames:
        print(f)
```

STEP 44

Print the indexes of the images belonging to the top 50 highest losses. Based on the image plot of the 50 top losses, select the "anomalous" images to be removed. *Note that this step is optional.*

```python
print("Row index of top 50 losses:")
print(idxs)
```

```
Row index of top 50 losses:
tensor([1165, 2050,  288, 1032, 2226,  871, 2365, 1227, 1020, 2252,   21,   38,
        1374, 2367, 1461,  229,  603, 1581, 1868, 2157,  926, 1453, 1959, 2071,
          11, 1061, 1256, 1177,  492, 2371, 2211, 1822,  424, 1837,  244,  907,
         320, 2145,  481, 1485, 1170, 2161, 1810, 2146,   98,   20,  628, 2063,
        1955, 1343])
```

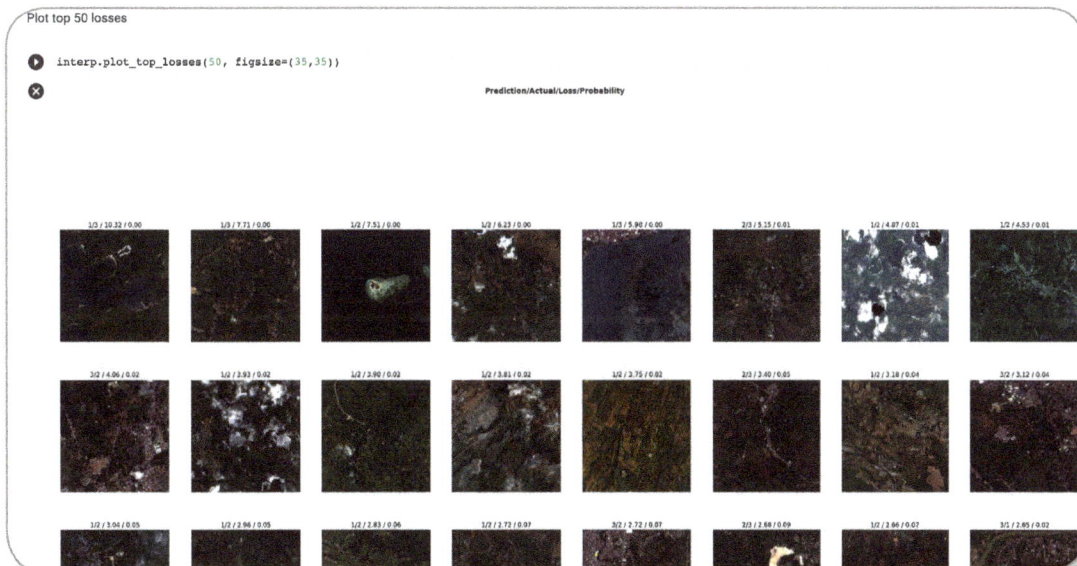

```
Plot top 50 losses
```

```
interp.plot_top_losses(50, figsize=(35,35))
```

Prediction/Actual/Loss/Probability

STEP 45

Assign the selection as a list data type to the variable **selected_index**. Call the **drop_image()** function to pass the index of images to be dropped.

```
[28] print("Row index of top 50 losses:")
     print(idxs)

  Row index of top 50 losses:
     tensor([1165, 2050,  288, 1032, 2226,  871, 2365, 1227, 1020, 2252,   21,   38,
             1374, 2367, 1461,  229,  603, 1581, 1868, 2157,  926, 1453, 1959, 2071,
               11, 1061, 1256, 1177,  492, 2371, 2211, 1822,  424, 1837,  244,  907,
              320, 2145,  481, 1485, 1170, 2161, 1810, 2146,   98,   20,  628, 2063,
             1955, 1343])

  selected_index=[2050,1032,244,2146,98,20,628,2063]

  drop_image(selected_index)
```

STEP 46

Execute the code cell.

The function will print out the data associated with the images.

```
selected_index=[2050,1032,244,2146,98,20,628,2063]

drop_image(selected_index)

      Unnamed: 0         x          y  ...  POV_2015  Highly_Urbanized  Is.City
id                                     ...
10740       2399  122.915742   7.872098  ...     36.45             False    False
8359        4639  124.546720   9.760598  ...     30.08             False    False
8132        4854  123.044503   9.932280  ...     52.82             False    False
7241        5652  124.031674  10.790689  ...     29.19             False    False
2083       10130  121.456446  16.456191  ...     10.81             False    False
2000       10208  121.799810  16.542032  ...     14.71             False    False
1649       10545  121.113082  16.842475  ...     32.35             False    False
1593       10594  120.855560  16.885395  ...     24.53             False    False

[8 rows x 20 columns]
Image filenames dropped from dataframe:
CNN_DIMG_PHI_2015_ST_384_3840_010740.jpg
CNN_DIMG_PHI_2015_ST_384_3840_008359.jpg
CNN_DIMG_PHI_2015_ST_384_3840_008132.jpg
CNN_DIMG_PHI_2015_ST_384_3840_007241.jpg
CNN_DIMG_PHI_2015_ST_384_3840_002083.jpg
CNN_DIMG_PHI_2015_ST_384_3840_002000.jpg
CNN_DIMG_PHI_2015_ST_384_3840_001649.jpg
CNN_DIMG_PHI_2015_ST_384_3840_001593.jpg
```

Confirm the filenames of the images.

```
selected_index=[2050,1032,244,2146,98,20,628,2063]

drop_image(selected_index)

      Unnamed: 0         x          y  ...  POV_2015  Highly_Urbanized  Is.City
id                                     ...
10740       2399  122.915742   7.872098  ...     36.45             False    False
8359        4639  124.546720   9.760598  ...     30.08             False    False
8132        4854  123.044503   9.932280  ...     52.82             False    False
7241        5652  124.031674  10.790689  ...     29.19             False    False
2083       10130  121.456446  16.456191  ...     10.81             False    False
2000       10208  121.799810  16.542032  ...     14.71             False    False
1649       10545  121.113082  16.842475  ...     32.35             False    False
1593       10594  120.855560  16.885395  ...     24.53             False    False

[8 rows x 20 columns]
Image filenames dropped from dataframe:
CNN_DIMG_PHI_2015_ST_384_3840_010740.jpg
CNN_DIMG_PHI_2015_ST_384_3840_008359.jpg
CNN_DIMG_PHI_2015_ST_384_3840_008132.jpg
CNN_DIMG_PHI_2015_ST_384_3840_007241.jpg
CNN_DIMG_PHI_2015_ST_384_3840_002083.jpg
CNN_DIMG_PHI_2015_ST_384_3840_002000.jpg
CNN_DIMG_PHI_2015_ST_384_3840_001649.jpg
CNN_DIMG_PHI_2015_ST_384_3840_001593.jpg
```

STEP 47

After removing the "anomalous" data, repeat steps to generate a ImageDataBunch, creating learner and training for 14 epochs with the dataset.

STEP 48

Unfreeze the last three layer groups of the model. Find the best learning rate and plot it.

```
learn.freeze_to(-3)
learn.lr_find()
learn.recorder.plot(suggestion=True)
```

0.00% [0/1 00:00<00:00]

epoch	train_loss	valid_loss	error_rate	time

53.33% [80/150 02:48<02:27 0.5969]

LR Finder is complete, type {learner_name}.recorder.plot() to see the graph.
Min numerical gradient: 2.75E-06
Min loss divided by 10: 3.31E-07

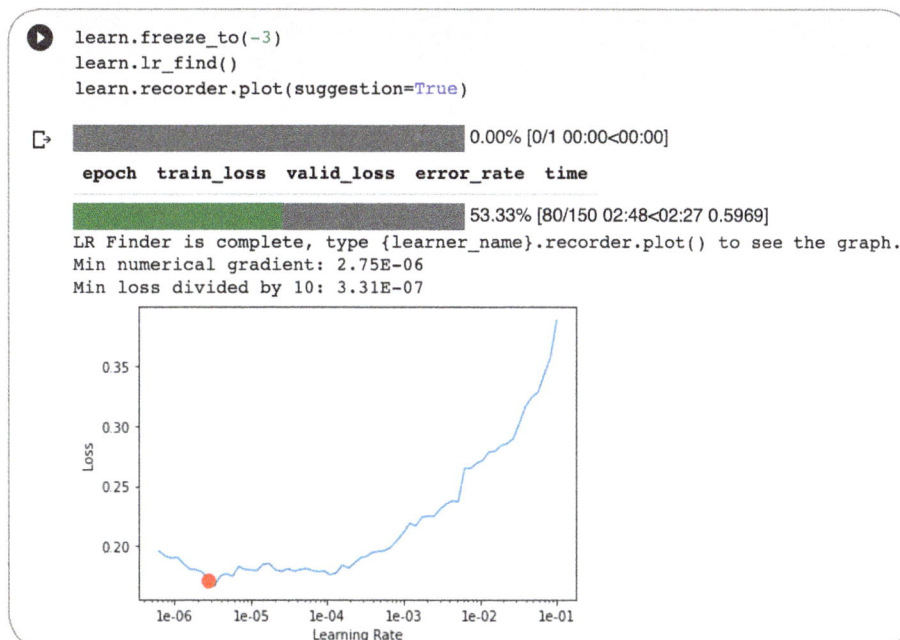

STEP 49

Unfreeze the last three layer groups and train for six more epochs using the learning rate range determined from the previous graph.

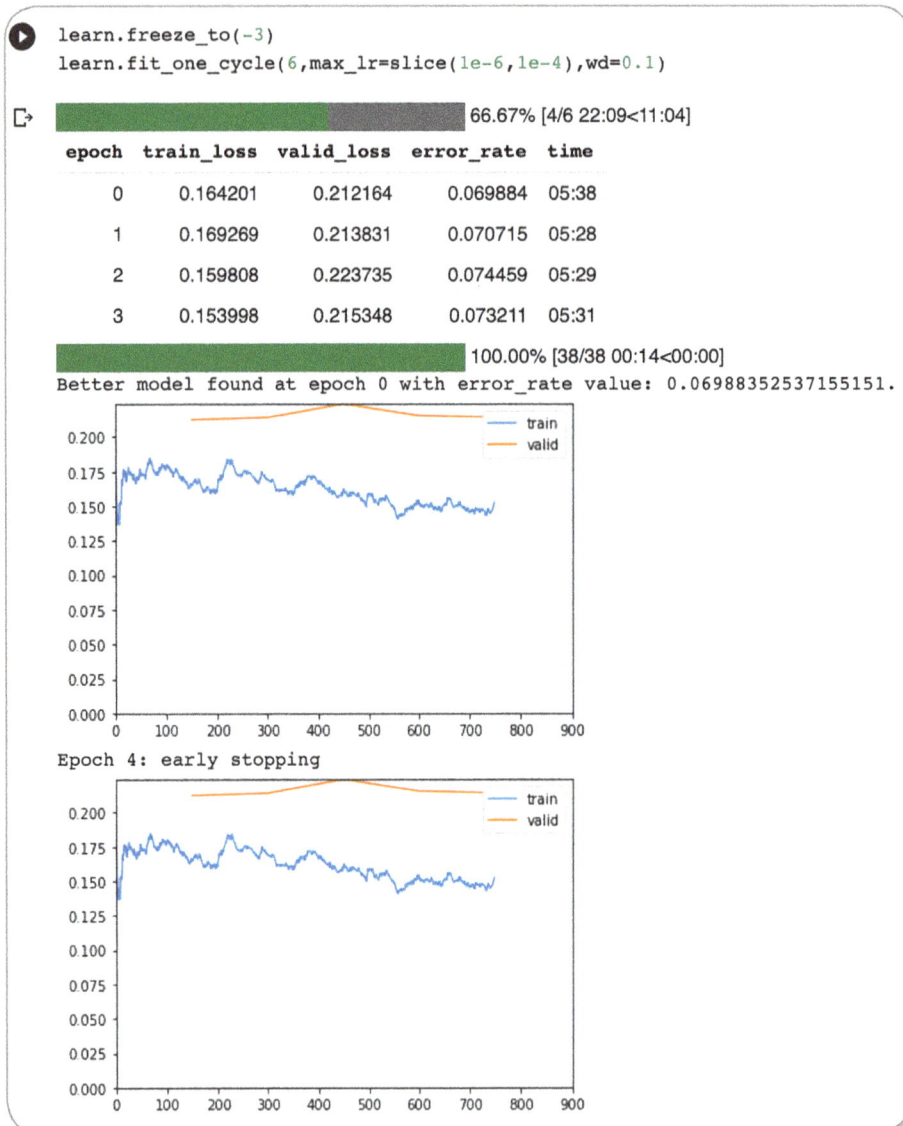

```
learn.freeze_to(-3)
learn.fit_one_cycle(6,max_lr=slice(1e-6,1e-4),wd=0.1)
```

66.67% [4/6 22:09<11:04]

epoch	train_loss	valid_loss	error_rate	time
0	0.164201	0.212164	0.069884	05:38
1	0.169269	0.213831	0.070715	05:28
2	0.159808	0.223735	0.074459	05:29
3	0.153998	0.215348	0.073211	05:31

100.00% [38/38 00:14<00:00]

Better model found at epoch 0 with error_rate value: 0.06988352537155151.

Epoch 4: early stopping

In this scenario, note that the model did not improve after three cycles, thus the training was terminated.

STEP 50

Unfreeze all layer groups and determine the best learning rate again.

```
learn.unfreeze()
learn.lr_find()
learn.recorder.plot(suggestion=True)
```
```
                                              0.00% [0/1 00:00<00:00]
epoch   train_loss   valid_loss   error_rate   time
                                              54.67% [82/150 03:53<03:13 0.5699]
LR Finder is complete, type {learner_name}.recorder.plot() to see the graph.
Min numerical gradient: 1.91E-06
Min loss divided by 10: 1.00E-06
```

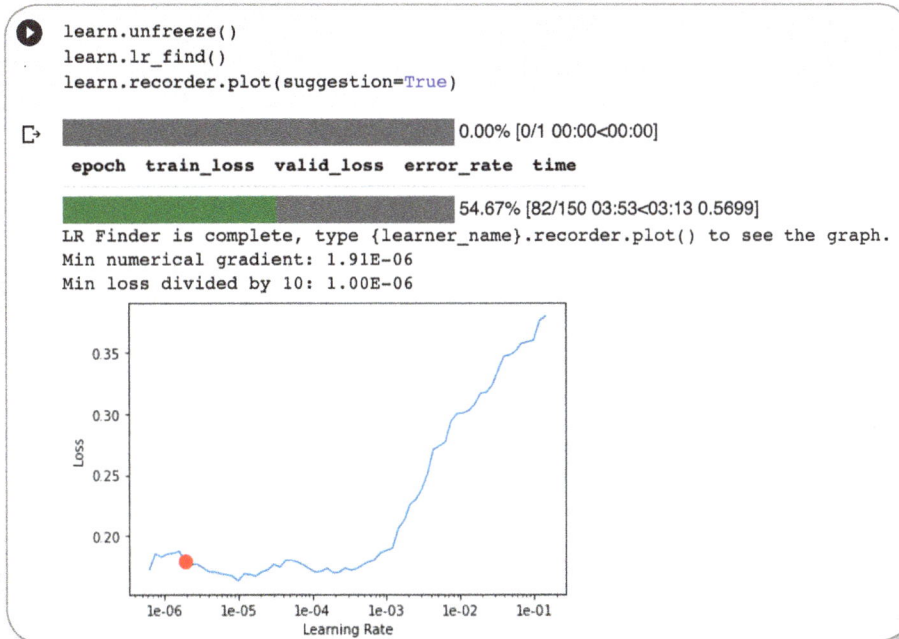

STEP 51

Unfreeze all the layers and train for three more epochs using the learning rate from the previous graph. *This step ensures the consistency of the whole network.*

```
learn.unfreeze()
learn.fit_one_cycle(3,max_lr=slice(1e-8,5e-6),wd=0.1)
```

epoch	train_loss	valid_loss	error_rate	time
0	0.403564	0.399175	0.141667	00:57
1	0.408957	0.400449	0.138333	00:57
2	0.409362	0.393298	0.128333	00:56

```
Better model found at epoch 0 with error_rate value: 0.14166666567325592.
```

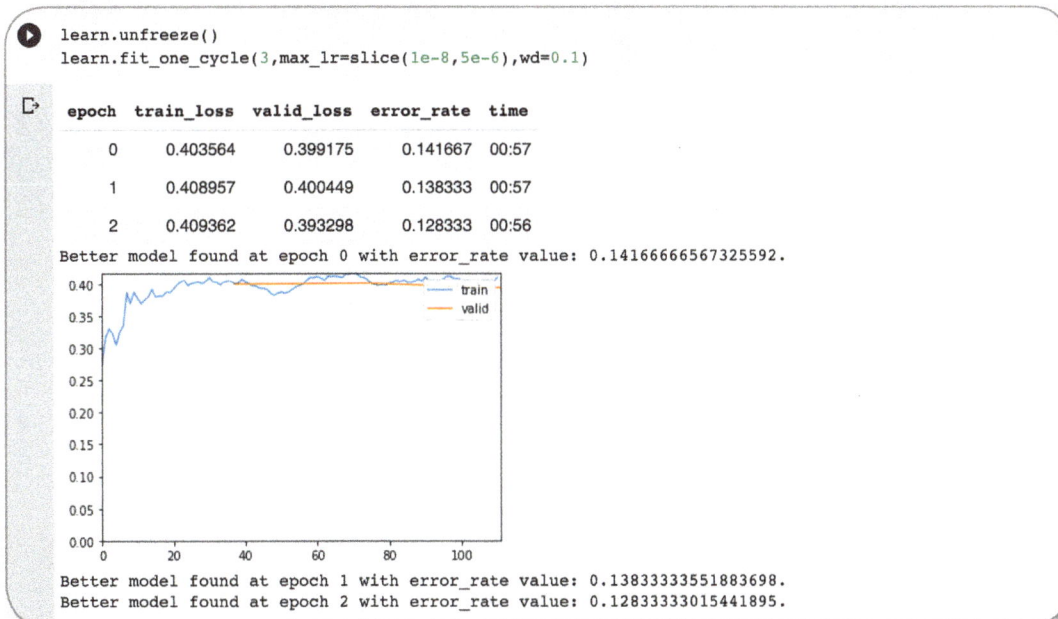

```
Better model found at epoch 1 with error_rate value: 0.13833333551883698.
Better model found at epoch 2 with error_rate value: 0.12833333015441895.
```

STEP 52

Define again the interpretation methods for classification of models. Extract the top losses and the corresponding image ID. Lastly, check if the validation dataset, losses, and image IDs (idx) are of the same length.

```
interp = ClassificationInterpretation.from_learner(learn)

losses,idxs = interp.top_losses()

len(data.valid_ds)==len(losses)==len(idxs)
```
```
True
```

STEP 53

View the images again showing the top losses from the model's prediction, actual value, training loss, and probability.

```
interp.plot_top_losses(50, figsize=(35,35))
```

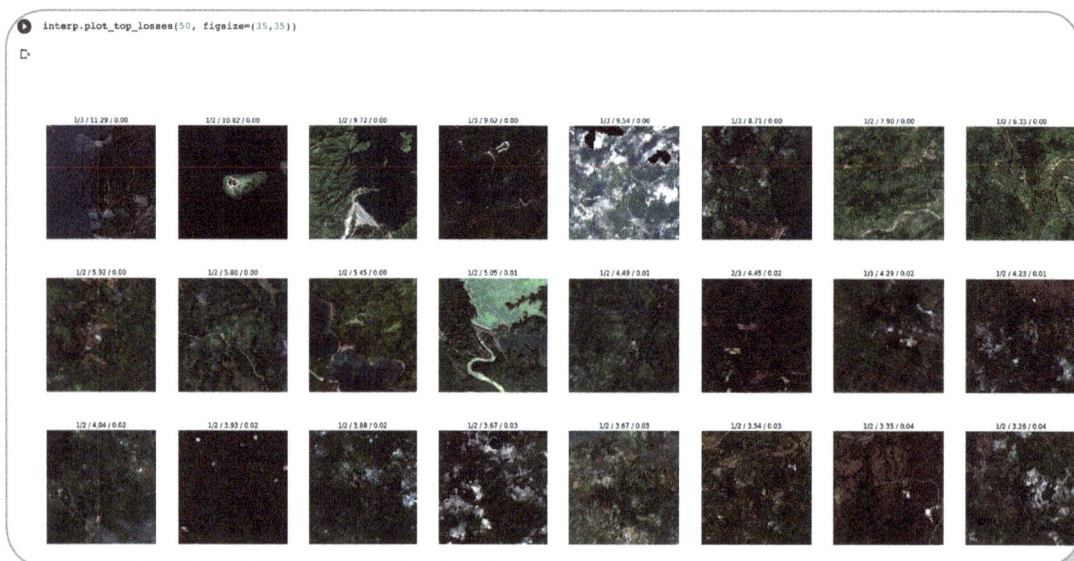

STEP 54

Generate the confusion matrix to validate the training process.

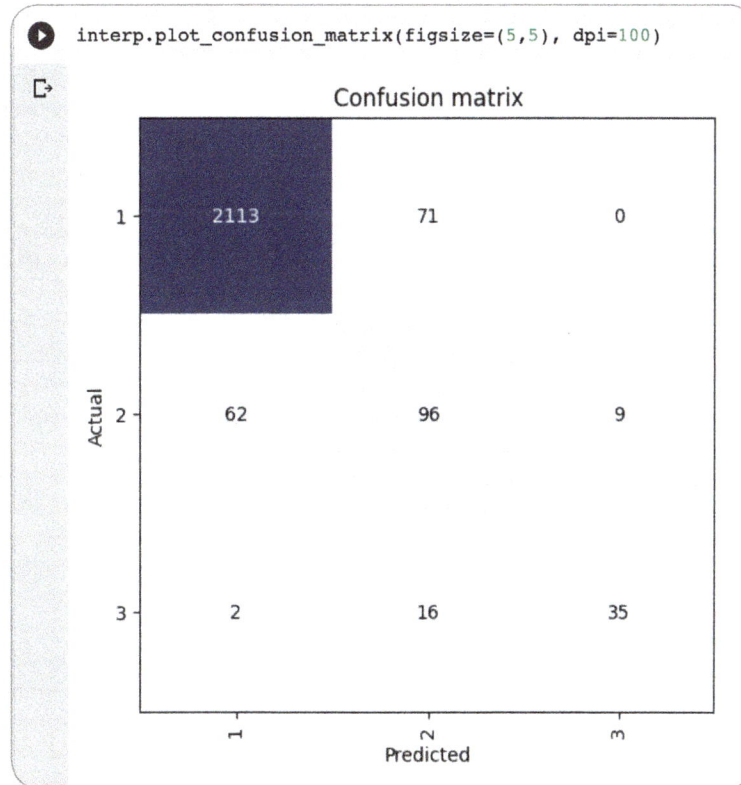

```
interp.plot_confusion_matrix(figsize=(5,5), dpi=100)
```

Confusion matrix

	Predicted 1	Predicted 2	Predicted 3
Actual 1	2113	71	0
Actual 2	62	96	9
Actual 3	2	16	35

STEP 55

Save the learner object and model weights in Google Drive.

```
learn.export(file=learner_filename) #train and export learner
learn.save(modelWt_filename)

# define folders
save_path = "/content/gdrive/MyDrive/models/"

os.makedirs(save_path, exist_ok=True)

shutil.copy(os.path.join('/content/',learner_filename), save_path)
shutil.copy(os.path.join("/content/models/",modelWt_filename+'.pth'), save_path)
```

STEP 56

Test the trained CNN model using the 10% test dataset.

4. CNN Model Testing and Evaluation

Fastai framework does not provide direct methods for holdout testing and evaluation. Therefore we will use a little trick and feed fastai's validation dataset with our holdout test set and perform standard validation as during CNN training. Interpreter will then display confusion matrix and top losses belonging to test set.

```python
#memory garbage collection: take object that stores a lot of mem -> avoid restarting notebook:
learn=None
gc.collect()
```

```python
bs_val = 64       # batch size, change to 16 if you run out of memory even after clicking Kernel->Restart

#create Databunch
df = pd.read_csv(test_dataset) #load test dataset with holdout images(10%) and labels(classes)
df_val = df[['bin_GMM','filename']]

#create ImageList with folder of all images and dataset of filenames and corresponding classes of our test set
img_list = ImageList.from_df(df=df_val, path='/content/data/', cols='filename', folder=imagery_folder, suffix='')
img_list_split = img_list.split_none() #all data on train set, not splitting to train and validation sets like in databunch during standard training of CNN
list_label = img_list_split.label_from_df(0)
list_label.valid = list_label.train # trick: load training dataset as validation dataset
print(list_label) #check what is inside train, validation and test set at the moment

list_label.transform(tfms=None,size=int(img_res)) # optional transforms
data = list_label.databunch(bs=bs_val);
data.normalize(imagenet_stats)

learn = cnn_learner(data, models.resnet34, metrics = error_rate)
learn = load_learner('/content/', file=learner_filename) #learner object must be used for inference purposes
learn.load(modelWt_filename) #load weights of the model, which we want to test
learn.data.valid_dl = data.valid_dl #override with inference data with transfroms and other..
learn.loss_func = torch.nn.CrossEntropyLoss()
```

First, clear the virtual memory.

```python
#memory garbage collection: take object that stores a lot of mem -> avoid restarting notebook:
learn=None
gc.collect()
```

```
118570
```

STEP 57

Prepare the ImageDataBunch for the test dataset and load the trained CNN model and learner objects.

```
bs_val = 64        # batch size, change to 16 if you run out of memory even after clicking Kernel->Restart

#create Databunch
df = pd.read_csv(test_dataset) #load test dataset with holdout images(10%) and labels(classes)
df_val = df[['bin_GMM','filename']]

#create ImageList with folder of all images and dataset of filenames and corresponding classes of our test set
img_list = ImageList.from_df(df=df_val, path='/content/data/', cols='filename', folder=imagery_folder, suffix='')
img_list_split = img_list.split_none() #all data on train set, not splitting to train and validation sets like in databunch
list_label = img_list_split.label_from_df(0)
list_label.valid = list_label.train # trick: load training dataset as validation dataset
print(list_label) #check what is inside train, validation and test set at the moment

list_label.transform(tfms=None,size=int(img_res)) # optional transforms
data = list_label.databunch(bs=bs_val);
data.normalize(imagenet_stats)

learn = cnn_learner(data, models.resnet34, metrics = error_rate)
learn = load_learner('/content/', file=learner_filename) #learner object must be used for inference purposes
learn.load(modelWt_filename) #load weights of the model, which we want to test
learn.data.valid_dl = data.valid_dl #override with inference data with transfroms and other..
learn.loss_func = torch.nn.CrossEntropyLoss()
learn.metrics #check which metrics is set up

interp = ClassificationInterpretation.from_learner(learn,ds_type=DatasetType.Valid) #perform interpretation for validation
interp.plot_confusion_matrix() #matrix representing predictions on holdout test set
```

STEP 58

The code cell will output information regarding the data split and confusion matrix.

```
LabelLists;

Train: LabelList (1323 items)
x: ImageList
Image (3, 384, 384),Image (3, 384, 384),Image (3, 384, 384),Image (3, 384, 384),Image (3, 384, 384)
y: CategoryList
1,1,1,1,1
Path: /content/data;

Valid: LabelList (1323 items)
x: ImageList
Image (3, 384, 384),Image (3, 384, 384),Image (3, 384, 384),Image (3, 384, 384),Image (3, 384, 384)
y: CategoryList
1,1,1,1,1
Path: /content/data;

Test: None
```

Confusion matrix

STEP 59

Plot the top 25 images with high losses and overlay a heatmap to indicate areas in the images that the CNN considers as important for actual nightlight class.

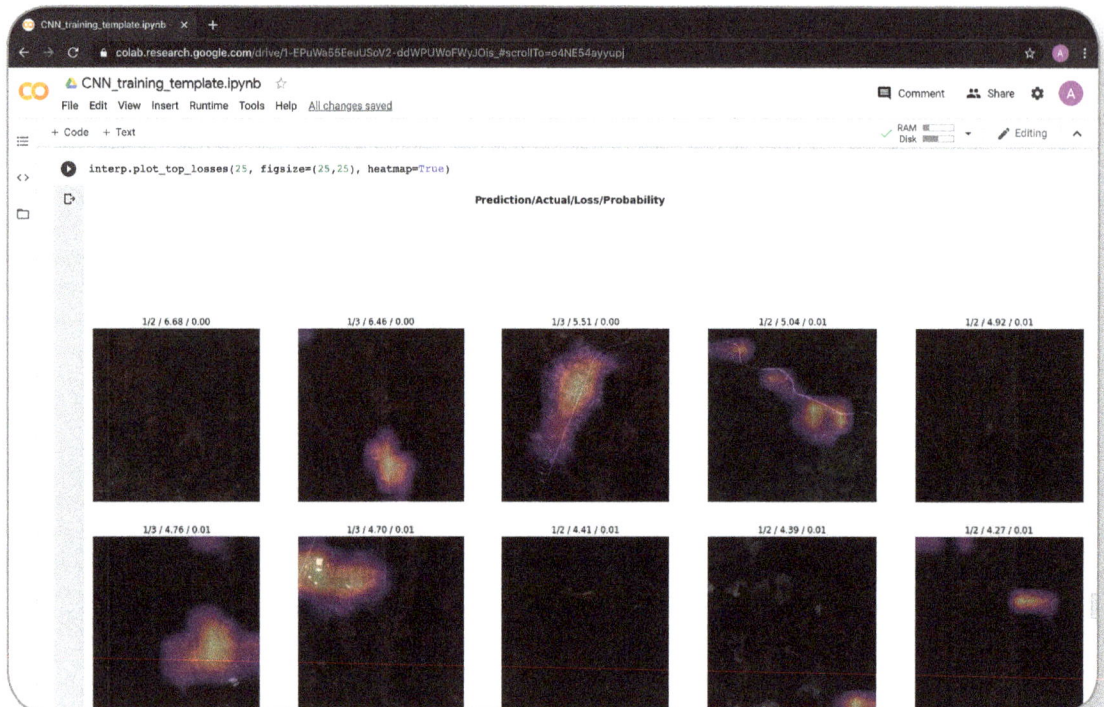

STEP 60

Then define the ***evaluate_model_from_interp()*** function to evaluate the overall accuracy of the model.

```python
tfms = None
data_test = data

def evaluate_model_from_interp(interp, data):
    # perform evaluation of the model to take a look at predictions vs. labels and compute accuracy
    print(f'Interp has {len(interp.y_true)} ground truth labels: {interp.y_true}')
    print(f'Interp yielded {len(interp.preds)} raw predictions. First two raw predictions are: {interp.preds[:2]}')
    print(f'The problem had {len(data.classes)} classes: {data.classes}') # data.c is just len(data.classes)
    print('')
    print(f'Pred -> GroundTruth = PredLabel -> GroundTruthLabel')

    ok_pred = 0

    for idx, raw_p in enumerate(interp.preds):
        pred = np.argmax(raw_p)
        if idx < 10: #display first 10 predictions and corresponding real labels
            print(f'{pred} -> {interp.y_true[idx]} = {data.classes[pred]} -> {data.valid_ds.y[idx]}')
        if pred == interp.y_true[idx]: #count correct predictions
            ok_pred += 1

    acc = ok_pred / len(interp.y_true) #calculate accuracy by correct predictions divided by total predictions
    print(f'Overall accuracy of the model: {acc:0.5f}')

#call function
evaluate_model_from_interp(interp, data_test)
```

```
Interp has 1323 ground truth labels: tensor([0, 0, 0, ..., 0, 0, 0])
Interp yielded 1323 raw predictions. First two raw predictions are: tensor([[9.6205e-01, 3.7922e-02, 3.2040e-05],
        [9.9941e-01, 5.9113e-04, 3.3564e-08]])
The problem had 3 classes: [1, 2, 3]

Pred -> GroundTruth = PredLabel -> GroundTruthLabel
0 -> 0 = 1 -> 1
0 -> 0 = 1 -> 1
0 -> 0 = 1 -> 1
0 -> 0 = 1 -> 1
0 -> 0 = 1 -> 1
0 -> 0 = 1 -> 1
0 -> 0 = 1 -> 1
0 -> 0 = 1 -> 1
0 -> 0 = 1 -> 1
0 -> 0 = 1 -> 1
Overall accuracy of the model: 0.93197
```

5 CONVOLUTIONAL NEURAL NETWORK MODEL FEATURE EXTRACTION

After training the CNN, the next step is to extract the abstract satellite image features that are correlated with the intensity of night lights. This is done by altering the model such that it generates the features from the last hidden layer as an output rather than as a regular classification category output. In this case, the feature vectors that the CNN uses to specify the intensity of night lights are extracted.

> **Data Requirements**
> - Archive file containing daytime satellite imagery (JPG)
> - CSV file containing binned luminosity values and government-published poverty estimates
> - Trained CNN model
>
> **Tools**
> - Google Colaboratory (footnote 7) (CNN_training_template.ipynb)

STEP 1

For feature extraction, open a new notebook file. Click **File**.

Then click **Upload Notebook**.

STEP 2

Click **Choose File**. Use the Jupyter Notebook file **CNN_feature_extraction.ipynb**.

Locate the file and Click **Open**.

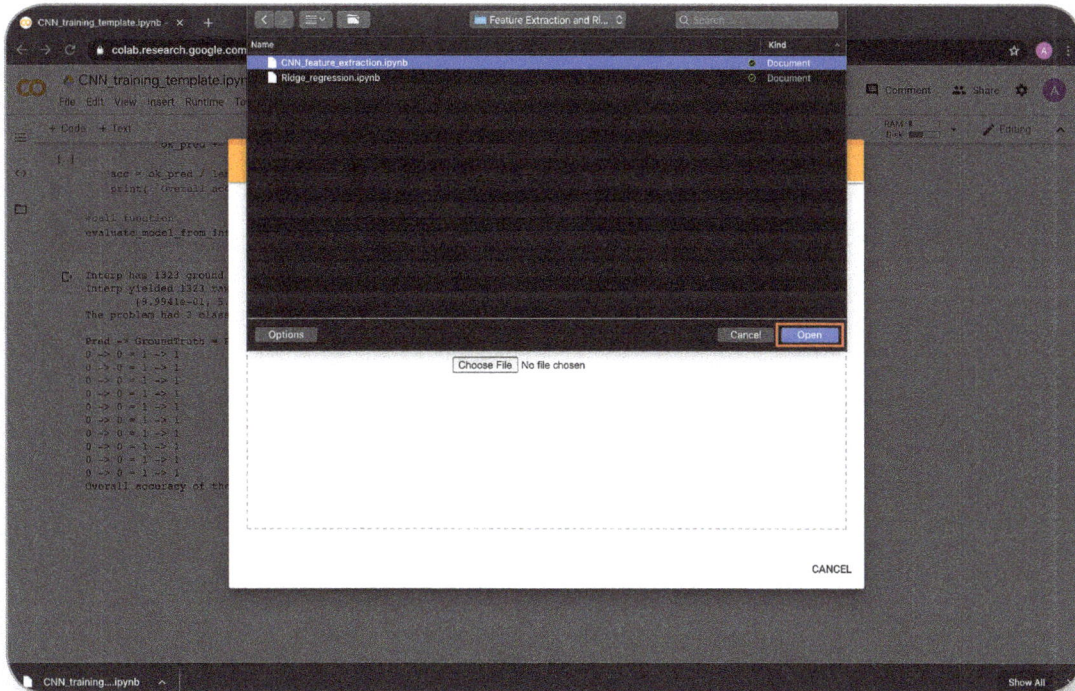

STEP 3

Setup the runtime type once the file has loaded. Click **Runtime** on the menu bar.

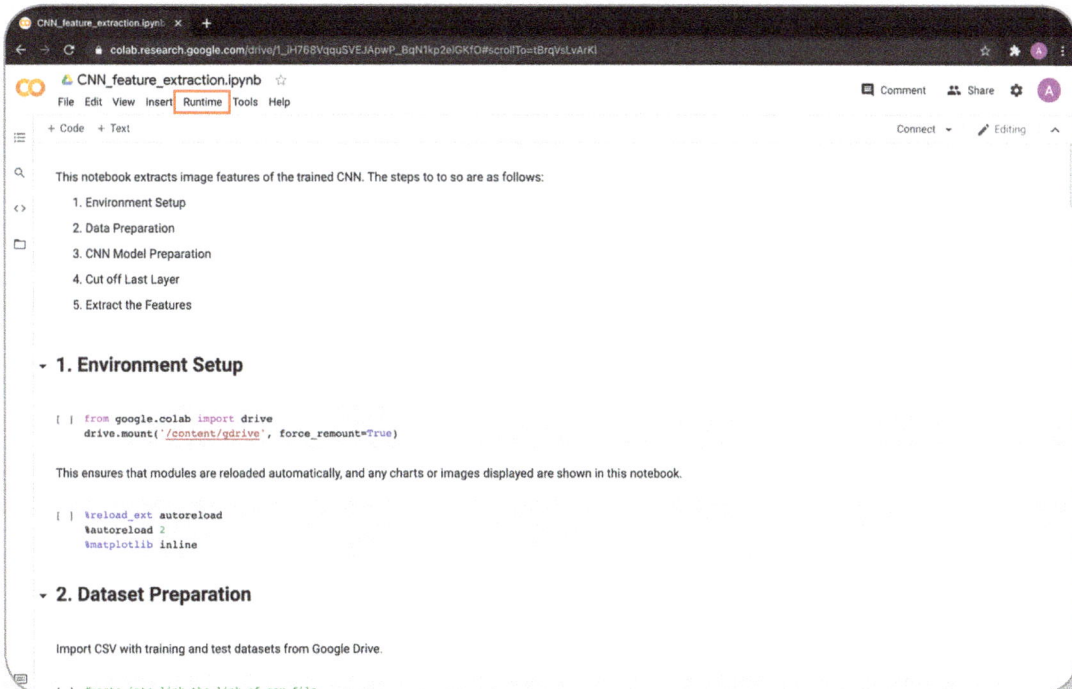

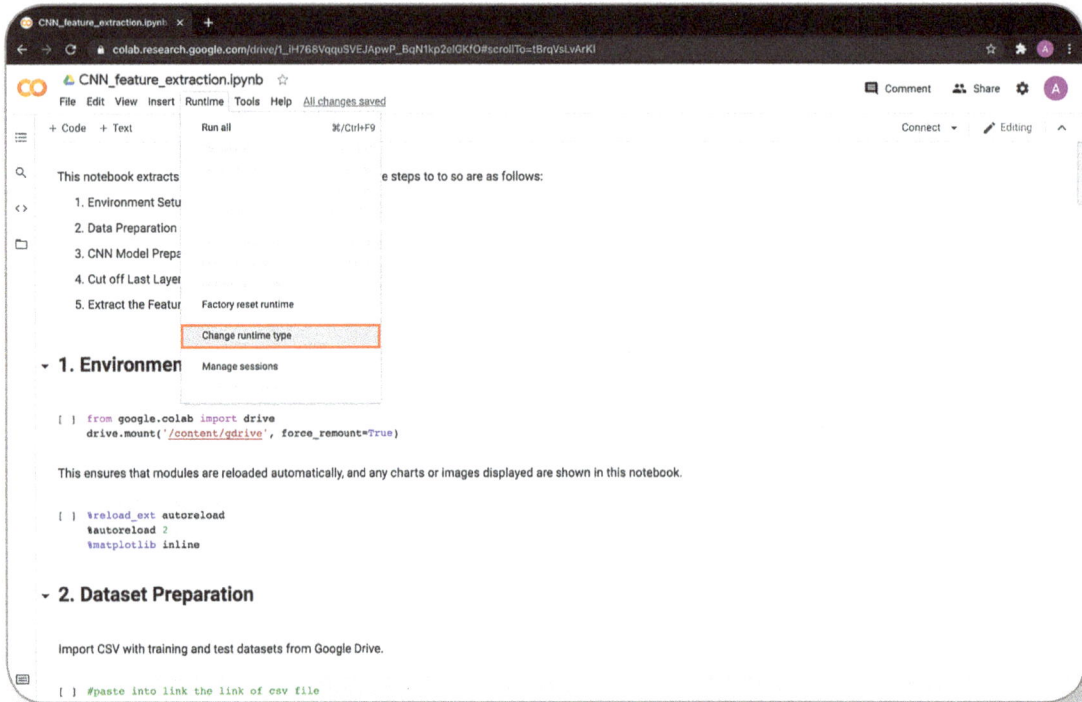

On the Notebook settings, change **Hardware accelerator** into **GPU**. Then click **Save**.

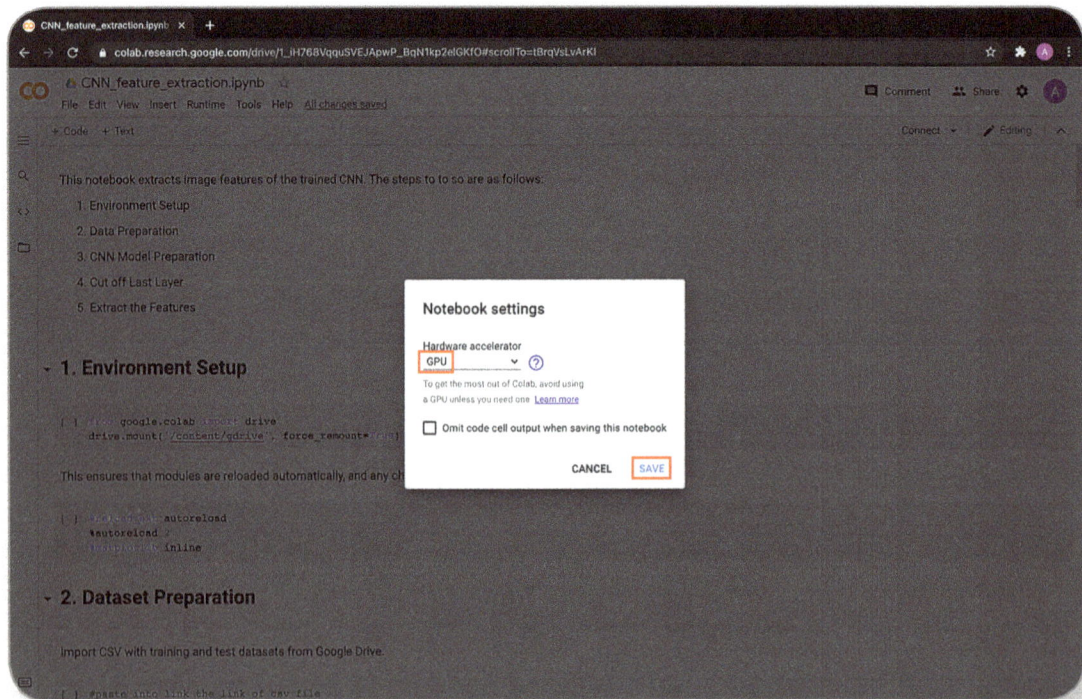

STEP 4

Click **Connect**.

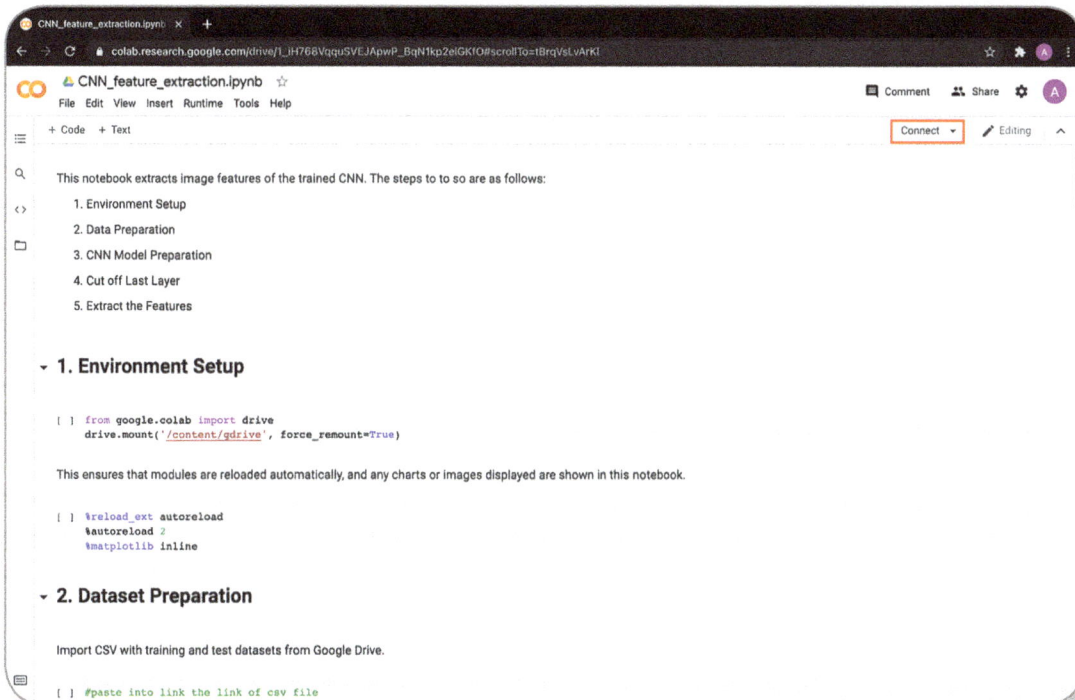

This will initialize the Colab environment.

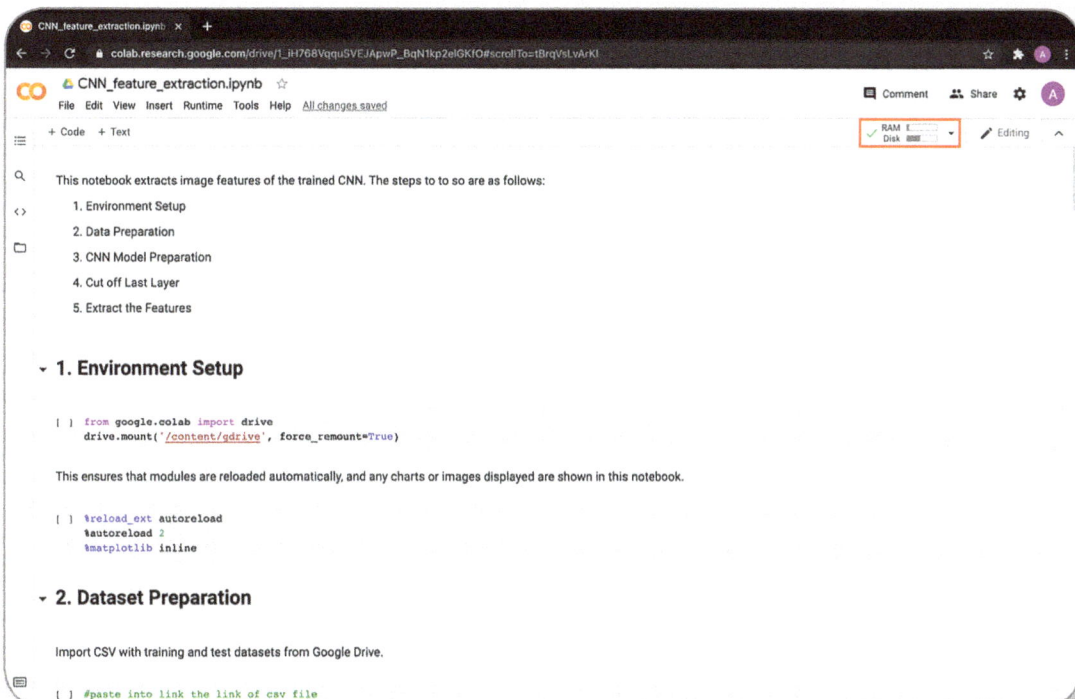

STEP 5

For environment setup, mount Google Drive (footnote 6) to Google Colab.

```
from google.colab import drive
drive.mount('/content/gdrive', force_remount=True)
```

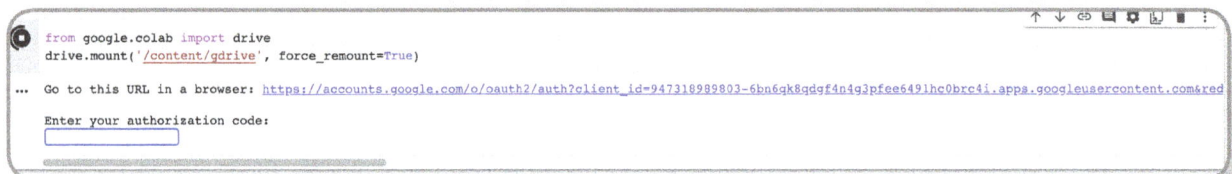

```
from google.colab import drive
drive.mount('/content/gdrive', force_remount=True)

... Go to this URL in a browser: https://accounts.google.com/o/oauth2/auth?client_id=947318989803-6bn6qk8qdgf4n4g3pfee6491hc0brc4i.apps.googleusercontent.com&red

    Enter your authorization code:
```

STEP 6

In the browser, sign in to Google account.

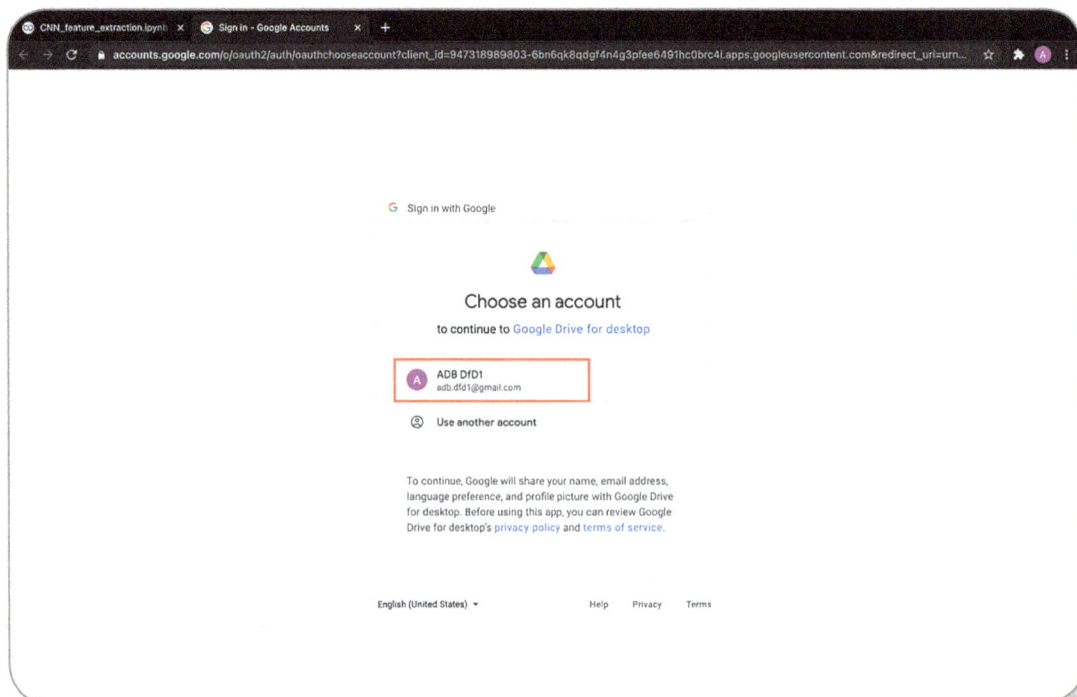

Click **Allow**.

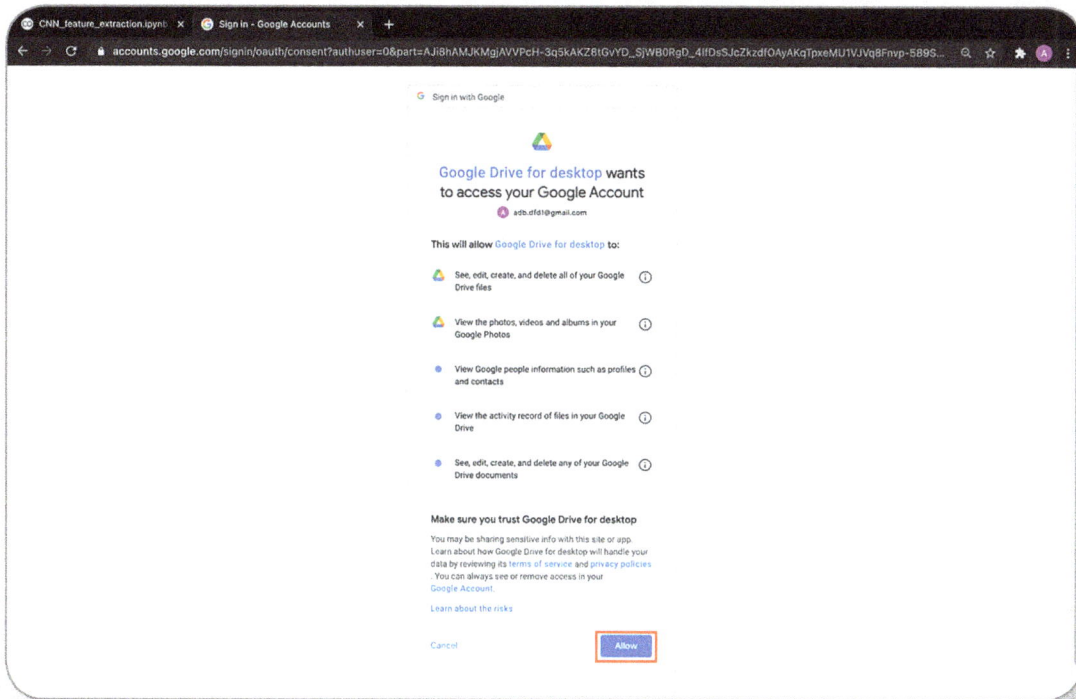

Click **Copy** icon to copy the code.

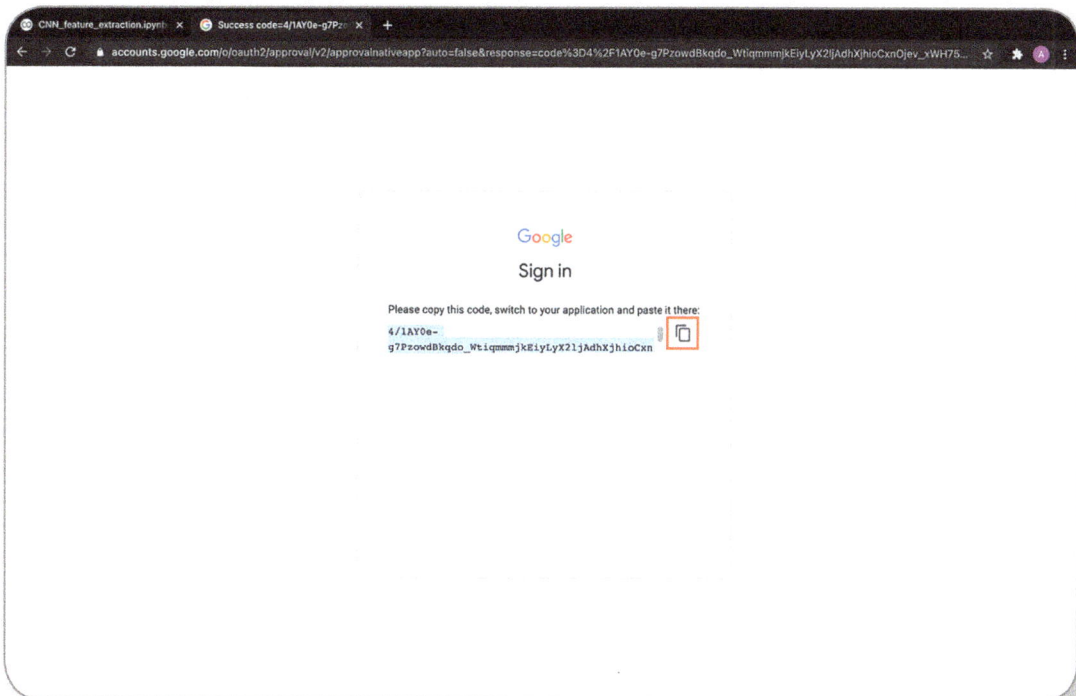

Return to the Colab browser tab. **Paste** the code in the text box. Then press **Enter**.

```
from google.colab import drive
drive.mount('/content/gdrive', force_remount=True)

...  Go to this URL in a browser: https://accounts.google.com/o/oauth2/auth?client_id=947318989803-6bn6qk8qdgf4n4g3pfee6491hc0brc4i.apps.googleusercontent.com&red

Enter your authorization code:
4/1AY0e-g7PzowdBkqdc
```

A status will show the path where Google Drive is mounted.

```
from google.colab import drive
drive.mount('/content/gdrive', force_remount=True)

Mounted at /content/gdrive
```

STEP 7

Ensure that modules are reloaded automatically and any charts or images displayed are shown in the notebook.

```
%reload_ext autoreload
%autoreload 2
%matplotlib inline
```

STEP 8

Locate the path of the training dataset's CSV file.

```
#paste into link the link of csv file
import pandas as pd
train_dataset = ''
test_dataset = train_dataset.replace('train90','test10')

df_train = pd.read_csv(train_dataset)
df_test = pd.read_csv(test_dataset)
```

STEP 9

Click Files icon ⬜ to show the **Files section**.

STEP 10

Click **gdrive** from the list of folders and expand the file directory tree to find the CSV file location.

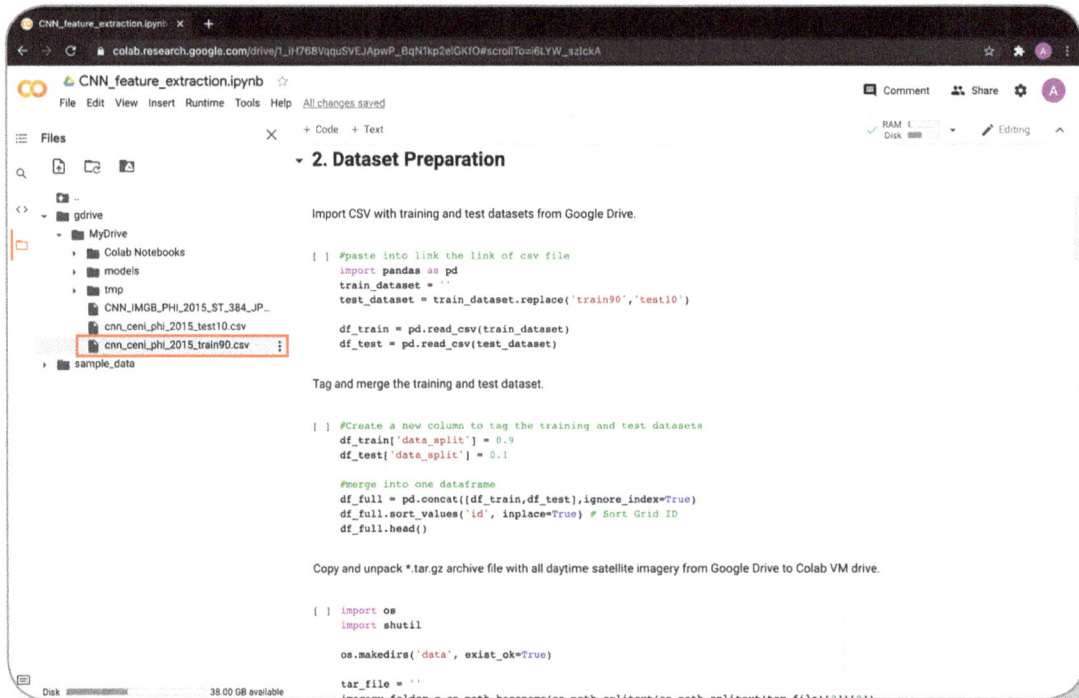

STEP 11

Click the vertical ellipsis to show more file options.

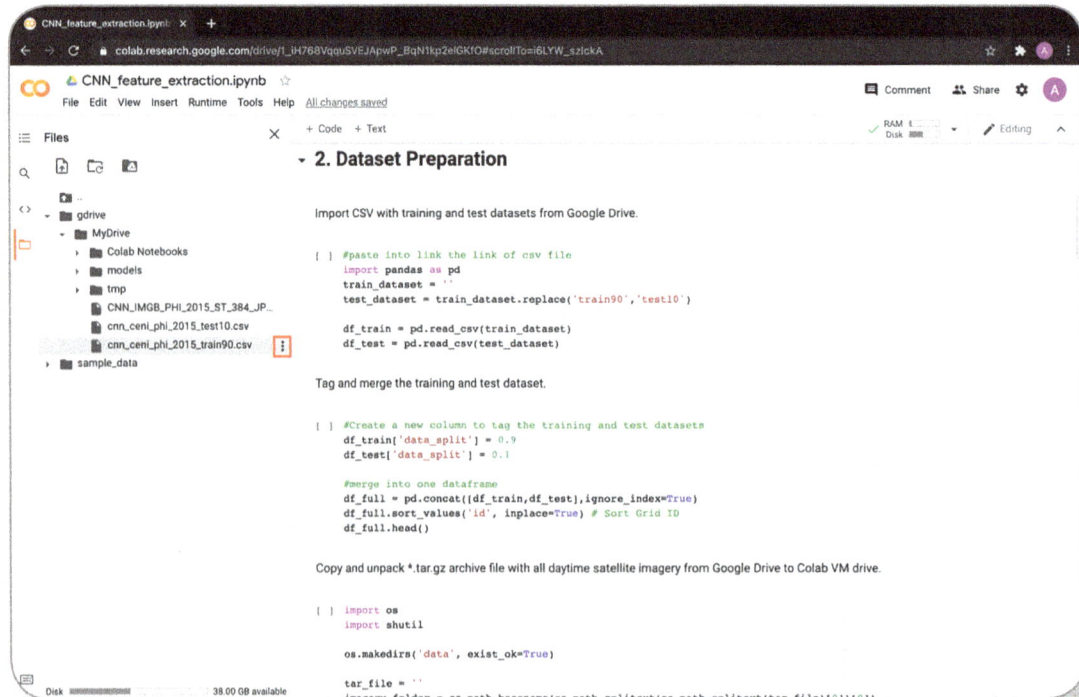

STEP 12

Click **Copy path**.

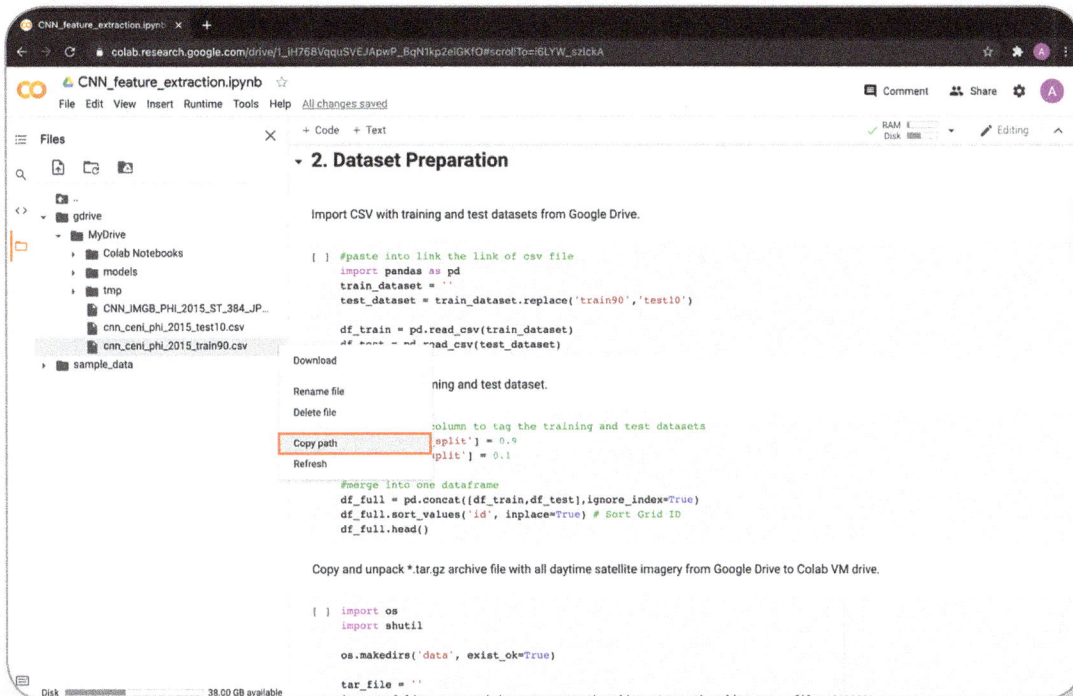

STEP 13

Paste the link on the blank space after the variable *train_dataset* and enclose in apostrophes.

```python
#paste into link the link of csv file
import pandas as pd
train_dataset = ''
test_dataset = train_dataset.replace('train90','test10')


df_train = pd.read_csv(train_dataset)
df_test = pd.read_csv(test_dataset)
```

```python
#paste into link the link of csv file
import pandas as pd
train_dataset = '/content/gdrive/MyDrive/cnn_ceni_phi_2015_train90.csv'
test_dataset = train_dataset.replace('train90','test10')


df_train = pd.read_csv(train_dataset)
df_test = pd.read_csv(test_dataset)
```

STEP 14

Create an identifying column in the training and test datasets, merge the two, sort the dataframe by grid ID, and print out the first four rows of the dataset.

```python
#Create a new column to tag the training and test datasets
df_train['data_split'] = 0.9
df_test['data_split'] = 0.1

#merge into one dataframe
df_full = pd.concat([df_train,df_test],ignore_index=True)
df_full.sort_values('id', inplace=True) # Sort Grid ID
df_full.head()
```

	id	lon	lat	geocode	avg_rad	bin_GMM	filename	City_Municipality	City_Municipality_PCODE	Province	Provinc
18686	1	121.856175	20.825723	20902000	0.0	1	CNN_DIMG_PHI_2015_ST_384_3840_000001.jpg	Itbayat	PH020902000	Batanes	PH0
5649	2	121.856175	20.790880	20902000	0.0	1	CNN_DIMG_PHI_2015_ST_384_3840_000002.jpg	Itbayat	PH020902000	Batanes	PH0
18687	3	121.821332	20.756037	20902000	0.0	1	CNN_DIMG_PHI_2015_ST_384_3840_000003.jpg	Itbayat	PH020902000	Batanes	PH0
5650	4	121.856175	20.756037	20902000	0.0	1	CNN_DIMG_PHI_2015_ST_384_3840_000004.jpg	Itbayat	PH020902000	Batanes	PH0
5651	5	121.786490	20.721195	20902000	0.0	1	CNN_DIMG_PHI_2015_ST_384_3840_000005.jpg	Itbayat	PH020902000	Batanes	PH0

STEP 15

Load **os** and **shutil** packages for operating system functionality and for unpacking archive files, respectively.

```python
import os
import shutil

os.makedirs('data', exist_ok=True)

tar_file = ''
imagery_folder = os.path.basename(os.path.splitext(os.path.splitext(tar_file)[0])[0])
imagery_path = os.path.join('data',imagery_folder)

shutil.unpack_archive(tar_file, 'data')
```

STEP 16

Click **Files** icon 🗀 to show the **Files section**.

STEP 17

From the list of folders, click **_gdrive_** and expand the file directory tree to find the targ.gz file location.

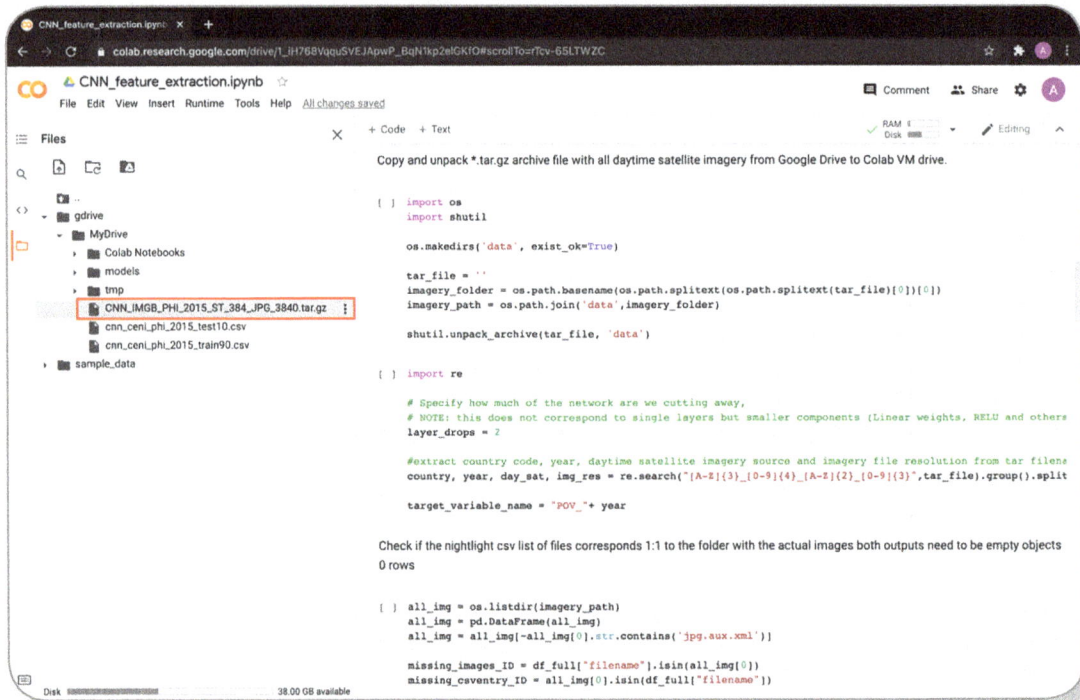

STEP 18

Click the vertical ellipsis to show more file options.

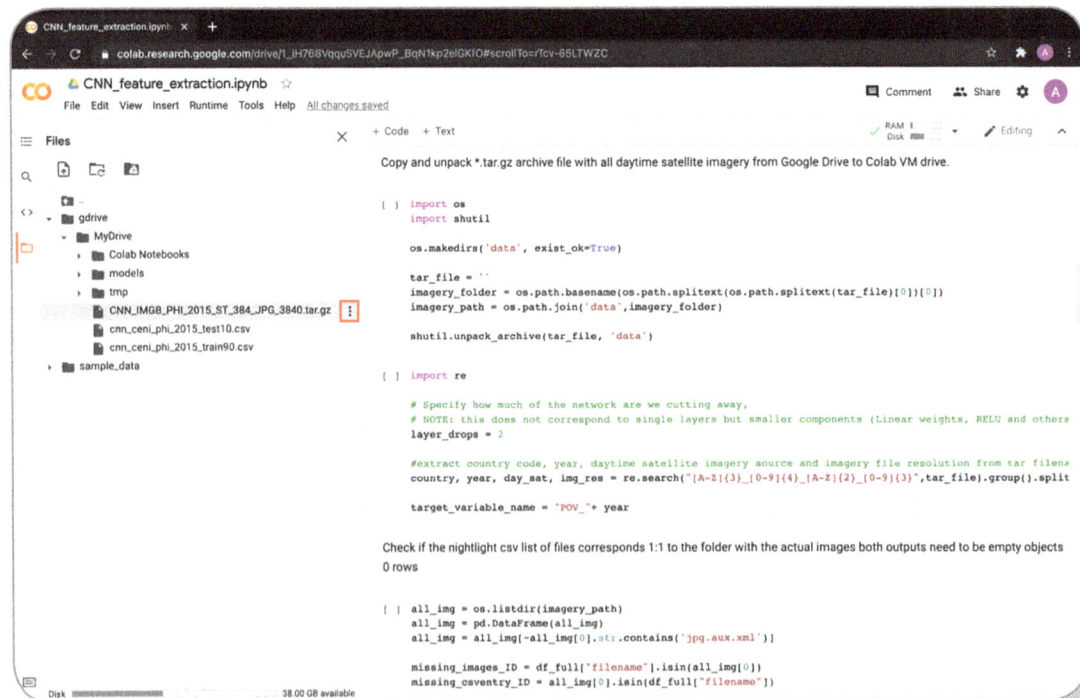

STEP 19

Click **Copy path**.

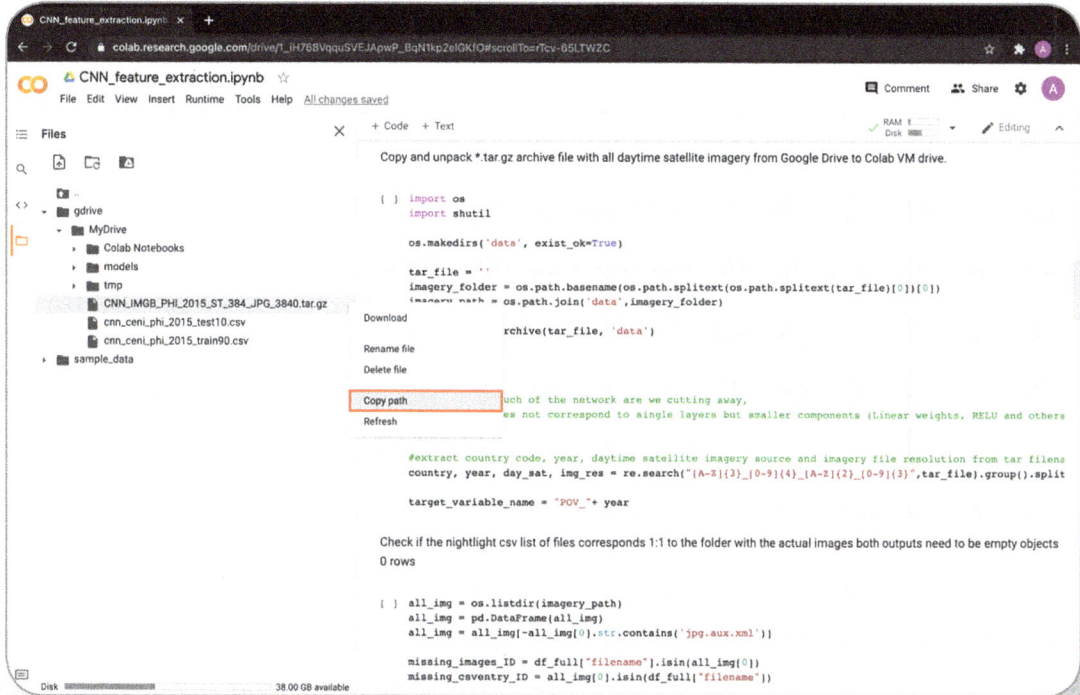

STEP 20

Paste the link beside the variable **tar_file** and enclose it in apostrophes.

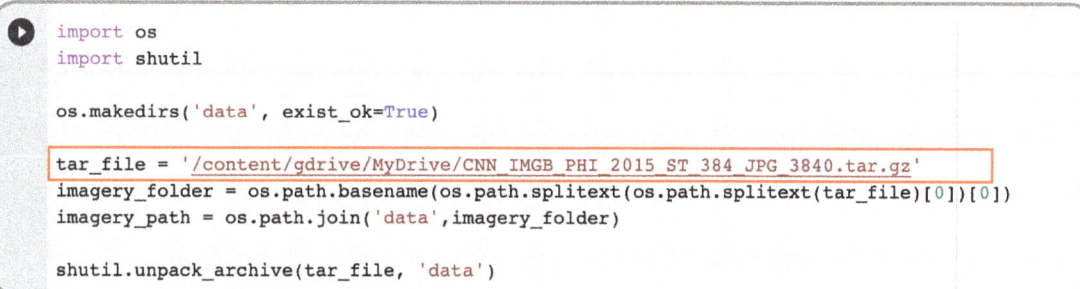

```python
import os
import shutil

os.makedirs('data', exist_ok=True)

tar_file = '/content/gdrive/MyDrive/CNN_IMGB_PHI_2015_ST_384_JPG_3840.tar.gz'
imagery_folder = os.path.basename(os.path.splitext(os.path.splitext(tar_file)[0])[0])
imagery_path = os.path.join('data',imagery_folder)

shutil.unpack_archive(tar_file, 'data')
```

STEP 21

Generate the different parameters for the CNN model.

```python
import re

# Specify how much of the network are we cutting away,
# NOTE: this does not correspond to single layers but smaller components (Linear weights, RELU and others)
layer_drops = 2

#extract country code, year, daytime satellite imagery source and imagery file resolution from tar filename
country, year, day_sat, img_res = re.search("[A-Z]{3}_[0-9]{4}_[A-Z]{2}_[0-9]{3}",tar_file).group().split("_")

target_variable_name = "POV_"+ year
```

Check if all satellite imagery in the CSV file are present in the folder.

```python
all_img = os.listdir(imagery_path)
all_img = pd.DataFrame(all_img)
all_img = all_img[-all_img[0].str.contains('jpg.aux.xml')]

missing_images_ID = df_full["filename"].isin(all_img[0])
missing_csventry_ID = all_img[0].isin(df_full["filename"])

missing_images = df_full[-missing_images_ID]
missing_entries = all_img[-missing_csventry_ID]
print("images in the df_full, but not in the folder: ")
print(missing_images)

print("_____")
print("")
print("Images in the folder, but not in the df_full: ")
print(missing_entries)


images in the df_full, but not in the folder:
Empty DataFrame
Columns: [id, lon, lat, geocode, avg_rad, bin_GMM, filename, City_Municipality, City_Municipality_PCODE, Province, Region, POCEN2010, POPCEN2015, POV_2009, P
Index: []
_____

Images in the folder, but not in the df_full:
Empty DataFrame
Columns: [0]
Index: []
```

STEP 22

Delete the rows in the dataframe that do not have a corresponding imagery, otherwise fastai's databunch will not work.

```python
df = df_full.copy(deep = True)[missing_images_ID]
print(df_full.shape)
print(df.shape)
```

STEP 23

Define the necessary parameters for creating ImageDataBunch.

3. CNN Model Preparation

Assign parameters needed for training the CNN model

```
root_col='/content/'
val_pct = 0.2        # percentage of dataset to be used for validation
label_col = 'bin_GMM'    # names of column containing the binned luminosity in dataset
filename_col = 'filename' # names of column containing the imagery filenamesin dataset

# Assemble learner and CNN model filenames
learner_filename = "_".join(["CNN_LRNR_RES34",country,year,day_sat,str(img_res)]) + ".pkl"
modelWt_filename = "_".join(["CNN_TCNN_RES34",country,year,day_sat,str(img_res)])
```

STEP 24

Import all libraries that are needed for the extraction of features from the trained CNN model.

```
from fastai import *
from fastai.vision import *
from fastai.metrics import error_rate
```

STEP 25

Load the dataset to the ImageDataBunch.

```
data = ImageDataBunch.from_df(df=df,                        # using df to define training dataset
                        path = root_col,
                        folder = imagery_path,
                        valid_pct = val_pct,       # percentage of data used for validation
                        fn_col = filename_col,     # filename column in dataset
                        label_col = label_col,     # classes column in dataset
                        size = int(img_res)        # image size
                        ).normalize(imagenet_stats) # use the normalization that was used to train the pretrained model
```

STEP 26

Create a learner object from the fastai library containing the datasets (i.e., images and labels) without the pre-trained CNN.

```
learn = cnn_learner(data, models.resnet34, metrics = error_rate, pretrained=False)
```

STEP 27

Copy the pre-trained model from Google Drive to the Google Colab virtual machine drive.

```
# define gdrive CNN model save path
source_path = "/content/gdrive/MyDrive/models/"

shutil.copy(os.path.join(source_path,learner_filename), root_col)
shutil.copy(os.path.join(source_path,modelWt_filename+'.pth'), root_col)
```

STEP 28

Load the trained CNN model and merge it with the dataset in the learner object. It also outputs the ImageDataBunch information and structure of the model layers.

```
learn.load(root_col + modelWt_filename )

Learner(data=ImageDataBunch;

  Train: LabelList (16072 items)
  x: ImageList
  Image (3, 384, 384),Image (3, 384, 384),Image (3, 384, 384),Image (3, 384, 384),Image (3, 384, 384)
  y: CategoryList
  1,1,1,1,1
  Path: /content;

  Valid: LabelList (4018 items)
  x: ImageList
  Image (3, 384, 384),Image (3, 384, 384),Image (3, 384, 384),Image (3, 384, 384),Image (3, 384, 384)
  y: CategoryList
  1,1,1,1,1
  Path: /content;

  Test: None, model=Sequential(
    (0): Sequential(
      (0): Conv2d(3, 64, kernel_size=(7, 7), stride=(2, 2), padding=(3, 3), bias=False)
      (1): BatchNorm2d(64, eps=1e-05, momentum=0.1, affine=True, track_running_stats=True)
      (2): ReLU(inplace=True)
      (3): MaxPool2d(kernel_size=3, stride=2, padding=1, dilation=1, ceil_mode=False)
      (4): Sequential(
        (0): BasicBlock(
          (conv1): Conv2d(64, 64, kernel_size=(3, 3), stride=(1, 1), padding=(1, 1), bias=False)
          (bn1): BatchNorm2d(64, eps=1e-05, momentum=0.1, affine=True, track_running_stats=True)
          (relu): ReLU(inplace=True)
          (conv2): Conv2d(64, 64, kernel_size=(3, 3), stride=(1, 1), padding=(1, 1), bias=False)
          (bn2): BatchNorm2d(64, eps=1e-05, momentum=0.1, affine=True, track_running_stats=True)
        )
```

STEP 29

Select two test images from the dataframe and load them into the python environment. This is helpful when trying out functions that operate on images.

```
path_one = df[df[target_variable_name]>0]["filename"][1000]
path_two = df[df[target_variable_name]>0]["filename"][51]

pic_one = open_image(os.path.join(imagery_path,path_one))
pic_two = open_image(os.path.join(imagery_path,path_two))
```

STEP 30

Insert the predict function as a method of the learner class. This method returns only the node values of the last layer in the model, which are normally probabilities of each output category.

```
def my_predict(self, item:ItemBase, return_x:bool=False, batch_first:bool=True, with_dropout:bool=False, **kwargs):
    "Return probabilities for `item`."
    batch = self.data.one_item(item)
    res = self.pred_batch(batch=batch, with_dropout=with_dropout)
    raw_pred,x = grab_idx(res,0,batch_first=batch_first),batch[0]
    return (raw_pred)

setattr(Learner, 'my_predict', my_predict)
```

STEP 31

Compare the result of the predict function with the custom predict function that was previously defined.

```
print(learn.    predict (pic_one))
print(learn.my_predict (pic_one))

(Category tensor(0), tensor(0), tensor([1.0000e+00, 1.6193e-06, 2.8243e-09]))
tensor([1.0000e+00, 1.6193e-06, 2.8243e-09])
```

STEP 32

Generate a new model without the last fully connected layer.

```
new_model = learn

print('Original fully-connected layer group length: '     + str(len(learn.model[1])))
print('------------')
print("Original fully-connected layer structure:")
print(learn.model[1])
print('')
print('')

new_model.model[1] = new_model.model[1][:-layer_drops]

print('New fully-connected layer group length: ' + str(len(new_model.model[1])))
print('------------')
print("New fully-connected layer structure:")
print(new_model.model[1])
```

```
Original fully-connected layer group length: 9
------------
Original fully-connected layer structure:
Sequential(
  (0): AdaptiveConcatPool2d(
    (ap): AdaptiveAvgPool2d(output_size=1)
    (mp): AdaptiveMaxPool2d(output_size=1)
  )
  (1): Flatten()
  (2): BatchNorm1d(1024, eps=1e-05, momentum=0.1, affine=True, track_running_stats=True)
  (3): Dropout(p=0.25, inplace=False)
  (4): Linear(in_features=1024, out_features=512, bias=True)
  (5): ReLU(inplace=True)
  (6): BatchNorm1d(512, eps=1e-05, momentum=0.1, affine=True, track_running_stats=True)
  (7): Dropout(p=0.5, inplace=False)
  (8): Linear(in_features=512, out_features=3, bias=True)
)


New fully-connected layer group length: 7
------------
New fully-connected layer structure:
Sequential(
  (0): AdaptiveConcatPool2d(
    (ap): AdaptiveAvgPool2d(output_size=1)
    (mp): AdaptiveMaxPool2d(output_size=1)
  )
  (1): Flatten()
  (2): BatchNorm1d(1024, eps=1e-05, momentum=0.1, affine=True, track_running_stats=True)
  (3): Dropout(p=0.25, inplace=False)
  (4): Linear(in_features=1024, out_features=512, bias=True)
  (5): ReLU(inplace=True)
  (6): BatchNorm1d(512, eps=1e-05, momentum=0.1, affine=True, track_running_stats=True)
)
```

STEP 33

Define a new function that extracts the tensor of the image features. Then measure the tensor length. **Tensors** are multidimensional arrays. It functions like a numpy array however it has an added benefit where it can be calculated on a graphics processing unit.[9]

```python
def Extract_Features (img):
    # Input:  A jpg with the correct size (we could resize but this usually happens before in our case)
    # return: A tensor of image features (second to last layer of the CNN)
    # those are the features that get weighted together to classify the image's nightlight class.

    img_feature_layer = new_model.my_predict(img).flatten()

    return(img_feature_layer)
```

```python
tensor_len = len(Extract_Features (pic_one))
print(tensor_len)
```
```
512
```

STEP 34

Before predicting image features, create an empty array for storing extracted features and a dataframe containing image file names.

```python
features_out = np.empty((len(df["id"]), tensor_len))
features_out_img = df["filename"]
print(features_out.shape)
```
```
(20090, 512)
```

STEP 35

Loop through the images and extract the features.

```python
for i, path_i in enumerate(features_out_img):
  # open the image with the fastai open image function
  temp_img = open_image(os.path.join(imagery_path, path_i))
  # extract the features of the single image
  tempfeatures = Extract_Features (temp_img).flatten().reshape(1, -1).numpy()
  # store them for output
  features_out[i,:] = tempfeatures
```

STEP 36

Merge the extracted features with the image file names.

```
features_out_pd = pd.DataFrame(data = features_out, index = features_out_img)
```

STEP 37

Save the CSV file to Google Drive, which will be used for ridge regression.

```
csv_path ="/content/gdrive/MyDrive/"
features_filename = "_".join(["CNN_FOUT_RES34",country,year,day_sat,str(img_res)])+".csv"
CENI_full_filename = "_".join(["CNN_CENI_RES34",country,year,day_sat,str(img_res)])+".csv"
```

```
[ ]  # save to disk
     features_out_pd.to_csv(features_filename)
     df_full.to_csv(CENI_full_filename)
     # copy from colab virtual drive to google drive
     shutil.copy(os.path.join('/content/',features_filename), csv_path)
     shutil.copy(os.path.join('/content/',CENI_full_filename), csv_path)
```

6 RIDGE REGRESSION

In the final training step, ridge regression is implemented to determine the relationship between the image features and the government-published poverty rates. The data derived from these features are aggregated by getting the element-wise average values of the vectors at the same geographic level as the government-published poverty rate. Ridge regression is linear like ordinary least squares regression, but it applies a squared penalty term (lambda) on the parameters to avoid overfitting in the case of a small ratio of observations to covariates. In principle, however, one may also consider using other model estimation methods like random forest to assess the sensitivity of estimates in the chosen estimation method.

> **Data Requirements**
> - CSV file containing binned luminosity and poverty estimates
> - CSV file containing image level features
>
> **Tools**
> - Google Colaboratory (Ridge_regression.ipynb)

STEP 1

For ridge regression, upload a new notebook file in Google Colab (footnote 7). Click **File**.

STEP 2

Click **Upload Notebook**.

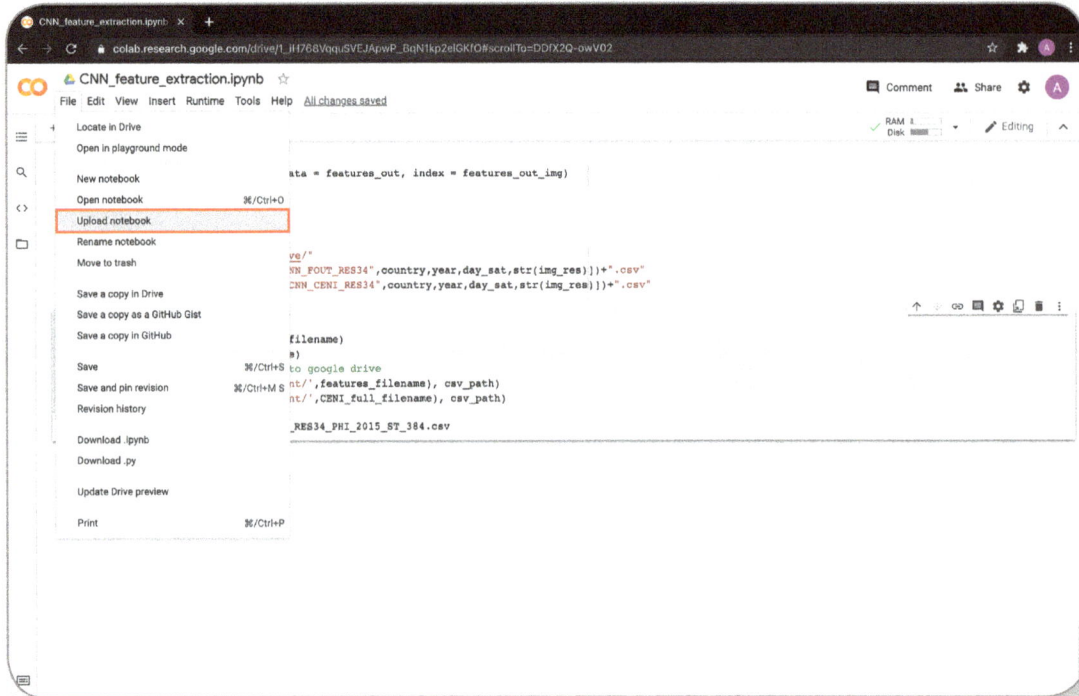

STEP 3

Click **Choose File**.

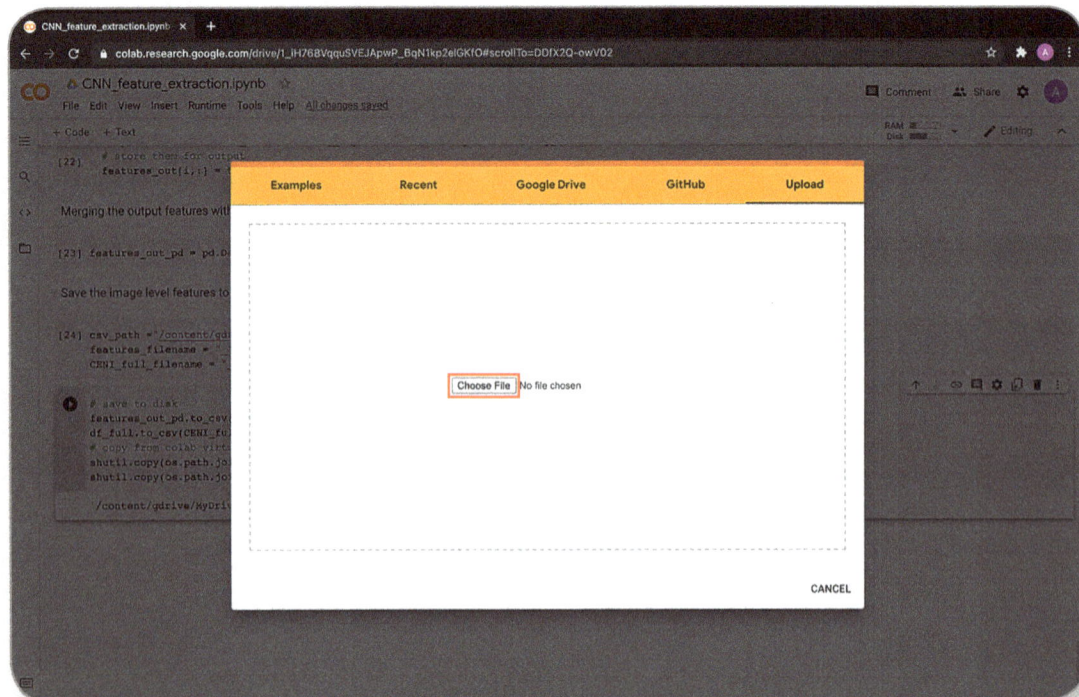

Use the Jupyter Notebook file **Ridge_regression.ipynb**. Locate the file and click **Open**.

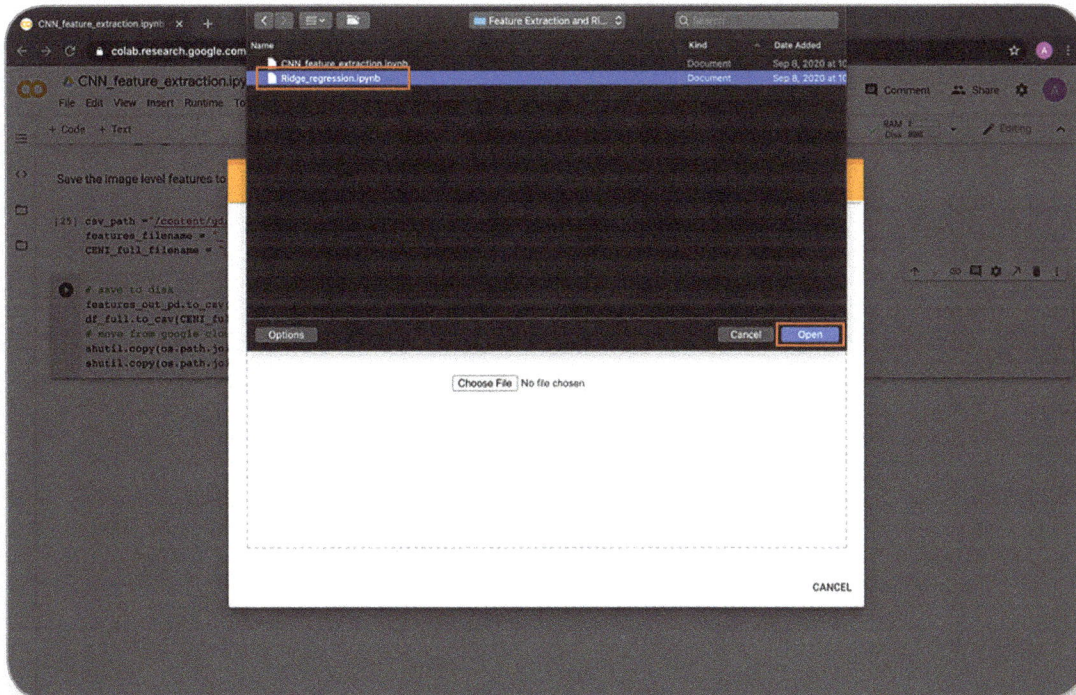

STEP 4

Click **Connect**. This will initialize the Colab environment.

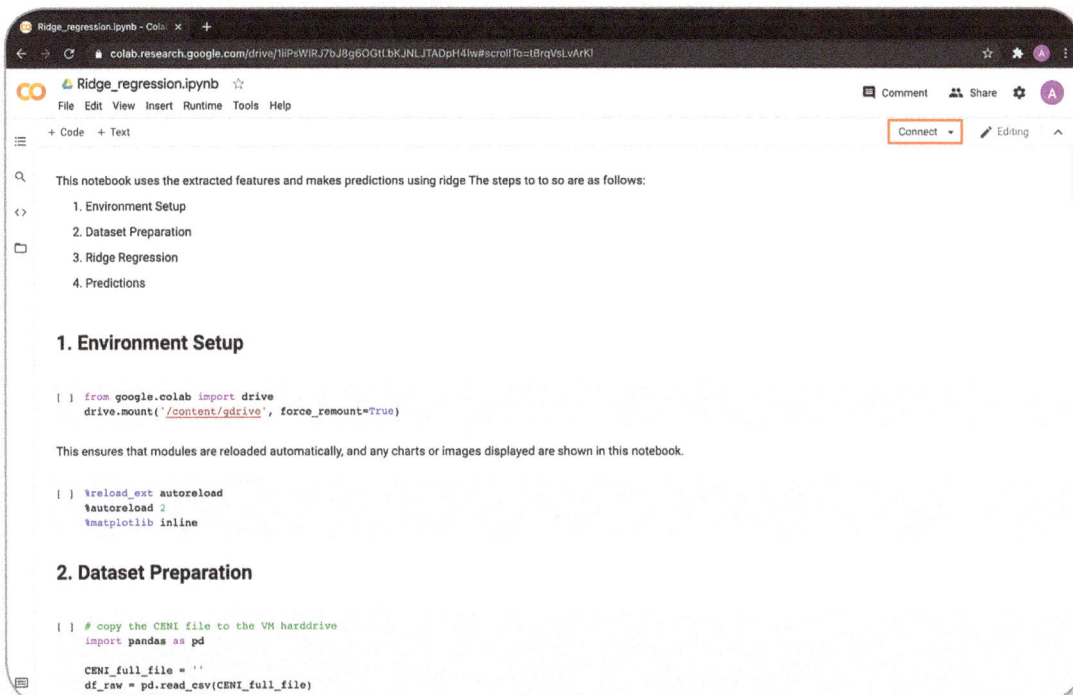

STEP 5

Mount Google Drive (footnote 6) to Google Colab.

```
from google.colab import drive
drive.mount('/content/gdrive', force_remount=True)
```

STEP 6

Click on the link.

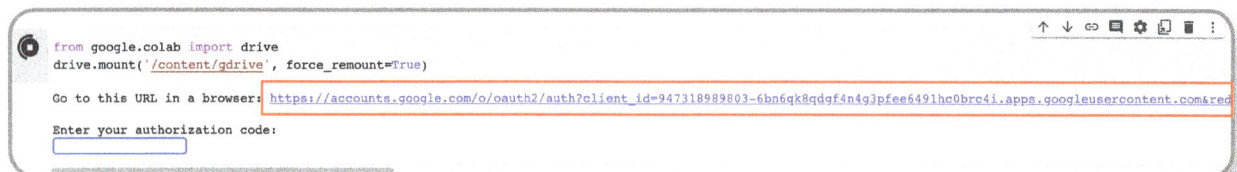

```
from google.colab import drive
drive.mount('/content/gdrive', force_remount=True)

Go to this URL in a browser: https://accounts.google.com/o/oauth2/auth?client_id=947318989803-6bn6qk8qdgf4n4g3pfee6491hc0brc4i.apps.googleusercontent.com&red

Enter your authorization code:
```

STEP 7

In the browser, sign in to Google account.

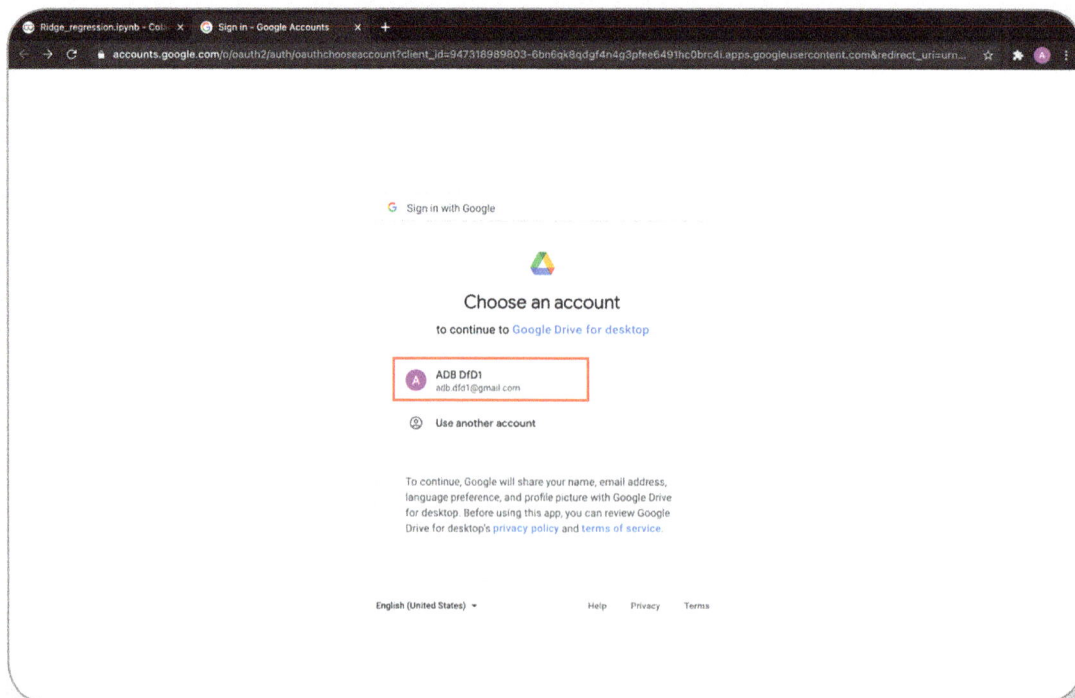

Click **Allow**.

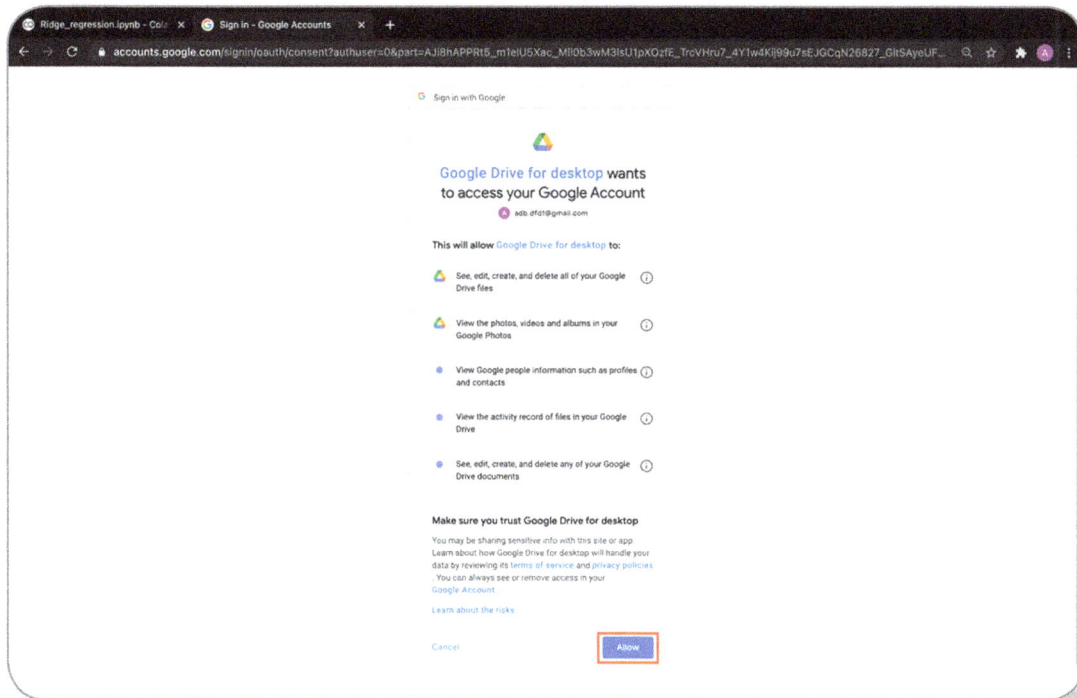

Click **Copy** icon 📋 to copy the code.

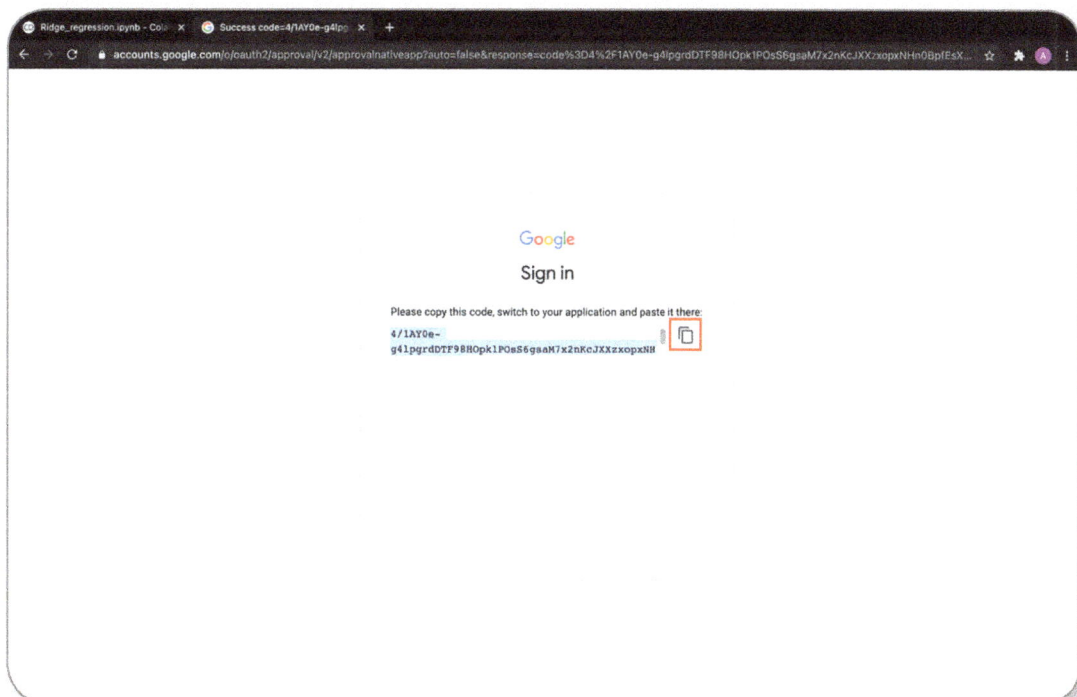

Return to the Colab browser tab. **Paste** the code in the text box. Then press **Enter**.

A status will show the path where Google Drive is mounted.

STEP 8

Ensure that any edits made on the libraries are reloaded automatically and any charts or images displayed are shown in this notebook.

STEP 9

Locate the path to the dataset containing the binned luminosity and poverty rates.

Click **Files** icon 📁 to show the **Files section**.

STEP 10

Click on **gdrive** from the list of folders and expand the file directory tree to find the CSV file location.

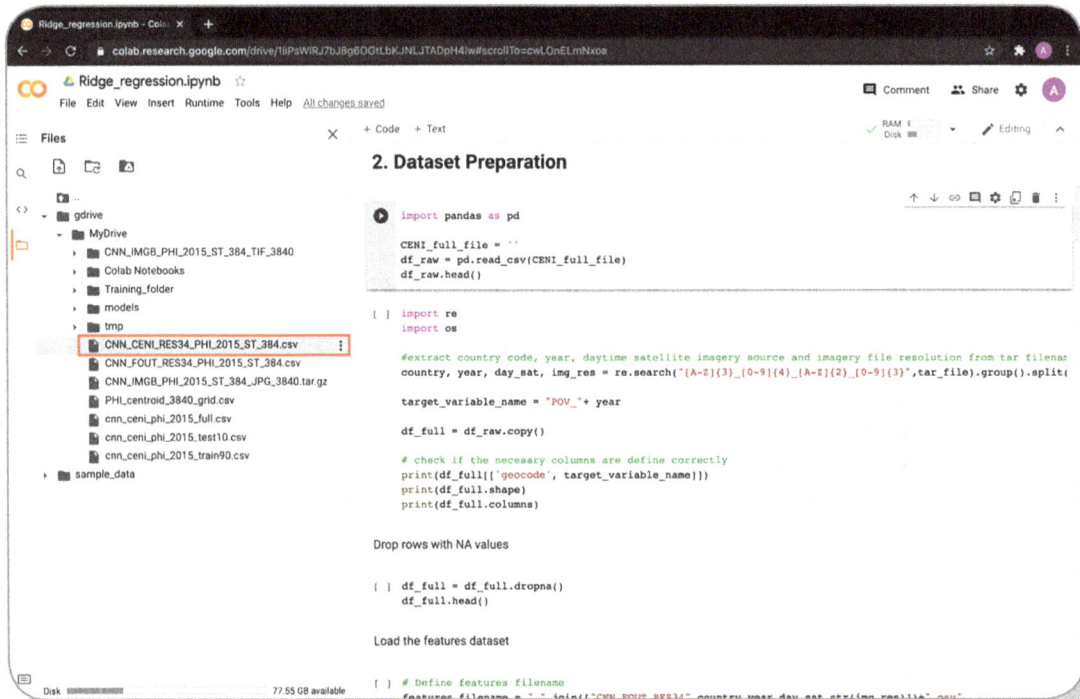

STEP 11

Click the vertical ellipsis to show more file options.

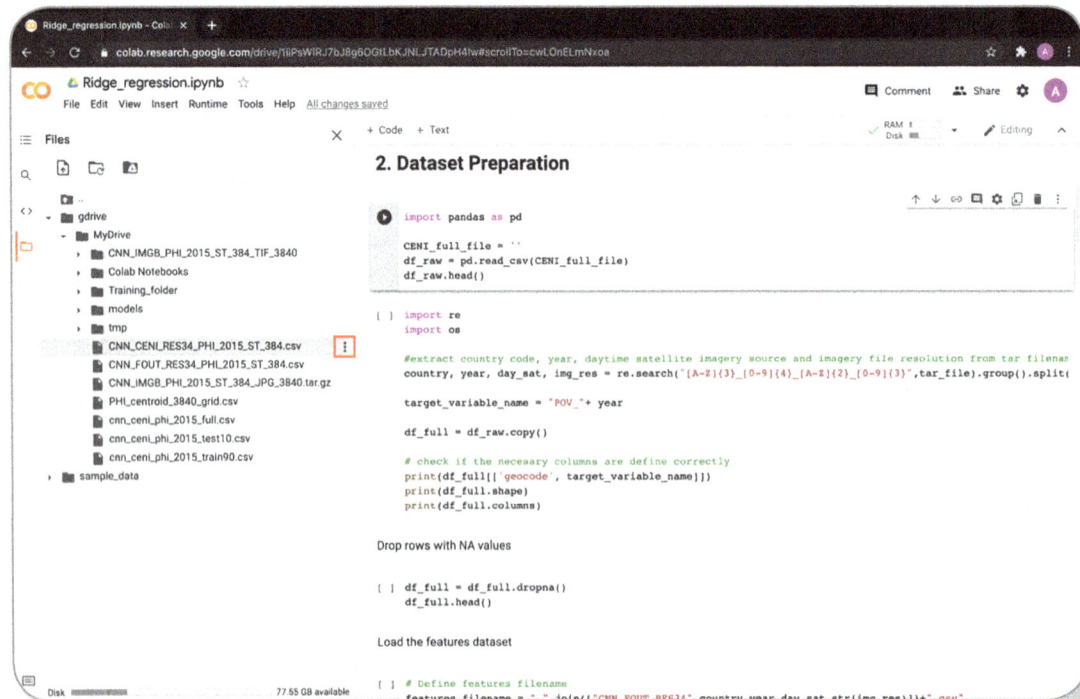

STEP 12

Click **Copy path**.

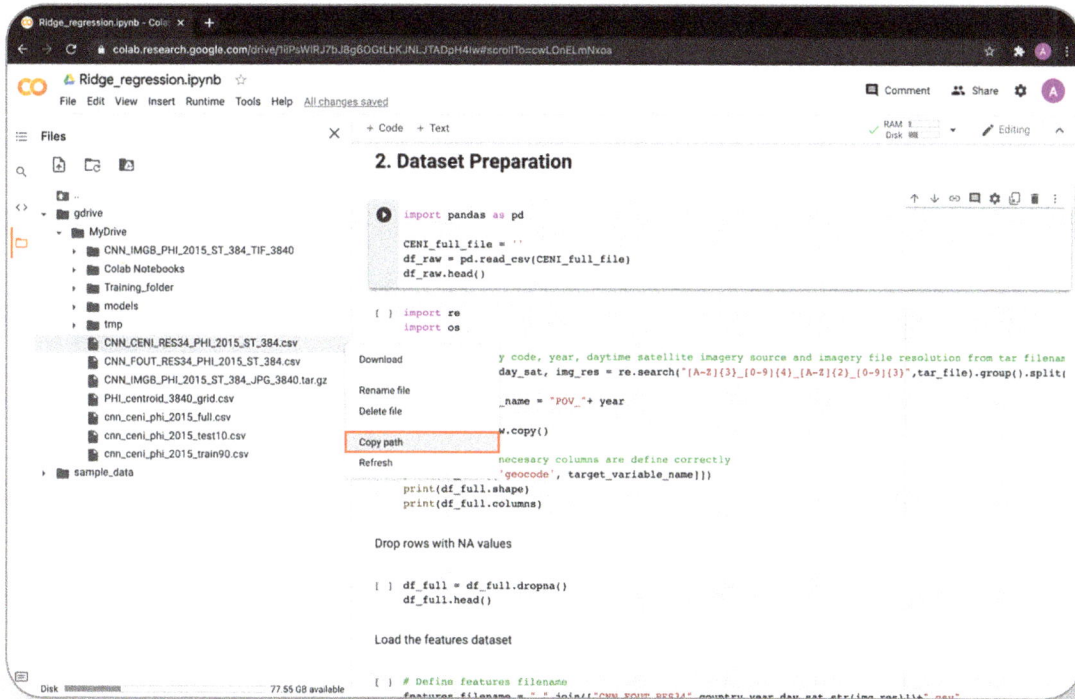

STEP 13

Paste the link on the blank space after the variable *CENI_full_file* and enclose in apostrophes.

```python
import pandas as pd

CENI_full_file = '/content/gdrive/MyDrive/CNN_CENI_RES34_PHI_2015_ST_384.csv'
df_raw = pd.read_csv(CENI_full_file)
df_raw.head()
```

Import the CSV file containing the merged training test dataset from Google Drive.

```python
import pandas as pd

CENI_full_file = '/content/gdrive/MyDrive/CNN_CENI_RES34_PHI_2015_ST_384.csv'
df_raw = pd.read_csv(CENI_full_file)
df_raw.head()
```

	Unnamed: 0	id	lon	lat	geocode	avg_rad	bin_GMM	filename	City_Municipality	City_Municipality_PCODE	Province
0	0	1	121.856175	20.825723	20902000	0.0	1	CNN_DIMG_PHI_2015_ST_384_3840_000001.jpg	Itbayat	PH020902000	Batanes
1	1	2	121.856175	20.790880	20902000	0.0	1	CNN_DIMG_PHI_2015_ST_384_3840_000002.jpg	Itbayat	PH020902000	Batanes
2	2	3	121.821332	20.756037	20902000	0.0	1	CNN_DIMG_PHI_2015_ST_384_3840_000003.jpg	Itbayat	PH020902000	Batanes
3	3	4	121.856175	20.756037	20902000	0.0	1	CNN_DIMG_PHI_2015_ST_384_3840_000004.jpg	Itbayat	PH020902000	Batanes
4	4	5	121.788490	20.721195	20902000	0.0	1	CNN_DIMG_PHI_2015_ST_384_3840_000005.jpg	Itbayat	PH020902000	Batanes

STEP 14

Define the different parameters needed for the model.

```
import re
import os

#extract country code, year, daytime satellite imagery source and imagery file resolution from tar filename
country, year, day_sat, img_res = re.search("[A-Z]{3}_[0-9]{4}_[A-Z]{2}_[0-9]{3}",CENI_full_file).group().split("_")

target_variable_name = "POV_"+ year

df_full = df_raw.copy()

# check if the necesary columns are define correctly
print(df_full[['geocode', target_variable_name]])
print(df_full.shape)
print(df_full.columns)
```

```
           geocode  POV_2015
0         20902000     26.38
1         20902000     26.38
2         20902000     26.38
3         20902000     26.38
4         20902000     26.38
...            ...       ...
20085    157005000     28.85
20086    157011000     26.26
20087    157005000     28.85
20088    157011000     26.26
20089    157011000     26.26

[20090 rows x 2 columns]
(20090, 20)
Index(['Unnamed: 0', 'id', 'lon', 'lat', 'geocode', 'avg_rad', 'bin_GMM',
       'filename', 'City_Municipality', 'City_Municipality_PCODE', 'Province',
       'Region', 'POCEN2010', 'POPCEN2015', 'POV_2009', 'POV_2012', 'POV_2015',
       'Highly_Urbanized', 'Is.City', 'data_split'],
      dtype='object')
```

STEP 15

Drop all rows with "NA" values.

```
df_full = df_full.dropna()
df_full.shape

(20068, 20)
```

STEP 16

Load the feature dataset, which is the output of the feature extraction notebook, in the virtual machine drive. *It is then loaded as a dataframe.*

```
# Define features filename
features_filename = "_".join(["CNN_FOUT_RES34",country,year,day_sat,str(img_res)])+".csv"

# load it into python
features_raw = pd.read_csv(os.path.join(os.path.dirname(CENI_full_file),features_filename ))
print(features_raw.shape)

(20090, 513)
```

STEP 17

Compare the filenames of the daytime satellite imagery that were processed during feature extraction with the filename list from the original CSV file containing binned luminosity and poverty rates.

```python
all_img = features_raw["filename"]
# all_img = pd.DataFrame(all_img)

missing_images_ID = df_full["filename"].isin(all_img)
missing_csventry_ID = all_img.isin(df_full["filename"])

missing_images = df_full[~missing_images_ID]
missing_entries = all_img[~missing_csventry_ID]
print("images in the df_full, but not in the features file: ")
print(missing_images)

print("_____")
print("")
print("images in the features file, but not in the df_full: ")
print(missing_entries)
```

```
images in the df_full, but not in the features file:
Empty DataFrame
Columns: [Unnamed: 0, id, lon, lat, geocode, avg_rad, bin_GMM, filename, Cit
Index: []
_____

images in the features file, but not in the df_full:
17868    CNN_DIMG_PHI_2015_ST_384_3840_017869.jpg
17869    CNN_DIMG_PHI_2015_ST_384_3840_017870.jpg
17940    CNN_DIMG_PHI_2015_ST_384_3840_017941.jpg
17941    CNN_DIMG_PHI_2015_ST_384_3840_017942.jpg
17942    CNN_DIMG_PHI_2015_ST_384_3840_017943.jpg
18016    CNN_DIMG_PHI_2015_ST_384_3840_018017.jpg
18786    CNN_DIMG_PHI_2015_ST_384_3840_018787.jpg
18787    CNN_DIMG_PHI_2015_ST_384_3840_018788.jpg
18788    CNN_DIMG_PHI_2015_ST_384_3840_018789.jpg
18835    CNN_DIMG_PHI_2015_ST_384_3840_018836.jpg
18836    CNN_DIMG_PHI_2015_ST_384_3840_018837.jpg
18837    CNN_DIMG_PHI_2015_ST_384_3840_018838.jpg
18889    CNN_DIMG_PHI_2015_ST_384_3840_018890.jpg
18890    CNN_DIMG_PHI_2015_ST_384_3840_018891.jpg
18891    CNN_DIMG_PHI_2015_ST_384_3840_018892.jpg
18892    CNN_DIMG_PHI_2015_ST_384_3840_018893.jpg
18948    CNN_DIMG_PHI_2015_ST_384_3840_018949.jpg
18949    CNN_DIMG_PHI_2015_ST_384_3840_018950.jpg
18950    CNN_DIMG_PHI_2015_ST_384_3840_018951.jpg
19004    CNN_DIMG_PHI_2015_ST_384_3840_019005.jpg
19005    CNN_DIMG_PHI_2015_ST_384_3840_019006.jpg
19006    CNN_DIMG_PHI_2015_ST_384_3840_019007.jpg
Name: filename, dtype: object
```

Delete all rows in the original CSV file that contain filenames that were not processed during feature extraction.

```
df = df_full.copy(deep = True)[missing_images_ID]
print(df_full.shape)
print(df.shape)

(20068, 20)
(20068, 20)
```

STEP 18

Generate a new dataframe containing only the geocode and filenames column and drop duplicate geocode entries.

```
# make a temporary file that only contains the filename and geocode columns
img_geocode = df[["filename", "geocode"]]
# drop the double rows we just want the relation between image and geocode
img_geocode = img_geocode.drop_duplicates()

img_geocode.head()
```

	filename	geocode
0	CNN_DIMG_PHI_2015_ST_384_3840_000001.jpg	20902000
1	CNN_DIMG_PHI_2015_ST_384_3840_000002.jpg	20902000
2	CNN_DIMG_PHI_2015_ST_384_3840_000003.jpg	20902000
3	CNN_DIMG_PHI_2015_ST_384_3840_000004.jpg	20902000
4	CNN_DIMG_PHI_2015_ST_384_3840_000005.jpg	20902000

STEP 19

Generate a new dataframe containing only the training poverty data.

```
df_LHS = df[['geocode', 'data_split' , target_variable_name]]
df_LHS = df_LHS.drop_duplicates(subset='geocode')
print(df_LHS.shape)

(1621, 3)
```

STEP 20

Merge the geocode-filename dataframe with the features dataframe.

```
# ensure that the datatypes align
img_geocode.filename.astype(str)
features_raw.filename.astype(str)
# merge
features = img_geocode.merge(features_raw, on = "filename")
```

STEP 21

Compute the average features by geocode group and generate one feature vector per geocode.

```
avg_features = features.copy(deep = True)
avg_features.drop(columns=['filename'])
avg_features = avg_features.groupby('geocode', as_index=False).mean()
```

STEP 22

Merge the training poverty and averaged features dataframes.

```
avg_features_full = df_LHS.merge(avg_features, on = 'geocode')

print(df_LHS.shape)
print(avg_features.shape)
print(avg_features_full.shape)
print(avg_features_full.iloc[:5,:6])

(1621, 3)
(1621, 513)
(1621, 515)
      geocode  data_split  POV_2015          0         1         2
0    20902000         0.9     26.38   0.002491  0.001594  0.001437
1    20901000         0.9     14.40   0.001808  0.001810  0.001680
2    20904000         0.1     17.96   0.001693  0.001549  0.001572
3    20903000         0.9     18.27   0.002649  0.001554  0.003831
4    20906000         0.9     19.48   0.001762  0.002304  0.001636
```

STEP 23

Load the packages needed to perform ridge regression.

```
from sklearn.model_selection import cross_val_score
from sklearn.linear_model import LinearRegression

from sklearn.model_selection import GridSearchCV
from sklearn.linear_model import Ridge
```

STEP 24

Implement the following steps:

- Determine geocodes of outliers from the averaged features based on the defined standard deviation specified in the variable **outlier_flag**.

```
import numpy as np

outlier_flag = 4 # standard deviation
validation_size_percent = 10

outliers = avg_features_full['geocode'][avg_features_full[target_variable_name] > avg_features_full[target_variable_name].mean() +
                              outlier_flag * avg_features_full[target_variable_name].std()].unique()
print("outlier Regions: ")
print(outliers)
print("number of outliers: " + str(len(outliers)))

validation_regions = avg_features_full['geocode'][avg_features_full['data_split'] == (validation_size_percent/100)].unique()

print("number of validation_regions: " + str(len(validation_regions)))

# combine validation and outlier regions to drop them at once
drop_regions = np.append(outliers, validation_regions)

# drop outliers and validation set
avg_features = avg_features_full[-avg_features_full['geocode'].isin(drop_regions)]
avg_features_validation = avg_features_full[avg_features_full['geocode'].isin(validation_regions)]

# training set
Xs = avg_features.drop([target_variable_name, 'geocode', 'data_split'], axis = 1)
y = avg_features[target_variable_name].values.reshape(-1,1)

# full dataset
Xs_full = avg_features_full.drop([target_variable_name, 'geocode', 'data_split'], axis = 1)
y_full = avg_features_full[target_variable_name].values.reshape(-1,1)

# only validation set
Xs_validation = avg_features_validation.drop([target_variable_name, 'geocode', 'data_split'], axis = 1)
y_validation  = avg_features_validation[target_variable_name].values.reshape(-1,1)

print(avg_features_full.shape)
print("Xs shape: " + str(Xs.shape))
print("y shape: " + str(y.shape))
print("Outlier flag: " + str(outlier_flag) + " sd")
print("Validation Xs shape: " + str(Xs_validation.shape))
print("Validation relative size: " + str(round( Xs_validation.shape[0] / avg_features_full.shape[0],2)) )
```

■ Extract the validation datasets and drop the outliers.

```python
import numpy as np

outlier_flag = 4 # standard deviation
validation_size_percent = 10

outliers = avg_features_full['geocode'][avg_features_full[target_variable_name] > avg_features_full[target_variable_name].mean() +
                                   outlier_flag * avg_features_full[target_variable_name].std()].unique()
print("outlier Regions: ")
print(outliers)
print("number of outliers: " + str(len(outliers)))

validation_regions = avg_features_full['geocode'][avg_features_full['data_split'] == (validation_size_percent/100)].unique()

print("number of validation_regions: " + str(len(validation_regions)))

# combine validation and outlier regions to drop them at once
drop_regions = np.append(outliers, validation_regions)

# drop outliers and validation set
avg_features = avg_features_full[~avg_features_full['geocode'].isin(drop_regions)]
avg_features_validation = avg_features_full[avg_features_full['geocode'].isin(validation_regions)]


# training set
Xs = avg_features.drop([target_variable_name, 'geocode', 'data_split'], axis = 1)
y = avg_features[target_variable_name].values.reshape(-1,1)


# full dataset
Xs_full = avg_features_full.drop([target_variable_name, 'geocode', 'data_split'], axis = 1)
y_full = avg_features_full[target_variable_name].values.reshape(-1,1)

# only validation set
Xs_validation = avg_features_validation.drop([target_variable_name, 'geocode', 'data_split'], axis = 1)
y_validation = avg_features_validation[target_variable_name].values.reshape(-1,1)


print(avg_features_full.shape)
print("Xs shape: " + str(Xs.shape))
print("y shape: " + str(y.shape))
print("Outlier flag: " + str(outlier_flag) + " sd")
print("Validation Xs shape: " + str(Xs_validation.shape))
print("Validation relative size: " + str(round( Xs_validation.shape[0] / avg_features_full.shape[0],2)) )
```

■ Create separate dataframes for full, training, and test datasets.

```python
import numpy as np

outlier_flag = 4 # standard deviation
validation_size_percent = 10

outliers = avg_features_full['geocode'][avg_features_full[target_variable_name] > avg_features_full[target_variable_name].mean() +
                            outlier_flag * avg_features_full[target_variable_name].std()].unique()
print("outlier Regions: ")
print(outliers)
print("number of outliers: " + str(len(outliers)))

validation_regions = avg_features_full['geocode'][avg_features_full['data_split'] == (validation_size_percent/100)].unique()

print("number of validation_regions: " + str(len(validation_regions)))

# combine validation and outlier regions to drop them at once
drop_regions = np.append(outliers, validation_regions)

# drop outliers and validation set
avg_features = avg_features_full[~avg_features_full['geocode'].isin(drop_regions)]
avg_features_validation = avg_features_full[avg_features_full['geocode'].isin(validation_regions)]

# training set
Xs = avg_features.drop([target_variable_name, 'geocode', 'data_split'], axis = 1)
y = avg_features[target_variable_name].values.reshape(-1,1)

# full dataset
Xs_full = avg_features_full.drop([target_variable_name, 'geocode', 'data_split'], axis = 1)
y_full = avg_features_full[target_variable_name].values.reshape(-1,1)

# only validation set
Xs_validation = avg_features_validation.drop([target_variable_name, 'geocode', 'data_split'], axis = 1)
y_validation  = avg_features_validation[target_variable_name].values.reshape(-1,1)


print(avg_features_full.shape)
print("Xs shape: " + str(Xs.shape))
print("y shape: " + str(y.shape))
print("Outlier flag: " + str(outlier_flag) + " sd")
print("Validation Xs shape: " + str(Xs_validation.shape))
print("Validation relative size: " + str(round( Xs_validation.shape[0] / avg_features_full.shape[0],2)) )
```

```
outlier Regions:
[]
number of outliers: 0
number of validation_regions: 161
(1621, 515)
Xs shape: (1460, 512)
y shape: (1460, 1)
Outlier flag: 4 sd
Validation Xs shape: (161, 512)
Validation relative size: 0.1
```

STEP 25

Set the parameter space for lambda (the ridge regression penalty term) that needs to be searched through.

```
max_lambda = 10
print("maximum lambda: " + str(max_lambda))
min_lambda = 0.01
print("minimum lambda: " +str(min_lambda))

parameters = {'alpha': 10**np.linspace(np.log10(min_lambda), np.log10(max_lambda), num = 15)}
print(parameters)
```

```
maximum lambda: 10
minimum lambda: 0.01
{'alpha': array([ 0.01      ,  0.01637894,  0.02682696,  0.04393971,  0.07196857,
        0.11787686,  0.19306977,  0.31622777,  0.51794747,  0.8483429 ,
        1.38949549,  2.27584593,  3.72759372,  6.1054023 , 10.          ])}
```

STEP 26

Perform ridge regression with tenfold cross validation (CV) to tune hyperparameters and measure performance.

```
ridge = Ridge(fit_intercept = True, normalize = True)
ridge_regressor = GridSearchCV(ridge, parameters, scoring = "neg_mean_squared_error", cv = 10)

%time ridge_regressor.fit(Xs,y)
```

```
CPU times: user 9.21 s, sys: 9.27 s, total: 18.5 s
Wall time: 9.4 s
GridSearchCV(cv=10, error_score=nan,
             estimator=Ridge(alpha=1.0, copy_X=True, fit_intercept=True,
                             max_iter=None, normalize=True, random_state=None,
                             solver='auto', tol=0.001),
             iid='deprecated', n_jobs=None,
             param_grid={'alpha': array([ 0.01      ,  0.01637894,  0.02682696,  0.04393971,  0.07196857,
        0.11787686,  0.19306977,  0.31622777,  0.51794747,  0.8483429 ,
        1.38949549,  2.27584593,  3.72759372,  6.1054023 , 10.          ])},
             pre_dispatch='2*n_jobs', refit=True, return_train_score=False,
             scoring='neg_mean_squared_error', verbose=0)
```

STEP 27

Identify the model with the best CV score.

```
print(ridge_regressor.best_params_)
best_ridge = ridge_regressor.best_estimator_
RMSE_valid = round((((y_validation/100 - 0.01*best_ridge.predict(Xs_validation))**2).mean()**0.5,4)
RMSE_full  = round((((y_full/100 - 0.01*best_ridge.predict(Xs_full))**2).mean()**0.5,4)

print("Validation RMSE: " + str(RMSE_valid))
print("Full RMSE: " + str(RMSE_full))
```

```
{'alpha': 0.8483428982440717}
Validation RMSE: 0.1107
Full RMSE: 0.1045
```

STEP 28

Define the function for computing R-squared and root mean square error (RMSE).

```python
import shutil

def Ridge_Rsquared (predicted, true):
  SSE = sum((predicted - true)**2)
  SST = sum((true - true.mean())**2)
  R_square = 1 - SSE / SST
  RMSE = (SSE/len(true))**0.5
  return round(float(R_square),4)

eval_valid = Ridge_Rsquared(0.01*best_ridge.predict(Xs_validation), 0.01*y_validation)
eval_full  = Ridge_Rsquared(0.01*best_ridge.predict(Xs_full), 0.01*y_full)
eval_train = Ridge_Rsquared(0.01*best_ridge.predict(Xs), 0.01*y)


ridgestats = pd.DataFrame({"stat": ['RMSE_valid', 'RMSE_full', 'R2_valid', 'R2_full', 'R2_train'],
                   "value": [RMSE_valid, RMSE_full, eval_valid, eval_full, eval_train]})
print(ridgestats)


ridgestats_file = "_".join(["CNN", "Ridgestats" , "RES34", country, year, day_sat, str(img_res)] ) + ".csv"

ridgestats.to_csv(ridgestats_file)

shutil.copy(os.path.join('/content/',ridgestats_file), "/content/gdrive/MyDrive/")
```

```
          stat   value
0   RMSE_valid  0.1107
1    RMSE_full  0.1045
2     R2_valid  0.5038
3      R2_full  0.5972
4     R2_train  0.6060
'/content/gdrive/MyDrive/CNN_Ridgestats_RES34_PHI_2015_ST_384.csv'
```

STEP 29

Implement the calculations for the training, validation, and the entire dataset.

```python
import shutil

def Ridge_Rsquared (predicted, true):
  SSE = sum((predicted - true)**2)
  SST = sum((true - true.mean())**2)
  R_square = 1 - SSE / SST
  RMSE = (SSE/len(true))**0.5
  return round(float(R_square),4)

eval_valid = Ridge_Rsquared(0.01*best_ridge.predict(Xs_validation), 0.01*y_validation)
eval_full  = Ridge_Rsquared(0.01*best_ridge.predict(Xs_full), 0.01*y_full)
eval_train = Ridge_Rsquared(0.01*best_ridge.predict(Xs), 0.01*y)


ridgestats = pd.DataFrame({"stat": ['RMSE_valid', 'RMSE_full', 'R2_valid', 'R2_full', 'R2_train'],
                "value": [RMSE_valid, RMSE_full, eval_valid, eval_full, eval_train]})
print(ridgestats)


ridgestats_file = "_".join(["CNN", "Ridgestats" , "RES34", country, year, day_sat, str(img_res)] ) + ".csv"

ridgestats.to_csv(ridgestats_file)

shutil.copy(os.path.join('/content/',ridgestats_file), "/content/gdrive/MyDrive/")
```

```
          stat    value
0   RMSE_valid   0.1107
1    RMSE_full   0.1045
2     R2_valid   0.5038
3      R2_full   0.5972
4     R2_train   0.6060
'/content/gdrive/MyDrive/CNN_Ridgestats_RES34_PHI_2015_ST_384.csv'
```

STEP 30

Generate the regression statistics outputs as CSV file and copy them in Google Drive.

```
import shutil

def Ridge_Rsquared (predicted, true):
  SSE = sum((predicted - true)**2)
  SST = sum((true - true.mean())**2)
  R_square = 1 - SSE / SST
  RMSE = (SSE/len(true))**0.5
  return round(float(R_square),4)

eval_valid = Ridge_Rsquared(0.01*best_ridge.predict(Xs_validation), 0.01*y_validation)
eval_full  = Ridge_Rsquared(0.01*best_ridge.predict(Xs_full), 0.01*y_full)
eval_train = Ridge_Rsquared(0.01*best_ridge.predict(Xs), 0.01*y)


ridgestats = pd.DataFrame({"stat": ['RMSE_valid', 'RMSE_full', 'R2_valid', 'R2_full', 'R2_train'],
                "value": [RMSE_valid, RMSE_full, eval_valid, eval_full, eval_train]})
print(ridgestats)

ridgestats_file = "_".join(["CNN", "Ridgestats" , "RES34", country, year, day_sat, str(img_res)] ) + ".csv"

ridgestats.to_csv(ridgestats_file)

shutil.copy(os.path.join('/content/',ridgestats_file), "/content/gdrive/MyDrive/")
```

```
          stat    value
0   RMSE_valid   0.1107
1    RMSE_full   0.1045
2     R2_valid   0.5038
3      R2_full   0.5972
4     R2_train   0.6060
'/content/gdrive/MyDrive/CNN_Ridgestats_RES34_PHI_2015_ST_384.csv'
```

STEP 31

Import the **matplotlib** library used for data visualization. Then define a function for plotting a 45-degree fit line.

```
import matplotlib.pyplot as plt

# add functionality to plot at 45° line
def abline(slope, intercept):
    """Plot a line from slope and intercept"""
    axes = plt.gca()
    x_vals = np.array(axes.get_xlim())
    y_vals = intercept + slope * x_vals
    plt.plot(x_vals, y_vals, '--')
```

STEP 32

Plot the government-published poverty rates against the predicted poverty rates.

```
plot_filename = "_".join(["CNN", "PLOT" , "RES34", country, year, day_sat, str(img_res), "validation"] ) + ".eps"

col_dict = {True: 'r', False: "b"}
col = [col_dict[valid] for valid in avg_features_full['data_split'] == (validation_size_percent/100)]

plt.scatter(y_full, best_ridge.predict(Xs_full), c = col)
plt.ylabel('Predictions')
plt.xlabel('Survey')
plt.suptitle(country + " " + year + " " + "Ridge Regression")
plt.title('Validation set: poverty share (%)')
txt=""
plt.figtext(0.5, -0.1, txt, wrap=True, horizontalalignment='center', fontsize=12)
abline(1,0)

plt.savefig(plot_filename, format='eps', dpi = 600)

shutil.copy(os.path.join('/content/',plot_filename), "/content/gdrive/MyDrive/")
```

```
'/content/gdrive/MyDrive/CNN_PLOT_RES34_PHI_2015_ST_384_validation.eps'
```

STEP 33

Load the Python **pickle** library, which then exports the ridge regression model. Copy the file to Google Drive.

```
import pickle
trained_ridge_regression_file = "_".join(["CNN", "RidgeModel" , "RES34", country, year, day_sat, str(img_res)] ) + ".pkl"
# Save to file in the current working directory
with open(trained_ridge_regression_file, 'wb') as file:
    pickle.dump(best_ridge, file)

#copy to gdrive
shutil.copy(os.path.join('/content/',trained_ridge_regression_file), "/content/gdrive/MyDrive/")
```

```
'/content/gdrive/MyDrive/CNN_RidgeModel_RES34_PHI_2015_ST_384.pkl'
```

STEP 34

Then reload the saved model parameters.

```
# Load from file
with open(trained_ridge_regression_file, 'rb') as file:
    best_ridge = pickle.load(file)
```

STEP 35

Extract the array of the image level features, collapse it into a one-dimension array to get the predicted poverty rates, and generate a dataframe with the corresponding imagery filename as the index.

Then, merge the poverty prediction dataframe with the data frame containing the government-published poverty rates using the imagery filename as the merging parameter.

```
[31] # Perform prediction for all grids
     pred_out  = best_ridge.predict(features_raw.loc[ : , "0":"511"])
     # make the prediction a pandas object with the corresponding filenames we used for looping
     pred_out_pd = pd.DataFrame({'prediction': pred_out.flatten()}, index = features_raw.filename)

     print(len(pred_out))
     print(len(features_raw.filename))

     20090
     20090
```

Take the prediction vector and bring it together with the rest of our data

+ Code   + Text

```
print(df.shape)
output = df_raw.join(pred_out_pd, on = "filename", how = "outer")
print(output.shape)

print("-----")
print(output[:5])

(20068, 20)
(20090, 21)
-----
   Unnamed: 0  id         lon  ...  Is.City  data_split  prediction
0           0   1  121.856175  ...    False         0.9   42.077561
1           1   2  121.856175  ...    False         0.9   22.352971
2           2   3  121.821332  ...    False         0.9   31.209596
3           3   4  121.856175  ...    False         0.9   21.770260
4           4   5  121.786490  ...    False         0.9   37.656852

[5 rows x 21 columns]
```

STEP 36

Generate the poverty prediction output file as a CSV file. Then copy these results to Google Drive.

```
poverty_prediction_file = "_".join(["CNN", "POV"  , "RES34", country, year, day_sat, str(img_res)] ) + ".csv"
output.to_csv(poverty_prediction_file)

shutil.copy(os.path.join('/content/',poverty_prediction_file), "/content/gdrive/MyDrive/")

'/content/gdrive/MyDrive/CNN_POV_RES34_PHI_2015_ST_384.csv'
```

7 RESCALING OF POVERTY ESTIMATES AND VISUALIZATION

Data Requirements

- CSV file containing poverty estimates
- Machine learning based population estimate raster

Tool

- R and RStudio (Rescaling_and_visualization.R)

STEP 1

In RStudio, use the R code: **Rescaling_and_visualization.R.**

```
Rescaling_and_visualization.R ×
     Source on Save   Q                                                    Run    Source ▾
  1  # Rescale poverty predictions, generate raster, and visualization
  2
  3 ▾ # Load packages----
  4  library(raster)
  5  library(tidyverse)
  6
  7  tmp_path <- "C:/temp"
  8
  9 ▾ if (!dir.exists(tmp_path)) {
 10    dir.create(tmp_path)          # Create the folder if not yet existing
 11 ▴ }
 12
 13 ▾ #Set raster options ----
 14  rasterOptions(tmptime = 4,
 15                progress = 'text',
 16                timer = TRUE,
 17                maxmemory = 10e+9,
 18                chunksize = 5e+9,
 19                tmpdir = tmp_path)
 20
 21 ▾ # Define CRS----
 22  WGS84<- "+proj=longlat +datum=WGS84 +no_defs +ellps=WGS84 +towgs84=0,0,0"
 23
 24  # select csv file containing the ridge regression predicted poverty
 25  pov_csv_path <- tcltk::tk_choose.files(filters = matrix(c("CSV",".csv","All files","*"),2,2,byrow = T),
 26                            caption = "Select Predicted Poverty CSV")
 27
 28  # set csv path's parent directory as working directory---
 29  setwd(dirname(dirname(pov_csv_path)))
 30
 31  #detect country and year from filename
 32  country_year <- str_extract(pov_csv_path,"[A-Z]{3}_[0-9]{4}")
 33
 34  country <- str_split(country_year,"_",simplify = T)[1]
 35  year <- str_split(country_year,"_",simplify = T)[2]
 36
 37  target_var <- paste0("POV_",year) #define column containing published poverty estimates
```

continued on next page

Step 1 *continued*

```
38
39   # load csv to dataframe
40   df_pov <- read.csv(pov_csv_path)
41
42 ▾ # Aggregate population into the grid----
43
44   # create centroids dataframe
45
1:66    (Top Level) ⬍                                                          R Script ⬍
```

STEP 2

Load **raster** and **tidyverse** packages.

```
2
3 ▾ # Load packages----
4    library(raster)
5    library(tidyverse)
6
```

STEP 3

Define the folder where the temporary raster files will be saved or create the folder if it does not exist.

For raster calculations, set several raster package options to improve the speed of calculation. The important options are as follows:

- **maxmemory** – maximum number of bytes to read into memory.
- **chunksize** – maximum number of bytes to read/write in a single chunk while processing (chunk by chunk) disk-based raster objects.

Other options are:

- **progress** – 'text': displays raster operation progress bar
- **tmptime** – number of hours before a temporatry file gets deleted from the tmpdir.
- **tmpdir** – location for writing temporary file.
- **timer** – TRUE: outputs the raster calculation duration.

```
 7   tmp_path <- "C:/temp"
 8
 9 ▾ if (!dir.exists(tmp_path)) {
10     dir.create(tmp_path)          # Create the folder if not yet existing
11 ▴ }
12
13 ▾ #Set raster options ----
14   rasterOptions(tmptime = 4,
15                 progress = 'text',
16                 timer = TRUE,
17                 maxmemory = 10e+9,
18                 chunksize = 5e+9,
19                 tmpdir = tmp_path)
```

STEP 4

Define the coordinate reference system for WGS84.

```
20
21 ▾  # Define CRS----
22    WGS84<- "+proj=longlat +datum=WGS84 +no_defs +ellps=WGS84 +towgs84=0,0,0"
23
```

STEP 5

Select the CSV file containing the ridge regression poverty estimates.

```
24   # select csv file containing the ridge regression predicted poverty
25   pov_csv_path <- tcltk::tk_choose.files(filters = matrix(c("CSV",".csv","All files","*"),2,2,byrow = T),
26                                   caption = "Select Predicted Poverty CSV")
```

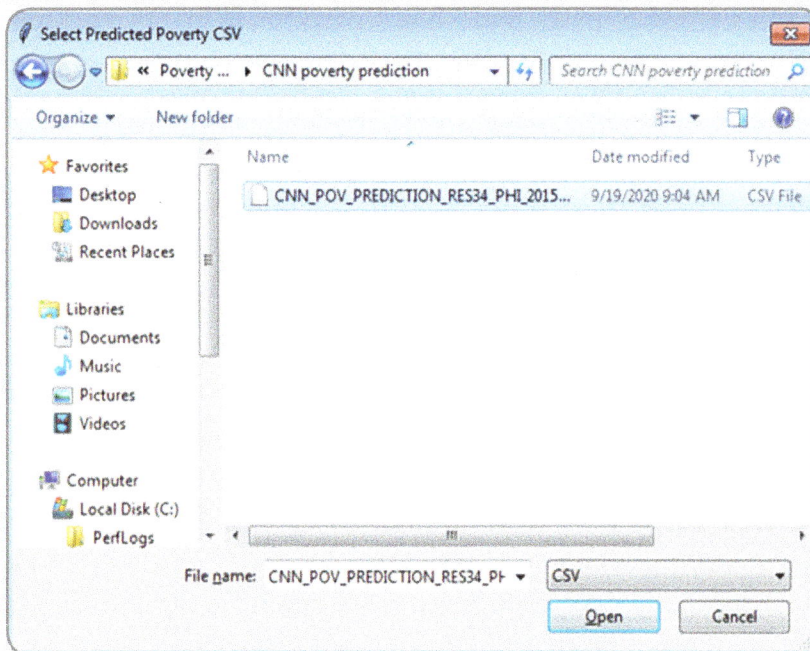

STEP 6

Set the CSV's parent directory as the working directory. Extract the country code and year of study using information from the CSV filename. Then, define the government-published poverty estimates' column name. Load the CSV file as a dataframe.

```
28   # set csv path's parent directory as working directory---
29   setwd(dirname(dirname(pov_csv_path)))
30
31   #detect country and year from filename
32   country_year <- str_extract(pov_csv_path,"[A-Z]{3}_[0-9]{4}")
33
34   country <- str_split(country_year,"_",simplify = T)[1]
35   year <- str_split(country_year,"_",simplify = T)[2]
36
37   target_var <- paste0("POV_",year) #define column containing published poverty estimates
38
39   # load csv to dataframe
40   df_pov <- read.csv(pov_csv_path)
```

STEP 7

Subset the predicted poverty dataframe to get the grid ID (id) and the latitude (lat) and longitude (lon), and rasterize the resulting dataframe using the function **rasterFromXYZ()**.

```
44   # create centroids dataframe
45   centroids <- df_pov %>%
46     select(id,lon,lat)
47
48   # make a raster from centroids
49   centroid_rast <- rasterFromXYZ(xyz = centroids[,c("lon","lat", "id")],  crs=WGS84)
```

The function **rasterFromXYZ()** generates raster from regular grids like the dataset used. The function assumes that the minimum distance between x and y coordinates is the raster resolution.

STEP 8

Load the machine learning population raster.

```
51 ▾ #load ML estimated population raster----
52   pop_raster_path <- tcltk::tk_choose.files(filters = matrix(c("TIF",".tif","All files","*"),2,2,byrow = T),
53                          caption = "Select Population Raster")
54   pop_raster <- raster(pop_raster_path)
```

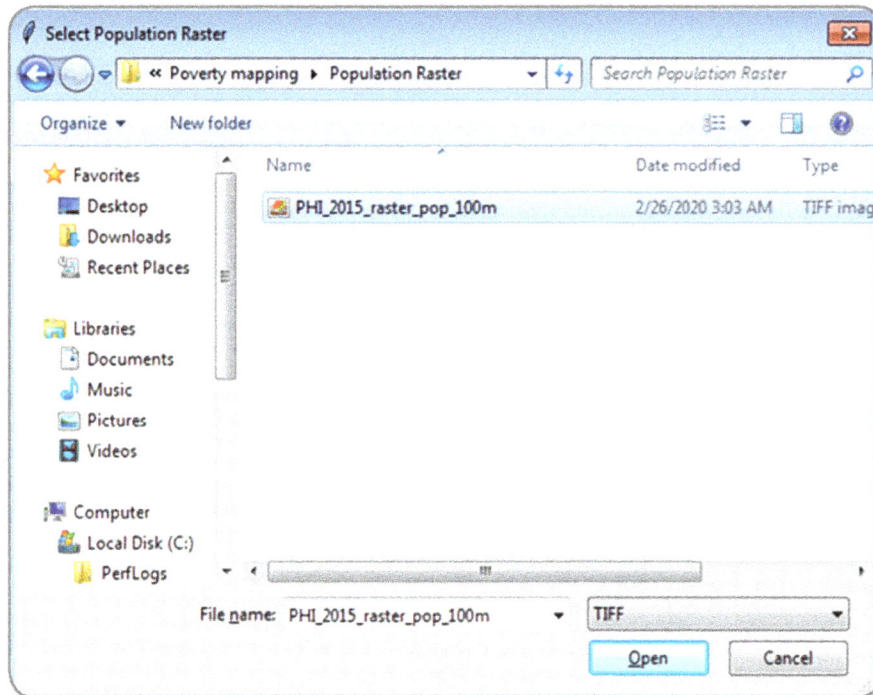

STEP 9

Check if the population raster is using WGS84 CRS. Otherwise, reproject the raster. Print out the new CRS of the population raster. Also, compare the resolution of the population and poverty grids. Note from the results that the population and centroid rasters have different resolutions.

```
56  #check if pop_raster projection is WGS84, otherwise reproject raster
57  if (compareCRS(pop_raster,WGS84)==FALSE) {
58    print("Raster CRS is not WGS84. Projecting raster to WGS84...")
59    pop_raster <- projectRaster(pop_raster,crs = WGS84)
60  }
61  print(crs(pop_raster))
62  print(paste0("Population Raster grid size: ",paste(res(pop_raster),collapse = ", ")))
63  print(paste0("Centroid Raster grid size: ",paste(res(centroid_rast),collapse = ", ")))
```

```
> #check if pop_raster projection is WGS84, otherwise reproject raster
> if (compareCRS(pop_raster,WGS84)==FALSE) {
+   print("Raster CRS is not WGS84. Projecting raster to WGS84...")
+   pop_raster <- projectRaster(pop_raster,crs = WGS84)
+ }
[1] "Raster CRS is not WGS84. Projecting raster to WGS84..."
361 seconds
> print(crs(pop_raster))
CRS arguments:
 +proj=longlat +datum=WGS84 +no_defs +ellps=WGS84 +towgs84=0,0,0
> print(paste0("Population Raster grid size: ",paste(res(pop_raster),collapse = ", ")))
[1] "Population Raster grid size: 0.000921, 0.000903000000000003"
> print(paste0("Centroid Raster grid size: ",paste(res(centroid_rast),collapse = ", ")))
[1] "Centroid Raster grid size: 0.0429204653119797, 0.0429204653119974"
>
```

STEP 10

Calculate the **adjustment_factor** first because the two rasters have different resolutions.

Aggregate the population headcount of the machine learning population raster at the poverty grid level, which will be used to rescale the ridge regression poverty prediction. Using the **aggregate()** function, aggregate the population in the poverty grid using the calculated adjustment_factor. Then, resample the aggregated population raster to match the resolution of the centroid raster.

```
65   # determine resolution ratio of centroid raster and population raster
66   adjustment_factor <- round(res(centroid_rast)/res(pop_raster))[1]
67
68   # aggregate population raster values to poverty grid by taking its sum
69   pop_agg <- aggregate(pop_raster, fact = adjustment_factor, fun = sum)
70
71   # resample pop_agg raster to match the extent and resolution of centroid_rast
72   pop_agg_resampled <- resample(pop_agg, centroid_rast)
```

STEP 11

Set the aggregated population raster layer's name to **"gridpop"**. Stack the centroid and aggregated population raster, then convert the raster stack as a dataframe. Merge the created dataframe with the predicted poverty dataframe.

```
74   # rename raster column
75   names(pop_agg_resampled) <- "gridpop"
76
77   # stack the two raster
78   pop_id_stack <- raster::stack(centroid_rast,pop_agg_resampled)
79
80   #convert the raster stack to dataframe
81   df_pop_id <- as.data.frame(pop_id_stack,na.rm=T)
82
83   # merge the aggregated population at poverty grid with the predicted poverty dataframe
84   df_grid_pov <- left_join(df_pov,df_pop_id,by="id")
```

STEP 12

Prior to rescaling, check if there are poverty prediction values that are either negative or more than 100%. Set the negative values to 0.0001 and adjust the values above 100% to 100%.

```
86 ▾ # Rescaling poverty estimates----
87
88   #list predictions with values less than zero
89   df_grid_pov$prediction[df_grid_pov$prediction<0]
90   #list predictions with values more than 100
91   df_grid_pov$prediction[df_grid_pov$prediction>100]
92
93   # set all negative and more than 100 prediction values to 0.0001 and 100, respectively
94   df_grid_pov$prediction[df_grid_pov$prediction<0] <- 0.0001
95   df_grid_pov$prediction[df_grid_pov$prediction>100] <- 100
```

```
> df_grid_pov$prediction[df_grid_pov$prediction<0]
  [1]   -9.76615276   -2.44891190   -2.11756679   -0.33303274   -3.09370659   -1.67311394   -0.13072355
  [8]   -0.06488157   -4.66824640   -4.54287004   -1.31282410   -0.96758935  -17.74339779   -2.78249089
 [15]   -3.70780614  -46.46954242   -7.49085999   -5.43519687  -12.30298783   -1.07066770   -2.17014635
 [22]   -2.34823957   -3.74335482   -2.10970982   -5.82334686   -0.90075623   -3.87349206   -7.57365484
 [29]  -10.52484519   -3.23173896   -3.97719036   -3.07286788   -0.56072147   -2.78270204   -1.81189565
 [36]  -16.27836149  -16.32787600  -13.83109915   -0.65088385   -2.62484320   -3.12055855   -5.52654036
 [43]   -1.40884846   -2.74597482   -1.12613739   -2.62847857   -5.97378568   -2.73238845   -1.69923546
 [50]  -14.95788028   -2.65768206   -0.31590220   -2.72752851   -1.01700032   -0.73631685   -3.69906196
 [57]   -3.17035178  -11.20606404   -2.23988866   -0.49158938   -1.07697913   -4.81580071   -1.46566070
 [64]   -0.26618075   -6.03245353   -3.67005747   -2.27726058   -2.35306144   -0.63171279   -6.83863028
 [71]   -0.61520243   -1.47657141   -1.96351253   -1.12781684   -0.38764935   -0.78226025   -0.63581880
 [78]   -2.23446817   -3.12026997   -4.22790189   -5.94424881   -1.35129182   -6.89809722   -4.03085238
 [85]   -0.48542614   -5.84422507   -1.75696018   -0.32208028   -1.01284010   -1.70427220   -0.99470605
 [92]   -1.65616706   -0.78161033   -0.50962936   -0.74728261  -12.05323645   -4.12564256   -8.78057057
 [99]   -1.97061892   -0.65292023   -3.02659539   -0.70654295   -7.55077973   -0.77817140   -1.88521730
[106]   -2.32702656   -0.84572781   -0.93529947   -0.32274265   -0.39417643   -1.86285201   -0.13672533
[113]   -2.65728878   -1.09520873  -10.63899570   -1.26016500   -1.38133152   -5.57652139  -10.33314256
[120]   -2.74571277   -7.56366834   -4.97146788  -14.00443877   -1.05094801   -1.42111790   -3.65463779
[127]   -0.34020028   -0.18592289   -4.33768258   -0.35663700   -5.85590182   -8.93088045   -7.57810217
[134]   -5.53394989   -3.40195403   -2.04033049   -1.51549486   -2.10078391   -1.83702723   -1.46783083
[141]   -2.86351434   -1.19690448   -0.12814693
> #list predictions with values more than 100
> df_grid_pov$prediction[df_grid_pov$prediction>100]
[1] 130.2866 112.5153 106.7372
>
```

STEP 13

Rescale the poverty predictions. Convert the predicted poverty rates to index values by dividing the values by 100.

```
97    #rescale poverty predictions based on published poverty estimates
98    df_grid_pov <- df_grid_pov %>%
99      mutate(pred_hci = prediction / 100) %>%
100     mutate(svy_hci  = get(target_var) / 100) %>%
101     mutate(pred_hc = gridpop * pred_hci) %>%
102     mutate(svy_hc = gridpop * svy_hci) %>%
103     group_by(geocode) %>%
104     mutate(pred_hc_rescale =  pred_hc * (sum(svy_hc) / sum(pred_hc))) %>%
105     mutate(pred_hci_rescale =  pred_hc_rescale / gridpop) %>%
106     ungroup()
```

STEP 14

Convert the government-published poverty rates to index values by dividing the values by 100.

```
97   #rescale poverty predictions based on published poverty estimates
98   df_grid_pov <- df_grid_pov %>%
99     mutate(pred_hci = prediction / 100) %>%
100    mutate(svy_hci  = get(target_var) / 100) %>%
101    mutate(pred_hc = gridpop * pred_hci) %>%
102    mutate(svy_hc = gridpop * svy_hci) %>%
103    group_by(geocode) %>%
104    mutate(pred_hc_rescale =  pred_hc * (sum(svy_hc) / sum(pred_hc))) %>%
105    mutate(pred_hci_rescale =  pred_hc_rescale / gridpop) %>%
106    ungroup()
```

STEP 15

Calculate the grid level poverty headcount by multiplying the grid population by the predicted poverty index.

```
97   #rescale poverty predictions based on published poverty estimates
98   df_grid_pov <- df_grid_pov %>%
99     mutate(pred_hci = prediction / 100) %>%
100    mutate(svy_hci  = get(target_var) / 100) %>%
101    mutate(pred_hc = gridpop * pred_hci) %>%
102    mutate(svy_hc = gridpop * svy_hci) %>%
103    group_by(geocode) %>%
104    mutate(pred_hc_rescale =  pred_hc * (sum(svy_hc) / sum(pred_hc))) %>%
105    mutate(pred_hci_rescale =  pred_hc_rescale / gridpop) %>%
106    ungroup()
```

STEP 16

Calculate the government-published poverty headcount.

```
97   #rescale poverty predictions based on published poverty estimates
98   df_grid_pov <- df_grid_pov %>%
99     mutate(pred_hci = prediction / 100) %>%
100    mutate(svy_hci  = get(target_var) / 100) %>%
101    mutate(pred_hc = gridpop * pred_hci) %>%
102    mutate(svy_hc = gridpop * svy_hci) %>%
103    group_by(geocode) %>%
104    mutate(pred_hc_rescale =  pred_hc * (sum(svy_hc) / sum(pred_hc))) %>%
105    mutate(pred_hci_rescale =  pred_hc_rescale / gridpop) %>%
106    ungroup()
```

STEP 17

Group the data according to geocode.

```
97   #rescale poverty predictions based on published poverty estimates
98   df_grid_pov <- df_grid_pov %>%
99     mutate(pred_hci = prediction / 100) %>%
100    mutate(svy_hci  = get(target_var) / 100) %>%
101    mutate(pred_hc = gridpop * pred_hci) %>%
102    mutate(svy_hc = gridpop * svy_hci) %>%
103    group_by(geocode) %>%
104    mutate(pred_hc_rescale =  pred_hc * (sum(svy_hc) / sum(pred_hc))) %>%
105    mutate(pred_hci_rescale =  pred_hc_rescale / gridpop) %>%
106    ungroup()
```

STEP 18

Derive the rescaled predicted poverty headcount for each grid by multiplying the grid's predicted poverty headcount by the ratio of the sum of the government-published and predicted poverty headcounts. *This is calculated for each geocode group.*

```
97   #rescale poverty predictions based on published poverty estimates
98   df_grid_pov <- df_grid_pov %>%
99     mutate(pred_hci = prediction / 100) %>%
100    mutate(svy_hci  = get(target_var) / 100) %>%
101    mutate(pred_hc = gridpop * pred_hci) %>%
102    mutate(svy_hc = gridpop * svy_hci) %>%
103    group_by(geocode) %>%
104    mutate(pred_hc_rescale =  pred_hc * (sum(svy_hc) / sum(pred_hc))) %>%
105    mutate(pred_hci_rescale =  pred_hc_rescale / gridpop) %>%
106    ungroup()
```

STEP 19

Calculate the rescaled poverty index by dividing the rescaled predicted poverty headcount by the grid level population counts.

```
97   #rescale poverty predictions based on published poverty estimates
98   df_grid_pov <- df_grid_pov %>%
99     mutate(pred_hci = prediction / 100) %>%
100    mutate(svy_hci  = get(target_var) / 100) %>%
101    mutate(pred_hc = gridpop * pred_hci) %>%
102    mutate(svy_hc = gridpop * svy_hci) %>%
103    group_by(geocode) %>%
104    mutate(pred_hc_rescale =  pred_hc * (sum(svy_hc) / sum(pred_hc))) %>%
105    mutate(pred_hci_rescale =  pred_hc_rescale / gridpop) %>%
106    ungroup()
```

STEP 20

Ungroup the dataframe.

```
97    #rescale poverty predictions based on published poverty estimates
98    df_grid_pov <- df_grid_pov %>%
99      mutate(pred_hci = prediction / 100) %>%
100     mutate(svy_hci  = get(target_var) / 100) %>%
101     mutate(pred_hc = gridpop * pred_hci) %>%
102     mutate(svy_hc = gridpop * svy_hci) %>%
103     group_by(geocode) %>%
104     mutate(pred_hc_rescale =  pred_hc * (sum(svy_hc) / sum(pred_hc))) %>%
105     mutate(pred_hci_rescale =  pred_hc_rescale / gridpop) %>%
106     ungroup()
```

STEP 21

Check if there are rescaled poverty indexes above 1; set to 1 if there are any.

```
101   #list rescaled predictions with values more than 1
102   df_grid_pov$pred_hci_rescale[df_grid_pov$pred_hci_rescale>1]
103
104   # If any, set all rescaled values more than 1 to 1
105   df_grid_pov$pred_hci_rescale[df_grid_pov$pred_hci_rescale>1] <- 1
```

```
> #list rescaled predictions with values more than 1
> df_grid_pov$pred_hci_rescale[df_grid_pov$pred_hci_rescale>1]
 [1] 1.066041 1.114437 1.002371 1.796617 1.020819 1.171022 1.046143 1.095574 1.034427 1.179695
[11] 1.015254 1.059618 1.114126 1.150759 1.377199 1.096228 1.298676 1.195739 1.088301 1.018356
[21] 1.114425 1.561659 1.023001 1.190219 1.063670 1.198248 1.074865 1.352508 1.047025 1.213172
[31] 1.101369 1.562566 1.156449 1.022488 1.146228 1.064639 1.000607 1.050016 1.049233 1.319102
[41] 1.042742       NA       NA       NA       NA       NA 1.215445 1.112034       NA 1.117670
[51] 1.174949 1.114226       NA       NA       NA       NA       NA       NA 1.179504       NA
[61]       NA       NA       NA 1.119742       NA       NA       NA       NA       NA       NA
[71] 1.022075 1.594319 1.122841
>
```

STEP 22

Generate the poverty raster.

```
115 ▾ # generate raster ----
116
117   pov_hci_raster <- rasterFromXYZ(xyz = df_grid_pov[,c("lon","lat", "pred_hci")],  crs=WGS84)
118   pov_hci_rescaled_raster <- rasterFromXYZ(xyz = df_grid_pov[,c("lon","lat", "pred_hci_rescale")],  crs=WGS84)
119
120 ▾ # Output raster----
121   # set raster destination path
122   raster_path <- "Output/Poverty Raster/"
123
124 ▾ if (!dir.exists(raster_path)) {
125     dir.create(raster_path, recursive = T)
126 ▴ }
127
128   writeRaster(pov_hci_raster ,
129               filename = paste0(raster_path, paste(country_year, "pov_hci.tif",sep = "_")),
130               overwrite=TRUE)
131   writeRaster(pov_hci_rescaled_raster,
132               filename = paste0(raster_path, paste(country_year,"pov_hci_rescaled.tif",sep = "_")),
133               overwrite=TRUE)
```

Generate poverty rasters for both predicted and rescaled predicted poverty index using the raster function **rasterfromXYZ()**.

The parameters supplied are the centroid coordinates (lat and lon) and the corresponding data to be rasterized.

STEP 23

Define the folder where the raster will be saved or create the folder if it does not exist.

```
115 ▾ # generate raster ----
116
117   pov_hci_raster <- rasterFromXYZ(xyz = df_grid_pov[,c("lon","lat", "pred_hci")],  crs=WGS84)
118   pov_hci_rescaled_raster <- rasterFromXYZ(xyz = df_grid_pov[,c("lon","lat", "pred_hci_rescale")],  crs=WGS84)
119
120 ▾ # Output raster----
121   # set raster destination path
122   raster_path <- "Output/Poverty Raster/"
123
124 ▾ if (!dir.exists(raster_path)) {
125     dir.create(raster_path, recursive = T)
126 ▴ }
127
128   writeRaster(pov_hci_raster ,
129               filename = paste0(raster_path, paste(country_year, "pov_hci.tif",sep = "_")),
130               overwrite=TRUE)
131   writeRaster(pov_hci_rescaled_raster,
132               filename = paste0(raster_path, paste(country_year,"pov_hci_rescaled.tif",sep = "_")),
133               overwrite=TRUE)
```

STEP 24

Output the raster using the **writeRaster()** function.

```
115 ▾ # generate raster ----
116
117   pov_hci_raster <- rasterFromXYZ(xyz = df_grid_pov[,c("lon","lat", "pred_hci")],  crs=WGS84)
118   pov_hci_rescaled_raster <- rasterFromXYZ(xyz = df_grid_pov[,c("lon","lat", "pred_hci_rescale")],  crs=WGS84)
119
120 ▾ # Output raster----
121   # set raster destination path
122   raster_path <- "Output/Poverty Raster/"
123
124 ▾ if (!dir.exists(raster_path)) {
125     dir.create(raster_path, recursive = T)
126 ▴ }
127
128   writeRaster(pov_hci_raster ,
129             filename = paste0(raster_path, paste(country_year, "pov_hci.tif",sep = "_")),
130             overwrite=TRUE)
131   writeRaster(pov_hci_rescaled_raster,
132             filename = paste0(raster_path, paste(country_year,"pov_hci_rescaled.tif",sep = "_")),
133             overwrite=TRUE)
```

STEP 25

Visualize the raster. Load another raster visualization package, **rasterVis** (aside from **ggplot2**, which was already loaded as part of the **tidyverse** package).

```
135 ▾ # Visualization----
136   #load packages
137   library(rasterVis)
138
139   #define plotting function
140 ▾ plot_raster <- function(rast,p_var){
141     theme_set(theme_bw())
142     hci_heat <- cut(rast, p_var$category/100, include.lowest = T)
143
144     plt_raster <- gplot(hci_heat) +
145       geom_tile(aes(fill = as.character(value)))+
146       scale_fill_brewer(name = p_var$scale_title,
147                         palette = "RdYlGn",
148                         direction = -1,
149                         labels = p_var$scale_label) +
150       labs( title = paste0(p_var$map_title),
151             x = "",
152             y ="") +
153       theme(axis.text = element_blank(),
154             axis.ticks = element_blank(),
155             panel.grid.major = element_blank(),
156             panel.grid.minor = element_blank(),
157             panel.border = element_blank())+
158       coord_fixed()
```

STEP 26

Define **plot_raster()** function that will aid in plotting the raster.

```r
135 ▾ # Visualization----
136    #load packages
137    library(rasterVis)
138
139    #define plotting function
140 ▾ plot_raster <- function(rast,p_var){
141      theme_set(theme_bw())
142      hci_heat <- cut(rast, p_var$category/100, include.lowest = T)
143
144      plt_raster <- gplot(hci_heat) +
145        geom_tile(aes(fill = as.character(value)))+
146        scale_fill_brewer(name = p_var$scale_title,
147                          palette = "RdYlGn",
148                          direction = -1,
149                          labels = p_var$scale_label) +
150        labs( title = paste0(p_var$map_title),
151              x = "",
152              y ="") +
153        theme(axis.text = element_blank(),
154              axis.ticks = element_blank(),
155              panel.grid.major = element_blank(),
156              panel.grid.minor = element_blank(),
157              panel.border = element_blank())+
158        coord_fixed()
159
160      #save map as png
161      ggsave(plt_raster,
162             filename = p_var$filename,
163             dpi = 300,
164             device='png')
165
166      return(plt_raster)
167 ▴ }
```

The function requires two objects, a raster (**rast**) and a list (**p_var**). **p_var** contains the following parameters:

- *category* – a vector object containing the interval classes for reclassifying the raster values,
- *scale_title* and *scale_label* – define the scale bar title and labels, respectively,
- *map_title* – defines the map title, and
- *filename* – specifies the filename of the map for saving as png image file.

Inside the function, set the theme to black and white.

```
135 ▾ # Visualization----
136   #load packages
137   library(rasterVis)
138
139   #define plotting function
140 ▾ plot_raster <- function(rast,p_var){
141     theme_set(theme_bw())
142     hci_heat <- cut(rast, p_var$category/100, include.lowest = T)
143
144     plt_raster <- gplot(hci_heat) +
145       geom_tile(aes(fill = as.character(value)))+
146       scale_fill_brewer(name = p_var$scale_title,
147                         palette = "RdYlGn",
148                         direction = -1,
149                         labels = p_var$scale_label) +
150       labs( title = paste0(p_var$map_title),
151             x = "",
152             y ="") +
153       theme(axis.text = element_blank(),
154             axis.ticks = element_blank(),
155             panel.grid.major = element_blank(),
156             panel.grid.minor = element_blank(),
157             panel.border = element_blank())+
158       coord_fixed()
159
160     #save map as png
161     ggsave(plt_raster,
162           filename = p_var$filename,
163           dpi = 300,
164           device='png')
165
166     return(plt_raster)
167 ▴ }
```

STEP 27

Using the supplied category, reclassify the raster values

```
135 ▾  # Visualization----
136    #load packages
137    library(rasterVis)
138
139    #define plotting function
140 ▾  plot_raster <- function(rast,p_var){
141      theme_set(theme_bw())
142      hci_heat <- cut(rast, p_var$category/100, include.lowest = T)
143
144      plt_raster <- gplot(hci_heat) +
145        geom_tile(aes(fill = as.character(value)))+
146        scale_fill_brewer(name = p_var$scale_title,
147                          palette = "RdYlGn",
148                          direction = -1,
149                          labels = p_var$scale_label) +
150        labs( title = paste0(p_var$map_title),
151              x = "",
152              y ="") +
153        theme(axis.text = element_blank(),
154              axis.ticks = element_blank(),
155              panel.grid.major = element_blank(),
156              panel.grid.minor = element_blank(),
157              panel.border = element_blank())+
158        coord_fixed()
159
160      #save map as png
161      ggsave(plt_raster,
162            filename = p_var$filename,
163            dpi = 300,
164            device='png')
165
166      return(plt_raster)
167 ▴  }
```

STEP 28

Create a **gplot** object and set the categorized raster as the data source. **gplot** is a wrapper for plotting raster.

```
135 ▾ # Visualization----
136   #load packages
137   library(rasterVis)
138
139   #define plotting function
140 ▾ plot_raster <- function(rast,p_var){
141     theme_set(theme_bw())
142     hci_heat <- cut(rast, p_var$category/100, include.lowest = T)
143
144     plt_raster <- gplot(hci_heat) +
145       geom_tile(aes(fill = as.character(value)))+
146       scale_fill_brewer(name = p_var$scale_title,
147                         palette = "RdYlGn",
148                         direction = -1,
149                         labels = p_var$scale_label) +
150       labs( title = paste0(p_var$map_title),
151             x = "",
152             y ="") +
153       theme(axis.text = element_blank(),
154             axis.ticks = element_blank(),
155             panel.grid.major = element_blank(),
156             panel.grid.minor = element_blank(),
157             panel.border = element_blank())+
158       coord_fixed()
159
160     #save map as png
161     ggsave(plt_raster,
162           filename = p_var$filename,
163           dpi = 300,
164           device='png')
165
166     return(plt_raster)
167 ▴ }
```

STEP 29

Specify the raster's value as the object fill using the **geom_tile()** function.

```
135 ▾  # Visualization----
136    #load packages
137    library(rasterVis)
138
139    #define plotting function
140 ▾  plot_raster <- function(rast,p_var){
141      theme_set(theme_bw())
142      hci_heat <- cut(rast, p_var$category/100, include.lowest = T)
143
144      plt_raster <- gplot(hci_heat) +
145        geom_tile(aes(fill = as.character(value)))+
146        scale_fill_brewer(name = p_var$scale_title,
147                          palette = "RdYlGn",
148                          direction = -1,
149                          labels = p_var$scale_label) +
150        labs( title = paste0(p_var$map_title),
151              x = "",
152              y ="") +
153        theme(axis.text = element_blank(),
154              axis.ticks = element_blank(),
155              panel.grid.major = element_blank(),
156              panel.grid.minor = element_blank(),
157              panel.border = element_blank())+
158        coord_fixed()
159
160      #save map as png
161      ggsave(plt_raster,
162             filename = p_var$filename,
163             dpi = 300,
164             device='png')
165
166      return(plt_raster)
167 ▴  }
```

STEP 30

Using the **scale_fill_brewer()** function, specify the following:

- **name** – scale title,
- **palette** – color palette of the map and scale, which is set to Red-Yellow-Green ("RdYlGn"),
- **direction = -1** – reverses the color palette order from "RdYlGn" to "GnYlRd", and
- **labels** – scale label to match the categorical grouping of the dataset.

```r
135 ▾ # Visualization----
136    #load packages
137    library(rasterVis)
138
139    #define plotting function
140 ▾ plot_raster <- function(rast,p_var){
141      theme_set(theme_bw())
142      hci_heat <- cut(rast, p_var$category/100, include.lowest = T)
143
144      plt_raster <- gplot(hci_heat) +
145        geom_tile(aes(fill = as.character(value)))+
146        scale_fill_brewer(name = p_var$scale_title,
147                          palette = "RdYlGn",
148                          direction = -1,
149                          labels = p_var$scale_label) +
150        labs( title = paste0(p_var$map_title),
151              x = "",
152              y ="") +
153        theme(axis.text = element_blank(),
154              axis.ticks = element_blank(),
155              panel.grid.major = element_blank(),
156              panel.grid.minor = element_blank(),
157              panel.border = element_blank())+
158        coord_fixed()
159
160      #save map as png
161      ggsave(plt_raster,
162             filename = p_var$filename,
163             dpi = 300,
164             device='png')
165
166      return(plt_raster)
167 ▴ }
```

STEP 31

Specify the map title and leave the x and y axes unlabeled.

```r
135 ▾  # Visualization----
136    #load packages
137    library(rasterVis)
138
139    #define plotting function
140 ▾  plot_raster <- function(rast,p_var){
141      theme_set(theme_bw())
142      hci_heat <- cut(rast, p_var$category/100, include.lowest = T)
143
144      plt_raster <- gplot(hci_heat) +
145        geom_tile(aes(fill = as.character(value)))+
146        scale_fill_brewer(name = p_var$scale_title,
147                          palette = "RdYlGn",
148                          direction = -1,
149                          labels = p_var$scale_label) +
150        labs( title = paste0(p_var$map_title),
151              x = "",
152              y ="") +
153        theme(axis.text = element_blank(),
154              axis.ticks = element_blank(),
155              panel.grid.major = element_blank(),
156              panel.grid.minor = element_blank(),
157              panel.border = element_blank())+
158        coord_fixed()
159
160      #save map as png
161      ggsave(plt_raster,
162             filename = p_var$filename,
163             dpi = 300,
164             device='png')
165
166      return(plt_raster)
167 ▴  }
```

STEP 32

Remove axis text, tick marks, gridlines, and borders (optional).

```
135  # Visualization----
136  #load packages
137  library(rasterVis)
138
139  #define plotting function
140  plot_raster <- function(rast,p_var){
141    theme_set(theme_bw())
142    hci_heat <- cut(rast, p_var$category/100, include.lowest = T)
143
144    plt_raster <- gplot(hci_heat) +
145      geom_tile(aes(fill = as.character(value)))+
146      scale_fill_brewer(name = p_var$scale_title,
147                        palette = "RdYlGn",
148                        direction = -1,
149                        labels = p_var$scale_label) +
150      labs( title = paste0(p_var$map_title),
151            x = "",
152            y ="") +
153      theme(axis.text = element_blank(),
154            axis.ticks = element_blank(),
155            panel.grid.major = element_blank(),
156            panel.grid.minor = element_blank(),
157            panel.border = element_blank())+
158      coord_fixed()
159
160    #save map as png
161    ggsave(plt_raster,
162           filename = p_var$filename,
163           dpi = 300,
164           device='png')
165
166    return(plt_raster)
167  }
```

STEP 33

Set the Cartesian coordinates to a fixed aspect ratio (**coord_fixed()**) which is a 1:1 ratio of x and y values.

```
135 ▾ # Visualization----
136   #load packages
137   library(rasterVis)
138
139   #define plotting function
140 ▾ plot_raster <- function(rast,p_var){
141     theme_set(theme_bw())
142     hci_heat <- cut(rast, p_var$category/100, include.lowest = T)
143
144     plt_raster <- gplot(hci_heat) +
145       geom_tile(aes(fill = as.character(value)))+
146       scale_fill_brewer(name = p_var$scale_title,
147                         palette = "RdYlGn",
148                         direction = -1,
149                         labels = p_var$scale_label) +
150       labs( title = paste0(p_var$map_title),
151             x = "",
152             y ="") +
153       theme(axis.text = element_blank(),
154             axis.ticks = element_blank(),
155             panel.grid.major = element_blank(),
156             panel.grid.minor = element_blank(),
157             panel.border = element_blank())+
158       coord_fixed()
159
160     #save map as png
161     ggsave(plt_raster,
162           filename = p_var$filename,
163           dpi = 300,
164           device='png')
165
166     return(plt_raster)
167 ▴ }
```

STEP 34

Save the plot as png image format using the filename to be supplied in the variable **p_var**.

Other supported image format are "eps", "ps", "tex" (pictex), "pdf", "jpeg", "tiff", "png", "bmp", "svg" or "wmf".

```
135 ▾  # Visualization----
136    #load packages
137    library(rasterVis)
138
139    #define plotting function
140 ▾  plot_raster <- function(rast,p_var){
141      theme_set(theme_bw())
142      hci_heat <- cut(rast, p_var$category/100, include.lowest = T)
143
144      plt_raster <- gplot(hci_heat) +
145        geom_tile(aes(fill = as.character(value)))+
146        scale_fill_brewer(name = p_var$scale_title,
147                          palette = "RdYlGn",
148                          direction = -1,
149                          labels = p_var$scale_label) +
150        labs( title = paste0(p_var$map_title),
151              x = "",
152              y ="") +
153        theme(axis.text = element_blank(),
154              axis.ticks = element_blank(),
155              panel.grid.major = element_blank(),
156              panel.grid.minor = element_blank(),
157              panel.border = element_blank())+
158        coord_fixed()
159
160      #save map as png
161      ggsave(plt_raster,
162            filename = p_var$filename,
163            dpi = 300,
164            device='png')
165
166      return(plt_raster)
167 ▴  }
```

STEP 35

Return the gplot object so that it will automatically show in the viewer pane upon function call.

```
135 ▾ # Visualization----
136   #load packages
137   library(rasterVis)
138
139   #define plotting function
140 ▾ plot_raster <- function(rast,p_var){
141     theme_set(theme_bw())
142     hci_heat <- cut(rast, p_var$category/100, include.lowest = T)
143
144     plt_raster <- gplot(hci_heat) +
145       geom_tile(aes(fill = as.character(value)))+
146       scale_fill_brewer(name = p_var$scale_title,
147                         palette = "RdYlGn",
148                         direction = -1,
149                         labels = p_var$scale_label) +
150       labs( title = paste0(p_var$map_title),
151             x = "",
152             y ="") +
153       theme(axis.text = element_blank(),
154             axis.ticks = element_blank(),
155             panel.grid.major = element_blank(),
156             panel.grid.minor = element_blank(),
157             panel.border = element_blank())+
158       coord_fixed()
159
160     #save map as png
161     ggsave(plt_raster,
162            filename = p_var$filename,
163            dpi = 300,
164            device='png')
165
166     return(plt_raster)
167 ▴ }
```

STEP 36

Set the maps' save path and create a folder if it does not exist.

```
169   map_path <- "Output/Poverty maps/"
170
171 ▼ if (!dir.exists(map_path)) {
172     dir.create(map_path,recursive = T)
173 ▲ }
```

STEP 37

Specify the parameters needed by the function and pass on the raster object and the parameters to the function.

```
175 ▼ #plot poverty rate map----
176
177   # define variables to be used for visualization
178   map_variables <- list(map_title = "2015 Machine Learning-Predicted Poverty Map",
179                         scale_title = "Poverty rate per 4km x 4km",
180                         category=c(0,20,40,60,80,100),
181                         scale_label=c("0-20","20-40","40-60","60-80","80-100"),
182                         filename = paste0(map_path,paste(country,year,"pov_hci_map.png",sep = "_")))
183
184   plot_raster(pov_hci_raster,map_variables)
185
186 ▼ #plot rescaled 4km poverty rate map----
187
188   # define variables to be used for visualization
189   map_variables <- list(map_title = "2015 Calibrated Machine Learning-Predicted Poverty Map",
190                         scale_title = "Poverty rate per 4km x 4km",
191                         category=c(0,20,40,60,80,100),
192                         scale_label=c("0-20","20-40","40-60","60-80","80-100"),
193                         filename = paste0(map_path,paste(country,year,"pov_hci_rescaled_map.png",sep = "_")))
194
195   plot_raster(pov_hci_rescaled_raster,map_variables)
```

The resulting poverty maps—machine learning (predicted and calibrated) and government-published—for the Philippines are shown in Figure 2 and for Thailand in Figure 3.

Figure 2: Machine Learning and Published Poverty Rate Maps of the Philippines, 2015

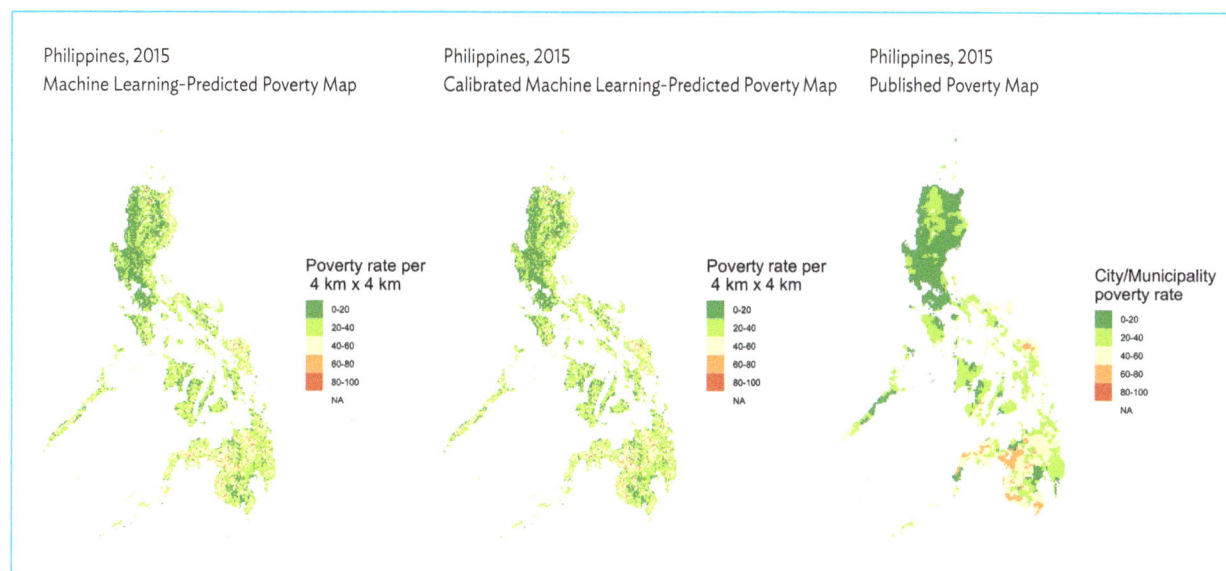

Note: The first two images present the uncalibrated and calibrated machine learning-based poverty rate estimates in (approximately) every 4 square kilometer grid, respectively. The third image shows the municipal or city-level poverty rates published by the Philippine Statistics Authority.

Source: Calculations and graphics generated by the study team.

Figure 3: Machine Learning and Published Poverty Rate Maps of Thailand, 2015

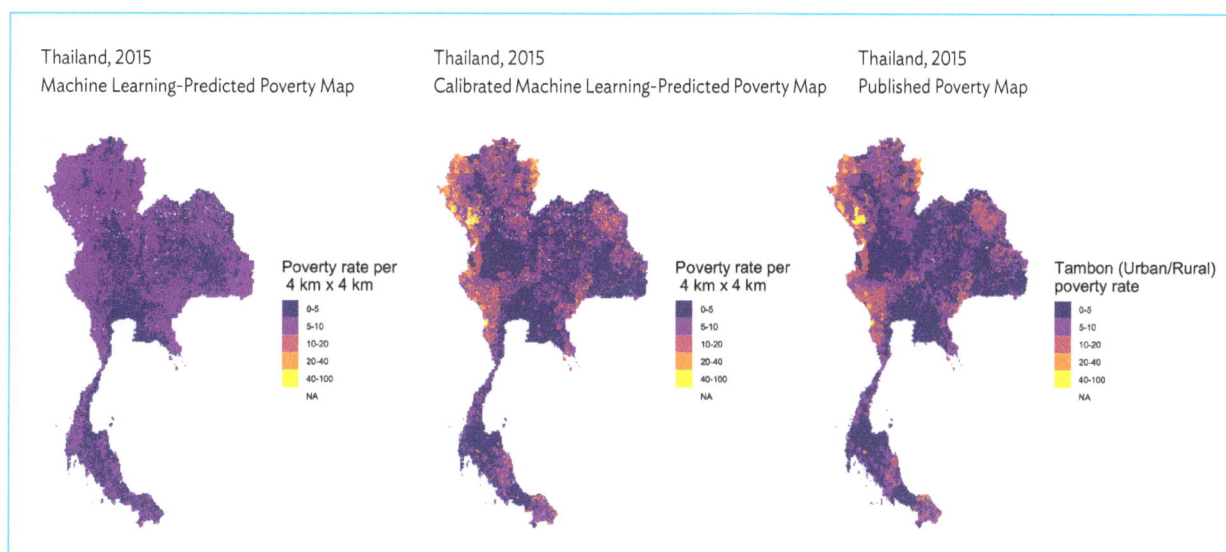

Note: The first two images present the uncalibrated and calibrated machine learning-based poverty rate estimates in (approximately) every 4 square kilometer grid, respectively. The third image shows the tambon-level poverty rates published by the National Statistical Office of Thailand.

Source: Calculations and graphics generated by the study team.

BIBLIOGRAPHY

Asian Development Bank (ADB). 2020. *Mapping Poverty through Data Integration and Artificial Intelligence: A Special Supplement of the Key Indicators for Asia and the Pacific*. Manila.

_____. 2021. *Mapping the Spatial Distribution of Poverty Using Satellite Imagery in the Philippines*. Manila.

_____. Forthcoming. *Mapping the Spatial Distribution of Poverty Using Satellite Imagery in Thailand*. Manila.

Database of Global Administrative Areas (GADM). GADM Data. https://gadm.org/data.html (accessed 20 February 2021).

Environmental Systems Research Institute (ESRI). 1998. ESRI Shapefile Technical Description: An ESRI White Paper – July 1998. https://www.esri.com/Library/Whitepapers/Pdfs/Shapefile.pdf.

N. Gorelick et al. 2017. Google Earth Engine: Planetary-Scale Geospatial Analysis for Everyone. *Remote Sensing of Environment*. 202. pp 18–27.

R. J. Hijmans. 2020. raster: Geographic Data Analysis and Modeling. R Package, Version 3.4-5. https://CRAN.R-project.org/package=raster.

Humanitarian Data Exchange (HDX). 2020. About the Humanitarian Data Exchange. https://data.humdata.org/faq.

N. Jean et al. 2016. Combining Satellite Imagery and Machine Learning to Predict Poverty. *Science*. 353 (6301). pp 790–794.

K. Jordahl. 2014. GeoPandas: Python Tools for Geographic Data. https://github.com/Geopandas/Geopandas.

M. Kuhn. 2008. Building Predictive Models in R Using the Caret Package. *Journal of Statistical Software*. 28 (5). pp. 1–26.

O. P. Lamigueiro and R. Hijmans. 2020. rasterVis. R Package, Version 0.49. https://oscarperpinan.github.io/rastervis/.

"Lesson 2 - Deep Learning for Coders (2020)", Youtube video, 1:31:04, posted by Jeremy Howard on 22 August 2020. https://www.youtube.com/watch?v=BvHmRx14HQ8.

"Lesson 3 - Deep Learning for Coders (2020)", Youtube video, 2:06:22, posted by Jeremy Howard on 22 August 2020. https://www.youtube.com/watch?v=5L3Ao5KuCC4.

"Lesson 5: Deep Learning 2019 - Back propagation; Accelerated SGD; Neural net from scratch", Youtube video, 2:13:33, posted by Jeremy Howard on 22 August 2020. https://www.youtube.com/watch?v=CJKnDu2dxOE.

W. McKinney. 2010. Data Structures for Statistical Computing in Python. *Proceedings of the 9th Python in Science Conference.* 445. pp. 56–61.

J. O'Brien. 2020. gdalUtilities: Wrappers for 'GDAL' Utilities Executables. R Package, Version 1.1.1. https://CRAN.R-project.org/package=gdalUtilities.

E. Pebesma. 2018. Simple Features for R: Standardized Support for Spatial Vector Data. *The R Journal.* 10 (1). pp. 439–446.

J. Reback et al. 2020. Zenodo: pandas-dev/pandas: Pandas 1.0.3, Version 1.0.3. http://doi.org/10.5281/zenodo.3715232.

R Core Team. 2020. R: A Language and Environment for Statistical Computing. https://www.R-project.org/.

N. Ross. 2020. fasterize: Fast Polygon to Raster Conversion. R Package, Version 1.0.3. https://CRAN.R-project.org/package=fasterize.

RStudio Team. 2020. RStudio: Integrated Development for R. RStudio. http://www.rstudio.com/.

L. Scrucca et al. 2016. mclust 5: Clustering, Classification and Density Estimation using Gaussian Finite Mixture Models. *The R Journal.* 8 (1). pp. 289–317.

H. Wickham et al. 2019. Welcome to the tidyverse. *Journal of Open Source Software.* 4 (43). p. 1686.

www.ingramcontent.com/pod-product-compliance
Lightning Source LLC
Chambersburg PA
CBHW061219270326
41926CB00032B/4774